# Oxford English Grammar Course
## Advanced

A grammar practice book for
advanced students of English

# OXFORD
UNIVERSITY PRESS

Great Clarendon Street, Oxford, OX2 6DP, United Kingdom

Oxford University Press is a department of the University of Oxford.
It furthers the University's objective of excellence in research, scholarship,
and education by publishing worldwide. Oxford is a registered trade
mark of Oxford University Press in the UK and in certain other countries

First published in 2011

2015 2014 2013 2012 2011

10 9 8 7 6 5 4 3 2 1

ISBN: 978 0 19 431391 9    Student's book with answers
ISBN: 978 0 19 431250 9    Student's book and CD-ROM pack with answers

Printed in China

This book is printed on paper from certified and well-managed sources

ACKNOWLEDGEMENTS

*Although every effort has been made to trace and contact copyright holders
before publication, this has not been possible in some cases. We apologise for any
apparent infringement of copyright and, if notified, the publisher will be pleased
to rectify any errors or omissions at the earliest possible opportunity.*

Michael Swan & Catherine Walter

# Oxford English Grammar Course

## Advanced

A grammar practice book for
advanced students of English

**With answers**

OXFORD
UNIVERSITY PRESS

# publisher's acknowledgements

The authors and publisher are grateful to those who have given permission to reproduce the following extracts and adaptations of copyright material:

p32 Extract from 'Wildlife Expedition Cruising FAQs' from www.oceansworldwide.co.uk. Reproduced by kind permission.

p39 Extract from 'How not to have a summer of discontent' by Sarah Vine, 26 July 2010, *The Times*. Reproduced by permission of NI Syndication.

p63 Excerpt from *Under Milk Wood* by Dylan Thomas, copyright © 1952 Dylan Thomas. Reprinted by permission of David Higham Associates and New Directions Publishing Corp.

p253 Extract from 'Errors & Omissions: Another distinctively British usage gets lost on its way across the Atlantic' by Guy Keleny, 28 August 2010, *The Independent*. Reproduced by permission.

p276 Extract from *As Others Hear Us* by E M Delafield © E M Delafield. Reproduced by permission of PFD www.pfd.co.uk on behalf of the Estate of E M Delafield.

Sources:
p277 www.expatax.nl

Illustrations by:

**Peter Lawrence**/Oxford Designers and Illustrators: pp: 15, 95, 25; **Ed McLachlan:** pp 118, 127, 141, 188; **Phillip Scramm**/Meiklejohn Illustration agency: pp 11 (communicator), 12, 128, 191, 199

The publisher would like to thank the following for their kind permission to reproduce photographs:

**Alamy Images** pp22 (red shoes/RTimages), 22 (plasma TV/Judith Collins), 22 (Ferrari Fiorano 599 GTB/Oleksiy Maksymenko), 216 (files/Caro), 231 (South African mask/ Stock Connection Blue), 274 (semi-detached house/ Nikreates); **Bridgeman Art Library Ltd** pp129 (Head of Statue of Man, Sodano, Sandro (b.1966)/Private Collection/© Special Photographers Archive), 143 (Roman woman, from floor of a house (mosaic), Roman, (3rd century AD)/Volubilis, Morocco/Hannah Armstrong), 231 (Viking Runestone, from Tjanguide, Alskog, Gottland (stone) by Swedish School/Ancient Art and Architecture Collection Ltd.); **British Museum Images** p231 (Sumerian Seal); **Corbis** pp32 (whale tail/Vivian Kereki), 77 (elephant/ Paul Souders), 77 (brown bear/Jami Tarris), 77 (dolphin/ Jeffrey Rotman), 77 (sperm whale/Denis Scott), 112 (Michael Jordan/Neal Preston), 172 (Strawberry and cream/Winkelmann, Bernhard/the food passionates); **Getty Images** pp22 (headphones/Business Wire), 37 (cave painting/Robert Frerck/Stone); Nature Picture Library pp77 (leafcutter ant/Stephen Dalton), 77 (frog/Kim Taylor); **Philip Hargraves** p22 (charger); **OUP** pp77 (cheetah/ Corbis/Digital Stock), 87 (Jefferson Memorial/Photodisc), 184 (businessman/Stockbyte), 184 (lingerie and pearls/ Photodisc), 216 (drill/Melba Photo Agency), 216 (pliers/ Ingram), 216 (wrench/Dennis Kitchen Studio, Inc.); **Photolibrary** p22 (bike/imagebroker RF); **Science Photo Library** pp77 (peregrine falcon/Jim Zipp), 86 (Portrait in oils of Sir Isaac Newton); **Wikimedia Commons** p231 (Photo of Kokopelli petroglyph, Embudo, NM USA/Einar Einarsson Kvaran).

Sourced cartoons:

**CartoonStock:** p250 ('I miss the good old days…')

**Private Eye**: p113 ('Aren't you supposed to take…?'/ Husband)

**Punch Cartoon Library:** pp14 ('You have a go…'/ Donegan); 16 ('The dog's being impossible again.'/ Haldane); 27 ('Things are looking bad.'/Ian); 27 ('I'm selling this…'/Anton); 38 ('I'm sorry…'/Darling); 57 ('Pembroke, have you…'/Barsotti); 57 ('When did you last feed…'/ Haldane); 87 ('All the exits…'/Duncan); 94 ('I'm thinking of leaving…'/Mike Williams); 109 ('Excuse me, but would you mind…?'/Honeysett); 110 ('I'm sorry to bother you…'/ Noel Ford); 110 ('Didn't we have some children…'/Ffolkes); 123 ('If you don't mind…'/Clive Collins); 199 ('Gerald, I don't think…'/Ffolkes); 199 ('I would be happy…'); 240 ('I'm sorry, but as your account…'/Heath); 249 ('Well, wherever he is…'/Graham); 269 ('Frankly Wallace…'); 269 ('Mind you, this is a tough area…'/Noel Ford); 288 ('You sold my what to who?'/Noel Ford);

**The New Yorker Collection**/ www.cartoonbank.com pp: 26 ('He's swearing…'/Pat Brynes); 29 ('Do these shoes…?'/ Cotham); 61 ('I can see…'/Drucker); 64 ('I wonder…'/BEK); 109 ('The problem with you…'/Victoria Roberts); 11 ('We have lots of information technology…'/S Harris); 207 ('We can't say new…'/Tuohy); 233 ('How to rob…'/Farley Katz); 269 ('It sort of makes…'/S Gross);

**The Spectator:** pp 6 ('Don't you ever switch off…'/Paul Wood); 11 ('Toast training school'/Linden); 14 ('How romantic…'); 43 ('I've wired his electric chair'/Husband); 43 ('Mrs Dunne is here…'/Husband); 48 ('That's an excellent idea…'/Moulson); 57 ('My baggage has gone to Hell.'/ Geoff Thompson); 110 ('Before you turned up…'/Austin; 113 ('No nurse…'/Nicholas); 124 ('No, kickboxing is down the hall…'/Nick Downes); 207 ('Listen, I'll call you back…'/ Baker); 223 ('How to eat while reading.'/S Harris);

**The Tessa Sayle Agency:** p.10 ('Do come out Rover…'/ Ronald Searle);

**New Woman:** p 2 ('I've spent…'/Cole)

Every effort has been made to trace the owners of the copyright material used in this book, but we should be pleased to hear from any copyright holder whom we have been unable to contact.

# contents

# authors' acknowledgements

This book, like the earlier volumes in the *Oxford English Grammar Course* series, has benefited enormously from the hard work and professionalism of our editorial and design team at Oxford University Press. In particular, we would like to acknowledge the contributions of our remarkable editor, Sarah Bleyer, and our equally remarkable designer, Phil Hargraves, who have once again made it possible for us to write and publish the book that we wanted to, and whose input is evident on every page.

# introduction

## Who is this book for?

The *Oxford English Grammar Course* (Advanced Level) is for people who have a good knowledge of English, but who want to speak or write more correctly, perhaps for academic or professional purposes.

## What kind of English does the book teach?

This book teaches modern British English. It deals with the grammar of speech and writing in both formal and informal styles.

## How is the book organised?

There are two parts.

1  **Word and sentence grammar**

    Part 1 deals with the structures that are important at this level for combining words into sentences. It has seventeen Sections, each covering a major topic and containing:
    * an introduction to the topic
    * a number of one- or two-page lessons with explanations and exercises
    * (in most Sections) two or three 'More Practice' pages.

2  **Grammar beyond the sentence**

    Part 2 contains lessons on the structures that are important for **writing and reading more complex texts.** Much of this material will be helpful to university students. Other lessons in Part 2 deal with the grammar of **natural informal conversation**.

    (Note that there is not always a clear dividing line between sentence grammar and text grammar, so some topics appear in both Part 1 and Part 2.)

## What about revision of elementary grammar?

Even advanced students can still make elementary mistakes. This book contains a number of 'revise the basics' lessons to help students consolidate their earlier learning. However, students who have serious problems with basic accuracy should work through the appropriate Sections of the *Intermediate Level* before studying this book.

## Does the book give complete information about English grammar?

Even the biggest grammars cannot contain everything that is known about English. The explanations and exercises in this book cover all the points that are really important for advanced students; there are additional notes giving further information on complex points. For more details, see *Practical English Usage* (Swan, Oxford University Press 2005), *The Cambridge Grammar of the English Language* (Huddleston and Pullum, Cambridge University Press 2002) or *A Comprehensive Grammar of the English Language* (Quirk and others, Longman 1985).

Some language problems come in the area between grammar and vocabulary. Grammars can only give limited information about the grammar of individual words; for detailed explanations, see The *Oxford Advanced Learner's Dictionary*.

## Does the book give enough practice?

This book gives a great deal of practice – more complete and varied than any similar book. Some exercises simply focus on structure; others make students think, solve problems, express opinions, talk about their experience etc. This is enough to fix the structures and rules in learners' minds and help them towards much more correct language use. But no single practice book can completely bridge the gap between conscious knowledge of a rule and the ability to apply it spontaneously in communication. This will come with further experience and language use; the exercises that are being developed for the *Oxford English Grammar Course* website www.oup.com/elt/oxfordenglishgrammar will help.

## Grammar and real life

The *Oxford English Grammar Course* shows how grammar is used in real-life communication, in authentic or adapted texts from newspapers and magazines, letters, quotations, advertisements and many other sources. (Please note that, when we quote a text that expresses an opinion, the opinion is not necessarily ours! The text is simply provided as an interesting and memorable example of the structure being studied.)

## Grammar and pronunciation

The 'Pronunciation for grammar' CD-ROM gives practice on:

- intonation
- word and sentence stress
- linking words together.
- unstressed words and syllables
- grammatical endings

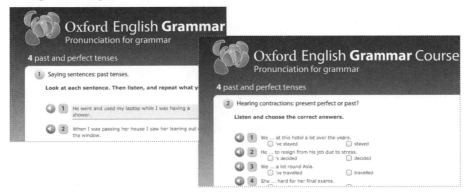

The exercises focus on hearing as well as speaking: for many language students, the main problem is not saying things correctly, but hearing exactly what is said. The CD-ROM also offers practice in listening to speakers with different native accents (English, Scottish, US American) and to speakers whose first language is not English.

## Examinations

This book teaches all the grammar (and more!) that is needed for Common European Framework Levels C1 and C2, and is suitable for learners studying for The Cambridge Advanced Examination in English, Cambridge Proficiency or the IELTS Examination.

With our best wishes for your progress in English.

*Michael Swan.*  *Catherine Walter*

# some useful grammatical terminology

**active** and **passive:** *I see, she heard* are **active** verbs; *I am seen, she was heard* are **passive** verbs.

**adjective clause:** the same as **relative clause**.

**adjective:** for example *big, old, yellow, unhappy*.

**adverb clause:** An adverb clause acts like an adverb in another clause. For example *We left **as soon as we could**.* (Compare *We left **immediately**.*)

**adverb particle:** A short adverb like *up, out, off*, often used as part of a phrasal verb (e.g. *clean up, look out*).

**adverb:** for example *quickly, completely, now, there*.

**affirmative sentences** or **statements** are not questions or negatives – for example *I arrived*.

**articles:** *a/an* ('indefinite article'); *the* ('definite article').

**auxiliary verbs** are used before other verbs to make questions, tenses etc – for example ***do** you think*, *I **have** finished, she **is** working*. See also **modal auxiliary verbs**.

**clause:** a part of a sentence with a subject and verb, usually joined to the rest of the sentence by a conjunction. ***Mary said** that **she was furious*** has two clauses. See also **sentence**.

**comparative:** for example *older, better, more beautiful, more slowly*.

**complement:** 1) a part of a sentence after a verb that gives more information about the subject or object. For example *John is **an engineer**; I feel **tired**; They elected Sandra **president***.
2) a word or expression needed after a noun, adjective, verb or preposition to complete its meaning. For example *the intention **to return**; full **of water**; They went **to Germany**; in **the garden***.

**conditional:** a structure using the conjunction *if*.

**conjunction:** for example *and, but, if, because, while*.

**consonant:** see **vowel**.

**contraction:** a short form like *I'm, you're, he'll, don't*.

**countable nouns:** the name of things we can count – for example *one **chair**, three **cars**;* **uncountable** (or 'mass') **nouns:** the names of things we can't count, like *oil, rice*.

**declarative question:** a question that has the form of a statement. For example *This is your car?*

**demonstrative:** *this, that, these* and *those* are demonstrative determiners or pronouns.

**determiner:** a word like *the, some, many, my*, which goes before (adjective +) noun.

**discourse markers** are words and expressions which help to structure spoken exchanges and written texts. For example *first of all, anyway, by the way, right*.

**ellipsis:** leaving words out. For example *'[Have you] Seen John?' 'No, I haven't [seen John].'*

**emphasis:** giving special importance to one part of a sentence, expression or word. For example *It was **the marketing manager** who phoned. No, I wanted **black** coffee.* Related words are *emphasise* and *emphatic*.

**formal, informal** We use **formal** language with strangers, in business letters etc: for example *'Good afternoon, Mr Parker. May I help you?'* We use **informal** language with family and friends: for example *'Hi, John. Need help?'*

**fronting:** moving part of a clause to the beginning to give it more emphasis or to focus on it. For example ***Annie** I quite like, but **her sister** I just can't stand.*

**gender:** (In English) the use of grammatical forms to show the difference between male and female, or between human and non-human. For example *he, she, it, who, which*.

**generalising:** talking about a whole class of people or things. For example *Penguins don't fly; I like chocolate*.

**identifying:** saying exactly who or what you are talking about. For example *Henry Bartlett; the woman over there in the corner; my first car; the woman who phoned just now*.

**imperative:** a form like ***Go** home, **Don't** worry*, which we use when we tell or ask people (not) to do things.

**indirect speech:** the grammar that we use to show what people say or think: for example *John said **that he was ill***.

**infinitive:** *(to) go, (to) sleep* etc.

**informal:** see **formal**.

**intransitive:** see **transitive**.

**inversion:** putting a verb before the subject. For example ***Are you** ready? So **do I**. Here **comes Arthur***.

**link verbs** connect subjects to complements, not to objects. For example *They **are** Russian; She **seems** nice*.

**modal verbs** or **modal auxiliary verbs**: *must, can, could, may, might, shall, should, ought to, will* and *would*.

**noun clause** A noun clause acts like the subject or object of another clause. For example *How she did it was a mystery; I understood what they wanted.* Noun clauses are common in indirect speech.

**noun**: for example *chair, oil, idea, sentence.*

**noun phrase**: a phrase based on a noun. For example *the first car that I bought.*

**object**: see **subject**.

**participle**: see **present participle, past participle**.

**participle clause**: a clause containing a participle, not a tense. For example *Walking to the window, I looked out.*

**particle**: see **adverb particle**.

**passive**: see **active**.

**past participle**: for example *gone, seen, stopped.* (In fact: 'past' participles can refer to the past, present or future).

**perfect infinitive**: *(to) have seen, (to) have started* etc.

**personal pronouns**: for example *I, you, us, them.*

**phrasal verb**: a two-part verb formed with an adverb particle □ for example *cut up, break down, run away.*

**phrase**: a group of words that belong together grammatically. For example *dead tired; would not have understood.*

**plural**: see **singular**.

**possessives**: for example *my, your; mine, yours; John's, my brothers'.*

**prediction**: saying what will happen. For example *I think we're going to lose; You'll be sorry.*

**preparatory subject/object**: *It* put in the place of a longer subject or object, which comes later. For example *It's important to believe in yourself; She made it clear that she was disappointed.*

**preposition**: for example *at, in, on, between.*

**prepositional verb**: a two-part verb formed with a preposition. For example *look at, listen to.*

**present participle**: for example *going, sleeping.* (In fact, 'present' participles can refer to the past, present or future).

**progressive** (or 'continuous'): for example *He's eating* (present progressive); *They were talking* (past progressive).

**pronouns**: for example *I, you, anybody, themselves.*

**quantifier**: a determiner that shows how much/ many we are talking about. For example *all, most, little.*

**question tag**: for example *isn't it?, doesn't she?*

**reduced relative clause**: for example the people invited (meaning 'the people who were invited').

**reflexive pronouns**: *myself, yourself* etc.

**relative clause**: a clause that begins with a relative pronoun. For example *the man who bought my car.*

**relative pronouns**: *who, which* and *that* when they join clauses to nouns. For example *the man who bought my car.*

**reply question**: for example *'I had a great time in Holland.' 'Did you? I am glad.'*

**rhetorical question**: a question with an obvious answer or with no answer. For example: *Who's a lovely baby, then?*

**sentence**: A written sentence begins with a capital letter (A, B etc) and ends with a full stop (.), like this one. A sentence may have more than one clause, often joined by a conjunction. For example: *I'll come and see you when I'm in London.* If one clause is part of another, it is called a 'subordinate clause'; the other is the 'main clause'. Clauses with equal weight are called 'co-ordinate clauses'.

**short answer**: for example *Yes, I am; No, we didn't; They will.*

**singular**: for example *chair, cat, man;* **plural**: for example *chairs, cats, men.*

**stress**: giving a syllable, word or phrase more importance by pronouncing it more loudly or on a higher pitch.

**subject** and **object**: In *She took the money – everybody saw her,* the **subjects** are *she* and *everybody;* the **objects** are *the money* and *her.*

**subjunctive**: a special verb form that is used to talk about possibilities rather than fact. For example *It's important that she inform the police. If I were you.* Modern English has very few subjunctives.

**superlative**: for example *oldest, best, most beautiful, most easily.*

**tense**: *She goes, she is going, she went, she was going, she has gone* are different tenses (for a list, see page 297).

**third person**: words for other people, not *I* or *you* – for example *she, them, himself, John, has, goes.*

**transitive** verbs normally have objects – for example *break, improve, tell.* **Intransitive** verbs don't usually have objects – for example *sleep, breathe, stay.*

**uncountable nouns**: see **countable nouns**.

**verb**: for example *sit, give, hold, think, write.*

**vowels**: *a, e, i, o, u* and their usual sounds; **consonants**: *b, c, d, f, g* etc and their usual sounds.

# list of topics

## Part 1 word and sentence grammar

# Part 2 grammar beyond the sentence

# Section 1 basic sentence types

The basic subject-verb-object structure of simple affirmative sentences should be well known at this level. Rules for the formation of questions, negatives, imperatives and exclamations are revised briefly in this section, and some more advanced points introduced. More complex types of spoken and written sentence structure are covered in other parts of the book: see the Table of Contents or the Index for details.

## questions: revise the basics ???

**word order** In most questions, we put an **auxiliary verb before the subject** – not the whole verb, even with long subjects.

*Are Annie and the rest of the family coming tomorrow?* (NOT *Are coming Annie …?*)
*Can all of the team be here at ten o'clock?*

If there is no other auxiliary verb, we use *do* (+ infinitive without *to*).

*What does 'hyperactive' mean?* (NOT *What means 'hyperactive'?*)

Note that *do* may come twice in questions: once as an auxiliary and once as a main verb.

*What does your brother do?*

**question-word subjects** When *who* and *what* are **subjects**, we normally make questions without *do*. Compare:

*'Who^{SUBJ} said that?' 'Lucy^{SUBJ} said that.'* (NOT *'Who did say that?'*)
*'Who^{OBJ} did you invite?' 'I invited Oliver^{OBJ}.'*
*'What^{SUBJ} happened?' 'Something strange^{SUBJ} happened.'* (NOT *'What did happen?'*)
*'What^{OBJ} did he say?' 'He said something strange^{OBJ}.'*

The same thing happens when subjects **begin with** question-words *which*, *what*, *whose*, *what sort of* or *how much/many*.

*Which team won?* (NOT *Which team did win?*)
*What country won the last World Cup?*
*How many students live here? (Compare How many students^{OBJ} did you^{SUBJ} invite?)*
*Whose dog dug up my flowers?*

However, *do* can be used with question-word subjects for special emphasis.

*'Ollie didn't get the job.' 'Really? So who did get it?'*

**1** **Correct the mistakes or write 'Correct'.**

▶ How ~~you~~ pronounce 'thorough'? ...*do you*...........................
▶ What happened? ...*Correct.*.......................
1 What time the train leaves? ...................................
2 What means 'understudy'? ...................................
3 Why she is crying? ...................................
4 Has the man from the Export Department telephoned? ...................................
5 What I must to do now? ...................................
6 Does the 9.30 train for Bristol leave from platform 7? ...................................
7 The postman has been? ...................................
8 Who does live next door? ...................................
9 Which car costs more? ...................................
10 What sort of music does help you to relax? ...................................

**2** **Make questions. Ask about the words** *in italics.*

▶ (a) *Mark* loves Emma.  (b) Mark loves *Emma*.
....(a) Who loves Emma?...(b) Who does Mark love?..................................................

1 (a) Rob bought *a jacket*.  (b) *Rob* bought a jacket.
...........................................................................................................................

2 (a) *Oliver* lost his credit card.  (b) Oliver lost *his credit card*.
...........................................................................................................................

3 (a) Kara has broken *her leg*.  (b) *Kara* has broken her leg.
...........................................................................................................................

4 (a) *This stuff* kills flies.  (b) This stuff kills *flies*.
...........................................................................................................................

5 (a) *Mike* caught the first plane.  (b) Mike caught *the first* plane.
...........................................................................................................................

6 (a) *His brother* collects Chinese paintings.  (b) His brother collects *Chinese* paintings.
...........................................................................................................................

7 (a) *Her* child broke our window.  (b) Her child broke *our* window.
...........................................................................................................................

**Prepositions often come at the end** of questions, especially in informal speech and writing.

*Who are you waiting **for**?     What's that book **about**?*

It is possible to begin with the preposition, but this is generally very formal.

***With whom** did Mozart collaborate?     **On what** do blue whales feed?*

This order is unusual or impossible in informal speech.

NOT *After whose children are you looking?*

Two-word questions ending with a preposition are common in conversation.

*'Rose is getting married.' '**Who to**?'     'I've been thinking.' '**What about**?'*

**3** **Write questions for these answers, beginning** *Who* **or** *What.*

▶ 'I went with Alex.' ..'Who did you go with?'.....................................
1 'The article's about microbiology.' ...............................................................
2 'She gave it to her sister.' ...............................................................
3 'I was talking to Emma.' ...............................................................
4 'You can open it with this.' ...............................................................
5 'The letter was from my bank manager.' ...............................................................
6 'She hit me with her shoe.' ...............................................................
7 'My brother works for Globe Advertising.' ...............................................................
8 'I'm thinking about life.' ...............................................................

**4** **Complete the conversations with two-word questions.**

▶ 'I'm writing a novel.' ..'What about?'.............. 'Love, life, art and death.'
1 'We're moving.' ..................................... 'North Wales.'
2 'I've mended the printer.' ..................................... 'Superglue.'
3 'I've bought a present.' ..................................... 'Myself.'
4 'Pete's in love again.' ..................................... 'His piano teacher.'
5 'I managed to stop the baby crying.' ..................................... 'Chocolate.'
6 'We're going to France for a week.' ..................................... 'Pat and Julie.'
7 'Sophie's got engaged.' ..................................... 'To an old school friend.'

**Note:  A few prepositions** do not normally come at the end of sentences (see page 195).
   ***During** whose lesson did you fall asleep?* (NOT *Whose lesson … during?*)

# negatives: revise the basics

**structure** To make **negative** verb forms, we put *not* or *n't* after an auxiliary verb or *be*. If there is **no other auxiliary**, we use *do*. In standard English, we don't normally use *not* or *do* with negative words like *never, hardly, nothing*. (But this is common in many dialects.)

The Minister **has not** made a decision.     She **couldn't** swim.     It **wasn't** raining.     I **don't** care.
He **never says** much. (NOT ~~He does never say much.~~ or ~~He doesn't never say much.~~)
I **hardly noticed** the interruption. (NOT ~~I didn't hardly notice~~ …)
We **saw nothing**. (NOT ~~We didn't see nothing.~~)

**1** **Correct the mistakes or write 'Correct'.**

▶ You ~~not understood~~. *did not understand* ........
▶ It hardly matters. *Correct* ........................
1 George never is in the office. ..................................
2 There wasn't nothing that I could do. ..................................
3 Fred not likes travelling. ..................................
4 The rooms have not been cleaned today. ..................................
5 Nothing didn't happen. ..................................
6 I do never drive at night. ..................................
7 We hardly didn't have time to think. ..................................
8 You don't must pay now. ..................................

**2** GRAMMAR IN TEXTS. **Put the letters of the expressions from the box into the texts.**

| A cannot be   B can't afford   C did not pay   D doesn't have   E doesn't open   F doesn't talk |
| G no longer   H not be allowed   I not be shown   J not been named   K not been paid |
| L nothing can justify   M wouldn't have to |

## A police anti-terrorism TV advertisement has been banned.

The advertisement asked people to look out for suspicious behaviour by their neighbours, describing a man who 1… to people, 2… his curtains, and 3… a bank card but pays for things in cash. The authority that regulates TV advertising banned the advertisement because this could offend or throw suspicion on innocent people, and ruled that the ad should 4… again.

**A 37-year-old Swedish motorist**, who has 5…, was caught driving his Mercedes sports car at 290km/h in Switzerland, and could be given a world-record speeding fine of SFr1.08m. Under Swiss law, the level of fine is determined by the wealth of the driver and the speed recorded. A local police spokesman said that "6 … a speed of 290km/h. The car 7… properly controlled. It must have taken 500m to stop."

## A travel company has collapsed, leaving over 1,000 customers stuck in Spain.

One holidaymaker said that he and his family had paid the company for an all-inclusive hotel on the Costa Brava, but they have now been asked to pay again for the whole week or leave. 'Well, we just 8… that," he said. "We paid everything in advance so we 9… spend any money while we're away." Another group in the resort of Lloret de Mar were notified as they were sunbathing that the all-inclusive deal they had paid for was 10… valid. One woman said her family of five was presented with a bill of 2,700 euros – more than the original cost of their holiday – and told they if they 11… it they would 12… any more food or drink. Hoteliers are also suffering; one said he had 100 rooms currently booked through the travel company, but had 13… for any of them. ●

**Note:** *do* and *not* with negative words  *Do* is possible with a negative for emphasis.
'I've split up with my girlfriend.' 'I'm not surprised. I **never did** like her.'
And *not* can **contradict** the meaning of another negative word.
I **didn't** say **nothing** – I said '**Hello**'.

# *not* and *no*

*Not* surprisingly, she failed her driving test. (NOT ~~No surprisingly~~ …)
I've worked in Scotland, but **not** in Ireland. (NOT … ~~but no in Ireland.~~)
She was talking to Andy, **not** you. (NOT … ~~no you.~~)    I do **not** agree.

*Not* can refer to different parts of a sentence. However, in a clause with a verb, *not* normally goes with the verb, whatever the exact meaning.

Peter **didn't study** art at Cambridge. (NOT ~~Not Peter studied art at Cambridge.~~ OR ~~Peter studied not art at Cambridge.~~ OR ~~Peter studied art not at Cambridge.~~)

**meaning of *no*** We use ***no*** with a **noun** or **-*ing*** form to mean '**not any**' or '**not a/an**'.

**No pilots** went on strike. (= 'There were**n't any** pilots on strike.')
We've got **no plans** for the holiday. (= '… **not any** plans …')
I know you're tired, but that's **no reason** to be rude. (= '… **not a** reason.')
***NO PARKING*** *AT WEEKENDS*.

**1** **Correct (✓) or not (✗)?**

▶ Not Bill phoned, but Pete. ✗
▶ I have no idea where Susie is. ✓
1 I speak Spanish, but no very well. …
2 There are no messages for you. …
3 We play tennis not on Sundays. …

4 We play tennis, but not on Sundays. …
5 No trains are running today. …
6 The trains are not running today. …
7 I'm sorry, Mary's no in today. …
8 Not this street is the right one. …

**2** **Complete the sentences with words from the box, and choose *not* or *no*.**
**Use a dictionary if necessary.**

| attend | cash | describe | entrance | excuse | humour | intend | office ✓ | repaired | revise | worry |

▶ We speak Spanish in the ..*office*.............. , but *no /* (*not*) at home.
1 There's *no / not* parking in front of the station ………………………… .
2 She was *no / not* able to ………………………… her attacker.
3 There's *no / not* ………………………… for that sort of behaviour.
4 They ………………………… my watch, but *no / not* properly.
5 We've got *no / not* time to ………………………… the schedule now.
6 I can ………………………… a meeting, but *no / not* tonight.
7 The receptionist obviously did *no / not* ………………………… to be helpful.
8 'Do you ………………………… a lot?' '*No / Not* usually.'
9 She's a woman with *no / not* sense of ………………………… .
10 I always pay ………………………… I've got *no / not* credit cards.

---

**NOTES**

***not*** The exact reference of *not* can be shown in speech by STRESS.
    *PETER didn't study medicine at Cambridge.* (It was Susan.)
    *Peter didn't study MEDICINE at Cambridge.* (He studied biology.)
In writing, we can use a special sentence structure if necessary (see page 260).
    *It was not Peter who studied medicine at Cambridge, but Susan.*

***not all*, *not every*** We most often put *not* **before** a subject beginning with *all* or *every*.
    **Not all** British people drink tea. (LESS COMMON: *All British people don't drink tea.*)
    **Not every** bird can fly. (LESS COMMON: *Every bird cannot fly.*)

# negative questions

**construction** Negative questions can be constructed in two ways.

| CONTRACTED (INFORMAL) | UNCONTRACTED (FORMAL, UNUSUAL) |
|---|---|
| *n't* after **auxiliary verb or** *be* | *not* after **subject** |
| Why **didn't** she answer? | Why did **she not** answer? |
| **Hasn't** Emma phoned? | Has **Emma not** phoned? |
| **Aren't** they at home? | Are **they not** at home? |

We say *aren't I?*, not ~~amn't I?~~

'**Aren't I** next?' 'No, Harry is.' (BUT NOT ~~I aren't next.~~)

**1** **Make these questions more conversational.**

▶ Why did you not phone? ...Why didn't you phone?...................

1 Who did they not tell? ...................................................................

2 Are you not well? ...................................................................

3 What did we not understand? ...................................................................

4 Was the office not open? ...................................................................

5 Do you not speak Chinese? ...................................................................

6 Are we not in the right place? ...................................................................

**answers to negative questions** Note how we use *Yes* and *No* in answers to negative questions. The choice depends on the answer, not the question. *Yes* goes with or suggests an **affirmative** verb; *No* goes with or suggests a **negative** verb.

'Don't you like it?' '**Yes** (I like it).'    'Aren't you ready?' '**No** (I'm not ready).'

**2** **Add *Yes* or *No* to the answers.**

▶ 'Can't you swim?' '...Yes......, I can.'

1 'Don't you understand?' '..............., I don't.'

2 'Didn't Ann tell you?' '..............., she did.'

3 'Wasn't the post office open?' '..............., it was.'

4 'Hasn't she phoned?' '..............., she has.'

5 'Didn't he agree?' '..............., he didn't.'

6 'Isn't this awful!' '..............., it is.'

7 'Aren't you hungry?' '..............., I am.'

8 'Can't you find the address?' '..............., I can't.'

'Don't you ever switch off, Jeremy?'

**checking negative ideas** We often use negative questions to check that something has not happened, is not true, etc. The meaning is like 'Is it true that … not … ?'

**Hasn't Mary phoned?** *I wonder if she's forgotten.* ( = 'Is it true that Mary hasn't phoned?') **Can't you come** *this evening?*

These questions can also express **surprise** that **something has not happened**, is not happening, etc.

**Haven't the tickets come** *yet?*    **Didn't he tell** *you he was married?*

The structure is often used in **rhetorical questions** – questions which don't ask for an answer (see page 287).

**Can't you read?** *It says 'closed'.*    **Don't you** *ever* **listen** *to what I say?*

**3** **Use negative questions to check the following negative ideas.**

▶ It looks as if she's not at home. *Isn't she at home?* ..............................................

1  It looks as if you don't understand. ......................................................................

2  So you haven't read this book? ..............................................................................

3  Do you mean that Magnus hasn't got a work permit? ..........................................

4  Perhaps you didn't get my message. ......................................................................

5  I think perhaps you didn't turn the lights off. ......................................................

6  It seems as if you can't understand English. I said 'Go away'. ..............................

7  Is it true that he didn't pass his driving test? ....................................................

8  I'm afraid you don't like English food. ................................................................

**checking positive ideas**  Negative questions can also check **that something is true**.

***Didn't you*** *see Peter yesterday? How is he?* (= 'I believe you saw Peter …')

**4** **Make negative questions to make sure that these things are true. Put in words from the box. Use a dictionary if necessary.**

| appointment  deposit  insurance ✓  interest  profit  reservation  washer |

▶ I think we paid the fire … last month.
   *Didn't we pay the fire insurance last month?* .....................................................

1  You made a … for dinner at 8.00, right?

   ...............................................................................................................................

2  I'm pretty sure Ann paid a 10% … with her order.

   ...............................................................................................................................

3  I thought you said you were going to put a new … on the tap.

   ...............................................................................................................................

4  I believe that this account pays 3% …

   ...............................................................................................................................

5  My … with Dr Masters is at 10.30, surely?

   ...............................................................................................................................

6  The firm made a … of half a million euros last year, no?

   ...............................................................................................................................

Negative questions are also common in **exclamations** (see page 13).

***Isn't it*** *hot!*     ***Doesn't the garden*** *look nice!*     ***Wasn't that lecture*** *boring!*

**Note:  polite invitations**  We can use *Won't/Wouldn't …?* in polite invitations.
   ***Won't you come*** *in?*     ***Wouldn't you like*** *something to drink?*
   *Why don't you …?* is also used in this way (BUT NOT *Why won't you …?*). Compare:
   *Why don't you join us for a drink?* (= 'Please join us …')
   *Why won't you join us for a drink?* (= 'Why don't you want to?')
We do not use negative questions to ask people to do things for us.
   ***Can you*** *help me?*     ***You couldn't*** *help me, could you?*
   BUT NOT ***Can't you*** *help me?* (This sounds like a criticism.)

# more about negatives

**I don't think** etc  We usually use **I don't think** + **affirmative verb**, not **I think** + **negative verb**. The same is true with **believe, suppose, imagine** and similar verbs.

*I **don't think** you know Joe.* (MORE USUAL THAN *I think you don't know Joe.*)
*I **don't believe** she's at home.*
*I **don't suppose** you can lend me some money?*

However, with **hope** we normally make the **following** verb negative.

*I **hope** it **doesn't rain.*** (NOT ~~I don't hope it rains.~~)

For expressions like *I hope so/not, I believe so/not*, see page 279.

**1** **Change the sentences and choose the best words to complete them.**
**Use a dictionary if necessary.**

▶ The laboratory hasn't completed the *analysis / inspection.* (*I / think*)
    *I don't think the laboratory has completed the analysis .*

1 Your report of the meeting isn't quite *exact / accurate.* (*we / believe*)
    ......................................................................

2 You didn't understand the *lecture / conference.* (*I / suppose*)
    ......................................................................

3 You don't know Ruth's *site / whereabouts.* (*I / suppose*)
    ......................................................................

4 John won't read the *instructions / lecture* I sent him. (*I / imagine*)
    ......................................................................

5 Emma doesn't have a driving *licence / record.* (*I / think*)
    ......................................................................

6 I didn't make my *intentions / inventions* clear. (*I / think*)
    ......................................................................

7 You didn't remember to *apply / book* our plane tickets. (*I / suppose*)
    ......................................................................

8 The company hasn't got enough *figures / funds* to continue trading. (*I / believe*)
    ......................................................................

There is a similar use of *not* and other negative words with **seem**, **expect** and **want** before an infinitive.

*He **doesn't seem** to like you.* (LESS FORMAL THAN *He seems not to like you.*)
*I **don't expect** to be back before Monday.* (LESS FORMAL THAN *I expect not …*)
*I **never want** to see you again.* (MORE NATURAL THAN *I want never to see …*)

**2** **Change the sentences.**

▶ He's probably not from around here. (*He doesn't seem …*)
    *He doesn't seem to be from around here.*

1 I don't think she's ready. (*She doesn't seem*)
    ......................................................................

2 I probably won't be home late. (*I don't expect …*)
    ......................................................................

3 I would hate to climb another mountain. (*I never want …*)
    ......................................................................

4 It doesn't rain much here, apparently. (*It doesn't seem …*)
    ......................................................................

5 I probably won't pass the exam. (*I don't expect …*)
    ......................................................................

6   He is determined not to get married. (*He never wants …*)

.........................................................................................................................................

7   I don't think the water's hot. (*The water … seem …*)

.........................................................................................................................................

8   I would hate to work with him. (*… never want …*)

.........................................................................................................................................

9   I don't think I'll be here tomorrow. (*… expect …*)

.........................................................................................................................................

10  I don't think the heating is working. (*… seem …*)

.........................................................................................................................................

**not … or**  When *not* refers to two or more verbs, nouns, adjectives etc, we usually join them with *or*.

*He doesn't smoke or drink.* (NOT ~~He doesn't smoke nor drink.~~)
*She wasn't angry or upset.*
*It's not on the table or in the cupboard.*

However, we can use *nor* after a pause, to separate and emphasise a second idea.

*Our main need is not food, nor money. It is education.*
*She didn't phone on Tuesday, nor on Wednesday.*

Note that *neither* cannot be used in this way.

For *neither … nor*, see page 203.

**3**  **Write about two things that you don't do (or like or want).**

▶   *I don't sing or play an instrument.*
    ......................................................................................................................

    .........................................................................................................................................

**NOTES**

**not … because**  Negative sentences with *because*-clauses can often be understood in two ways.
    *I **didn't sing** because Pat was there.* (= 'I didn't sing' or 'I sang, but for another reason'.)
The confusion can be avoided by reorganising the sentence.
    *Because Pat was there, I didn't sing.*  OR  *I sang, but not because Pat was there.*

**extra not**  In informal speech, expressions like *I don't think* or *I don't suppose* are often added after
a negative statement. This makes no difference to the meaning of the statement.
    *She hasn't got much chance of passing her driving test, **I don't think**.*
    *We won't be home before midnight, **I don't suppose**.*
Also in informal speech, a negative verb (without a negative meaning) is sometimes used after
expressions of doubt or uncertainty.
    *I shouldn't be surprised if they **didn't** get married soon.* (= '… if they got married.')
    *I wonder whether I **oughtn't** to see the doctor.* (= '… whether I ought …')

**ain't**  The word *ain't* is very common in many English dialects (but is not used in modern standard English). It means
'am/are/is not' or 'have/has not'.
    *We **ain't** ready yet.*    *I **ain't** got a clue what she wants.*

**We use *nor* and *neither*** rather than *also not*. Note the word order.
    *The chief engineer was not in the building, and **nor was his assistant**.*
    (NOT *… and his assistant was also not.*)
    *'I didn't think much of the game.' '**Neither did I.**'*

For negative subjunctives (e.g. *It is important that she not be disturbed*), see page 224.

# imperatives

**structure and meaning  Imperatives** look the same as **infinitives without** *to*. We use imperatives to tell people what to do, advise them, encourage them etc.

**Get** *some butter while you're out.*      **Look** *again.*      **Have** *another cup.*

**Negative imperatives** begin with ***do not / don't***. (Note: these can be used before *be*.)

*Please* **do not park** *in front of this garage.*      **Don't listen** *to him.*
**Don't be** *afraid.*

***Always*** and *never* come **before** imperatives.

**Always check** *your change.* (NOT ~~Check always your change.~~)
**Never start** *something you can't finish.*

**1** (Circle) **the best way of completing each sentence (in your opinion), or write 'It depends'.**

1  *Always / Never* say 'Yes' if you don't understand. ...........................
2  *Always / Never* read the small print on a contract. ...........................
3  *Always / Never* do today what you could put off till tomorrow. ...........................
4  *Always / Never* keep cheese in the fridge. ...........................
5  *Always / Never* wear a hat at mealtimes. ...........................
6  *Always / Never* expect the best from people. ...........................
7  *Always / Never* think twice before you buy something you want. ...........................
8  *Always / Never* trust your first impressions of people. ...........................

**2** **Write a piece of advice for people, beginning** *Always* **or** *Never*.

...........................................................................................................................

**Emphatic imperatives** begin with ***do*** (this can be used before *be*).

**Do stop** *shouting!*      **Do come** *in and sit down.*      **Do be** *careful.*

**3** **What might somebody say in the following situations? Make sentences beginning** *Do*,
**using the words and expressions in the box.**

| be back by midnight   be careful   come again   have some more coffee   let me help |
| shut up   use my car   use my phone ✓ |

▶  Somebody needs to contact her mother.
   *Do use my phone.* ...........................................
1  Their child is going to cycle to school through heavy traffic.
   ...........................................................
2  Their guest has just finished her coffee.
   ...........................................................
3  Their fourteen-year-old child is going out to a party.
   ...........................................................
4  Somebody needs to fetch her mother from the station.
   ...........................................................
5  Somebody has got too much to do.
   ...........................................................
6  A child is screaming non-stop.
   ...........................................................
7  They would like another visit from their friend.
   ...........................................................

'Do come out, Rover,
Susan won't bite.'

**imperatives with subjects**  If it is necessary to make it clear who is meant or who we are speaking to, an imperative can have a subject (usually *you* or an **indefinite pronoun**).

*John, **you** take the car, and Mary, **you** take the children on the bus.*
***Somebody** answer the phone, please, I've got my hands full.*

Note the position of subjects in negative imperatives.

***Don't you** come in here or I'll call the police.* (NOT ~~You don't come~~ ...)
***Don't anybody** say a word.* (NOT ~~Anybody don't say~~ ...)

A subject can also be used to make an order, invitation etc more emphatic.

***You** take your hands off me!*    ***You** just sit down and relax for a bit.*

We don't put subjects in emphatic imperatives.

***You** come here.* OR ***Do** come here.* BUT NOT ~~Do you come here.~~

**imperative + *and/or***  An imperative followed by *and* or *or* can have a conditional meaning, like an *if*-clause.

*Come in here **and** I'll call the police.*  (= 'If you come in here, I'll call the police.')
*Walk down our street any day **and** you'll see kids playing.*
*Stop singing **or** I'll scream.* (= 'If you don't stop singing, I'll scream.')

**4** **Correct (✓) or not (✗)?**

1   Say always what you think.  ...
2   Do be careful when you're driving.  ...
3   Open somebody the door, please.  ...
4   Don't you talk to me like that.  ...
5   Do you be quiet.  ...
6   Don't anybody interrupt, please.  ...
7   Buy me a drink and I'll tell you my life story.  ...
8   Never drink and drive.  ...
9   Answer you the door, John, can you?  ...
10  Don't never interrupt Andy when he's working.  ...

'No, no, always land buttered side down!'

**5** **Here are some of the instructions for using a universal communicator (in 2150 everybody will have one). Put in the missing words from the box.**

| hold down    press    press    receive    select    slide    type |

To turn the communicator on, [1]............... the on/off button. To turn the communicator off or restart it, [2].............. the on/off button for two seconds. To put the communicator to sleep, [3]............... the on-off button once. To open communication with another communicator, [4].............. your finger across the screen, then [5].............. the number from your connections list or [6].............. the number into the keypad. To [7].............. an incoming call from another communicator, tap anywhere on the screen once.

'Always aim at complete harmony of word and deed.' (*Mahatma Gandhi*)

'Never underestimate the power of human stupidity.' (*Robert A Heinlein*)

'Always do right. This will please some people and astonish the rest.' (*Mark Twain*)

'Never, never, never give up.' (*Winston Churchill*)

'Always end the name of your child with a vowel, so that when you yell the name will carry.' (*Bill Cosby*)

'Never follow the crowd.' (*Bernard Baruch*)

'Never bend your head. Always hold it high. Always look the world straight in the eye.' (*Helen Keller*)

# let's; let me etc

**structure and meaning** We can use **let's** (or *let us* – very formal) + **infinitive without to** to make **suggestions** or give **orders** to a group **that includes the speaker** (like a kind of **imperative**).

*Let's play poker.*    *Let's go out this evening.*    *Let's be quiet and listen to Carl.*

The normal **negative** is **Let's not** … .

*Let's not spend too much on the holiday.*

*Don't let's* … is informal; *Let us not* and *Do not let us* are very formal.

*Look, don't let's get upset, OK?*    *Let us not forget those who came before us.*

**question tag** The usual question tag (see pages 284–285) for *let's* is **shall we?**

*'Let's have a party, shall we?' 'Yes, let's.'*

**Let me …** When we say what we are going to do, we can soften the announcement, and make it more polite, with *Let me* … .

*This doesn't taste very nice. **Let me try** adding some sugar.*
*I'm sorry that wasn't clear. **Let me put** it another way.*

Two very common expressions for gaining time are **Let me see …** and **Let me think …**.

*So how many potatoes should I cook? **Let me see**. Suppose each person eats two …*
*When are we going to have Granny round? **Let me think** – Tuesday's no good …*

**Let's see** is common with a similar meaning.

*What shall we have for supper? **Let's see**. There's some left-over chicken. Or I could cook up some pasta. Or we could phone for an Indian …*

**1** **Put in *let's* or *let me* with words from the box.**

| have   go   invite   see   take   tell   think   worry |

1  ..................................... a game of tennis.
2  ..................................... the boss what we think of him.
3  A meeting? ..................................... – I'm free from 10.00 onwards.
4  ......................... not ......................... about the price – I want to buy it.
5  ..................................... out for a pizza, shall we?
6  Don't ............... Josie – she's so boring.
7  'What would you like to do on your birthday?' '..................................... for a minute.'
8  ......................... not ......................... the bus – I'd rather walk.

**2** **Correct (✓) or not (✗)?**

1  Not let's start arguing.  …
2  Let's have a game of snooker, will we?  …
3  Let me try to explain.  …
4  Let us be silent for a moment.  …
5  Let's don't forget to phone Annie.  …
6  Who can we invite? Let's see.  …

'Spring is nature's way of saying, "Let's party!".'
(Robin Williams)

**Note:** **Let him …** etc A structure with a third-person noun or pronoun is also possible.
*'The kid says he doesn't like the fish.' 'That's his problem. **Let him** starve.'* (informal)
**Let our enemies** *be under no illusions: we can and will defend ourselves.* (formal)
Note also the structure with *there*.
*And God said: '**Let there be** light'.*
**Let there be** *no doubt in your minds about our intentions.*

# exclamations: revise the basics

*How ...!* and *What ...!*: **word order**  Note the word order in these exclamations.
The **complete expression** with *How ...* or *What ...* goes **before** a subject and verb (if any).

*How difficult* this is! (NOT ~~How this is difficult!~~)
*How convincingly* he argues! (NOT ~~How he argues convincingly!~~)
*What a lot of nonsense* Andy talks!

We don't drop articles after *What*.

*What a* brilliant idea ! (NOT ~~What brilliant idea!~~)

**1** **Change the sentences into exclamations with *How* or *What*.**

▶ These grapes are sweet.
   *How sweet these grapes are!*

▶ She wears lovely jewellery.
   *What lovely jewellery she wears!*

1 It was a waste of time.
   ......................................................................................................

2 This computer loads slowly.
   ......................................................................................................

3 The days seemed long then.
   ......................................................................................................

4 I made a big mistake.
   ......................................................................................................

5 We all played well on Saturday.
   ......................................................................................................

6 The time goes fast.
   ......................................................................................................

7 His poetry is boring.
   ......................................................................................................

8 Those people make a lot of noise.
   ......................................................................................................

We can use negative questions (see page 6) as exclamations.

*Isn't she* sweet!     *Doesn't he* look happy!     *Wasn't it* strange!

**2** **Change the sentences from Exercise 1 into exclamations with negative questions.**

▶ *Aren't these grapes sweet!*
▶ *Doesn't she wear lovely jewellery!*
1 ......................................................................................................
2 ......................................................................................................
3 ......................................................................................................
4 ......................................................................................................
5 ......................................................................................................
6 ......................................................................................................
7 ......................................................................................................
8 ......................................................................................................

# more practice

**1 Five of sentences 1–10 are quite formal, and would be uncommon or unnatural in conversation. The others are normal. Write 'F' or 'N'.**

▶ I want never to see you again. ~~F~~

▶ What do they want? N

1  The dog seems not to like you. …
2  I don't believe him. …
3  I think you haven't met my sister. …
4  Let us consider what we are to do next. …
5  Are you ready? …
6  Why did you not wait for me? …
7  I don't suppose you're hungry. …
8  From where do you come? …
9  Do come in. …
10  I don't eat meat or fish. …

**2 Seven of sentences 1–12 are wrong. Correct the mistakes or write 'Correct'.**

▶ Where ~~you put~~ the newspaper? *did you put* ...............

▶ Never tell her she's wrong. *Correct* ...............

1  I'm not hardly awake yet. ...............
2  Do be quiet, children! ...............
3  Why you are asking me? ...............
4  You wait here for a minute. ...............
5  Where you've been all day? ...............
6  Why do not these lights work? ...............
7  What beautiful eyes she's got! ...............
8  Answer somebody the phone, please. ...............
9  I don't hope it'll rain. ...............
10  Don't you believe him. ...............
11  'Don't you want some coffee?'  'No, I do.' ...............
12  I don't smoke nor drink. ...............

**3 Which speaker wants to leave?**

Speaker 1: Would it be better for me to leave now? …
Speaker 2: Wouldn't it be better for me to leave now? …

**4 Choose the correct forms of the cartoon captions.**

'*You have / Have you* a go in ours,
and we'll have a go in yours, okay?'

'*What / How* romantic! Breakfast in bed!'

**5** Can you complete these typical children's questions, using words from the boxes? And can you answer any of them? (Parents usually can't.)

blue   built   different   each other ✓   flying fish   Grand Canyon   how   round
stars are there   they make   what

▶ animals ever help   *Do animals ever help each other?* ............................
1 why every animal ....................................................................
2 really fly ..............................................................................
3 why the Earth ........................................................................
4 why the sky ...........................................................................
5 how deep ..............................................................................
6 light year .............................................................................
7 how bulletproof glass ...............................................................
8 why the Eiffel Tower ................................................................
9 how many .............................................................................
10 birds fly ...............................................................................

come from   frogs eat   God   make you cry   tails   time   what
when you die   who invented   why water

11 why cutting onions ..................................................................
12 where babies ..........................................................................
13 where go ...............................................................................
14 real ......................................................................................
15 football ................................................................................
16 makes thunder ........................................................................
17 what ....................................................................................
18 why cats ...............................................................................
19 wet ......................................................................................
20 what ....................................................................................

**6** INTERNET EXERCISE. Use a search engine to find out which expression is more common in each of the following pairs.

1  **A** "seems not to be"        **B** "does not seem to be"
2  **A** "seems not to have"       **B** "does not seem to have"
3  **A** "Is it not beautiful?"      **B** "Isn't it beautiful?"
4  **A** "I hope not."              **B** "I don't hope so."

These three verbs live a double life. They can be **auxiliary verbs** used to form questions, negatives, emphatic forms, perfect and progressive tenses and passives. They can also be **ordinary full verbs**. For this reason, each of them can appear twice in a single phrase.

I *am being* served.     **Have** you **had** an invitation?     What **do** you **do**?

Some of the basic uses can benefit from revision even at this level, and are covered in the following pages, along with other more advanced points.

## *be*: progressive forms; *do be*

**progressives**  We use *am being, are being* etc for **actions** and **behaviour,** but not feelings. Compare:

* *You're being* stupid. (= 'You're **doing** stupid things.')
  I *was being* careful. (= 'I **was doing** something carefully.')
* *I'm depressed just now.* (NOT ~~I'm being depressed just now.~~)
  She **was** very cheerful yesterday. (NOT ~~She was being~~ …)

**1  Put in the best form of *be*.**

1  The baby ..................................... very good today.
2  I ..................................... a bit lonely these days.
3  John ..................................... difficult about money again – it's a real problem.
4  Really! The children ..................................... absolutely impossible this morning.
5  I don't know why I ..................................... so tired this week.
6  You ..................................... very careless with those glasses.
7  I didn't really mean what I said. I ..................................... silly.
8  She ..................................... excited about her birthday – it's sweet.

**Note:  *do(n't) be*  Do** can be used with *be* in negative and emphatic imperatives (see page 10).
   ***Don't be*** sad.     ***Do be*** careful.

For progressive *be* in passive structures (e.g. *I'm being served*), see pages 78 and 297.

| 'To be is to do.' (*Socrates*) | 'To do is to be.' (*Jean-Paul Sartre*) | 'Dobedobededo.' (*Frank Sinatra*) |

'The dog's being impossible again.'

# *there is*: revise the basics

**1** **Check your knowledge. Put in the correct form of *there is (not)*.**

▶ *There will not be* ................ (OR *There won't be* ................) a meeting tomorrow.

▶ How many Prime Ministers *have there been* ................ since 1950?

1 ................................ no Europeans in Australia in 1700.

2 ................................ any messages for me while I was out?

3 This has been a relatively mild winter. ................................ no snow at all.

4 I'm hungry. ................................ anything to eat in the house?

5 I got back home to find that ................................ a burglary.

6 I don't think ................................ any reason to get upset.

7 Sorry – ................................ any more decaf.

8 Dr McPherson is ill, so ................................ a lecture tomorrow.

9 ................................ going ................................ an enormous row when your father gets home.

10 Why ................................ so many strikes this year?

**2** **Complete the sentences with your own ideas.**

1 2000 years ago there weren't any ................................................................

2 There have always been ................................................................

3 There have never been ................................................................

4 Next year there ................................................................

5 In 100 years, perhaps there ................................................................

> ***there is* and *it is*** ***There is*** introduces something **new**. ***It is*** usually refers to something that we have **already talked about**, or that people **already know about**.

'*There's* a taxi outside.' '*It's* for me.' (NOT ~~*It's a taxi outside.*~~)

**3** **Put in *there's* or *it's*.**

1 ................................ a new student in the class.

2 ................................ ice on the lake.

3 'What's that smell?' '................................ Pete's aftershave.'

4 '................................ a funny noise outside.' '................................ just the wind.'

5 'Whose is that coat? '................................ mine.'

6 Would you like some of this coffee? ................................ still hot.

7 ................................ a bus stop just round the corner.

8 I've got a new car. ................................ pretty fast.

9 ................................ a problem with the cooker.

10 ................................ a message for you at the reception desk.

# *there is*: more complex structures

| | |
|---|---|
| with *seem/appear* | *There seems to be a hold-up.* |
| with **modal verbs** | *There may be a job for you.* |
| | *There can't be two people with that name.* |
| with *certain/sure/likely* | *There's certain to be an inquiry.* |
| | *Are there likely to be more strikes?* |
| with *any/no need/sense/point/use* | *Is there any point in talking to him?* |
| | *There's no need to shout.* |
| with *something/anything/etc + wrong* | *Is there something wrong?* |
| in **question tags** | *There won't be a test, will there?* |
| **infinitive** | *We want there to be a referendum.* |
| | *I'd like there to be more time to think.* |
| ***-ing* form** | *What's the chance of there being an agreement?* |
| with **auxiliary** *be* | *There were some people singing in the street.* |
| | (= 'Some people were singing …') |

**1** **Complete the sentences as shown.**

▶ <u>There may be</u> ......................................... a change of government. (*may*)

▶ I don't want <u>there to be</u> ......................................... any trouble. (*infinitive*)

1 ......................................... a restaurant open somewhere. (*must*)

2 ......................................... a problem with the electricity. (*seem*)

3 Thank you, it's OK. ......................................... (*wrong*)

4 ......................................... in making a fuss now – it's too late. (*point*)

5 I've given up hope of ......................................... an improvement in the situation. (*-ing* form)

6 Do you think ......................................... any more customers tonight, or can we close the shop? (*likely*)

7 Don't drive so fast. ......................................... a speed camera ahead. (*could*)

8 ......................................... enough food for everybody, ......................................... (*will*; question tag)

9 I'd like ......................................... plenty of time for discussion. (*infinitive*)

10 ......................................... too many people talking at yesterday's meeting, and not enough listening. (*auxiliary be*)

**2** **GRAMMAR IN TEXTS.** **Put the letters of the boxed expressions into the texts.**
**(Some expressions are needed more than once.)**

| |
|---|
| A there being *(twice)*    B there has never been *(twice)*    C there may have been *(three times)* |
| D there might be *(twice)*    E there will be *(once)*    F will there be *(once)* |

1 … a time when you could tell what part of the island someone came from by the way they talked, but you'd be hard-pressed to do it now.

2 … a time when people got married at 13 and had a child by age 16, but that was when the average life span was something like 35.

3 … a worse time to spend money on a holiday abroad. The pound has gone through the floor, and you may not have a job when you come back.

4 In the words of the Bhagavad Gita: … a time when you and I have not existed, nor … a time when we will cease to exist.

5 **What is the current thinking about … more than one Universe?**
I've been reading about how black holes

6 You are also right about … more than two sides to the story: his side, her side, and the truth.

7 What are some of the signs that … problems in your electrical system? Some older houses

8 Why do scientists believe that … water on the moon? The latest research seems to show

9 One day … more people from India or from China on the Internet than the rest of the world.

10 Some experts believe … as many as four ice ages. Geological evidence from

# *have*: revise the basics

**progressive** When *have* is used to talk about **actions** (e.g. *have dinner*) and **experiences** (e.g. *have problems*), **progressive** forms arc oftcn possible.

'Where's Sue?' 'She'**s having** a shower.'    I'**m having** difficulty understanding this.

With **auxiliary uses** and most **other meanings** of *have* (e.g. possession, relationships, suffering from illnesses), **progressive** forms are **not possible**.

**Have you** seen Steve? (NOT ~~Are you having seen Steve?~~)
**Have you** got my scissors? (NOT ~~Are you having my scissors?~~)
Maurice **has** flu. (NOT ~~Maurice is having flu.~~)

**1  Correct (✓) or not (✗)?**

1  She phoned while we were having lunch. …
2  My sister's having a bad cold. …
3  I'm having trouble with my computer. …
4  Are you having any money on you? …
5  Are you having a table for two? …
6  I'm having a bad headache. …
7  We're having a party tonight. …

**got-forms and do-forms** In modern British English, **shorter present-tense** forms of *have* (e.g. *I have*, *have you*, *she has*) are often **avoided**, especially in informal speech. Instead, we use **longer forms** made with *do* or *got*.

I'**ve got** tickets for tomorrow. (More natural in BrE than *I have tickets for tomorrow*.)
**Do you have** a headache? OR **Have you got** a headache? (More natural than **Have you** a headache?)

*Got* adds nothing to the meaning: **I have got** is **present**, and simply means 'I have'.

**got-forms not used** *Got*-forms are not common in the past, and *got* is not normally used in infinitives or -*ing* forms, in short answers or question tags.

I **had** a bad cold last week. (NOT ~~I had got a bad cold~~ …)
'Have you got any money?'    'No, I **haven't**.' (NOT '~~No, I haven't got.~~')

*Got*-forms are not used with auxiliary *have*, or in expressions like *have dinner*, *have a shower*. And *got*-forms are not used to talk about repeated or habitual actions.

I **don't** often **have** colds. (NOT ~~I haven't often got colds.~~)

**2  Could the verbs be changed to got-forms?**

▶  Do you have a cold? ..Yes......
▶  Let's have a party. ..No.......
1  Have you a moment? ..............
2  I'd like to have more time. ..............
3  I'll have the answer tomorrow. ..............
4  I like having friends round. ..............
5  We often had money problems. ..............
6  I don't have your address. ..............
7  She never has doubts. ..............
8  Do you have a car? ..............

**British and American usage** In AmE, shorter affirmative present-tense forms are common in speech.

**We have** tickets for tomorrow.    **I have** a headache.

In very informal AmE, *I've got* often becomes *I got*, and *got*- and *do*-forms may be mixed.

'I(**'ve**) **got** a new apartment.' 'You **do**?'

For structures like *have something done*, see page 120.  For *have to*, see page 63.

# *do*: emphasis

**emotive emphasis** We can use *do* with affirmative verbs to to show that we **feel strongly** about what we are saying.

*That cake **does** look good!    I **did** enjoy the concert.*

**1** **Complete the sentences with words and expressions from the box; make them more emphatic by using *do/does/did*.**

> cold   depressed   for not phoning   is the right way   long hours   nonsense ✓
> the way she looks at you   the weekend in Scotland   to talk to somebody
> you're mistaken   your new shoes

▶ Julie talks   *Julie does talk nonsense.* ...........................................................

1 I think .................................................................................

2 I hate ..................................................................................

3 This room feels ...................................................................

4 I like ...................................................................................

5 You work ...........................................................................

6 Mary needed ......................................................................

7 We enjoyed .........................................................................

8 I apologise ..........................................................................

9 She looked ..........................................................................

10 I wonder if this ..................................................................

**contrastive emphasis.** *Do* can show a **contrast** – between false and true, appearance and reality, or a general statement and an exception.

*You think I don't care, but I **do** care.*
*It looks simple, but it **does** take a long time to prepare.*
*We didn't have much time to spare, but I **did** visit the cathedral.*

We can also use *do* to compare **expectations** with **reality**.

*I said I would get to the top, and I **did** get to the top.*

**2** **Join the beginnings and ends and write the sentences, adding the idea of contrast by using *do/does/did*.**

| BEGINNINGS | ENDS |
|---|---|
| ▶ I've forgotten her address, | Mind you, it uses a lot of petrol. |
| 1 'You don't understand me.' | She said 10.15, didn't she ? |
| 2 I may not be good at sport, | 'I understand you.' |
| 3 I'll come round this evening, | ▶ but I remember she lives near the park. |
| 4 I'm not sure he speaks English, | but I have to get back home early. |
| 5 It's a nice car to drive. | She goes to jazz concerts sometimes. |
| 6 I do all the housework, | and he had a tooth that needed filling. |
| 7 Although he didn't send me a card, | but Peter helps with the cooking. |
| 8 She doesn't like most music. | he phoned. |
| 9 I told him to see the dentist, | but he speaks some French. |
| 10 She's not on this train. | but I enjoy football. |

▶ *I've forgotten her address, but I do remember she lives near the park.* ...........................

1 ......................................................................................................

2 ......................................................................................................

3 ..................................................................................................................................................................

4 ..................................................................................................................................................................

5 ..................................................................................................................................................................

6 ..................................................................................................................................................................

7 ..................................................................................................................................................................

8 ..................................................................................................................................................................

9 ..................................................................................................................................................................

10 .................................................................................................................................................................

**3** **Put together words and expressions from the box to make sentences like the one in the example, using *do/does/did*.**

| Shakespeare ✓  make films ✓  write plays ✓  sell beer    Italians    lend money    fight against England |
| In England    fight against China    eat potatoes    banks    eat mice    speak Italian    speak Japanese |
| cats    rains a lot    snows a lot    Napoleon |

▶ .....*Shakespeare didn't make films, but he did write plays.*..................................................

1 ..................................................................................................................................................................

2 ..................................................................................................................................................................

3 ..................................................................................................................................................................

4 ..................................................................................................................................................................

5 ..................................................................................................................................................................

**4** GRAMMAR IN TEXTS. **These are extracts from three real letters. Complete them with the expressions from the box. Use a dictionary if necessary.**

| We do appreciate    We do in fact take good care    We do hope |

Dear ...

For the past seven years the Society has benefited from the tax rebate on your covenanted subscription, but unfortunately the covenant has now expired. 1................................... you will renew it.

Dear ...

Thank you for your letter of 14th November. I am extremely sorry that you have been troubled and I entirely agree that writing to you was discourteous and a bad use of our funds.

2................................... to ensure that this does not happen and I am making enquiries as to why we slipped up in your case.

Dear ...

I am writing to thank you for your gift of £200.00 by banker's standing order under your covenant, received on 5th October 2010.

3................................... all your support – it is vital to our expanding work.

For more about emphasis, see pages 260–261. For *do* as a substitute verb (e.g. *'Give him my love.'* *'I will do'*) and *do so*, see pages 276–277.

# Section 3 present and future

## present tenses

English has two 'present' tenses. The **simple present** (*I play, I work* etc) is used especially to talk about regular or permanent activities and situations. The **present progressive** (also called 'present continuous') is used especially to talk about things that are going on around the moment of speaking. For details, see pages 23–29.

Note that in academic grammars, a distinction is made between 'tense' (present or past) and 'aspect' (for example progressive). Tense shows time; progressive aspect typically shows whether an event is seen as ongoing or completed at a particular time. In more practical grammars such as this, it is common to use the term 'tense' in both cases.

## talking about the future

There are several ways to talk about the future in English (see pages 30–37). Three common structures are the ***will*-future**, ***be going to*** and the **present progressive**. The differences between these are complicated (and not generally very important). The explanations on pages 30–33 give some guidelines, but it is not possible to give simple precise rules for the use of these structures – often we can use two or three different forms to express the same idea.

The only bike you'll ever need

recharges up to 3 devices simultaneously

You'll love these shoes

Puts the fun back into driving

... will revolutionise your listening

It makes sense to go for the latest TV technology

# present tenses: revise the basics

| | SIMPLE PRESENT | PRESENT PROGRESSIVE |
|---|---|---|
| + | *I/you/we/they* **work**   *he/she/it* **works** | *I* **am**, *you* **are** etc *work***ing** |
| ? | **do** *I/you/we/they* work?   **does** *he/she/it* work? | **am** *I*, **are** *you* etc *work***ing**? |
| - | *I/you/we/they* **do not** work   *he/she/it* **does not** work | *I* **am not**, *you* are not etc *work***ing** |

- things that are **always true**
- things that happen **all the time**, **repeatedly**, **often**, **sometimes**, **never** etc.

- things that are happening **now**
- things that are happening **around now**
- things that are **changing**

*You **live** in Brighton, don't you?*
*No thanks. I **don't drink** coffee.*
*The Danube **runs** into the Black Sea*
*Oliver **works** for a bank.*
*What **do** giraffes **eat**?*
*I **play** tennis every Wednesday.*
*The sun **rises** in the east.*

*My **parents are living** with me just now.*
*Look – Peter's **drinking** your coffee.*
*Why **is** that child **running** away?*
*Harry's **not working** at the moment.*
*I'm **trying** to eat more vegetables.*
*She's **not playing** much tennis these days.*
*Interest rates **are rising** again.*

**1** CHECK YOUR KNOWLEDGE. **Match the beginnings and ends.**

- ▶ What do you write? C.
- ▶ What are you writing? F.
1  What do you do? …
2  What are you doing? …
3  Where do you work? …
4  Where are you working? …
5  Does your son play the violin? …
6  Is your son playing the violin? …
7  What language does she speak? …
8  What language is she speaking? …
9  Who drinks champagne? …
10  Who's drinking champagne? …

A  Actually, that's the radio.
B  French – she's from Switzerland.
C  Computer manuals.
D  I need to get this car started.
E  I'm an architect.
F  A letter to my mother.
G  I'm in Cardiff this week.
H  In a big insurance company.
I  It sounds like Russian.
J  Me – can I have some more?
K  Me, when I can afford it.
L  No, the piano.

**non-progressive verbs**  Remember: some verbs are mostly used in **simple** tenses even if we mean 'just now' (see pages 28–29).

*I **like** your dress.* (NOT ~~I'm liking your dress.~~)     *What **do they mean**?* (NOT ~~What are they meaning?~~)

**2** CHECK YOUR KNOWLEDGE. **Circle the correct verb forms.**

1  I *think / am thinking* we're going to be late.
2  Look – *it snows / it's snowing*.
3  *Do you look / Are you looking* for the bus station?
4  I *don't understand / am not understanding* this application form at all.
5  *Do you know / Are you knowing* whether they take dollars here?
6  What *do you want / are you wanting*?
7  I *hate / am hating* this programme.
8  Why *do you drive / are you driving* on the wrong side of the road?
9  Who *do you look / are you looking* at?
10  I *don't remember / am not remembering* why I came into the kitchen.

# instructions, commentaries, stories

**Present tenses** are common in instructions, commentaries and stories. The **simple present** is used for things that happen **one after another**, and the **present progressive** for **longer background situations**. (This is exactly like the way the simple past and past progressive are used together – see page 41.)

*'How **do** I **get** to the police station?' 'You **go** straight on for half a mile, then you **come** to a garage. You **take** the next left, then as you**'re coming** up to a railway bridge, look out for a sign on the right.'*
*I **put** some butter in a frying pan. While the butter **is melting**, I **break** three eggs into a bowl and **beat** them …*
*Chekhov **shoots**, Burns **punches** it away, and it's a corner. Meanwhile Fernandez **is warming up**, ready to replace …*
*So he**'s** just **having** breakfast when the doorbell **rings**. He **opens** the door and **sees** this beautiful woman outside. She**'s wearing** …*

Note the use of the present progressive for slower-moving commentaries.

*The Oxford boat **is moving** further and further ahead. And what**'s happening** now? Cambridge **are getting** very low in the water. **Are** they **sinking**? …*

**1** Put in simple present or present progressive verbs.

1 While the meat ....................................., I ..................................... the potatoes and
..................................... them in cold water. (*roast, peel, put*)
2 Giacomo ..................................... Miller deliberately ..................................... the ball away
with his hand. But the referee ..................................... (*shoot, knock, not look*)
3 So he ..................................... into the bar. And there's his girlfriend.
She ..................................... to a good-looking guy with a beard. So he
..................................... to them and ..................................... 'Hi!' (*walk, talk, go up, say*)

**2** Explain how you boil an egg or start to drive a car. Begin 'First I …'

..................................................................................................................................................
..................................................................................................................................................
..................................................................................................................................................
..................................................................................................................................................

**3** Write instructions to tell somebody how to get from one place to another (for example, from the nearest station to your home). Begin 'You …'

..................................................................................................................................................
..................................................................................................................................................
..................................................................................................................................................
..................................................................................................................................................

**4** Write the beginning of a short present-tense story.

..................................................................................................................................................
..................................................................................................................................................
..................................................................................................................................................
..................................................................................................................................................

# more about present tenses

**repeated actions** Repeated actions just **around the moment of speaking: present progressive.**
**Other** repeated actions: **simple present**.

*Why **is** he **hitting** the dog?     Jake's **seeing** a lot of Felicity these days.*
*I **go** to the mountains about twice a year.     Water **boils** at 100° Celsius.*

**1** Write about two or three things that you're doing a lot just around now; and some other things that you do from time to time.

......................................................................................................................
......................................................................................................................
......................................................................................................................
......................................................................................................................
......................................................................................................................
......................................................................................................................

**changes** We use the present progressive for **changing and developing situations**, even if these are **not** just **around the moment of speaking**.

*The political situation **is getting** worse.     Children **are growing up** faster.*
*Scientists say the universe **is expanding**, and has been since the beginning of time.*

**2** Write some sentences about some things that are changing (for example, some of the things in the box).

cities   computers   education   the economic situation   transport   travel
TV programmes   your English

......................................................................................................................
......................................................................................................................
......................................................................................................................
......................................................................................................................
......................................................................................................................
......................................................................................................................
......................................................................................................................
......................................................................................................................

**not around the moment of speaking** The simple present and present progressive can be used together even when we are talking about things going on **around other moments**, not the moment of speaking. This is common with *when* (meaning 'whenever').

*You **look** lovely when you**'re smiling**.*
*When the post **comes** I**'m** usually **having** breakfast.*

**3** Put in the correct forms.
   1  I hate it if people ................................... me when I ...................................
      (*interrupt, work*)
   2  I ................................... some of my best ideas while I ................................... in the
      country. (*get, walk*)
   3  When Alice ................................... about something, she ................................... funny
      grunting noises. (*think, make*)
   4  Our house ................................... really cold when the wind ...................................
      from the east. (*get, blow*)

→

# more about present tenses (continued)

**progressive with *always*** We can use a progressive form with *always* and similar words to talk about repeated but unpredictable or unplanned events.

*She's **always turning up** with little presents for the children.*
*I'm **always running into** Joanna in the supermarket.*

The structure is often used to make complaints and criticisms.

*This computer's **continually crashing** at the most inconvenient moments.*
*She's **forever taking** days off because of one little illness or another.*
*This government **is always thinking** of new ways to take your money.*

 Write a sentence about somebody you know who is always doing something annoying.

..................................................................................................................

**NOTES**

***I hear/see; it says*** We often use *I hear* or *I see* in the sense of 'I have heard/seen' to introduce pieces of information.
   ***I hear** Karen's getting married.*      ***I see** they're closing High Street again.*
Note also the similar use of *It says.*
   ***It says** in the paper there's a rail strike tomorrow.*
   *Where **does it say** that I need a visa?*

**here comes; there goes** We use the **simple present** in these two expressions.
   ***Here comes** the postman.*      *This wind! **There goes** my hat!*

**performatives** Sometimes we **do** something by **saying** something.
Verbs used like this are called **performatives**: they are normally **simple present**.
   *I won't do it again – I **promise**.*      *I hereby **declare** you man and wife.*
   *I **swear** to tell the truth.*      *I **name** this ship 'Spirit of Adventure'.*

**informal progressives** Progressives can sometimes make statements sound more friendly and informal (see page 291). Compare:
   *We **look forward** to further discussions in due course.*
   *I'm really **looking forward** to our week with you and the kids in July.*

**duration** Remember that we use a **present perfect**, not a present tense, to say **how long** things have continued up to the present.
   *I've **been waiting** since six o'clock.* (NOT ~~I'm waiting since ...~~)

'He's swearing in full sentences now.'

# Prison death rates • *rise / (are rising)* alarmingly

A GOVERNMENT COMMITTEE [1] *calls / is calling* for an investigation into the number of people who [2] *now die / are now dying* from natural causes inside the prison system. It [3] *appears / is appearing* that because of poor healthcare and a sedentary lifestyle, more and more prisoners [4] *die / are dying* prematurely. The increase is not due to a rise in the prison population or an increase in the age of inmates.

A recent report [5] *finds / is finding* that the average age of male prisoners who [6] *die / are dying* from natural causes is 56; the average for women is 47. In the general British population, the average age of death for men is 78 and for women 81. Death rates are thought to be higher in prison because prisoners [7] *take / are taking* less exercise and [8] *eat / are eating* less well than most of the population. They [9] *also suffer / are also suffering* higher levels of stress, and some [10] *receive / are receiving* substandard healthcare. Although the government [11] *currently invests / is currently investing* substantial funds in order to improve prisoner welfare, the focus is on reducing levels of suicide and self-harm, and the expenditure [12] *has / is having* little or no effect on the more general problem of rising death rates. ■

6 (Circle) **the correct verb forms for the cartoon captions.**

'Things *look / are looking* bad.'

'I *sell / I'm selling* this for a friend.'

# non-progressive verbs

Some verbs are rarely or never used in progressive forms, even if we are talking about what is happening at a particular moment.

I **don't like** her hairstyle. (NOT ~~I'm not liking her hairstyle.~~)
I called because I **need** to talk. (NOT … ~~because I'm needing to talk.~~)

Many of these verbs refer to states rather than actions. Here is a list of the most common ones.

**mental and emotional states; use of the senses**
*assume, believe, doubt, feel (= 'have an opinion'), hate, hear, imagine (= 'suppose'), know, (dis)like, love, prefer, realise, recognise, regret, remember, see, smell, suppose, taste, think (= 'have an opinion'), understand, want, wish.*

'I **love** you.' 'I **don't believe** you.' (NOT ~~'I'm loving you.' 'I'm not believing you.'~~)
I **doubt** if the train will be on time.     Who **do** you **think** will win?
I **feel** it's time for a break.

**communicating, causing reactions**
*(dis)agree, appear, astonish, deny, impress, mean, please, promise, satisfy, seem, surprise.*

What **do** you **mean**?     We **seem** to have a problem.     Your attitude **surprises** me.

**other state verbs**
*be, belong, concern, consist, cost, depend, deserve, fit, have (= 'possess'), include, involve, lack, matter, measure (= 'have length etc'), need, owe, own, possess, resemble, weigh (= 'have weight').*

Who **does** this car **belong** to?     I **need** help.     'I'm late.' 'It **doesn't matter**.'

**1** **Choose the best verbs from the boxes to complete the sentences.**

| consist   contain   depend   imagine   include   lack   not deserve   own |

1  'Can you do me a favour?' 'It ...........................'
2  This jam ........................... of 50% sugar, 10% fruit, and a lot of other stuff.
3  If that cake ........................... nuts, I can't eat it.
4  I'm too good to you. You ........................... me.
5  The soup's nice, but it ........................... salt.
6  I wonder who ........................... that dog.
7  No need to tip – the bill ........................... 15% service.
8  I ........................... you'd like a rest soon.

| appear   concern   deny   impress   matter   mean   owe   recognise |

9   'Don't we know that man?' 'Maybe. I don't ........................... him.
10  Do you know what 'incomprehensible' ...........................?
11  We're going to be late, but I don't think it ........................... much.
12  I'll pay you what I ........................... you tomorrow, if that's OK.
13  'How much money is the company making?' 'That doesn't ........................... you.'
14  There ........................... to be a problem with the train.
15  The police are questioning three men about the attack, but they ........................... everything.
16  'I've got my own helicopter.' 'You don't ........................... me.'

**progressive and non-progressive uses**  Some of these verbs may occasionally be used in progressive forms, especially to emphasise the idea of **change**, **development** or **novelty**.

*As I get older, I'm remembering less and less.     I didn't expect to like this place, but I'm really **loving** it.*

Some others are used in progressive forms with particular meanings. Compare:

*What **do** you **think** of her singing?     What **are** you **thinking** about?*
*I **weigh** too much these days.     I got a shock when I **was weighing** myself this morning.*

**Look** (meaning 'seem') can often be progressive or not, with little difference.

*You **look** / You're **looking** a bit tired today.*

**Smell** and **taste** can be progressive when we are talking about the deliberate use of the senses to find something out. Compare:

- *This meat **smells** funny.     I (can) **smell** smoke*
  *'What are you doing?'  'I'm **smelling** the fish to see if it's OK.'*

- *The soup **tastes** wonderful. I think I (can) **taste** garlic in it.*
  *'Leave that cake alone!'  'I'm just **tasting** it to see if it's OK.'*

**Feel** (referring to physical sensations) can be progressive or not, with little difference.

*I **feel** / I'm **feeling** fine.*

**See** can be progressive when it means 'meet'. Compare

*I (can) **see** John over there.     I'm **seeing** the doctor tomorrow.*

**2  Correct (✓) or not (✗)?**

1  Of course I'm believing you!  …
2  We're seeing your point.  …
3  Why is everybody looking at the sky?  …
4  I'm feeling you're both wrong.  …
5  What do you think about at this moment?  …
6  She may win, but I doubt it.  …
7  Does this milk taste sour to you?  …
8  I'm feeling quite depressed these days.  …
9  I'm remembering your face, but not your name.  …
10  We see the bank manager soon.  …
11  I'm supposing you'd like coffee.  …
12  I think it's time to go.  …
13  John's aftershave is smelling strange.  …
14  How much are you weighing?  …

'Do these shoes taste funny to you?'

---

**NOTES**

**use of *can***  Can is often used with *see, hear, feel, taste, smell, understand* and *remember* to give a progressive meaning, especially in British English. (See page 61.)
> *I **can see Sue** coming down the road.     **Can** you **smell** burning?*
> *I **can remember** when there were no houses here.*

**perfect tenses**  *Want, need* and *mean* can have present perfect progressive uses; *need* and *want* can have future progressive uses.
> *I've **been wanting** to meet you for years.     **Will** you **be needing** the car today?*
> *There's something I've **been meaning** to tell you.*

**-*ing* forms**  Even verbs which are never progressive have *-ing* forms which can be used in other kinds of structure.
> ***Knowing** her tastes, I bought her chocolate.*
> *I got all the way to the station without **realising** I was wearing my slippers.*

# future: revise the basics:
## *will, going to* or present progressive?

**future in the present**  We generally use **present** forms (present progressive or *am/are/is going to*) when we can **see the future in the present**: we already see things coming or starting.
We prefer *will* (the most common form) when we are simply giving information about the future, with no special reason for using present forms. Compare:

- *I'm seeing* Janet on Tuesday. (the arrangement exists now.)
  *I wonder if she'll recognise me.* (not talking about the present)
- *We're going to* get a new car. (The decision already exists.)
  *I hope it will be better than the old one.* (not talking about the present)

**plans**  *Be going to* and the **present progressive** can both be used to talk about plans.
We use the **present progressive** mostly when the **time** and/or **place** are **fixed**. Compare:

*I'm going to* take a holiday some time soon.     *Joe's spending* next week in France.
*Emma's going to* study biology.     *Phil's starting* work on Monday.

**1**  Rewrite the sentences, putting in expressions from the box and using the present progressive. (Different answers are possible.)

| for tomorrow's concert    from March 1st    next month    next week |
| next year    on Saturday    on Tuesday    this evening    tomorrow morning |

▶  I'm going to play tennis with Andy.
   *I'm playing tennis with Andy on Saturday.* ..............................................................

1  We're going to see Sarah.
   ....................................................................................................................

2  I'm going to start fencing lessons.
   ....................................................................................................................

3  We're going to meet the accountants.
   ....................................................................................................................

4  I'm going to get the car serviced.
   ....................................................................................................................

5  They're going to close the road for repairs.
   ....................................................................................................................

6  Everybody's going to get a free ticket.
   ....................................................................................................................

7  The air traffic controllers are going to strike.
   ....................................................................................................................

8  All the train companies are going to put their prices up.
   ....................................................................................................................

**decisions**  We prefer *be going to* and the **present progressive** for decisions and plans (see above) that exist **in the present** – they have already been made. We prefer *will* to announce decisions **as we make them**. Compare:

'We've got a lot of bills to pay.'  'I know. *I'm going to* do them all on Monday.'
'The plumber's bill has just come in.'  'OK, *I'll pay* it.'

**2** **Put in *I'll* or *I'm going to.***

▶ I've decided. ..*I'm going to*.................. take a week off.

1 'Is Alice coming round?' 'Wait a minute. ..................................... phone and ask her.'

2 'I've left my money at home.' 'Again? OK. .................................... pay.'

3 'Do you want to go for a walk?' 'No, .................................... get some work done.'

4 'I've got a headache.' '.................................... get you an aspirin.'

5 .................................... sell this car – it's giving me nothing but trouble.

6 Can you answer the phone if it rings? .................................... have a shower.

7 .................................... change my job soon.

8 'There's the doorbell.' '.................................... go.'

---

**predictions: what we expect** We prefer *going to* when we can already **see the future in the present**: we can see things coming or starting, or they are already **planned**. We prefer *will* to say what we **think or believe** about the future. Compare:

*Careful! The meat's going to burn.* (I can see it now.)
*Don't ask Pete to cook the steak – he'll burn it.* (I'm sure, because I know him.)

We don't use the present progressive to predict events which are outside our control.

*It's going to rain soon.* BUT NOT ~~It's raining soon.~~

**3** **(Circle) the best form.**

▶ Claire (*is going to*)/ *will* have a baby.

1 Perhaps *I'm going to / I'll* see you at the weekend.

2 Look at the sky: *it's going to / it will* snow.

3 Look out – *we're going to / we'll* hit that car!

4 Ask John – *he's probably going to / he'll probably* know the answer.

5 You'd better put a coat on, or *you're going to / you'll* get cold.

6 If you press this key, the computer *is going to / will* shut down.

7 You can see from Barbara's face that *there's going to / there'll* be trouble.

8 It's no use telling Andy about your problems; *he's going to / he'll* tell everybody else.

---

**simple present** We sometimes use the **simple present** to talk about the future; for instance when we talk about **timetables**, routines and schedules.

*The meeting starts at ten o'clock.*     *What time does the train arrive in Paris?*
*My plane leaves from Heathrow.*

We can also use the **simple present** to give and ask for **instructions**.

'*Where do I get an application form?*' '*You go to the main office on the second floor.*'

In other cases we **don't** use the **simple present** in simple sentences to talk about the **future.**

*Emma's coming round later.* (NOT ~~Emma comes ...~~ )     *I'll write – I promise.*
*There's the phone. I'll answer it.* (NOT ... ~~I answer.~~)

For the simple present with a future meaning after *if, when* etc, see pages 204 and 232.

**4** **Choose the best tense.**

▶ The film (*ends*)/ *will end* at midnight.

▶ I *phone* /(*will phone*) you soon.

1 I *start / will start* dieting after Christmas.

2 Rob *comes / is coming* round after 7.00.

3 *Do you / Will you* post my letters?

4 I *have / will have* a French class at 9.00 tomorrow.

5 The train isn't direct – you *change / will change* at Manchester.

6 My final exam *is / will be* in May.

7 What time *does / will* the concert start?

8 I *play / am playing* hockey tomorrow.

# more about the present progressive, *going to* and *will*

**spoken and written English** *Be going to* and the **present progressive** are particularly common in **spoken** English, as ways of talking about the future. This is because conversation is often about future events that we can **see coming**, so present forms are natural. In written English, these forms are less often used. *Will* is extremely common in **writing**, because written language tends to deal with less immediate future events, when we do not see the future in the present. *Will* is also preferred when giving information about **impersonal,** fixed arrangements – for example official itineraries. Compare:

*We're meeting* Sandra at 6.00.
*The President* **will arrive** *at the airport at 14.00. He* **will meet** …

**pronunciation of *going to*.** In informal speech, *going to* is often pronounced as /gənə/. This is often shown in writing as *gonna*.

**1** **GRAMMAR IN A TEXT.** **Put the letters of the boxed expressions into the text.**

> A it will be   B there will be   C will be introduced   D will be presented
> E will be welcomed   F will cast off   G will cover   H will play   I you will be

**O**n a wildlife cruise with Wildlife Worldwide, ¹… on a small vessel (the vessels we work with generally accommodate between 20 and 128 passengers), just enough to be able to meet new people and get to know them over the course of the trip, and to be able to recognise and greet all of the other passengers onboard. Not so many that every time you see a face ²… be a new one!

On a wildlife cruise the vessels have been specially adapted and refitted to accommodate guests, since many of them were actually research vessels in a former life. On a wildlife cruise, ³… illustrated talks and presentations throughout the journey. These ⁴… a whole range of topics from birds and mammals, to geography, history and astronomy, and they ⁵… by the onboard guides and experts who ⁶… such an important role in making your trip a special one.

To begin with you ⁷… aboard with a glass of champagne and a bite to eat. The crew ⁸… the boat, and once you are under way you ⁹… to the captain and his crew. Departures are generally late afternoon/early evening. Passengers are free to visit the ship's bridge any time of the day or night.

It is fascinating seeing how the ship's course is plotted, and to observe the monitors of depth, wind speed and wave height! (*Adapted from Oceans Worldwide website.*)

**2** **GRAMMAR IN A TEXT.** **Put the letters of the boxed expressions into the text.**

> A going to be happy   B going to be there   C going to see   D It's going to be
> E there are going to be   F we're catching   G we're leaving

Well, ¹… tomorrow, Sandra. ²… amazing! It's quite a small boat – about 50 passengers, so we'll soon get to know everybody. And ³… half a dozen experts on this and that giving lectures in the evenings, and going ashore with us and answering our stupid questions when we land. Tony Soper's ⁴…, believe it or not, so the bird-watchers are ⁵… ! And there's a terrific woman called Ingrid Visser who's red-hot on killer whales. I can't remember the others, but I know there's a marine mammal expert, and an astronomer. And we're definitely ⁶… whales – lots and lots of whales, they've promised! Can't wait!

Well, must go and pack – ⁷… a very early flight. Looking forward to seeing you in July. Prepare yourselves for a long photo evening!

Love from both to both

Jane

***shall*** **and** ***will*** In modern English *I/we will* and *I/we shall* can generally be used with no difference of meaning. *Will* is more common, and *shall* is dying out. (In any case, the commonest forms in speech are the contractions *I'll* and *we'll*.)

***shall*** **in questions** In older English, *shall* was used to talk about **obligation** (rather like *should*). This meaning still survives in **first-person questions**, where *shall* is used to **ask for instructions or suggestions,** or **offer services**.

*What time* ***shall we*** *come round?*    ***Shall I*** *take your coat?*

Compare the use of *will* to ask for information:

*What time* ***will we*** *get into London?*

**legal language** Legal documents, such as contracts, often use *shall* to express obligation.

*The hirer* ***shall be*** *responsible for maintenance of the vehicle.* (from a car-hire contract)

**3** **Put in** *shall* **or** *will*.

1 Where ........................... we go on holiday this year?

2 Where ........................... I be this time next year?

3 Sending out the invitations ........................... be Jim's responsibility.

4 The tenant........................... be wholly responsible for all decoration and repairs.

5 ........................... I put the kettle on?

6 What time ........................... I need to be at the airport?

7 What ........................... I cook for supper?

8 How soon ........................... we hear about the application?

The Hirer shall, during the period of the hiring, be responsible for: supervision of the premises, the fabric and the contents; their care, safety from damage however slight or change of any sort; and the behaviour of all persons using the premises whatever their capacity, including proper supervision of car parking arrangements. The Hirer shall make good or pay for all damage (including accidental damage) to the premises or to the fixtures, fittings or contents and for loss of contents. The Hirer shall not use the premises for any purpose other than that described in the Hiring Agreement and shall not allow the premises to be used for any unlawful purpose or in any unlawful way nor

For other (non-future) uses of *will*, see pages 65 and 72.

**NOTES**

**different forms possible** The differences between the three main structures used to talk about the future are not always very clear-cut. *Will* and present forms (especially *going to*) are often both possible in the same situation, when 'present' ideas like intention or fixed arrangement are a part of the meaning but not very important. The choice of structure will depend on which part of the meaning we want to emphasise. In the following examples all of the different forms would be correct, with no important difference of meaning.

- *What will you do next year?*
  *What are you doing next year?*
  *What are you going to do next year?*
- *All the family will be there.*
  *All the family are going to be there.*
- *If your mother comes, you'll have to help with the cooking.*
  *If your mother comes, you're going to have to help with the cooking.*
- *You won't believe this.*
  *You're not going to believe this.*

# be + infinitive: *I am to … etc*

**official plans etc** We often say that something **is to happen** when we talk about **official plans** and fixed arrangements.

*The Prime Minister **is to visit** British soldiers in Antarctica.*
*Our firm **is to merge** with Universal Export.*

**pre-conditions** The structure is common in ***if*-clauses**, where the main clause expresses a **pre-condition** – something that must happen first if something else **is to happen**.

*We'd better hurry if we**'re to get** there by lunchtime.*
*You'll need to start working if you**'re to pass** your exam.*

**orders** The structure can also be used (for example by parents) to give orders.

*You**'re to do** your homework before you go to bed.*
*Tell Jenny she**'s not to be** back late.*

**1** Here are some (mostly) real spoken or written sentences. Use the *be* + infinitive structure to complete them with verbs from the box. Use a dictionary if necessary.

| assemble   bloom   continue   deliver   follow   get through   inspect   plan   report   tidy up |
|---|

1 Professor Loach ………………………………… eight lectures on classical mythology next term.
2 On his arrival at the airport, the general ……………………………… a guard of honour.
3 If we ……………………………… providing care for homeless children, we need your support today.
4 Young soldiers quickly learn that a good breakfast is vital if they ……………………………… another demanding day.
5 Any new diet has to be simple if you ……………………………… it for any length of time.
6 You have to know where you're going if you ……………………………… the best way of getting there!
7 The chrysanthemums must be planted right away if they ……………………………… for Christmas.
8 The children ……………………………… their room before they watch TV.
9 In case of fire, all staff ……………………………… in the front courtyard.
10 All visitors ……………………………… to the reception desk.

For the past form of this structure (*I was to … etc*), see page 37.
For passive uses (e.g. *to be taken three times a day*), see page 103.

**2** Imagine you are a parent who is going out for the evening, leaving two teenagers alone in the house. Write three instructions beginning 'You're to' and three beginning 'You're not to'.

……………………………………………………………………………………………………………………………………………
……………………………………………………………………………………………………………………………………………
……………………………………………………………………………………………………………………………………………
……………………………………………………………………………………………………………………………………………
……………………………………………………………………………………………………………………………………………
……………………………………………………………………………………………………………………………………………

# future progressive

We use the future progressive (*will be ...ing*) to say that something will be **in progress at a certain time in the future**.

*This time next Tuesday I'll be lying on the beach.*
*You won't be able to park here tomorrow; they'll be mending the road.*

**1** **What will you be doing at ten o'clock tomorrow morning (or some other time, if you prefer)?**

.................................................................................................................

**2** **Write three things that you will certainly not be doing at ten o'clock tomorrow morning (or some other time, if you prefer).**

.................................................................................................................
.................................................................................................................
.................................................................................................................

**polite enquiries** A common use of the **future progressive** is to **ask politely** 'What have you already decided?' Compare:

*Will you write to Oliver?* (request or order)
*Are you going to write to Oliver?* (perhaps pressing for a decision)
*Will you be writing to Oliver?* (just asking about plans)

**3** **Make future progressive questions to ask somebody politely:**

▶ when they are planning to go shopping. *When will you be going shopping?* .......

1 when they intend to pay the rent.
.................................................................................................................

2 who they plan to invite.
.................................................................................................................

3 how soon they intend to come back.
.................................................................................................................

4 when they plan to go home.
.................................................................................................................

5 where they are planning to stay.
.................................................................................................................

6 what time they are planning to have breakfast.
.................................................................................................................

7 what they plan to study at university.
.................................................................................................................

8 whether they expect to use the car.
.................................................................................................................

## Will you be watching the leaders' TV debate?

The first ever prime ministerial TV debate in a UK general election campaign will take place on Thursday.

**Will you be watching?**

"I'll be watching. I want to see how professional liars work."

"Yes, I shall be watching and it will be an interesting test of the party leaders."

"I will be watching until the end of the first question. When none of them have answered simply, openly and honestly, along with millions of other viewers I will switch off and then go to the pub."

(*postings from a website discussion before a British general election*)

# future perfect

The **future perfect** (*I will have driven/worked* etc) can be used to say that something will have been **completed by a certain time in the future.**

We'**ll have finished** planting the new trees by Wednesday.
This government **will have ruined** the country before the next election.

**1** Here are some sentences taken from newspaper articles and reports. Complete them with verbs from the box, using the future progressive. Use a dictionary if necessary.

drive   drop   host   pass   put on   quadruple   rise

1 When this year's competition in Nottingham is completed, Great Britain, like Japan, ...................................... it on 3 occasions.
2 In a few weeks' time, the fallen leaves .................................... from ankle to knee deep.
3 Frank, Mr Andrews' chauffeur, .................................... his boss more than 12,000 miles by the end of the campaign.
4 If a traveller goes eastwards round the Earth, when he gets halfway he .................................... through 12 time zones and gained 12 hours.
5 The decision means that annual government support for the railways .................................... from well over £1 billion to around £300 million in 10 years.
6 Within 100 years the human population ....................................
7 If you do not weigh yourself for a year and you eat just an extra 500 calories each day during that time, you .................................... a full 21.8 kg; rather a nasty shock!

The **future perfect progressive** (*I will have been driving/working* etc) is not very common. We can use it to say **how long** something will have continued by a certain time.

By next summer I'**ll have been working** here for eight years.

**2** Write three sentences about yourself with the future perfect progressive. For example, say how long you will have been learning English / working / living in your house.
1 By the end of this year, ....................................................................................................
2 By ......................................................................................................................................
3 By ......................................................................................................................................

**Note: other uses** These tenses, and other structures with *will*, can be used not only to talk about the future, but also to express **certainty** about the past and present (see page 65).
As you **will have heard** by now, we are planning to open a new branch in Liverpool.
The world's top skiers **will have been studying** the course all morning, in preparation for the first big event this afternoon.

'When you have lost your Inns, drown your empty selves, for you will have lost the last of England.'
(*Hilaire Belloc*)

# future in the past

present progressive → **past progressive**     *am/is/are going to* → **was/were going to**
*will* → **would**     *am/is/are to* → **was/were to**

*I was in a state of panic, because I **was sitting** my final exams in two days.*
*We **were going to** start a business if we could raise enough capital.*
*I had a feeling that things **would** soon turn difficult.*
*So this was the town where I **was to spend** the winter. I didn't like the look of it.*

*She treated me like dirt. But she **would live** to regret it.*
*I thought we were saying goodbye for ever. But we **were to meet** again under very strange circumstances.*

**1** **Write some things that were in the future when you were ten years old, and that you could not have expected.**

▶ *I would become a teacher. I was to spend eight years in France.* ...........
...............................................................................................
...............................................................................................
...............................................................................................
...............................................................................................
...............................................................................................

**2** **About 30,000 years ago, someone painted this picture on a cave wall. Write some of the things that were in the future, and that he/she could never have imagined. Use *would.***

▶ *People would learn how to make metal tools. Empires would come*
   *and go. There would be ...* ......................................................
...............................................................................................
...............................................................................................
...............................................................................................
...............................................................................................

# more practice

**1** **Correct the mistakes or write 'Correct'.**

▶ Penguins ~~aren't flying~~. *don't fly* ..................

▶ Nobody's listening to me. *Correct* ..................

1 'What do you write?' 'A report for the Managing Director.' ..................

2 I'm thinking this is the wrong address. ..................

3 Why is that man jumping up and down? ..................

4 Iron is melting at 1536°. ..................

5 How do your tai-chi lessons go? ..................

6 We're seeing a lot of Peter and Susan just now. ..................

7 He's always criticising! ..................

8 It's saying in today's paper that the pilots are going on strike. ..................

9 'Is it going to snow?' 'I'm doubting it.' ..................

10 Julie's not feeling very well today. ..................

11 This cheese is tasting funny. ..................

12 I'm not working next Friday. ..................

13 We should leave now if we're to catch the train. ..................

14 Will you be seeing Edward when you're in Glasgow? ..................

15 This time tomorrow I'm lying on the beach. ..................

16 Do you know what time the film starts? ..................

17 Next July we have been together for five years. ..................

18 I'll never be knowing what he thinks of me. ..................

19 Sorry I'm late – the train I was going to catch was cancelled. ..................

20 They showed me the room where I would have stayed. I said it was OK. ..................

**2** **Choose the correct form of the cartoon caption.**

'I'm sorry, *he doesn't see / he's not seeing* anyone today.'

**3** **Write four predictions for next week. (You can use *will* or *going to*.)**
**Check them at the end of the week to see how many were right.**

..................
..................
..................
..................

**4** **Write two things that you are certainly going to do one day, and two things that**
**you are certainly never going to do.**

..................
..................
..................
..................

**5** DO IT YOURSELF. **Which of these rules are wrong?**

1 We use *will* especially when we can see the future in the present.
2 *Going to* is often pronounced 'gonna'.
3 The future perfect progressive is very common in conversation.
4 *Shall* is not used in modern English.
5 We don't normally use the present progressive for fixed future arrangements.

**Rules ……………………………… are wrong.**

**6** GRAMMAR IN A TEXT. **Put in simple present or present progressive forms of the verbs in the box.**

| arrive decide fall find give go out hide live light lose sing start |
| stay tell try work write |

### Puccini's opera La Bohème: what happens in Act 1

It is a bitterly cold winter in 19th-century Paris. Marcello, a painter, and Rodolfo, a writer, [1] …………………………to keep warm. Their musician friend Schaunard [2] ………………………… with food, firewood, wine, cigars, and money: he [3] ………………………… lessons to an eccentric Englishman and has just been paid. They [4] ………………………… to eat, but then [5] ………………………… to go out and spend the money at a café. Rodolfo [6] ………………………… behind for a moment to finish an article that he [7] ………………………… While he [8] ………………………… , there is a knock at the door. It is Mimi, who [9] ………………………… in another room in the building. Her candle has blown out, and she has no matches. Rodolfo [10] ………………………… it for her. Then Mimi [11] ………………………… her key. Both candles [12] ………………………… Rodolfo [13] ………………………… her key but [14] ………………………… it. They [15] ………………………… each other their life stories in two songs; while they [16] ………………………… they [17] ………………………… in love.

**7** GRAMMAR IN A TEXT. **Put in the verbs from the boxes.**

| helped read started taken will have been will have tidied |

### School Holidays

By ten o'clock this morning my children [1] ………………………… off school for 67 hours. During that time they [2] ………………………… their rooms, [3] ………………………… several books, [4] ………………………… our elderly neighbour with his garden, [5] ………………………… a box of unwanted toys to charity and [6] ………………………… their holiday diaries. Later in the week they will visit the Science Museum, go on a nature trail and have a dental check-up. They will go to bed at 8.30pm on the dot and watch only half an hour of BBC4 a day.

| broken up cleaned up given up have spent hidden spent unloaded will have baked |

Yeah, right. This is the more likely scenario: I [7] ………………………… several batches of cupcakes, [8] …………………………the dishwasher 20 times, [9] ………………………… almost three hours looking for tiny lost bits of Lego, and [10] …………………………trying to interest my eldest in reading a book. I will have [11] ………………………… several paint-related disasters, [12] ………………………… fights, and [13] ………………………… the remote control. Like millions of other parents, I will also [14] ………………………… an unbelievable sum of money on plastic rubbish in a museum shop. And there are several more weeks of this to look forward to. School holidays!

(*Sarah Vine, The Times, adapted*)

# Section 4  past and perfect tenses

English uses six different verb forms to refer to past events and situations. They are:

| NAME | EXAMPLE |
|---|---|
| (simple) present perfect | I have worked |
| present perfect progressive | I have been working |
| simple past | I worked |
| past progressive | I was working |
| (simple) past perfect | I had worked |
| past perfect progressive | I had been working |

Another common name for 'progressive' is 'continuous'.

In academic grammars, a distinction is made between 'tense' (present or past) and 'aspect' (perfective and/or progressive). Tense shows time; aspect shows, for example, whether an event is seen as ongoing or completed at a particular time. In more practical grammars such as this, it is common to use the term 'tense' for all of these different forms.

The uses of the six past and perfect tenses are covered in the following pages. Note in particular that the English **present perfect** (e.g. *I have seen*) is **constructed** in the same way as a tense in some other Western European languages (e.g. *j'ai vu, ich habe gesehen, ho visto, jeg har set*), but that it is **not used** in exactly the same way (see page 42).

For past and perfect **passive** tenses, see page 78.

**Maxwells** have been established for over twenty years. We have grown and expanded from a small printing firm into an internationally known organisation.

FOR OVER THIRTY YEARS WE HAVE BEEN DEDICATED TO PRODUCING THE HIGHEST QUALITY GOURMET COFFEE.

For over forty years we have been designing and manufacturing test equipment for car manufacturers.

*For over half a century we have supplied our customers with the very best in soft furnishings. More recently we have added bed linens and dress fabrics to our ever expanding product range.*

For over sixty years we have been producing high quality herbal medicines and food supplements for dogs and cats.

For over seventy years we have cared for the needs of the holiday visitor. We have welcomed guests from all over the world.

Children have been treated at the **Nuffield Orthopaedic Centre** for over eighty years. We have extensive long-term experience in treatment of complex disorders.

WE HAVE BEEN TRADING FOR OVER NINETY YEARS, AND WE HAVE NOW BECOME ONE OF THE LARGEST FOOD MANUFACTURERS IN CANADA.

For over a century, we have built up customer relationships built on strength, stability, integrity, and service.

# simple past and past progressive: revise the basics

**the difference** We use the **simple past** for **completed actions** (long or short, repeated or not).

*Pam **phoned** this morning.*    *When I was younger I **played** football most days.*
*I **painted** the kitchen yesterday. It **took** all day*

We use the **past progressive** to say that actions were **not complete** at a particular time.

*At ten o'clock last night I **was still painting** the kitchen.*

Note the difference when we use the **past progressive** and the **simple past** together.
**Past progressive: longer** action or situation.
**Simple past: complete shorter** action that **happened** while the longer action **was happening**.

*At 1.00, when I **got** home from the hospital, Pete **was cooking** lunch.*

**1** **Put in the correct tenses.**

▶ This time yesterday I ..*was running*..... in a half-marathon. (*run*)
▶ We ..*were having*....... a great time yesterday evening, but then the neighbours ..*came*............... round and ..*complained*........ about the noise. (*have; come; complain*)

1 I ................................. my girlfriend while we ................................. in Italy. (*meet; work*)
2 When I walked in they ................................. cards. (*all play*)
3 When I ................................. to work this morning I ................................. to buy a new raincoat. (*go; stop*)
4 Oliver ................................. his arm while he ................................. (*break; ski*)
5 I can't remember what I ................................. when I ................................. the news about the crash. (*do; hear*)
6 While we ................................. TV upstairs, somebody ................................. into the house and ................................. my mother's jewellery. (*watch; break; steal*)
7 I ................................. in a rock group when I was at school. (*sing*)
8 He ................................. to find that three policemen ................................. by his bed. (*wake up; stand*)
9 When I was a child, we ................................. our own amusements. (*make*)

**2** **GRAMMAR IN A TEXT.** **Read the news report and (circle) the correct tenses.**

**D**RIVERS ON a Chinese motorway in Sichuan had to stop suddenly because an ostrich [1] *ran / was running* along the road. It [2] *turned out / was turning out* to belong to a Mr Liu, of Meishan, who [3] *explained / was explaining* that the ostrich [4] *ran / was running* away when he [5] *fed / was feeding* it. "I [6] *just left / was just leaving* his pen after giving him his food when he suddenly [7] *ran / was running* out and [8] *dashed / was dashing* into the street," he [9] *said / was saying*. The giant bird [10] *kept on / was keeping on* running, and Liu [11] *followed / was following* it on his motorbike, reports Sichuan News Online. Passing drivers [12] *helped / were helping* him to chase the ostrich into a petrol station, where workers [13] *caught / were catching* it with ropes. ■

# present perfect and simple past: revise the basics

> **meanings** Both these tenses are used to talk about **finished** actions, situations and events. There is a difference.
> The **present perfect** suggests that a finished action has some **connection with the present**.
> The **simple past** does **not** suggest a **connection with the present**.

*I've made a cake. Would you like a slice?*
*I didn't have much to do this morning, so I made a cake.*

**1** Read the sentences and choose the best answers to the questions.

▶ 'I've broken my glasses.' *Are the speaker's glasses broken?* (A) Yes.   B Don't know.   C No.

▶ 'Anna went to London.' *Is Anna in London?*   A Yes.   (B) Don't know.

1 'Sam has been elected chairman.' *Is Sam chairman?*   A Yes.   B Don't know.   C No.

2 'Mum has gone to church.' *Is she in church?*   A Yes.   B Don't know.   C No.

3 'Dad went to the pub.' *Is he in the pub?*   A Yes.   B Don't know.

4 'The cat's caught a mouse.' *Has the cat got the mouse?*   A Yes.   B Don't know.   C No.

5 'Maggie caught a cold.' *Has Maggie got a cold?*   A Yes.   B Don't know.

6 'Marlowe has written a novel.' *Is this a new novel?*   A Yes.   B Don't know.   C No.

7 'Holmes wrote a novel.' *Is this a new novel?*   A Yes.   B Probably not.

8 'I've finished cutting the grass.' *Is the grass short?*   A Yes.   B Don't know.   C No.

9 'She's travelled all over Africa.' *Is she still alive?*   A Yes.   B Don't know.   C No.

> **time words** We **don't** often use the **present perfect** with words for a **finished time**.

*I **went** out four evenings **last week**.* (NOT ~~I've been out … last week.~~)
*Jamie **phoned yesterday**.* (NOT ~~Jamie has phoned yesterday.~~)

> We often use the **present perfect** with words for **time up to now**.

*I've **been** out three evenings **this week**.*     *I've **never seen** a fox.*
***Have** you **read** this **before**?* (= 'at any time up to now')

**2** (Circle) the correct verb form.

1 Several government ministers *were / have been* involved in a big bribery scandal last year.

2 The people in the flat upstairs *disturbed / have disturbed* us every night this week.

3 The aid agencies *distributed / have distributed* 2,000 tonnes of food to the refugees since May.

4 All of our students *achieved / have achieved* excellent exam results last summer.

5 I think I *saw / have seen* this film before.

6 Most of yesterday's newspapers *commented / have commented* critically on Thursday's budget.

7 The 1944 Education Act *attempted / has attempted* to ensure equal educational opportunities for everyone.

8 We're all very pleased that the Managing Director *decided / has decided* to retire next autumn.

'I've spent 25 years making a name for myself and now you want me to CHANGE it?!'

**news and details** We often announce a piece of **news** with the **present perfect**, and then use the **simple past** for the **details** of time and place.

*I've found your glasses. They were in the car.*
*The President has arrived in London. He was met by the Prime Minister ...*

**3** GRAMMAR IN TEXTS. **Read the reports and put in verbs from the box in the correct tenses.**

| be   clash   dig   fire   have   identify   reach   take |

1   Police in France ............................ with protesters striking over wage cuts. Riot police ............................ tear gas at a group of part

2   An oil spill ............................ the Welsh coast. The spill ............................ place early on Tuesday morn

3   Police ............................ eight suspects in last month's Birmingham car bomb attack. Six of the suspects ............................ non-British passports as

4   The fossilised remains of a giant shark ............................ found in Nebraska, US. Scientists ............................ up a gigantic jawbone, teeth and scales

**4** **Find a news report with similar tense use to the examples in Exercise 3 (for example on an internet news page). Write the first two or three sentences here.**

..............................................................................................................................................................
..............................................................................................................................................................
..............................................................................................................................................................
..............................................................................................................................................................

'Mrs Dunne is here for your lesson, Ralph. Where have you hidden the piano?'

'I've wired his electric wheelchair to this control . . . . Want a go?'

'I've never won an argument with her, and the only times I thought I had, I found out the argument wasn't over yet.'
(*US President Jimmy Carter, talking about his wife Rosalyn*)

'Do I like vegetables? I don't know. I have never eaten them. No, that is not quite true. I once ate a pea.'
(*Beau Brummel, 1778–1840*)

# present perfect progressive: revise the basics

**duration** We can use the **present perfect progressive** to talk about actions and situations **continuing up to now**. This is common when we talk about **duration**: how long things have been going on. Compare:

*'**Are** you **waiting** for a table?'* *'Yes. I**'ve been waiting** since eight o'clock.'*
(NOT ~~I'm waiting since eight o'clock.~~)
*Mark**'s studying** engineering. He**'s been doing** practical work for the last six months.*

Remember that some verbs are not normally used in progressive forms; for example *have* and *be*.

*We've had this car for ten years.* (NOT ~~We've been having this car …~~)
*How long have you been in England?* (NOT ~~How long have you been being …?~~)

Don't confuse *How long have you been here for?* (meaning 'up to now') and *How long are you here for?* (meaning 'until when').

**filling time** We often use the **present perfect progressive** to say how we have been filling our time **up to now**.

*Sorry I haven't been to see you. I**'ve been working** very hard.*
*'You're all wet!'* *'Yes, I**'ve been swimming**.'*
*'What **have** you **been doing** with yourself since I last saw you?'* *'Travelling.'*

**1** Here are some sentences from real and fictional conversations. Complete them with the verbs from the box, using the present perfect progressive.

| behave   chase   cry   escape   farm   make   sell   tell   talk |
| --- |

1 For some time it seems that I ................................................. to myself.
2 I................................................. you for eight miles.
3 I................................................. for the last 70 years and never seen anything like it.
4 I................................................. from myself all my life.
5 I................................................. badly for two years, and you know it, and you don't even mind.
6 I................................................. some inquiries about nightclubs.
7 I.................................................cars for some time now.
8 I'll rub my face quickly so she doesn't see I .................................................
9 I................................................. Veronica about that week we had in Scotland.

**2** Complete this sentence with information about yourself (true or false). Use the present perfect progressive.
I ................................................................. for .................................................

**Note: permanent states** We **don't** often use the present perfect progressive to talk about **permanent unchanging states** (see page 50). Compare:
    *'Where have you been?'* *'We**'ve been looking** at the castle.'*
    *Chedlow Castle **has looked** down on this peaceful valley for 800 years.*

# simple past and present perfect: summary

SIMPLE PAST: *I worked/wrote/drove* etc

**finished actions**

- **finished actions, no connection with present**
  *My grandfather **worked** for a newspaper.*     *I **hated** school.*

- **with words for a finished time, like *yesterday, in 2002, ago, then, when***
  *I **saw** Ann yesterday.* (NOT ~~I have seen Ann yesterday.~~)     *Bill **phoned** three days ago.*
  *When **did** you **stop** smoking?* (NOT ~~When have you stopped smoking?~~)

- **stories**
  *A man **walked** into a café and **sat** down at a table. The waiter **asked** …*

- **details (time, place etc) of news**
  *The cat has eaten your supper. She **took** it off the table.*
  *Bill has had an accident. He **fell** off his bicycle when he was going to work.*

(SIMPLE) PRESENT PERFECT: *I have worked/written/driven* etc

**A finished actions**

- **thinking about past and present together**
  *I've **written** to John, so he knows what's happening now.*     *Jane **has found** my glasses, so I can see again.*

- **news**
  *A plane **has crashed** at Heathrow airport.*     *The Prime Minister **has left** for Paris.*

- **up to now: how much/many; how often**
  *I've **drunk** six cups of coffee today.*     *My father **has** often **tried** to stop smoking.*

- **up to now: things that haven't happened; questions; *ever* and *never***
  *John **hasn't phoned**.*     ***Has** Peter **said** anything to you?*     ***Have** you ever **seen** a ghost?*
  *I've never **seen** one.*

- ***already, yet* and *just***
  *'Where's Peter?' 'He's already **gone** home.'*     ***Has** the postman **come** yet?*     *'Coffee?' 'I've just **had** some.'*

- NOT **with words for a finished time**
  *I **saw** Penny yesterday. She's getting married.* (NOT ~~I have seen Penny yesterday.~~)

**B unfinished actions continuing up to now**
**(especially with *be, have, know* and other non-progressive verbs)**

- **to say how long (often with *since* and *for*)**
  *How long **have** you **been** in this country?*     *We've **had** our car for seven years.*
  *I've **known** Jake since 2005.* (NOT ~~I know Jake since 2005.~~)

PRESENT PERFECT PROGRESSIVE: *I have been working/writing/driving* etc

**unfinished actions continuing up to now (most verbs)**

- **to say how long (often with *since* and *for*)**
  *Have you **been waiting** long?*     *I've **been learning** English since last summer.*
  *We've **been driving** for three hours – it's time for a rest.*
  DON'T **use a present tense to say how long.**
  *I've **been living** here since January.* (NOT ~~I'm living here since January.~~)

- **to say how we have been filling our time up to now**
  *Sorry I haven't written. I've **been travelling**.*     *'You look tired.' 'Yes, I've **been working** in the garden.'*

- NOT USUALLY **to talk about long, unchanging states**
  *The castle **has stood** on this hill for 900 years.*

# more about the simple past and past progressive

**past situations that have not changed** If we are talking about the past, we tend to use past tenses even for situations that have not changed.

*Those people we met in Paris **were** very nice.*
*I got that job because I **spoke** French.*

**past progressive for repetition** We generally use the **simple past** for repeated past actions.

*My father **travelled** a lot when I was young.*   *I **ran** away from school regularly.*

But we can use the **past progressive** for repeated actions **around a particular time**.

*I **was playing** a lot of tennis when I got to know Peter.*
*It was hard to get a free half-hour in July, because we **were rehearsing** non-stop.*

**1** Complete the sentences with verbs from the box. Use a past progressive (three times) or a simple past (six times).

| be   demonstrate   drink   give   go   interpret   play   speak   work |
|---|

1  I got really tired last week. There was a big conference, and I ..................................... for eight or ten hours a day most days.
2  I've just finished 'Death in the Sand'. That ..................................... a really good book.
3  At the time of the election, people ..................................... daily against the government's policies.
4  In Shakespeare's time, only a few children ..................................... to school.
5  Jo and Carl had some Japanese friends staying at the weekend, and they invited me because I ..................................... Japanese.
6  Things were difficult at home at that time. Her brother was in trouble with the police, and her father ..................................... very heavily.
7  When I was at school they ..................................... us Latin lessons five times a week. They never explained why.
8  What was the name of that man we were talking to who ..................................... in a garage?
9  Have you heard anything from your cousin who came to see us? The one who ..................................... the guitar professionally?

**2**  **GRAMMAR IN A TEXT.** Read the text. There are twenty expressions *in italics* with past verbs. Circle the ones that are used for situations that have certainly or probably not changed.

I first *got to know* my friend Alex, nearly 40 years ago, when I *was living* in Geneva. I *was working* in a translation agency, and he *had a job* in an insurance company. We *met* at a party, *started* chatting, and found that we *had a remarkable amount* in common. To start with, we *were the same age* – in fact, we *had the same birthday*. We *were both very tall*, we both *had long fair hair*, and we both *played hockey*. We *had pretty similar tastes*: we both *had vintage sports cars* that we *spent* too much money on, and we also both *had expensive girlfriends*. We both *liked classical music*, we both *sang in local choirs*, and we both *liked parties* that *went on* all night. It was the beginning of a long and important friendship.

**backgrounding** We can make a fact seem less central, not the main 'news', by using the past progressive.

*I **was having** lunch with the President yesterday. She said …* (This makes it sound as if the lunch with the President was an everyday occurrence – not 'news'. A good way of making oneself sound important.)
*John **was saying** that there are going to be some important changes.* (This takes the focus away from John, and puts the emphasis on what he said – the changes.)

**progressive with *always*** We can use a progressive form with *always* and similar words to talk about repeated but unpredictable or unplanned events. Compare

*My grandmother **always came** to see us on Tuesdays.*
*Andy **was always coming round** at the most inconvenient moments.*

The structure is often used to make complaints and criticisms.

*That car **was continually breaking down** miles from home.*
*John **was forever buying** one useless new gadget or another.*

This is also possible with present progressives (see page 26).

**distancing** We can make requests, personal questions and so on less direct by using a past tense instead of a present (see page 290).

*I **thought** you might like to pay now.*
*We **were wondering** if you needed any help.*

**3** Complete the sentences with verbs from the box. One sentence must have a simple past; use a past progressive in the others.

> always bring   always complain   always forget   always have   ask
> hope   say   sing   think   wonder

1  The Prime Minister ...................................................... me only the other day what I thought of his economic policies.
2  My grandmother......................................................about the neighbours – they couldn't do a thing right.
3  We ...................................................... if you could give us some advice.
4  I ...................................................... you might have some free time at the weekend.
5  In my last job, we ...................................................... meetings first thing on Friday mornings.
6  My maths teacher ...................................................... my name. It used to drive me crazy.
7  I ...................................................... perhaps you and I ought to have a serious talk.
8  John ...................................................... that he thinks Anna's in love again.
9  When my sister was at home she ...................................................... us little presents.
10 I ...................................................... at the Royal Opera House the other evening, and there was this gorgeous woman in the front row …

**4** Correct (✓) or not (✗)? One sentence is not correct.
1  I used to have trouble buying football boots because I had very wide feet. …
2  We didn't see much of Dad last month, because he was going backwards and forwards to America most of the time. …
3  Pete wasn't studying very hard when he was at university. …
4  I was talking to the Governor of the Bank of England the other day, and he thinks we're in deep trouble. …
5  When my sister was in her teens, she was always falling in love with really nasty boys. …
6  You know, I was thinking that it might be time to get a new car. …

# more about the present perfect

*Who **wrote** that?* (NOT ~~Who has written that?~~)
*Bill **gave** me this necklace.*     ***Did** you **put** this here?*
*Whose idea **was** it to come here on holiday?*

***Has** Barbara **phoned** today?*     *Barbara **phoned** today. She needed some advice.*
*I **haven't seen** John this week.*     *I **saw** John this week, and he said …*

**1** **Choose the best way(s) to complete each sentence: A, B or both.**

1  That's a nice picture. Who … it?  **A** *has painted*  **B** *painted*  **C** both
2  … on holiday this year?  **A** *Have you been*  **B** *Did you go*  **C** both
3  …Emma's first email today?  **A** *Have you seen*  **B** *Did you see*  **C** both
4  Stop fighting, kids. Now: who … it?  **A** *has started*  **B** *started*  **C** both
5  It was a shock when the police … today.  **A** *have turned up*  **B** *turned up*  **C** both
6  I … my appointment with the physiotherapist this week.  **A** *have missed*  **B** *missed*  **C** both
7  …those flowers?  **A** *Has Susie brought*  **B** *Did Susie bring*  **C**  both
8  Mark … earlier this evening – he needs to talk to you.  **A** *has turned up*  **B** *turned up*  **C** both
9  …that glass?  **A** *Have you broken*  **B** *Did you break*  **C** both
10  I … a really terrible time today.  **A** *have had*  **B** *had*  **C** both

**2** **Write about where some of your possessions came from.**

▶ My brother gave me my silver bracelet. I bought my new jeans in Paris. ................

................................................................................................................................

................................................................................................................................

................................................................................................................................

................................................................................................................................

................................................................................................................................

'That's an excellent idea, Miss Jones. Who gave it to you?'

**tenses with *since*** Different tenses are possible in sentences with *since*.
In the **main part** of the sentence, a present perfect (simple or progressive) is normal:

*We've **lived** here since our marriage.*
*I've **been studying** French since last May.*

But there may be a **past** tense in the **time expression** after *since*.

*We've lived here since we **got** married.*
*We've visited my parents every week since we **bought** the car.*

A **present perfect** is also possible in the time expression, to talk about **continuation** up to now.

*We've lived here since we've **been** married.*
*We've visited my parents every week since **we've had** the car.*

And a **present** tense is sometimes used in the main part of the sentence, especially to emphasise changes.

*You're **looking** much better since your operation.*

**3** **Choose the right tense.**

1 The company has doubled its profits since James … as manager.
   **A** *has taken over*   **B** *took over*   **C** both
2 The company has doubled its profits since James … manager.   **A** *has been*   **B** *is*   **C** both
3 Sue … much happier since she split up with Carl.   **A** *has been*   **B** *is*   **C** both
4 Since the new baby …, nobody has had much sleep.   **A** *has arrived*   **B** *arrived*   **C** both
5 I've been saving a lot of money since I … the new job.   **A** *have started*   **B** *started*   **C** both
6 We've all been eating much better since the new chef … doing the cooking.
   **A** *has been*   **B** *was*   **C** both
7 Everybody … going around singing since the weather turned nice.   **A** *has been*   **B** *is*   **C** both
8 The house has been much quieter since Helen … out.   **A** *has moved*   **B** *moved*   **C** both

**4** **Complete one or more of these sentences in any way you like.**

1 My life has been very different since I ………………………………………………………… (past tense)
2 My life has been very different since I've …………………………………………………………………
3 'What's that?'  'I don't know. And I don't know who …………………………………………………………

---

**NOTES**

**present perfect + past time expression** The present perfect is unusual with expressions of finished
time (see page 42). This is because the present perfect is used when we are focusing more on the
present than on the past details – for example when we give somebody a piece of news. But the structure
is not impossible. Some real examples:

> Police **have arrested** more than 900 suspected drugs traffickers in raids throughout the country **on Friday
> and Saturday**.
> A 24-year-old soldier **has been killed** in a road accident **last night**.

**British and American English** In **American** English, the **simple past** is often used to give **news**.
This is less common in British English.

> *Honey, I **crashed** the car.* (BrE: … *I've **crashed*** ….)

And some indefinite time-adverbs are used more often with a simple past in American English than
in British English: for example *yet, already, before, ever, just.*

> ***Did* you *eat*** yet? / ***Have* you *eaten*** yet? (BrE: ***Have* you *eaten*** yet?)
> *His plane just **landed** / **has** just **landed**.* (BrE: *His plane **has** just **landed**.*)

# more about the present perfect progressive

**progressive or simple?** The **present perfect progressive** is normal when we are talking about **temporary** actions and situations continuing **up to now.**

*It's **been raining** all week.     Granny's **been staying** with us since Easter.*

The **present perfect progressive** can also be used for **longer, more permanent** situations, especially when the emphasis is on activity or change.

*The Dutch **have been reclaiming** land from the sea for centuries.*
*The universe **has been expanding** steadily since its origin.*

However, we often prefer a **simple present perfect** in these cases, especially when we are talking about unchanging states rather than actions. Compare:

*I've **been living** here since August.*
*I've **lived** in this village all my life.*
*Lucy's **been covering** cushions all afternoon.*
*An ice-cap **has covered** Greenland for something like 5 million years.*

*Want* and *mean* are not normally used in the present progressive (see page 28), but they can be used in the **present perfect progressive**.

*I've **been wanting** to meet you for ages.*
*I've **been meaning** to tell you – there's a problem with the central heating.*

**1** **Complete the sentences with verbs from the box.**

| analyse   assume   create   debate   design   ensure   predict   run   substitute   want |
|---|

1   Our statistics department has recently ...................................... the last year's marketing performance. (*progressive*)
2   Right through human history, people ...................................... works of art based on the natural world. (*progressive*)
3   As far back as our records reach, people ...................................... the end of the world. (*progressive*)
4   My friend Alistair ........................... always ...................................... that he is right and everybody else is wrong. (*simple*)
5   For the last ten years, I ...................................... advanced computer systems. (*progressive*)
6   It seems that for a long time some wine producers ...................................... cheap wines for more expensive ones – it's a very profitable business. (*progressive*)
7   The same family ........................... always ...................................... this business. (*simple*)
8   Parliament ...................................... the question for three days now without reaching a conclusion. (*progressive*)
9   For nearly 1,000 years, Britain's island situation ...................................... its freedom from invasion. (*simple*)
10   Since I first met her, I ...................................... to ask her out, but I'm too shy. (*progressive*)

**2** **Write a sentence (true or false) about yourself, using the present perfect progressive.**

.......................................................................................................................................

**3** INTERNET EXERCISE. **Use a search engine to find some sentences beginning "All through history, people ...". Which tense is most often used?**

.................................................................................

# past perfect: revise the basics

**use** We use the **past perfect** when we are already talking about the **past**, and want to talk about an **earlier past** time.

I **tiptoed** into the room and **sat** down. But the meeting **had** already **finished**.
He **found** a seat on the train, **opened** his newspaper and **started** to read. Then a terrible thought **struck** him.
**Had** he **turned** off the gas?
We **couldn't understand** why Ellie **hadn't phoned**.

**1** Complete the sentences with the verbs in the box (past or past perfect).
Use a dictionary if necessary.

| affect apply check enclose obtain participate publish select |

1 I ..................................... for the job, although I wasn't sure I wanted it.
2 David & Davis rejected Martin's new book, although they.................................... three of his novels before.
3 Jones ..................................... in two earlier expeditions, and was clearly the best person to lead the group.
4 I sent off the form, and then realised I ..................................... the wrong photograph.
5 We did not think we would have an opportunity to see the match, but Penny told us she ..................................... some free tickets and invited us to go with her.
6 The committee interviewed six of us for the job, but I was sure they ..................................... the person they wanted already.
7 The fire started because nobody ..................................... the electrical wiring for years.
8 The doctor told my father that working with chemicals all his life ..................................... his eyesight.

**2** Complete these sentences in any way you like, using a past perfect.
1 I couldn't get a job, although .....................................
2 He went to prison for five years, because .....................................
3 We were two hours late, because .....................................

**3** GRAMMAR IN TEXTS. Put the letters of the expressions from the box into the news reports.
Use a dictionary if necessary.

| A had been asked   B had been given   C had been overcharged   D had moved   E had replied   F had requested |

A caller to Surrey council complained that the phone number he ¹... for their library was out of order – only to be told that '0900 1800' were in fact its opening hours.

A Lancaster man phoned the town hall to say that the city-centre car park was haunted, because his car ²... to a different parking space while he was shopping.

A woman rang the emergency number 999 to say that she ³... in the local supermarket.

A TOURIST RETURNING home, who wanted to get from London to Heathrow Airport, arrived at Torquay in south-west England at two o'clock in the morning. It seems that she ⁴... information at Paddington Station, ⁵... where she wanted to go, and ⁶... 'Turkey'.

For the past perfect in indirect speech, see page 220.

# more about the past perfect: time conjunctions

**not always necessary**  With time conjunctions like *after*, *as soon as*, *once*, a past perfect is not always necessary, because we are not going back to an earlier past, but simply moving forward from one event to the next.

*After the new government came in, things were very different.*
*As soon as Mary arrived we all sat down to dinner.*
*Once it stopped raining we started playing again.*

However, we can use the past perfect with these conjunctions if we want to emphasise that the first action was separate, finished before the second started.

*After the plane had landed they discovered bullet holes in the wings.*
*As soon as I had finished my exams I took a long holiday.*
*Once they had checked all my bags I was allowed into the building.*

**use with *when***  This 'separating' use of the past perfect is common with *when*. Compare:

- *When I opened the window, the cat jumped out.*
  *When I had opened the windows, I sat down and had a cup of tea.*
- *When I phoned her, she came at once.*
  *When I had made all my phone calls, I did some gardening.*

**1** **Rewrite the sentences using *when* and the past perfect.**

▶ I cleaned up the kitchen, and then I sat down and had a cup of coffee.
  *When I had cleaned up the kitchen, I sat down and had a cup of coffee.*

1  I considered all the alternatives and then decided to sell my car.
  ........................................................................

2  We looked at eight houses and then we were completely exhausted.
  ........................................................................

3  She explained the problem, and then there was a long silence.
  ........................................................................

4  I paid for the meal, and then I didn't have enough money for the bus.
  ........................................................................

5  Everybody said what they thought, and then we voted.
  ........................................................................

**2** **Choose the best way of completing each sentence.**

1  After I *tried / had tried* to phone her six times, I gave up and went out.
2  As soon as he *saw / had seen* me he gave me a big smile.
3  Once the dogs *went / had been* for their walk, they settled down quietly.
4  When I *called / had called* Annie, she pretended not to hear.
5  After I *painted / had painted* the kitchen ceiling I decided to stop for a rest.
6  When everybody *voted / had voted*, the results were announced almost immediately.
7  When Lucy *came in / had come in*, everybody stopped talking.
8  When I *sent / had sent* the email, I realised I had made a terrible mistake.
9  Once I *telephoned / had telephoned* everybody, I wondered what to do next.
10  When I *got / had got* home, I went straight to bed.
11  When I *opened / had opened* the door, the children ran in.
12  When they *mapped / had mapped* the whole territory, they returned to their headquarters.

**Note:  We don't use the past perfect** when we simply mean 'some time before now'.
  *Hello. I left a suit to be cleaned. Is it ready yet?* (NOT … *I had left a suit* …)

# past perfect progressive

**use** When we are talking about a **past time**, we can use the **past perfect progressive** to talk about **earlier situations** which had continued **up to that time**.

*All the roads were flooded: it **had been raining** solidly for three days.*
*She got ill because she **hadn't been sleeping** enough.*
*When I looked at the books, I saw that the firm **had been losing** money for years.*

**1** Here are some sentences taken from books and newspapers. Complete them with verbs from the boxes, using the past perfect progressive. Use a dictionary if necessary.

| cry expect hold see sit think wait |
| --- |

1  She fetched herself a packet of sandwiches from the counter and then came back to where she
.....................................

2  My next call was to the company that ..................................... some of my things in storage, just to warn them that I was coming round.

3  And since her birthday, she ..................................... more of Dionne than she had for years.

4  Olive ..................................... so many horrors that hearing the question she almost laughed with relief.

5  It was the music that brought me in from the hall where I .....................................

6  For a long, long time I ..................................... of getting out of that awful place.

7  Everybody was looking at me. And I simply couldn't explain why I .....................................

| carry carry go on knit look photograph play watch |
| --- |

8  Police said that the two men arrested in Ireland ..................................... several addresses of safe houses in France.

9  I ..................................... tennis for about five minutes when there was a very loud explosion very close at hand.

10  At the big house I met the Officer who ..................................... for me earlier on.

11  She couldn't really remember anything, only that she ..................................... a sweater and then she had woken up in this bed with her nosy, bossy sister sitting beside her.

12  The rucksack and the rifle I ..................................... since yesterday evening seemed like a ton weight.

13  Their affair ..................................... for years before she decided to tell her husband.

14  Believe it or not, he was arrested because he ..................................... the Houses of Parliament.

15  When her escape was discovered, it turned out that everybody thought somebody else
..................................... her.

**2** GRAMMAR IN TEXTS. **Put the letters of four of the expressions from the box into the news reports. Use a dictionary if necessary.**

| A had been arriving   B had been forgetting   C had been hoping   D had been navigating |
| --- |
| E had been trying   F had been watching   G had been working |

An illegal immigrant has been arrested inside the Houses of Parliament. He ¹... illegally for months as a cleaner in one of the country's most secure buildings. He was only discovered when a police officer based at the House carried out a random check on the Police National Computer.

A man who thought he was sailing along the coast of southern England had to be rescued by emergency services after his motor boat ran out of fuel while repeatedly circling a small island in the Thames estuary. The man, who had only a roadmap to navigate by, ²... to sail from Gillingham to Southampton. He told his rescuers he ³... by keeping the coastline to his right.

A DRUG RUNNER who ⁴... to pay off his own drug debt with one last trip was stopped by police officers at Newton Abbot station. When searched, he was found to be carrying £16,000 worth of heroin.

# this is the first time etc

> **first time etc** We use **perfect tenses** in sentences with **this/it/that is/was the first/second/third/only/best/worst** etc.

*This is the first time that I've been here.* (NOT ~~This is the first time that I'm here.~~)
*This is the second time you've been late this week.*
*That was the fifth job he had had that year.*
*It was one of the worst meals I have/had ever eaten.*

**1** **Complete the sentences, using verbs from the box.**

| ask   be   drink   feel ✓   have   have   meet   play   see   see |
|---|

▶ This is the first time I ...*have felt*............ well for months.
1 This is the best film we ................................... for ages.
2 It was the first time I ................................... champagne, and I really didn't like it.
3 It's the third time she ................................... in love this year.
4 I played terribly. I think it was the worst game I ........................... ever ...............................
5 That week in Spain was the best holiday I ................................... in my life.
6 This is the first warm day we ................................... this year.
7 It was the first time she ................................... her boyfriend's family.
8 In the bath was the biggest spider I ........................... ever ...........................
9 That's the third time you ................................... me the same question.

**2** **Write three sentences about experiences you have had, using *It was the first/best/worst* etc.**
*When I went to Germany, it was the first time I had ever travelled by air.*
*I saw 'Hercules Unchained' years ago. It was the worst film I had ever seen.*
................................................................................................................
................................................................................................................
................................................................................................................

**3** **GRAMMAR IN TEXTS. Put the letters of three of the expressions from the box into the texts. Use a dictionary if necessary.**

| A  had been away from home    B  had been sent    C  had been used |
|---|
| D  had danced    E  had held a gun    F  had seen those people    G  had sung |

> *I was called up for war work on 31st December 1943 and sent to Stirling in Scotland. Well, they said they needed, me so I went. I didn't have much choice, really. It was awful at first, and it was the first time I* [1].... *What a mess we looked in our uniforms! Blue skirt, khaki tunic, brown shoes, woollen stockings and a hat that came over my ears.*

> "It was the first time I [2]... by myself in front of an audience. I was five years old. It was the school Christmas play and I had to sing '*Silent Night*'. They pushed me to the front of the stage and shone a bright light on me, and when I had finished all the people stood up and clapped."

> One of the reasons for the Peasants' Revolt in 1381 was the Poll Tax. There had been a long war with France. Wars cost money and that money usually came from the peasants through the taxes that they paid. In 1380, Richard II introduced a new tax called the Poll Tax. This made everyone who was on the tax register pay 5p. It was the third time in four years that such a tax [3].... By 1381, the peasants had had enough.

# more practice

**1** Which is/are correct or normal: A, B, (C) or both / all three?

1  Naval search vessels have rescued the Culligan family, whose yacht …… after hitting an ice floe off Newfoundland. (**A** *sank*  **B** *has sunk*)

2  When Andrew came into my life, I …… from one dead-end job to another, without much idea of what I really wanted in life. (**A** *moved*  **B** *was moving*)

3  I …… lunch with the Prime Minister yesterday, and during our conversation he gave me some interesting information. (**A** *had*  **B** *was having*)

4  We …… whether you would be interested in going skiing with us next month.
(**A** *wonder*  **B** *wondered*  **C** *were wondering*)

5  He wasn't a bad teacher, except that he …… to tell jokes, and they were never funny.
(**A** *always tried*  **B** *was always trying*)

6  I like your hair. Where …… it done? (**A** *did you have*  **B** *have you had*  **C** *were you having*)

7  The bank manager …… today. She'd like you to call back. (**A** *phoned*  **B** *has phoned*)

8  Things …… much better since Alex left. (**A** *are*  **B** *have been*)

9  I've had six different jobs since …… school. (**A** *I left*  **B** *I've left*)

10  The Talbot family …… in this town since the 11th Century. (**A** *lived*  **B** *have lived*  **C** *have been living*)

**2** Correct (✓) or not (✗)?

1  I've been meaning to ask you this for ages.  …

2  How long were you waiting when Pam finally arrived?  …

3  Is this the first time you're in Ireland?  …

4  We visit my parents every week since we've had the car.  …

5  Look what Alice has given me!  …

6  Have you seen the match between France and Scotland?  …

7  When I did all the shopping I went round to see Maggie.  …

8  As soon as we got into the car the children started fighting.  …

9  I was hoping we could have a few minutes to talk.  …

**3** DO IT YOURSELF. **Here are four examples of correct use and six rules. Four rules are bad. Look at the examples and decide which.**

> 1  Among the people who have had the greatest influence on our quality of life, the 19th-century French scientist Pasteur stands out.
> 2  I've finished my exams, at last!
> 3  We've been waiting here for exactly four hours and twenty minutes.
> 4  Once upon a time there was a clever little girl called Susie.

**Rules**

**A.** Use the present perfect for recent actions, and the simple past for actions that took place longer ago. ***good  bad***

**B.** Use the present perfect for finished actions that have some present importance, and the simple past for other finished actions. ***good  bad***

**C.** Use the present perfect for unfinished actions and the simple past for finished actions. ***good  bad***

**D.** Use the simple past, not the present perfect, when you talk about a definite time. ***good  bad***

**E.** Use the present perfect, not the simple past, when you talk about an indefinite time. ***good  bad***

**F.** Use the simple past, not the present perfect, when you talk about a finished time. ***good  bad***

# more practice (continued)

**4** GRAMMAR IN TEXTS. **Put the verbs into the text: simple past or past progressive.**

| arrive | become | dance | do | fight | pick up | play | play | reach | say | smash |
|---|---|---|---|---|---|---|---|---|---|---|
| stare | take out | tear | try | walk | | | | | | |

This was told to me as a true story. A woman I know, a teacher, took a job in a tough inner-city secondary school in South London. On her first day, she [1].................. at her classroom to find complete chaos. Loud rock music [2].................., some of the kids [3].................., others [4].................. cards, two of them [5].................. The noise level was incredible. My friend [6].................. to the front of the classroom and [7].................. to get the children's attention. Things [8].................. a little less noisy, but not much, and she had a lot of difficulty making herself heard – she is quite a small woman, with a quiet voice. Most of the children, in fact, simply went on with what they [9].................. as if she was not there. So she [10].................. a vase off the table and [11].................. it on the floor. That did get their attention. While they [12].................. at her with their mouths open, she [13].................. into her bag, [14].................. a medium-sized telephone directory, and slowly [15].................. it in half. (She is quite a small woman, but extremely strong.) 'Now,' she [16]..................., 'Today's lesson …' . She had no further trouble with that class.

**5** GRAMMAR IN TEXTS. **Circle the correct tenses.**

1

A British Formula 1 driver *was / has been* fined A$500 (£288) for performing car stunts for fans outside Melbourne's motor racing circuit. The driver *was / has been* caught by police executing "burnout" and "fishtail" tricks in a borrowed Mercedes.

2

Detectives *arrested / have arrested* a teenager in connection with the shooting of a 45-year-old man in Liverpool. Emergency services *found / have found* the man with injuries to his left thigh.

3

THE THEFT of a Picasso painting worth about $50m from a museum on Saturday *was / has been* blamed on poor security. A museum official *said / has said* that none of the alarms and only 25 out of 43 security cameras were working.

4

Canadian workers *discovered / have discovered* large dinosaur bones while digging a sewer tunnel in the city of Edmonton. A tooth and limb bone, which experts believe belong to the Albertosaurus and the Edmontosaurus species, *were / have been* found by drainage crews in the Quesnell Heights neighbourhood.

5

B acteria taken from cliffs in Devon *showed / have shown* themselves to be hardy space travellers. The microbes *were / have been* put on the exterior of the space station to see how they would survive in the hostile conditions that exist above the Earth's atmosphere. When scientists inspected them a year and a half later, they found many were still alive.

**6** INTERNET EXERCISE. **Use a search engine to find some sentences beginning "The English have never …". Write them here. Do you think they are true? Try some other nationalities.**

.................................................................................................................................
.................................................................................................................................
.................................................................................................................................
.................................................................................................................................
.................................................................................................................................

**Choose the correct forms of the cartoon captions.**

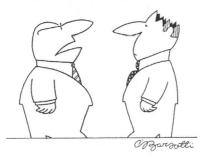

'Pembroke, have you *tried / been trying* to make decisions again?'

'My luggage *went / has gone* to hell.'

'When *did you last feed / have you last fed* that goldfish?'

'Television has brought back murder into the home – where it belongs.'
(*Alfred Hitchcock*)

'I have never killed a man, but I have read many obituaries with great pleasure.'
(*Clarence Darrow*)

'I have never been hurt by what I have not said.'
(*Calvin Coolidge*)

'His Majesty does not know what the band has just played, but it is *never* to be played again.'
(*King George V, after the Grenadier Guards band had played a piece by Richard Strauss*)

'I have never met a man so ignorant that I couldn't learn something from him.'
(*Galileo Galilei*)

'I have never found a companion that was so companionable as solitude.'
(*Henry David Thoreau*)

# Section 5 modal verbs

## What are modal verbs?

Modal verbs are a group of auxiliaries: *can, could, may, might, shall, should, will, would, must* and *ought*. They are used **before other verbs**, and in **tags** and **short answers**.

'*You can swim, can't you?*' '*Yes, I can.*'
'*She shouldn't be late, should she?*' '*No, she shouldn't.*'

## meanings

Modal verbs have **two** main kinds of meaning.

1. **Certainty:** we can use modal verbs to say for example that a situation is **certain**, **probable**, **possible** or **impossible**.

   *You **must** be tired.     Emma **should** be home by now.     We **might** go to Russia in June.     It **can't** be true.*

2. **Obligation and freedom:** we can use modal verbs for example to **tell** or **advise** people (not) to do things, and to talk about **freedom** or **ability** to do things. With these meanings they are important in the expression of **instructions**, **requests**, **suggestions** and **invitations**.

   *Students **must** register today.     **Can** I go now?     You **should** take a break.*
   ***Would** you like to join us for a drink?*

Modal verbs are not generally used to **report** situations and events, but simply to talk about their **probability**, **possibility** etc. So, for example, we say that something *could happen* in general, or that it *could not* happen, but to say that somebody actually did something on a particular occasion, we use a different verb (see page 60). Compare:

*I **could** read when I was four.     I **couldn't read** his handwriting.*
*I **managed to open** the tin with a screwdriver.* (NOT ~~I could open the tin~~ …)

## tense

Note that *could, might, should* and *would* are not generally used as **past** forms of *can, may, shall* and *will* (though this can happen in indirect speech – see page 221). Mostly, they are used for **less definite** meanings. Compare:

***Can** I go now? (direct request)     **Could** I go now? (less direct, more polite)*

**This Section** covers most uses of modal verbs, but a few uses are dealt with in other Sections (see the Index for details). This section also includes information on ***be able to**, **have (got) to**, **be supposed to**, **had better**, **used to*** and ***need (to)***, which are similar to modals in some ways.

---

'Rock journalism is people who can't write interviewing people who can't talk for people who can't read.'
(*Frank Zappa*)

'Go and see what that child is doing and tell her she mustn't.'
(*Traditional*)

'This is not a novel to be tossed aside lightly. It should be thrown with great force.'
(*Dorothy Parker*)

'The English may not like music, but they absolutely love the noise it makes.'
(*Thomas Beecham*)

'A cucumber should be well sliced and dressed with pepper and vinegar, and then thrown out, as good for nothing.'
(*Samuel Johnson*)

'There seems to be a natural instinct to imagine that where there is a wrong, there must be a right to balance it. Thus, if we condemn one act, we might feel inclined to praise another that constitutes a kind of counterweight in some global-historical moral scale. In reality there can often just be wrong as far as the eye can see.'
(*Steven Poole*)

'As we journey through life, discarding baggage along the way, we should keep an iron grip, to the very end, on the capacity for silliness. It preserves the soul from dessication.'
(*Humphrey Lyttelton*)

'Any fool can reinvent the wheel. The trick is to relabel it as a rotary transmission device.'
(*Neil MacShaw*)

# modals: revise the basics

**grammar** The grammar of modal verbs is special in several ways:

- The third person singular present has **no** -s.

  It **must** be lunchtime. (NOT It ~~musts~~ …)

- Questions and negatives are made **without** *do*.

  **Should she?** (NOT ~~Does she should?~~)     It **cannot** be true. (Note the spelling of *cannot*.)

- After modals (except *ought*) we use **infinitives without** *to*.

  I can't **sing**. (NOT ~~I can't to sing.~~)

- Modals have **no infinitives or participles**. Instead we use forms of other expressions such as **be able to**, **have to** or **be allowed to**.

  I want **to be able to** travel. (NOT ~~I want to can travel.~~)
  I've often **had to** lend my brother money.
  She's always **been allowed to** do what she wanted.

- Modals have a special **past** form made with a **perfect infinitive** (see pages 89–91).

  You **should have told** me.     Lucy **must have missed** her train.

**1** CHECK YOUR KNOWLEDGE. **Five of sentences 1–10 are wrong. Correct the mistakes or write 'Correct'.**

▸ I shouldn't to have much difficulty with this exercise. ..*shouldn't have*..........
▸ Must you go now? ..*Correct*.......................
1 He's never had to work hard in his life. ....................................
2 I'm sorry to must tell you this. ....................................
3 We ought to phone William this evening. ....................................
4 Will you be able to find the place by yourself? ....................................
5 Does everybody must pay now? ....................................
6 They say it mights snow tomorrow. ....................................
7 Do you think the children might be allowed to go camping? ....................................
8 Would you like some more coffee? ....................................
9 I'm sorry, but I really oughtn't stay any longer. ....................................
10 Don't tell me I can't have a ticket – I must to have a ticket. ....................................

**infinitives after modals** Modals can be followed by all kinds of infinitive, including **perfect** (see above), **progressive** and **passive** (all without *to*).

*I should be working, not playing computer games.*
*The police must be informed as soon as possible.*     *This door must not be opened.*

**2 Put in the right kind of infinitives of the verbs in the box.**

| get   mug   open   plan   tidy up   understand |

1 'Incomprehensible' means 'cannot ....................................'
2 'Where's Paul?' 'I think he may .................................... the garage.'
3 You shouldn't go out wearing that jewellery – you could ....................................
4 I'm afraid the management might .................................... to close some branches.
5 This door should not .................................... except in an emergency.
6 Shall I phone Emma? She must .................................... worried.

# ability: *can* and *could*

**past: *could* not always possible** We use *could* for **general ability**, to say that somebody was able to do something at any time, whenever he/she wanted.

*When I was younger I **could** run 10km in under 40 minutes.*

But we do **not** normally use *could* to say that somebody did something **on one occasion**. Instead, we use other expressions.

*I **managed to** run 10km yesterday in 55 minutes.* (NOT *I could run 10 km yesterday …*)
*How much steak **were** you **able to** buy?* (NOT *How much steak could you buy?*)
*After three days' climbing they **succeeded in** getting to the top.*
(NOT *After three days' climbing they could get to the top.*)
*I **found** a good pair of cheap jeans in the market.* (NOT *I could find …*)

However, we can use ***couldn't*** to say that something **did not happen** on one occasion.

*I looked everywhere, but I **couldn't** find my wallet.*

**1** **Correct the mistakes using *managed to* or write 'Correct'.**

▶ The town was crowded, but we ~~could find~~ a room in a small hotel. ....*managed to find*....
▶ She could read when she was four. ...*Correct*...............
1 I could pass my driving test at the third try. ...................................
2 Where I grew up, everybody could ride a horse. ...................................
3 I could get some really good bargains in the sale yesterday. ...................................
4 We couldn't find seats on the train. ...................................
5 Believe it or not, I could sing beautifully when I was younger. ...................................
6 I worked really fast, and I could finish everything by 4.00. ...................................
7 We had a fire in the attic on Saturday, but the firemen could put it out. ...................................
8 I couldn't understand the instructions at all. ...................................
9 The door was locked, but I could get in through a window. ...................................
10 Four centuries ago, only a few people could read. ...................................

**future: when *can* is possible** We use ***can*** to talk about future actions which depend on **present** ability, circumstances, agreements, decisions etc. In other cases, we use ***be able to***.

*I **can** come in tomorrow evening if you like.* (a present decision)
*The doctor says I **will be able** to walk properly in three months.*
(NOT *The doctor says I can walk properly in three months.*)

**2** **Put in *can* or *can't* if possible; if not, use *will/won't be able to*.**

▶ I ...*can*............................ let you have a cheque tomorrow, if that's OK.
▶ I think I ...*will be able to*............ do some skiing next winter.
1 I've no time today. Let me see. I ................................... see her on Wednesday.
2 Do you think one day machines ................................... read our thoughts?
3 'The manager ................................... see you at eleven o'clock.' 'Thank you.'
4 There's no way people ................................... travel to Mars in my lifetime.
5 It's no use going to Canada – you ................................... get a residence permit.
6 'We need some superglue.' 'OK, I ................................... get some this afternoon.'
7 I'll take the car to the garage next week, but I don't think they ...................................
  fix the steering.
8 I'm sorry, but I ................................... come to your party – I'll be away.
9 We're not free today, but we ................................... manage a meeting next week.
10 'What are we going to eat?' 'Well, I ................................... do steak and chips.'

> **can see etc** *Can* is often used with **see**, **hear**, **feel**, **taste**, **smell**, **understand** and **remember** to give a **progressive** kind of meaning.

*I **can see** Susan coming down the road.* (NOT ~~I'm seeing~~ ...)
*Through the window, I **could hear** a man singing.*    ***Can** you **smell** burning?*
*What's in the soup? I **can taste** something funny.*
*I **(can) remember** when there were no houses here.*
***Do/Can** you **understand** why Alice left so suddenly?*

**3** **Complete the sentences, using *can see* etc.**

1  I ........................ definitely ........................ something burning. What do you think it is?
2  He opened his eyes, but to his horror he .................................... absolutely nothing.
3  I .................................... Susan practising the piano next door; it sounds nice.
4  This isn't my coffee – I ........................ distinctly ........................ sugar in it.
5  He thought he .................................... something crawling up his leg, but when he looked he .................................... anything.
6  I knew he had been with another woman. I .................................... her perfume.
7  There was somebody in the room. She .................................... them breathing.
8  I ........................ vaguely ........................ dreaming last night that we were all living on the moon.
9  When she talks fast I .................................... one word in three, maximum.

'I can see why they made February the shortest month of the year.'

---

**NOTES**

**can with *speak* and *play*** We use ***I can speak/play*** and ***I speak/play*** with very little difference.
   *I **(can) speak** Greek quite well.*    ***Can/Does** anybody here **play** the piano?*

**typical behaviour** Another use of *can/could* is to talk about what is **typical** (see page 67).
   *A female crocodile **can** lay 30–40 eggs.*    *It **could** get very cold in our old house.*

**suggestions** We can use both *can* and *could* to make **suggestions** about what to do. *Could* is 'softer', less definite than *can*.
   *'What shall we do at the weekend?' 'Well, we **can** go down to Brighton. And we **could** see if Harry wants to come – what do you think?'*
Note the expression ***can always***.
   *'I don't know what to give Olivia for her birthday.' 'You **can always** give her a gift token.'*
   *(= ' ... if you can't think of anything better.')*

**criticism** We can use ***could*** (often with a strong stress) to **criticise** people for not doing things.
   *You **COULD** wipe your feet when you come in!*    *You **COULD** smile sometimes!*
   *You **COULD** have phoned to say you were coming!*
***Might*** can be used in the same way (see page 67).

# permission: *can, could, may* and *might*

**asking for permission** All four of these verbs can be used to **ask for permission**. *Can* is the **least polite/formal**; *could* is a little more polite/formal. These two are both used between people who know each other well, or when asking strangers for small things.

*Can/Could I have some more tea?     Excuse me – **can/could** I just get past?*

*Could* is common in more formal situations, or when asking for more important things.

*Could I stop work half an hour early?     Could I take your car for the afternoon?*

Adding **possibly** or **Do you think ...** makes a request even more polite.

*Could I possibly take your car for the afternoon?*
*Do you think I could leave my bags here for half an hour?*

*May* is similar to *could*, but less common. *Might* is extremely polite, and unusual.

*May I use your phone?     May I help you?     Might I make a suggestion?*

**giving permission** We **give** or **refuse permission** with *can* or *may*, not *could* or *might*.

*'Could I start late tomorrow?' 'Of course you **can**.'* (NOT ~~Of course you could.~~)
*Sorry, you **can't** have the car today – I need it.* (NOT ... ~~you couldn't have the car~~ ...)
*You **may** stroke the horses, but you **may not** feed them.*

**1** CHECK YOUR KNOWLEDGE. (Circle) the best description.

1  Hi, John. **Might I possibly look** at your newspaper?     *too polite / OK / not polite enough*
2  Excuse me, madam. **Can you watch** my luggage?     *too polite / OK / not polite enough*
3  **Can I have** three tickets for tomorrow night?     *too polite / OK / not polite enough*
4  **Could I borrow** your pen for a moment?     *too polite / OK / not polite enough*
5  Hello, Mr Parker. **Can I use** your office to work in today?     *too polite / OK / not polite enough*
6  'Dad, can I use your computer?' 'No, you **can't**.'     *too polite / OK / not polite enough*
7  'May I use your phone?' 'Yes, **you might**.'     *right / wrong*
8  Sorry, Louise. but I'm afraid **you couldn't go** out tonight.     *right / wrong*
9  **You can get** a passport application form from a post office.     *right / wrong*
10  **You may not make** personal phone calls from the office.     *right / wrong*

**asking about permission** *May* is not normally used to **ask about permission** that **already exists** – about what is **normally allowed**, or about **rules** and **laws**. Compare:

*May/Can I park here?     Can you park here on Sundays?* (NOT ~~May you park here on Sundays?~~)
*Can children go into pubs in Scotland?* (NOT ~~May children go into pubs~~ ...)

**past permission: *could* not used** We do not use *could* to say that somebody **was allowed** to do something **on one occasion**. Compare:

*When I was a child I **could** watch TV whenever I wanted to.* (not just one occasion)
*Yesterday evening the children **were allowed to** stay up late to watch the football.*
(NOT ~~Yesterday evening the children could stay up late~~ ...)

**2** Correct (✓) or not (✗)?

1  May people vote at age 17? ...
2  Can you download these books free, or do you have to pay? ...
3  I could do the exam late because I was ill. ...
4  At school, we could choose classics or science, but we couldn't mix them. ...
5  Everybody was allowed to go home early on Monday. ...
6  May anybody join this club? ...

# obligation: *must* and *have (got) to*

I **must** apply for a visa this week. OR I **have to** apply for a visa this week.
**Must** you play that dreadful music? OR **Do** you **have to** play that dreadful music?
We **must** leave now. OR We**'ve got to** leave now.

I **must** get my hair cut: it's too long.     My wife says I**'ve got to** get my hair cut.
You **have to** drive on the left in Britain. (MORE NATURAL THAN You must drive …)

All drivers **must** have adequate insurance.

**1** **Read this with a dictionary; see how must reflects the hearer's wishes.**
(In a dream, Mrs Ogmore-Pritchard is talking to her two dead husbands, Mr Ogmore and Mr Pritchard.)

MRS O-P:  Tell me your tasks in order.
MR O:   I must put my pyjamas in the drawer marked pyjamas.
MR P:   I must take my cold bath which is good for me.
MR O:   I must wear my flannel band to ward off sciatica.
MR P:   I must dress behind the curtain and put on my apron.
MR O:   I must blow my nose in a piece of tissue-paper which I afterwards burn.
MR P:   I must take my salts which are nature's friend.
MR O:   I must boil the drinking water because of germs.
MR P:   I must make my herb tea which is free from tannin.
MR O:   I must dust the blinds and then I must raise them.
MRS O-P:  And before you let the sun in, mind it wipes its shoes.
*Dylan Thomas: Under Milk Wood (adapted)*

*In soccer, players **must not** touch the ball with their hands. (It's not allowed.)*
*In rugby, players can pick up the ball, but they **do not have to**; they can also kick it.*

**2** **Put in expressions from the box with *must (not)*, *have/has (got) to* or *don't have to*.**

| answer   come round   do military service ✓   find out   get   go to bed   go to work |
|---|
| hit your opponent   pay taxes   take off   throw out   turn down   vote |

▶ In some countries, both men and women ..*have (got) to do military service.*..............

1  I'm really tired. I ...................................................................

2  Sophie hasn't been in touch for days. I ........................................................ why.

3  You ........................................................ the questions if you don't want to.

4  In my country, everybody ........................................................ in elections.

5  You really ........................................................ that old coat. Please!

6  In boxing, you ........................................................ below the belt.

7  We haven't had a talk for ages. You really ........................................................ one evening.

8  You ........................................................ a licence to watch TV.

9  When you go through airport security you ........................................................ your coat.

10  Harry – you ........................................................ that music. We're all going deaf!

11  We all ........................................................, one way or another.

12  Saturday tomorrow: I ........................................................, thank goodness.

# obligation: *should* and *ought to*

*Should* is used for **suggestions**, **advice** and **opinions**. It is **less strong** than *must*. Compare:

*All drivers **must** have adequate insurance: it's the law.*
*You **should** insure your computer against accidental damage – it's sensible.*

**Orders** and **instructions** can be made **more polite** by using ***should*** instead of *must*.

*Applications **should** be sent before 30 June.*      *Visitors **should** report to the office.*

For other uses of *should*, see pages 225, 237 and 239.

*Ought* is similar to *should*, but less common. It is followed by ***to***.

*You **ought to** insure your computer.*      *People **ought to** smile more.*

**1** (Circle) the best word or expression.

1   Do you think I *should / must* go and see Paul?
2   The house is on fire! Everybody *ought to / must* get out at once!
3   *Should / Must* we take the bus or get a taxi?
4   You *should / must* be 18 or over to vote in a general election.
5   I'm sorry, but you *ought to / must* wait in the queue like everybody else.
6   I think you *should / must* try to take a holiday.
7   We absolutely *should / must* clean up the kitchen – it's filthy.
8   Everybody *ought to /must* know more than one language.
9   They say you *should / must* eat five portions of fruit or vegetables a day.
10  People *should / must* take regular exercise.

**2** Write a question asking for advice for yourself.

▸   .....Should I go on studying or give up?.........What should I do this evening?.....
    ..............................................................................................................................

**3** Write a few sentences saying what you think other people should do: for example the government, parents, teachers, everybody.

..............................................................................................................................
..............................................................................................................................
..............................................................................................................................
..............................................................................................................................
..............................................................................................................................

Note:  Question forms of *ought* are
rather formal. In conversation people
prefer, for example,
   *Do you think I ought to …?* or
   *Should we …?* (NOT USUALLY *Ought I
   / we to …?*).

# certainty: *must, can't, will, should*

*must, can't* We say that something **must** be true if we are certain, not from direct experience, but from deduction: from thinking about it logically. Compare:

*She's at home: I saw her go in.*
*She **must be** at home – her car's outside and the lights are on.*

The usual negative of *must*, with this meaning, is **cannot/can't**.

*She **can't be** at home: her car's gone and there are no lights on.*

*should* We use *should* (*not*) when we are not certain, but think that there are **good reasons** to think that something is true or not.

*He left an hour ago. He **should be** home by now.*
*'Who can I ask about the dates?' 'Try Jessica – she **should know**.'*
*I'm going to service the car myself – it **shouldn't be** too difficult.*

**Ought to** is possible with the same meaning.

*'Try Jessica – she **ought to know**.'*

**1** **Choose the best form.**

1   If A is bigger than B, and B is bigger than C, then C *must / can't be* bigger than A.
2   Gemma *must / should* be able to translate this for you – she knows some Arabic.
3   'You've won first prize.' 'It *can't / shouldn't* be true!'
4   Look at their house. They *must / ought to* have plenty of money.
5   Look at those clouds. We *must / should* get some rain soon.
6   I'm going out for a bit. I *can't / shouldn't* be home too late.
7   That *must / can't* be her mother – they're more or less the same age.
8   'We're off to Turkey for a week.' 'That *must / should* be nice.'
9   Can I have a few words with you? It *should / shouldn't* take long.
10  That *mustn't / can't* be Daniel – he's in Morocco.

*will* We can use *will* and *will not / won't* with a similar meaning to *must/can't*. This is most common when we are certain of something because it's what is **expected**, or what is **normal/typical**.

*'There's somebody coming up the stairs.' 'That'll be Mary.'*
*'Can you ring John?' '**Will** he **be** there now?' 'Yes, he always starts work at 8.00.'*
*'Shall we go and have something to eat?' 'No, the canteen **won't be** open yet.'*

**2** **Put in *will* or *won't*.**

1   Chloe ........................... still be in the office: she's always the last to leave.
2   The chair isn't all that big. It ........................... fit in the car all right.
3   It's no use phoning Alan – he ........................... be at home now.
4   George saw William yesterday, so he ........................... know what's happening.
5   Jenny ........................... be out of hospital yet – her operation was only yesterday.
6   'There's a letter from you.' 'That ........................... be from the bank, I expect.'
7   As you ........................... know from my report, we are losing money heavily.
8   Jack had a very late night. He ........................... be feeling too good today, I imagine.
9   We'd better phone Helen. She ........................... be wondering where we've got to.
10  Excuse me. You ........................... remember me, but we met in Dublin last year.

# probability and possibility: *may, might, can, could*

**probability** To talk about the **probability** that something is true, or will happen, we can use *may*.

*Let's hurry – the shop **may** still be open.*
*We **may** go to Japan this summer.* (= 'There's a chance that we'll go.')

*Might* and *could* express a **smaller probability**.

*It **might/could** rain later, but I don't really think it will.*

**1** Write two things that you may do, or that may happen, in the future; and two things
(a little less probable) that you might/could do or that might/could happen.

.................................................................................................................................................
.................................................................................................................................................
.................................................................................................................................................
.................................................................................................................................................

**can not used** *Can* is **not** normally used to talk about probability.

*Andy **may** be in Joe's office.* (BUT NOT ~~Andy can be in Joe's office.~~)

**may not used in questions** We **don't** use **question** forms of *may* with this meaning.

*Do you think the firm may lose money?* (NOT ~~May the firm lose money?~~)

**2** Correct (✓) or not (✗)?
1 'Where's Jessica?' 'She may be with Lewis.' …
2 'Where's Jessica?' 'She can be with Lewis.' …
3 'Where's Jessica?' 'She could be with Lewis.' …
4 'Where's Jessica?' 'She might be with Lewis.' …
5 May you be in London next week? …
6 Do you think you may be in London next week? …
7 I may start Chinese lessons in the autumn. …
8 I think it might rain. …
9 Tomorrow could be a really busy day. …
10 Tomorrow can be a really busy day. …
11 May there be an election next year, do you suppose? …
12 'Where's Sally?' 'Ask her secretary. He can know.' …

**may not** and **can't**. Note the difference.

*Isabelle **may not** be at home.* (= 'Perhaps she's not at home.')
*Isabelle **can't** be at home – she's in Spain this week.* (= 'She's certainly not at home.')

**3** Put in *may not* or *can't*.
1 Our team ............................ possibly win on Saturday – they haven't got a chance.
2 I ............................ be here tomorrow. I'll let you know later.
3 That child ............................ want more food. He's just had three plates of stew.
4 There's a possibility of a strike, so the trains ............................ be running tomorrow.
5 I'll ask her, but she ............................ want to see you.
6 We ............................ be out of petrol. I filled the car up last night.
7 'I never want to see you again.' 'You ............................ mean that.' 'Oh, yes I do.'
8 We can try the restaurant round the corner, but they ............................ have a table free.

**can for what is typical** *Can* is not used to talk about probability (see page 66), but we can use *can* to talk about what is **typically** or normally **possible**.

*A female crocodile **can** lay 30–40 eggs.*
*Silver birch trees **can** grow up to 30m tall.*
*A divorce **can** be a disastrous experience for children.*
*It **can** get very cold in our old house.*

**4 Correct (✓) or not (✗)?**

1 Volcanic ash can damage aeroplane engines.  …
2 Ann can need some help – let's ask her.  …
3 The car's running badly. It can be time for a service.  …
4 Animals can take up a lot of your time.  …
5 You can get a lot of snow in the mountains in February.  …
6 'I can't find the sales report.' 'Ask Maggie. She can know where it is.'  …
7 Good wine can be quite cheap if you know where to shop.  …
8 Some parrots can live for over 50 years.  …
9 Emma can be really bad-tempered at times.  …
10 The baby's coughing a lot. I think she can have a cold.  …

**may … but** *May* (and sometimes *might*) can be used in arguing, to say that something is (not) true, but that this does not make a difference to the main point (see page 265).

*He **may** know a lot, **but** he's got no common sense.*
*She **may** be good with children, **but** she's hell to live with.*
*He **may not** like teaching, **but** he's very good at it.*

**5 Rewrite these pairs of sentences with *may … but*.**

▶ I'm slow. I'm not stupid.  *I may be slow, but I'm not stupid.*
1 She doesn't come to all the meetings. She knows what's going on.
   ..............................................................................
2 You have a degree. That's no substitute for practical experience.
   ..............................................................................
3 I don't know much about art. I know rubbish when I see it.
   ..............................................................................
4 The government makes impressive promises. Nothing is going to change.
   ..............................................................................

**NOTES**

*May well* is often used to say that something is quite probable.
   *He'll certainly pass the exam, and he **may well** get a really good result.*

*May, might* and *could* are possible with *if* + **present** (see page 232).
   *If he **carries** on like this, he **may/might/could** find himself in deep trouble.*
*May* is **not** possible with *if* + **past**.
   *If I **had** more time, I **might/could** study Chinese.* (NOT ~~If I had more time, I may…~~)

*May you …etc* *May* can introduce **wishes**.
   ***May** you both be very happy together.*      ***May** the best man win.*

**critical *might*** We can use *might* (often STRESSED) to criticise people for not doing things.
   *You **MIGHT** close the door behind you!*      *You **MIGHT** help with the washing up!*
   *You **MIGHT** have remembered Pam's birthday!*
*Could* can be used in the same way (see page 61).

# may have gone, should have told etc

modal verbs with perfect infinitives are used mostly to talk about 'unreal' past situations –
things which are the opposite of what happened, or which did not certainly happen.

*You **should have told** me earlier.*     *She **may have gone** home.*

the opposite of what happened  ***Should have** ..., **ought to have** ..., **would have** ..., **could have** ...*
and ***might have** ...* can be used to talk about **'unreal'** past situations that are the **opposite of what
really happened**.

*You **should have been** here an hour ago.* (But you weren't.)
*Alice **oughtn't to have bought** that car.* (But she did.)
*I was so angry I **could have killed** her.* (But I didn't.)
*If I'd known you were coming, I **would have stayed** in.*
*Jumping out of the window like that – he **could/might have broken** his leg.*

We can use the structure to **criticise** people for not doing things.

*You **could have helped** me!* (Why didn't you?)
*You **might have let** me know you weren't coming – I stayed in all evening!*

**1** **Complete the sentences with *should have ... could have ... , might have ...* or *would have ...* .
More than one answer may be possible.**

▸ He ...*should have paid*......... me last week. (*pay*)
1 When he said that to me I ..................................... him. (*hit*)
2 You ..................................... somebody, driving like that. (*kill*)
3 I ..................................... you, but I didn't have your number. (*phone*)
4 If my parents hadn't been so poor, I ..................................... to university. (*go*)
5 It's his fault she left him; he ..................................... nicer to her. (*be*)
6 I ..................................... more garlic in the soup. (*put*)
7 If you needed money, you ..................................... me. (*ask*)
8 'We got lost in the mountains.' 'You fools – you ..................................... a map.' (*take*)
9 It's a good thing they got her to hospital in time. She ..................................... (*die*)
10 You ..................................... me you were bringing your friends to supper! (*tell*)

not certain  ***May have** ..., **could have** ...* and ***might have** ...* can be used to talk about **possible** situations,
when we are **not sure what (has) happened**.

*I **may have left** my keys here this morning. Have you seen them?*
*'Why isn't he here?' 'He **could have missed** the train, I suppose.'*
*They're not home. They **might have gone** away for the weekend.*

**2** **Rewrite the sentences using *may/could/might have* ....**

▸ Perhaps she's got lost. ..*She may have got lost.*....... (OR ..*She could/might have got lost.*.......)
1 Perhaps Peter forgot to lock the door. ...................................................................................
2 Perhaps your mother sent these flowers. ...............................................................................
3 It's possible that the builders have finished. .........................................................................
4 There's a chance that I've found a new job. ...........................................................................
5 It seems possible that Alex has changed her mind. .............................................................
6 Somebody has been in my room, possibly. ...........................................................................
7 Perhaps we've come to the wrong house. .............................................................................

*Must/Can't have ...* are used to talk about what we know or believe from **logical deduction**, from **reasoning about things** (see page 65).

*Julie's crying. Something bad* **must have happened**.
*Joe isn't here. He* **can't have got** *my message.*

**3** Rewrite the sentences *in italics* using *must/can't have ...*

▶ 'We went to Dublin for the weekend.' *'I'm sure that was a nice change.'*
 *That must have been a nice change.* ...............................................................

1 'The car's got a big dent in the side.' *'It looks as if Bernie's had an accident.'*
 ...................................................................................................................

2 There's nothing in the fridge. *Obviously Luke hasn't been shopping.*
 ...................................................................................................................

3 'Lucy isn't here.' 'I reminded her yesterday. *Surely she hasn't forgotten.'*
 ...................................................................................................................

4 'There's a lot of water around.' *'That means it rained in the night.'*
 ...................................................................................................................

5 He had plenty of money last week. *I don't believe he's spent it all.*
 ...................................................................................................................

6 'I've finished the report.' 'Already? *I guess you worked all weekend.'*
 ...................................................................................................................

*must have ...* and *had to ...*  Note the difference.

*Joe* **must have gone** *home.* (It seems certain that he has gone home.)
*Joe* **had to go** *home.* (It was necessary for him to go home.)

*can't have ...* and *may not have ...*  Note the difference.

*They* **can't have arrived** *yet.* (They certainly haven't arrived.)
*They* **may not have arrived** *yet.* (Perhaps they haven't arrived.)

**4** Put in *must have ... , had to ... , can't have ...* or *may not have ...* .

1 Shakespeare ................................... to Australia, because Europeans didn't know about it. (*go*)
2 King Arthur.................................... – nobody's sure. (*exist*)
3 Castles in the Middle Ages .................................... cold in the winter. (*be*)
4 Poor people five hundred years ago .................................... easy lives. (*have*)
5 Sorry I'm late. I .................................... for a phone call. (*wait*)
6 She didn't answer. She .................................... what I said. (*understand*)
7 I .................................... two years' military service – a complete waste of time. (*do*)
8 You .................................... pleased when you heard you'd won the prize. (*be*)
9 'My ankle really hurts.' 'Well, you .................................... it if you can still walk.' (*break*)
10 I'm very sleepy. I .................................... at four this morning. (*get up*)

→

# *may have gone, should have told* etc (continued)

***needn't have …*** Note the difference between ***needn't have …*** and ***didn't need to …*.**

*I **needn't have cooked** so much food. Nobody was hungry.* (I did it, but it was unnecessary.)
*We had plenty of food left over from lunch, so I **didn't need to cook**.* (It was unnecessary, so I didn't do it.)

**5** **Choose the best way to complete the sentences.**

1 We *needn't have hurried / didn't need to hurry* – we got there much too early.
2 I *needn't have watered / didn't need to water* the flowers: Emma had already done it.
3 We *needn't have bought / didn't need to buy* the encyclopaedia. The kids never open it.
4 We had enough petrol, so I *needn't have filled up / didn't need to fill up*.
5 Luckily we had plenty of food, so I *needn't have gone / didn't need to go* shopping.
6 I *needn't have studied / didn't need to study* Latin at school; it hasn't been any use to me.
7 I *needn't have bothered / didn't need to bother* to get her a birthday present. She didn't even thank me.
8 Where I grew up we *needn't have locked / didn't need to lock* our doors; there was no crime.

**6** **Choose the right modal verbs.**

A DOG breeder has had five French bulldog pups stolen from her home. She believes she was being watched by thieves who knew the value of her dogs, which were stolen during a short period when she went out. She said "The dogs *may / might / must / should* have been taken soon after I left because their food and water were still there. I *may / could / should / must* have sold the female pup for as much as £2,200, and the male dogs were worth around £1,500 each." •

## NOTES

***Can have …*** is unusual except in questions and negatives.
*What **can have happened** to Julia? She **can't have forgotten**.*
*I suppose she **may have missed** the train.* (NOT *… she can have missed the train.*)

***Will have …*** and ***should have …*** are used to talk about what we can **reasonably expect** to have happened (see pages 36 and 65). ***Will have …*** is **more certain** than *should have …*.
*Dear Sir, You **will** recently **have received** our new price list …*
*Rebecca **should have arrived** home by now. Let's phone her.*

**present or future meaning** These structures can also be used to talk about unreal or uncertain situations in the present or future.
*I **should have been** on holiday this week, but they had a problem at work.*
*She **could have been** in the team for the next Olympics if she'd trained properly.*
*By the end of this year **I may have saved** enough money to go to America.*

***may have*: a change** The normal use of *may have …* is to say that things **possibly happened**: we are not certain.
*I'm not sure where she is. She **may have gone** out for a walk.*
But in modern English, some people use *may have …* to talk about things that were possible but **did not happen**.
*You were stupid to try climbing up the cliff. You **may have killed** yourself.*
This meaning is more traditionally expressed with *might/could have …*.
*… You **might/could have killed** yourself.*

For *will have …* (future perfect tense), see page 36. For *would have …* with *if*, see page 239.

# had better

*Had better,* like some modal verbs, is used to give **strong advice** to people (including ourselves). It is **not past** or **comparative**: it means 'This is a **good thing** to do **now**'.

*You'd **better** tidy your room before your father gets home.*
*Six o'clock – I'd **better** put the chicken in the oven.*

*Had better* is **not** used in **polite requests**. Compare:

***Could you** go out and buy something for supper?* (NOT ~~You'd better go out~~ ...)
*You'd **better** go now, or the shops will be closed.*

We use *had better* for **immediate** advice, not to say what people should **usually** do.

*You'd **better** get an eye test.* (BUT NOT ~~People had better get eye tests regularly.~~)

Compare *People should get eye tests regularly.*)

**1** **Correct (✓) or not (✗)?**

▶ It's getting late – we'd better think about going home. ✓
▶ You'd better let me use your phone. ✗
1 I'd better get my hair cut. ...
2 You'd better give me some more coffee. ...
3 Everybody had better give money to charity. ...
4 If you've got toothache again, you'd better see the dentist. ...
5 You'd better start working – the exam's next Tuesday. ...
6 We'd better hurry. The train leaves in ten minutes. ...
7 You'd better lend me some money. ...
8 It's getting late. I'd better get back home. ...


# be supposed to

**meanings** We use *be supposed to* to talk about what is **expected**; what **should** happen.

*You're **supposed to** have a licence to watch TV.*
*John **was supposed to** come at 6.00.*

We can use the structure to talk about what is **believed**.

*She's **supposed to** be a singer.*      *Is that **supposed to** be funny?*

**1** **Make sentences with *be supposed to*, using expressions from the box.**
**Different answers may be possible.**

| be efficient   be good communicators   be good with figures   forget things   go to mass on Sundays |
| have a lot of imagination   like children   make us laugh ✓   serve the people |

▶ Comedians *are supposed to make us laugh.*
1 Politicians ...................................................................
2 Teachers ...................................................................
3 Business people ...................................................................
4 Artists ...................................................................
5 Mathematicians ...................................................................
6 Linguists ...................................................................
7 Catholics ...................................................................
8 Old people ...................................................................

# *will* and *would*: willingness; typical behaviour

We can use *will* to talk about **willingness** to do something.

*Will you come this way, please?     What will you have to drink?*
*He'll do anything for money.     She won't tell us anything.*

**Would** is less direct, and can be used to make a request more polite.

*Would you come this way, please?*

**1** **Rewrite these sentences using *will*, *won't* or *would*.**

▶ Please wait here. ...*Will/Would you wait here?*.....................................

1 The car refuses to start. ....................................................

2 Please take a seat. .......................................................

3 Do you want tea or coffee? ...............................................

4 Please tell me your name. ................................................

5 Nobody wants to tell us the truth. ......................................

6 I am ready to help you. ..................................................

7 The computer refuses to recognise my password. ...........................

8 The bank is not willing to lend us any more money. ........................

9 Please sign the form at the bottom. ......................................

**habits** We can use *will* to talk about **habits** and **typical behaviour.**

*The neighbours will always babysit if you have to go out.*
*He'll watch TV all day, but he won't spend five minutes doing housework.*

If we **stress *will*** it can sound **critical**.

*If you WILL eat so much, it's not surprising you feel ill.*

**would** **Would** is used in the same way, to talk about the past.

*On Sundays all the family would come to our place for lunch.*
*They were nice people, but they WOULD play loud music all night.*

**2** **Choose the best ways of completing these laws of nature, using *will* / *won't* with expressions from the box.**

| always move faster   be enough   get lost   go off   go wrong   lose   misunderstand it   roll |
|---|

1 If something can go wrong it .......................................

2 However much you do, it ...........................................

3 The other queue ..................................................

4 If you are in charge of a group of children, one ....................................

5 If you make something so clear that even an idiot will understand it, some idiot

.......................................

6 If you drop a tool or small part while working on a car, it ...............................
to the exact centre underneath the vehicle.

7 If you have to get up early for a very important reason, your alarm

.......................................

8 If you watch your team during an important match, they ..............................

**3** **Think of somebody you know, and somebody you once knew. Write sentences about their typical behaviour, using *will* and *would*.**

.......................................................................

.......................................................................

# used to

forms  *Used to* can have the forms of an ordinary verb (questions and negatives with *did*), or the forms of a modal verb. The forms with *did* are more common. The following infinitive always has **to**.

**Did you use** to smoke?     **Used you** to smoke? (very uncommon)
We **didn't use** to go away on holiday.     We **used not** to go away on holiday.

meaning  The structure is used to talk about **past** situations and habits. There is **no present**.

I **used to play** tennis a lot. Now I **play** golf. (NOT ~~Now I use to play golf.~~)
We always **used to have** dogs. Now we **have** a cat.

**1** **Write a few sentences about the way people used to live hundreds of years ago.**

▶  Most people used to live in the country. Children didn't use to go to school.

......................................................................

......................................................................

......................................................................

......................................................................

......................................................................

**2** **Write a few sentences about things that you *used to do*, or *didn't use to do*, when you were younger. The words in the box may help.**

| believe   go to   like   listen to   play   read   think   watch   wear |
| --- |

......................................................................

......................................................................

......................................................................

......................................................................

......................................................................

**3** **Here are the answers to questions about somebody's schooldays. What do you think the questions might be? (There are different possibilities.)**

▶  'What languages did you use to study?' ............................................ 'Only French.'
1 ............................................................................ 'Rugby and tennis.'
2 ................................................................. 'No, but I used to play the violin.'
3 ...................................................................... 'No, I used to do very badly.'
4 ............................................................................ 'No, I used to hate it.'
5 ................................................................................ 'Yes, we did.'

**used to** and *would*  There is a difference. **Would** is only used to talk about **habits** – things that people **did repeatedly – in particular time frames.** Compare:

At weekends we **used to / would go** camping in the mountains.
I **used to play** the violin. BUT NOT ~~I would play the violin.~~ (no time-frame)
I **used to have** a Volkswagen. BUT NOT ~~I would have a Volkswagen.~~ (not a habit)

Note:  Some people write *used* instead of *use* in questions and negatives: for example *Did you used to …*
and *I didn't used to …*. (There is no difference in pronunciation.) This is not considered correct.

# *need*

**forms** *Need* can have the forms of an **ordinary verb** (questions and negatives with *do*, third-person *-s*, following infinitive with *to*).

*Do* we **need** to book?    *I think Alex **needs** to take a break.*

However, **modal** auxiliary forms are also possible, especially in **questions** and **negatives**.

*Need we* book?    *Tell her she **needn't come** in tomorrow.*

**use** Modal forms are most common when we are talking about things that are necessary at the time of speaking. Compare:

*Need I send / Do I need to send in the application now?*
*When **do people need** to send in the application?* (NOT *When need people send* …)

Note the difference between **mustn't** and **needn't / don't need to**.

*In bridge, you **mustn't** look at other people's cards.* (It's not allowed.)
*You **needn't** play for money, but you can if you like.* (It's not necessary.)

**1** | CHECK YOUR KNOWLEDGE. **Correct (✓) or not (✗)?**

1   Do we need to reserve a table for tonight?  …
2   Need we reserve a table for tonight?  …
3   Tell John he need reserve a table for tonight.  …
4   Pam needsn't work tomorrow.  …
5   Need I get a visa for my trip to Hungary?  …
6   Need people get a visa if they want to go to Hungary?  …
7   Just come when you like – you mustn't phone first.  …
8   Just come when you like – you don't need to phone first.  …
9   In a race, you mustn't start before the gun.  …
10   Do I need pay you now?  …

For *need* + perfect infinitive (e.g. *You needn't have bothered*), see page 70.  For *need …ing*, see page 95.

**Note** the structures *need hardly/scarcely/only* + infinitive without *to*.
  *I **need hardly emphasise** the importance of complete secrecy.*
  *If you have any problems, you **need only give** me a ring.*

'My grandfather took a bath every year, whether he needed to or not.'
(*Harry Lewis*)

'I seldom end up where I wanted to go, but almost always end up where I need to be.'
(*Douglas Adams*)

'What we think determines what happens to us, so if we want to change our lives, we need to stretch our minds.'
(*Wayne Dyer*)

'The Ten Commandments should be treated like an examination. Only six need to be attempted.'
(*Bertrand Russell*)

'If we really want liberty, then we need to go out and get it, we need to take it, because nobody is going to give it to us.'
(*Michael Badnarik*)

'Even very young children need to be informed about dying. Explain the concept of death very carefully to your child. This will make threatening him with it much more effective.'
(*P. J. O'Rourke*)

'It's often just enough to be with someone. I don't need to touch them. Not even talk. A feeling passes between you both. You're not alone.'
(*Marilyn Monroe*)

'You do not need to leave your room. Remain sitting at your table and listen. Do not even listen, simply wait, be quiet, still and solitary.'
(*Franz Kafka*)

'All I really need to know… I learned in kindergarten.'
(*Robert Fulghum*)

# more practice

**1** **Correct the mistakes, or write 'Correct'.**

▶ You ~~not must~~ park here. .....*must not*..........

▶ May I ask you something? ...*Correct*..........

1 I had to hurry, but I could get there in time. .....................................

2 'Could I use your phone?' 'Yes, of course you could.' .....................................

3 Could you watch my bags for a minute? .....................................

4 May people visit the cathedral? .....................................

5 The children could stay up late last night to watch the football. .....................................

6 You mustn't pay now if you don't want to – later is OK. .....................................

7 He can't be at home – there are no lights on. .....................................

8 We may go to Ireland in July. .....................................

9 May you be in London next week? .....................................

10 Ask Peter – he can know. .....................................

11 That woman can be really bad-tempered. .....................................

12 I might not have time to see you tomorrow. .....................................

**2** **Choose the best explanation of the words** *in italics*.

*He may be clever*, but he's got no common sense.

**A** 'I agree that he's clever'   **B** 'Perhaps he's clever'   **C** 'Perhaps he'll be clever one day'

**3** **Choose the best explanation of the words** *in italics*.

Phil *may not be here* tomorrow.

**A** 'isn't allowed to be here'   **B** 'will possibly not be here'   **C** both

**4** **Choose the most probable explanation of this sentence.**

I must get myself a new suit.

**A** I want a new suit.   **B** Somebody has told me to get a new suit.

**5** **DO IT YOURSELF.** **Which of the 'past' modal verbs have past meanings in these sentences?**

| | |
|---|---|
| ▶ Could I see you tomorrow? | ...No....... |
| ▶ Nobody could understand him. | ...Yes....... |
| 1 I might have a problem. | ............... |
| 2 We should try again. | ............... |
| 3 With a bit of luck, they could win. | ............... |
| 4 He would say nothing for hours. | ............... |
| 5 Alice thought she might be ill. | ............... |
| 6 If you asked me nicely, I might say 'Yes'. | ............... |
| 7 We really ought to ask somebody for advice. | ............... |

**6** **Choose the most probable explanation of this sentence.**

James isn't at home – he must be working late.

**A** It seems certain that James is working late.   **B** James has to work late.   **C** both

➜

**7** Choose the best answers to the questions.

1 She should have told her mother. *Did she tell her mother?*   YES   NO   MAYBE
2 We must have missed the turning. *Did we miss the turning?*   YES   NO   PROBABLY
3 Anna can't have got my message. *Did she get the message?*   YES   NO   PROBABLY NOT
4 He needn't have rented a car. *Did he rent a car?*   YES   NO   MAYBE
5 Harry may have gone home. *Has he gone home?*   YES   NO   MAYBE
6 The meeting may not have finished. *Has the meeting finished?*   YES   NO   MAYBE
7 Really! She might have told us! *Did she tell us?*   YES   NO   MAYBE
8 That was stupid – he might have caused an accident. *Did he cause an accident?*   YES   NO   MAYBE
9 They ought to have arrived by now. *Have they arrived?*   YES   NO   PROBABLY
10 They shouldn't have opened a new branch. *Did they open one?*   YES   NO   MAYBE

**8** Choose the best explanation of this use of *will*.

> She will sit talking to herself for hours.

**A** It refers to habitual behaviour.   **B** It predicts future behaviour.   **C** It describes a wish. …

**9** Choose the best explanation of this stressed use of *will*.

> She WILL buy things she can't afford.

**A** It refers critically to habitual behaviour.   **B** It refers neutrally to habitual behaviour.
**C** It makes a critical prediction of future behaviour.

**10** What does this sentence mean?

> You WOULD tell Peter about my accident – I didn't want him to know.

**A** You wanted to tell Peter about my accident.
**B** You were going to tell Peter about my accident but you didn't.
**C** It was typical of you to tell Peter about my accident.

**11** Put in *would*, *used to*, or both if possible.

1 When we lived in France we ………………………………… go skiing every winter.
2 I ………………………………… have an old Ford car that kept breaking down.
3 Robert ………………………………… play a lot of chess when he was younger.

**12** Circle the forms that are more normal or more correct.

1 What *did people use / used people* to do in the evenings before TV? …
2 I *didn't used / didn't use* to like opera. …
3 *Used you / Did you use* to play football? …
4 You *used not / didn't use* to like him, *did / used* you? …

**13** Choose the best explanation of this sentence.

> Phil had better get his hair cut.

**A** It was important that Phil should get his hair cut.   **B** It was best that Phil should get his hair cut.
**C** Phil should get his hair cut.   **D** It's best that Phil gets his hair cut.

**14** Choose the best explanation of this sentence.

> You were supposed to be here this morning.

**A** Everybody thinks you were here this morning.   **B** You should have been here this morning.
**C** You were definitely here this morning.

**15** Put the verbs into the texts.

| dive | extend | grow | grow | jump | jump | lift | live | reach | run | stay | swim | weigh |

1 Alaskan brown bears, the world's largest meat-eating animals that live on land, can ............... as much as 1,700 pounds (771 kilograms).

2 The fastest human swimmer can ........................... at just under 9 km per hour. The fastest mammal – the dolphin - can do 56 km per hour.

3 Some ants can ........................... 50 times their own body weight.

4 Elephants can't ...........................

5 Frogs can ........................... over 20 times their own length.

6 Ant supercolonies can ........................... for 100km.

7 There are trees that can ........................... for 20,000 years.

8 Cheetahs can ........................... at 110 km per hour.

9 In a dive, a peregrine falcon can ........................... 320 km per hour.

10 Sequoias can ........................... to be over 100m tall.

11 Sperm whales can ........................... to 3000m below the surface, and can ........................... under water for 90 minutes.

12 Bamboo can ........................... 1m in 24hrs.

**16** INTERNET EXERCISE. Use a search engine to find some interesting sentences containing the words "should have said" and "should not have said" (or change the verb if you prefer). Write them here.

.........................................................................................................................
.........................................................................................................................
.........................................................................................................................
.........................................................................................................................
.........................................................................................................................

## active and passive verbs

In many situations there are two participants: one that does something, or has an effect (the 'agent') and another that something happens to, or that is affected (the 'patient'). English, like many languages, has different sets of verb forms for these situations.

- If we want to focus on the **agent**, we make the agent the **subject** and use **active** verbs.
  *Harry invited everybody.*     *The volcano destroyed six villages.*
- If we want to focus on the **patient**, we make the patient the **subject** and use **passive** verbs. The agent is backgrounded or not mentioned.
  *Everybody was invited (by Harry).*     *Six villages were destroyed (by the volcano).*

# revise the basics

**passive tenses**  We make **passive verbs** with forms of *be* + **past participle** (*made, stolen* etc). **Passive** verbs have the **same tenses** (simple present, present progressive, present perfect etc) as active verbs (see page 297 for a list).

*These cars **are made** in Japan.*     *Your room **is being cleaned** now.*
*Nobody **has been told** about the problems.*     *The contract **will be signed** next week.*

**1  CHECK YOUR KNOWLEDGE.  Correct the mistakes or write 'Correct'.**
- ▶ Has my suit ~~cleaned~~ yet? ...*been cleaned*......    ▶ Nobody was asked. ...*Correct.*...............
- 1  Tomorrow's meeting has been cancelled. ...................................
- 2  You will told where to go. ...................................
- 3  We were taught to be polite to older people. ...................................
- 4  The road was closed because it was being repaired. ...................................
- 5  I'm afraid you have not selected for interview. ...................................
- 6  I heard that my friends had being arrested. ...................................

**passive infinitives and -*ing* forms**  *(to) be* + **past participle**; *being* + **past participle**.

*I want **to be paid** now.*     *We expect **to be informed** of your results.*
*He loves **being photographed**.*     *I got in without **being seen**.*

**Modal verbs** are often followed by passive infinitives.

*Something **must be done**.*     *I'm afraid the date **can't be changed**.*

**2  CHECK YOUR KNOWLEDGE.  Correct the mistakes or write 'Correct'.**
- ▶ She dislikes being ~~touching~~. ...*touched*...............    ▶ Everybody must be told. ...*Correct.*...............
- 1  I really think the whole family must to be consulted. ...................................
- 2  John hates being rushed. ...................................
- 3  I didn't expect been stopped. ...................................
- 4  Do you enjoy being massage? ...................................
- 5  I hope to be promoted soon. ...................................
- 6  Alice should be told immediately. ...................................

**use of *by***  We use *by* … in passive structures if we need to say who or what did something; but most often this is unnecessary. (Only about 20% of passives have *by*-phrases.)

***Who** was this picture painted **by**?*     *It was painted **by Rembrandt**.*
*Your room has been cleaned ~~by the cleaner~~.*     *These cars are made in Japan.*

**verb + preposition** In passive structures, **verb + preposition** groups **stay together**.

*The plan was **thought about** very carefully.* (NOT ~~About the plan was thought~~ …)
*I don't like **being shouted at**.*

**3** CHECK YOUR KNOWLEDGE. **Correct the mistakes or write 'Correct'.**
1 For everything will be paid at the end of the month. ....................................
2 Emma's novel has been translated into German by a translator. ....................................
3 I hate being spoken as if I was a servant. ....................................
4 My mother was very well looked after in hospital. ....................................
5 I'm afraid John can't be relied on to keep his promises. ....................................
6 By who was the new cathedral built? ....................................

**Verbs with two objects** like *give* or *send* have two possible active and passive structures.

| ACTIVE | PASSIVE |
|---|---|
| *They gave/sent **Joe a gold watch**.* | ***Joe** was given/sent a gold watch.* |
| *They gave/sent **a gold watch** to Joe.* | ***A gold watch** was given/sent to Joe.* |

We choose the structure which fits best with what comes before and after (see page 80).
The structure with the **person** as subject (e.g. *Joe was given* …) is very common.

**4** **Correct (✓) or not (✗)? (One sentence is wrong.)**
1 Peter was given a new car when he passed his exam. …
2 The builders are being given another month to finish the work. …
3 You were lent a bicycle last week – where is it? …
4 To my mother has just been sent a wonderful bouquet of flowers. …
5 I think Sally will be given the manager's job. …
6 Harold was awarded a medal for long service. …

**get-passives** We often make passives with **get** instead of *be*, especially in spoken English.

*My suitcase **got stolen** at the airport.     We never **get invited** to her parties.*

The *get*-passive often suggests that things happen by accident, unexpectedly, or outside our control.
It is not often used for longer, more deliberate, planned actions. Compare:

*My sister **got bitten** by a dog yesterday.*
*Don't worry about the repairs; they'll **get done** sooner or later.*
*The Emperor Charlemagne **was crowned** in 800 AD.* (It would be strange to say '*Charlemagne got crowned* …')
*The new school **will be opened** by the Prime Minister on May 25th.*

The **get-passive** is **often** (not always) used to talk about **bad** things that happen; perhaps because unexpected or unplanned events are mostly unwelcome.

**5** **Five of the passive verbs in sentences 1–8 would also be natural with *get*. Change them.**
▶ Maggie was hit by a car this morning. ..*Maggie got hit* ..............
▶ Mount Everest was first climbed in 1953. ..*Not natural with got*....
1 We were burgled last night. ....................................
2 Our roof was damaged in the storm. ....................................
3 St Paul's Cathedral was built by Sir Christopher Wren. ....................................
4 If you are caught, don't tell the police anything. ....................................
5 If there is one mosquito in the house, I am always bitten. ....................................
6 Dr Lee was awarded the Nobel prize for physics last year. ....................................
7 We were all sent home early because of the strike. ....................................
8 These cars are manufactured by a Japanese firm. ....................................

# reasons for using passives

There are several different **reasons** for using passives. This text illustrates some of them.

---

## A DRIVER has been sent to jail for 90 days for speeding.

GRAHAM SMITH, 29, of North Street, Barton, was driving at over 60mph (96kph) near a Barton primary school last November when he was stopped by police officers, Didcot magistrates heard on Thursday.

Twelve months earlier Smith had been disqualified from driving for three years for driving at 70mph in the Barton town centre. He was banned for twelve months in 2004 for a similar offence.

Mr Peter Jones, defending, said Smith had been using the car to visit a sick friend. He said Smith was depressed after the visit, and was anxious to get home as soon as possible.

He was caught by police during a routine speed check in Wantage Road, Barton. ■

---

**1** **DO IT YOURSELF.** Look at the way these passive verbs are used in the text: *has been sent; was stopped; had been disqualified; was banned; was caught.* Then look at the following explanations for why the writer chose passives. Two of them are right – which? The other three are wrong.

A The writer was most interested in **what happened**, not **who it happened to**. ☐

B Most of the text is about what **was done** to somebody, not what he/she/it **did**. ☐

C It is not known, not important or obvious **who did** something. ☐

D The writer was **giving details** of past events. ☐

E The writer wanted to go on talking about Smith. Active verbs (*magistrates have sent …, police stopped …* etc) would mean changing the subject and taking the focus away from Smith. ☐

**Explanations … and … are right.**

---

**same subject** A passive verb can make it possible to go on talking about the **same person or thing** (see explanation E, above).

*He waited for two hours; then he **was seen** by a doctor; then he **was sent** back to the waiting room. He sat there for another two hours – by this time he was getting angry. Then he **was taken** upstairs …*

**2** Choose the best ways of continuing each sentence.

1 He lives in a small house.
   **A** Somebody built it about forty years ago.   **B** It was built about forty years ago.

2 English is well worth learning.
   **A** People use it for international communication.   **B** It is used for international communication.

3 He got a sports car, but he didn't like it.
   **A** So he sold it again.   **B** So it was sold again.

4 My nephew is an artist.
   **A** He has just painted another picture.   **B** Another picture has just been painted by him.

5 The new Virginia Meyer film is marvellous.
   **A** They are showing it at our local cinema.   **B** It is being shown at our local cinema.

6 'How are your brothers?'
   **A** 'Fine. Peter's restoring an old boat.'   **B** 'Fine. An old boat is being restored by Peter.'

**another reason: heavy subjects** We don't like to begin sentences with long and heavy subjects. One way of avoiding this is to use passive structures. Compare:

*John trying to tell everybody what he thought* annoyed me.
*I was annoyed* by John trying to tell everybody what he thought.

*That she had not written to her parents for over two years* surprised me.
*I was surprised* that she had not written to her parents for over two years.

**3 Change these sentences. Can you see how this makes them better?**

1 George ringing me up me up at three o'clock in the morning to tell me he was in love again didn't please me.

.................................................................................................................................
.................................................................................................................................

2 Caroline telling me that she had always wanted to be a singer surprised me.

.................................................................................................................................

3 That nobody was prepared to take him to hospital shocked us.
We.............................................................................................................................

4 That Mary thought she was better than everybody else irritated everybody.

.................................................................................................................................

**formality and style** Passives are very common in some kinds of formal writing where the writer keeps him/herself in the background – for example business or scientific reports.

*The Department has been reorganised over the last year.* (RATHER THAN *We have reorganised the Department …* )
*Three different compounds* **were investigated** for their resistance to oxidation. (RATHER THAN *I investigated three …*)

Passives are also used to make rules and instructions seem less personally directed.

*Bicycles* **may not be parked** against these railings. (RATHER THAN *You may not park bicycles …* )

For some more complex formal passive structures, see pages 82–83.

**4 Rewrite these sentences using passive verbs.**

1 You must send applications to the Central Office before August 1. You must attach all supporting documentation, and you must enclose a cheque in payment of the full fee. You must also enclose a stamped addressed envelope.

.................................................................................................................................
.................................................................................................................................
.................................................................................................................................

2 We selected fifty workers at random and gave them a thorough physical examination. We took blood samples from all fifty and analysed them. We found no traces of lead poisoning.

.................................................................................................................................
.................................................................................................................................
.................................................................................................................................

**indefinite agents** Passives are often used in a formal style where the person or thing that does an action is unknown or indefinite. In a less formal style, we often prefer an active verb with a general pronoun like *they* or *you*. Compare:

*Road repairs* **are being carried** out.     *They're digging up* the damned road again.
*The police* **are** never successfully **sued**.     *You* **can't win** a case against the police.

# complex passive structures

**Note** these passive structures. They are mostly rather formal.

## A Passive of verbs followed by *that*-clauses

*They know that he is abroad.* → **It is known that** *he is abroad.* / *He is known **to be** abroad.*

**Many verbs that are followed by *that*-clauses** (e.g. *think, believe, say*) can be used in passive structures with **introductory it**. They are mostly rather formal, but common in news reports.

*It is thought that the Minister will resign.*
*At that time, **it was believed that** the sky was a crystal sphere.*
*It is expected that the company will become profitable in the New Year.*
*It was said that the gods were angry.*

Another way of expressing the same ideas is with **subject + passive verb + infinitive**.

*He is known to be in Wales.*     *They are said to own several houses.*
*She is understood to have left home.* (Note the perfect infinitive.)

This structure is also possible with **there** as a subject.

*There are thought to be fewer than twenty people still living in the village.*
*There were said to be ghosts in the house, but I never heard anything.*

1 **Make the sentences passive.**

▶ People think the government will fall. (*It*) .....It is believed that the government will fall.

▶ Everybody knows he is violent. (*He*) .....He is known to be violent.

▶ They say there is bad weather on the way (*There*) .....There is said to be bad weather on the way.

1 They believed that fresh air was bad for sick people. (*It*)
.................................................................................

2 Some people claim that there are wolves in the mountains. (*There*)
.................................................................................

3 They think that the man holding the hostages is heavily armed. (*The man*)
.................................................................................

4 They say he is in an agitated state. (*He*)
.................................................................................

5 People suggest that the rate of inflation will rise. (*It*)
.................................................................................

6 They report that she died in a plane crash. (*She – perfect infinitive*)
.................................................................................

7 People believe that there are 6,000 different languages in the world. (*There*)
.................................................................................

8 We understand that she left the country on Friday. (*It*)
.................................................................................

9 They think that there is oil under Windsor Castle. (*There*)
.................................................................................

10 People believed that the earth was the centre of the universe. (*The earth*)
.................................................................................

11 They know that he has been married four times. (*He*)
.................................................................................

12 We expect that there will be an announcement on Friday. (*It*)
.................................................................................

## B Passive of verbs followed by object + infinitive

> They asked **me to give** my name. → I was asked **to give** my name.

**Many verbs that are followed by object + infinitive** (e.g. *ask, tell, expect, choose*) can be used in passive structures with infinitives.

*I was asked to give* my name and date of birth.     *We were told to take* the 9.15 train.
*You are not expected to work* on Sundays.     *Ann was chosen to represent* our street.

Note that *see, hear* and *make* are followed by *to*-infinitives in this structure.

*He was **seen to come** out of her house at two o'clock.* .
*She has never been **heard to say** a kind word.*     *We were **made to lie** on the floor.*

Verbs that refer to **wanting** and **liking** are not generally used in this passive structure.

(NOT ~~I was wanted to reply.~~ OR ~~Everybody is liked to make suggestions.~~)

**2 Write true or false continuations for these sentences.**

1  I have never been asked to .......................................................
2  I have often been told to .......................................................
3  I am not usually expected to .......................................................
4  I will never be chosen to .......................................................
5  I have never been seen to .......................................................
6  I have sometimes been heard to .......................................................
7  I would not like to be made to .......................................................

## C Passive of verbs with object + noun/adjective complement

> They considered **him a genius**. → **He** was considered **a genius**.

**Many verbs that are followed by object + noun/adjective complement** (e.g. *consider, elect, make, call, regard ...as, see ... as*) can be used in passive structures.

*He **was considered a genius** by many people.*     *Mrs Robins **was elected President**.*
*We **were made very happy** by the decision.*     *He **was generally regarded as stupid**.*

**3 Make the sentences passive.**

1  They appointed Mr Evans secretary.

...............................................................................................................

2  We considered Louise a sort of clown.

...............................................................................................................

3  People regarded Dr Hastings as an expert on criminal law.

...............................................................................................................

4  The new owners have made the house much more attractive.

...............................................................................................................

5  The villagers called her a witch.

...............................................................................................................

6  They elected Professor Martin Vice-President.

...............................................................................................................

---

**NOTES**

**A few verbs that are followed by infinitives** (most commonly *decide, agree*) can be used in passive structures beginning with *it*.

*It **was decided not to advertise** again.*     *It **was agreed to hold** a meeting in April.*

But most verbs cannot be used in this way.

(NOT ~~It is started to make a profit.~~ OR ~~It is not expected to have difficulty.~~)

For the passive structures that are possible with a particular verb, see a good dictionary.

# other advanced points

**prepositional structures** The objects of prepositional verbs can become passive subjects.

*We have looked carefully **at the plan**.* → ***The plan** has been carefully looked at.*

But this is not usually possible if a verb already has another object before the preposition.

*They threw **stones** at him.* → ***Stones** were thrown at him.* BUT NOT *~~He was thrown stones at.~~*

**1 Correct (✓) or not (✗)?**

1 That table mustn't be put cups on. …
2 Your brother's a lovely guy, but I'm afraid he can't be relied on. …
3 His ideas haven't been talked about enough. …
4 These school desks have been written names on for generations. …
5 I think I've been told some lies about. …
6 This house hasn't been very well looked after. …

**adjectival past participles** Some past participles can be followed by other prepositions instead of *by*, especially if they are used more or less like adjectives. Compare:

*She was **frightened by** a spider.*    *Are you **very frightened of** spiders?*

Other common examples: *shocked at, surprised at, known to, filled with, covered with.*
For the structures possible with particular past participles, check in a good dictionary.

**2 Complete the sentences with words from the box.**

| covered   frightened   known   stuffed   surprised   surprised |
| --- |

1 I'm not ........................... of flying – just of crashing.
2 We're all feeling ........................... at the election result.
3 When he was arrested, his pockets were ........................... with jewellery.
4 When I looked out of the window I saw that the garden was ........................... with snow.
5 We were terribly ........................... at the news of Alice's death.
6 Jones has been ........................... to the police for some time.

**perfective past participles** With verbs that express **completion**, a present tense of *be* + **past participle** can have a similar meaning to a perfect tense.

*My suitcase **is packed** and I'm ready to go.* (= *… has been packed.*)
*The translation **is finished**.*    *Everything **is washed**.*

**3 One of these is wrong. Which one?**

1 The chicken is just about cooked.
2 My car is hit; it's going to cost a fortune to get it repaired
3 OK. The report is written; now you all have to read it.
4 Smiths rang to say your watch is mended.
5 I'm afraid your trousers are completely ruined.
6 The repainting's done. I hope you're happy with it.

**Number … is wrong.**

## NOTES

**verbs that can't passivise** Not all verbs can be made passive – check in a good dictionary.

> *A high wall encloses the garden.* ➔ *The garden is enclosed by a high wall.*
> *Our advisers recommend further investment.* ➔ *Further investment is recommended.*

BUT NOT:

> *John resembles Peter.* ➔ ~~*Peter is resembled by John.*~~
> *That suit doesn't fit you.* ➔ ~~*You aren't fitted by that suit.*~~
> *The government lacks confidence.* ➔ ~~*Confidence is lacked by the government.*~~

**active verbs with passive meanings** Some active verbs are used intransitively with a passive kind of meaning.

> *The cup **broke**.    Suddenly the door **opened**.    Your book's **selling** well.*
> *The ice **is melting**.    My new tee-shirts **have** all **shrunk**.*

This is common with verbs that describe things that can be done to materials.

> *This table **scratches** easily.    These knives **don't polish** well.    The bulb **won't unscrew**.*

**active and passive with the same meaning** Some verbs can be used in both active and passive structures with little difference. Common examples: *worry* and *drown*.

> *I **worry** / I'm **worried** when you don't phone.*
> *He fell into the lake and **drowned** / **was drowned**.*
> *They **married** / **were married** in June, and **divorced** / **were divorced** a year later.*

**Get-passives** are common with some of these expressions: for example *get drowned, get married/divorced, get dressed*.

**other languages** Some English passive verbs have active equivalents in other languages, and vice versa: for example *be born, die*.

**4** **Put the numbers of the boxed expressions in the right places in the newspaper cuttings.**

| | | | | |
|---|---|---|---|---|
| 1 are allowed | 2 get found out | 3 to be published | 4 to be reviewed | 5 to have been hit |
| 6 was also affected | 7 was delayed | 8 was found dead | 9 held up | 10 was mistakenly injected |
| 11 was ordered | 12 was yesterday charged | 13 were affected | 14 were disqualified | 15 were relocated |

**A** A woman ... with the murder of a 28-year-old man who ... in a hotel bedroom.

**B** Leading universities warned yesterday that unless they ... to set their own fees for undergraduate courses, they will lose their world-class reputations.

**C** Every spending decision taken by Labour in the last four months before the election is ... by the Treasury.

**D** A hospital trust ... to pay £100,000 yesterday after a patient died when an anaesthetic ... into a vein.

**E** PUBLICATION of a study into mobile phones and brain cancer was ... for years because scientists could not agree on its findings. The World Health Organisation's Interphone report was ... in 2006, but ... until yesterday because scientists from 13 countries interpreted the results differently.

**F** Many parts of China ... by heavy rain last week. Tens of thousands of people ... due to flooding, and the province of Jiangxi ... by some landslides after the heaviest rainfall in over 25 years. The North Island of New Zealand is reported ... by at least 8,000 lightning strikes during last Saturday afternoon,

**G** THIRTY of the top 100 runners in an international marathon in January ..., many for using cars. In the long run you will ....

# more practice

**1** **Choose the best sentences to build up a continuous text.**

1  a. HOW BOOKS ARE MADE *(circled)*
   b. HOW PEOPLE MAKE BOOKS

2  a. First of all, the printers print big sheets of paper.
   b. First of all, big sheets of paper are printed.

3  a. Each sheet contains the text of a number of pages (e.g. 32).
   b. The text of a number of pages (e.g. 32) is contained in each sheet.

4  a. People fold and cut the sheets to produce sections of the book.
   b. The sheets are folded and cut to produce sections of the book.

5  a. These sections are called signatures.
   b. We call these sections signatures.

6  a. The printers put all the signatures together in the correct order.
   b. All the signatures are put together in the correct order.

7  a. Then they are bound together and their edges are trimmed.
   b. Then they bind the signatures together and trim the edges.

8  a. Finally, the cover – which has been printed separately – is attached.
   b. Finally, they attach the cover – which they have printed separately.

9  a. Now the publishers can publish the book.
   b. Now the book can be published.

**2** **GRAMMAR IN A TEXT. This text has a bad mixture of actives and passives. Rewrite it twice, once just using passives and once just with actives.**

In 1665, an experiment was carried out to investigate the nature of colour. Newton darkened a room and made a hole in the window shutter, so that a narrow ray of sunlight was allowed to enter the room. A glass prism was taken and placed in the ray of light. The result was that the prism split the light into a band of colours like a rainbow – a spectrum. When he placed a second prism upside down in front of the first prism, it recombined the different colours of the spectrum into white light. At last, someone had scientifically demonstrated the relationship between light and colour.

*In 1665, an experiment was carried out to investigate the nature of colour. A room ...*

..............................................................................................................................
..............................................................................................................................
..............................................................................................................................
..............................................................................................................................
..............................................................................................................................
..............................................................................................................................

*In 1665, Newton* .......................................................................................................
..............................................................................................................................
..............................................................................................................................
..............................................................................................................................
..............................................................................................................................
..............................................................................................................................
..............................................................................................................................

**3** INTERNET EXERCISE. Use a search engine to find five or more sentences with *get*-passives. Write them down.

1 ......................................................................................................................................
2 ......................................................................................................................................
3 ......................................................................................................................................
4 ......................................................................................................................................
5 ......................................................................................................................................

**4** Write sentences about the man in the text, using *was said*, *was thought*, *was believed*, *was reported* and *was understood*.

The man was a legend. Nobody knew the truth about him; everybody had a story. He had been a bank robber in his younger days. He was immensely rich. He was a friend of the President. He advised governments. He had mistresses in three different countries. He was a mathematical genius. He spoke fourteen languages. He had climbed Everest in winter. He had a bath with gold taps. He had lived with wolves. He ran marathons to keep fit. And on top of all that, he was terribly nice.

▶ *He was said to have been a bank robber in his younger days.*..............................................
▶ *He was believed to be immensely rich.*.......................................................................................

1 ......................................................................................................................................
2 ......................................................................................................................................
3 ......................................................................................................................................
4 ......................................................................................................................................
5 ......................................................................................................................................
6 ......................................................................................................................................
7 ......................................................................................................................................
8 ......................................................................................................................................
9 ......................................................................................................................................
10 .....................................................................................................................................

**5** Put in the missing word from the cartoon caption.

'All the exits have ................................. sealed off.
He must have got out through the entrance.'

# Section 7  infinitives and *-ing* forms

## uses

**Infinitives** like *(to) break* and *-ing* **forms** like *breaking* have various uses.

- They can help to make verb forms:

    *I didn't **break** it.     You're **breaking** my heart.*

- They can be used rather like **nouns**, as subjects and after verbs.

    ***To wait** around makes me nervous.     **Talking** is easier than listening.*

    *I want **to see** you again soon.     Do you enjoy **cooking**?*

    **Infinitive subjects** are more often put later, in a structure with *it* (see page 228).

    *It makes me nervous **to wait** around.*

- **Infinitives** can also follow certain **adjectives** and **nouns**.

    *I'm **anxious to see** the new baby.     Have you any **plans to move** house?*

- *-ing* **forms** are used **after prepositions**, and can follow some **adjectives** and **nouns** in prepositional structures.

    *You can't live for long **without drinking**.     I'm **tired of listening** to him.*

    *I hate the **thought of getting** old.* (NOT *... the thought to get old.*)

- *-ing* **forms** can also be used rather like **adjectives** or adverbs.

    *I can smell **burning leaves**.     She ran out of the room **crying**.*

**Section 7** deals mainly with infinitives and *-ing forms* in their more **noun-like uses**, as subjects and after verbs. For other uses, see the Index.

## terminology

When *-ing* forms are used like nouns, they are often called 'gerunds' in grammars; when they are used in other ways, they are called 'present participles.' These are not very helpful names, and the distinction between the two kinds of use is not always completely clear. In this book we prefer the general term '-ing forms'.

## 'split infinitives'

There is an old 'rule' which says that adverbs should not be put between *to* and the rest of the infinitive. So for example *He began **slowly to get** up off the floor* is supposed to be 'more correct' than *He began **to slowly get** up off the floor*. This rule was invented in the 19th century by grammarians who thought English should imitate Latin (in which an infinitive is one word), and has little value. However, some people still avoid 'split infinitives' of this kind in formal writing.

## *try and* etc

With *try*, *wait*, *come* and *go*, a structure with *and* can be used instead of an infinitive (e.g. *I'll **try and get** home early*). See pages 202 and 307.

---

*'To be or not to be, that is the question.'*
(Shakespeare, Hamlet)

'Parting is such sweet sorrow.'
(*Shakespeare, Romeo and Juliet*)

'I love being a writer. What I can't stand is the paperwork.'
(*Peter de Vries*)

'Programming today is a race between software engineers striving to build bigger and better idiot-proof programmes, and the universe trying to produce bigger and better idiots. So far the universe is winning.'
(*Rick Cook*)

*'Beethoven tells you what it's like to be Beethoven and Mozart tells you what it's like to be human. Bach tells you what it's like to be the universe.'*
(*Douglas Adams*)

# revise the basics

| INFINITIVES | | | |
|---|---|---|---|
| **simple** | *(to) write* | **passive** | *(to) be written* |
| **progressive** | *(to) be writing* | **perfect passive** | *(to) have been written* |
| **perfect** | *(to) have written* | | |
| **perfect progressive** | *(to) have been writing* | **negative** | *not (to) write, be writing* etc |

**1** **Put a suitable infinitive of the verb *write* into each sentence. (One infinitive is without *to*.)**

1 I'm going ....................................................... some postcards this afternoon.

2 This letter appears ....................................................... by a very young child.

3 Dickens is said ....................................................... three novels that were never published.

4 These days, academic articles need .......................................................in English if they are to be widely read.

5 Please memorise these instructions, but be careful ....................................................... anything down.

6 I seem ....................................................... for ever – my hand really hurts.

7 This time tomorrow, I'll ....................................................... answers to exam questions.

| *-ING* FORMS | | | |
|---|---|---|---|
| **simple** | *writing* | **passive** | *being written* |
| **perfect** | *having written* | **perfect passive** | *having been written* |
| | | **negative** | *not writing* etc |

**2** **Put a suitable *-ing* form into each sentence. More than one answer may be possible.**

1 I enjoy .................................... children's stories.

2 Please forgive me for .................................... earlier – I've been away.

3 'Where's the report?' 'I'm afraid it's still ....................................'

4 After the great writer's death, his wife admitted .................................... all of his novels.

5 This article shows signs of .................................... in a great hurry.

**3** **Put infinitives from the box into the text, with or without *to*.**

| die die die hear live make read |
|---|

'I was at a reading by a very famous poet. I put my head back and closed my eyes in an attitude of deep concentration. I had lost the will [1]............................ I wanted [2]............................ I tried [3]............................ myself [4]............................ by sheer will-power. I made myself [5]............................ . I was instantly reincarnated as myself, just in time [6]............................ her say "And now I'd like [7]............................ an extract from my verse drama".'
(*Ian Duhig*)

# perfect infinitives and -*ing* forms

**Perfect infinitives** (*to have gone* etc) have the same kind of meaning as **perfect** or **past** tenses.

*I'm pleased* **to have met** *you.* (= '… that I **have met** you.')
*We were sorry* **not to have seen** *the cathedral.* (= '… that we **had not seen** the cathedral.')
*I expect* **to have finished** *everything by tomorrow.* (= ' … that I **will have finished** …')
*Shakespeare is believed* **to have travelled** *in Italy.* (= 'It is believed that Shakespeare **travelled** in Italy.')
*The picture seems* **to have been painted** *around 1600.* (= 'It seems that the picture **was painted** around 1600.')

**1  Rewrite these sentences using perfect infinitives.**

1  It seems that you misunderstood the directions. (*You seem …* )

...................................................................................................................................

2  We were sorry that we had upset her.

...................................................................................................................................

3  It seems that the rain has stopped.

...................................................................................................................................

4  I'm glad that I've got to know your family.

...................................................................................................................................

5  Max was disappointed that he had failed his exam.

...................................................................................................................................

6  We expect we'll have moved house before September.

...................................................................................................................................

7  Alice was very happy that she had left school.

...................................................................................................................................

8  I'm fortunate that I grew up bilingual.

...................................................................................................................................

9  It is believed that the terrorists have left the country.

...................................................................................................................................

10  It appears that the car was stolen last night.

...................................................................................................................................

**unreal situations**  With *was/were*, *meant* and *would like / would have liked*, we can use perfect infinitives to show that we are referring to the **opposite** of what really happened.

*They* **were to have got** *married in June, but she broke it off.*
*We* **meant to have asked** *you to dinner, but Pete had to go to France.*
*I'd like* **to have been sitting** *there when she walked in.*
(OR *I'd have liked* **to have been sitting** *there when she walked in.*)

Simple infinitives are also possible after *was/were* and *meant*.

*They* **were to get** *married in June, but …*
*We* **meant to ask** *you to dinner, but …*

'It is curious how, from time immemorial, man seems to have associated the idea of evil with beauty.'
(*Richard le Gallienne*)

'It's been a long road back to health and fitness for me. I am just glad to have been given the opportunity to do what I love most.'
(*Mohandas Gandhi*)

'Fortunately, it doesn't seem to have made a lot of difference to my audiences that I'm as bald as a billiard ball.'
(*James Taylor*)

'I will be glad to have done with this life forever.'
(*Taylor Caldwell*)

'Loneliness seems to have become the great American disease.'
(*John Corry*)

**2** **Rewrite the sentences using perfect infinitives.**

▶ She didn't go to university. (*was to*)
  _She was to have gone to university._

1 I didn't hear what he said when he found the frogs in his bed. (*would like to*)
  ..............................................................................................................

2 He didn't compete in the Olympics. (*was to*)
  ..............................................................................................................

3 We didn't see the Grand Canyon. (*were to*)
  ..............................................................................................................

4 It wasn't a quiet weekend. (*was to*)
  ..............................................................................................................

5 I didn't send her flowers for her birthday. (*mean*)
  ..............................................................................................................

6 I didn't tidy the house before the visitors arrived. (*mean*)
  ..............................................................................................................

7 I didn't live in Ancient Rome. (*would like*)
  ..............................................................................................................

---

**Perfect -*ing* forms** also have the same kind of meaning as **perfect** or **past tenses**.

*I am not aware of **having broken** any law.* (= '… that I **have broken** any law.')
*I apologise for **not having been** here earlier.* (= '… that I **wasn't** here earlier.')
*She had a vague memory of **having seen him** somewhere before.*
(= '… that she **had seen** him somewhere before.')

Simple -*ing* forms are also possible with the same meaning in most cases.

*I apologise **for not being** here earlier.*

**3** **Change the simple -*ing* forms to perfect forms, or vice versa.**

▶ I apologise for not having written.
  _I apologise for not writing._

▶ She didn't remember taking the car.
  _She didn't remember having taken the car._

1 The government was not responsible for having given false information.
  ..............................................................................................................

2 All three were found guilty of having committed armed robbery.
  ..............................................................................................................

3 I had no memory of being in his house.
  ..............................................................................................................

4 Several students were accused of cheating in their exams.
  ..............................................................................................................

5 I feel really bad about not having sent you a birthday card.
  ..............................................................................................................

For perfect infinitives after modal verbs (e.g. *should have gone*), see pages 68 – 70. For perfect infinitives in sentences with *if* (e.g. *would have gone*), see pages 232 – 234.

# infinitive without *to*

**basics** Remember that we use infinitives without *to* after *do*, after modal verbs (except *ought*), and in the structure *Why (not) …?*

*Do you **drink** coffee?    I must **go** now.    Why not **try** our all-you-can-eat buffet?*

**dropping to after conjunctions** When two infinitive structures are joined by *and, or, except, but, than, as* or *like*, the second infinitive is usually without *to*.

*I'm going to sit and **read** for a bit.    Do you want to talk now or **wait** till later?*

**after expressions with do** Expressions like *All I did was, What I do is* etc can be followed by an infinitive without *to*.

*All I did was (to) **give** him a little push.*

**1** Put in infinitives from the box without *to*.

| clean   delay   explain   frown   look after   look at   work |

1  We had nothing to do except ........................... the cinema posters.
2  I'm ready to do anything except ........................... on a farm.
3  It's easier to do it yourself than ........................... to somebody else how to do it.
4  It's as easy to smile as ...........................
5  I have to feed the animals as well as ........................... the children.
6  Why don't you do something useful like ........................... the flat?
7  What a fire door does is ........................... the spread of a fire.

**2** Put the numbers of the boxed expressions in the right texts.

| 1 accept   2 beg   3 believe   4 obstruct   5 read   6 see   7 sit   8 steal   9 wait   10 work |

A
It's time for investors to be patient and … Don't feel you have to do any buying or selling.

E
HE'S A LOVELY BOY. REALLY. I CAN GET HIM TO DO ANYTHING BUT … WHEN HE HEARS THE WORD HE JUST GRINS.

B
HOLIDAYMAKERS from Northern Ireland who fear they may be caught up in disruption caused by BA cabin crew strike action have been advised to wait and …

F
On the one hand, there are the Republicans who have said 'no' since the summer, refusing to do anything but …. progress. On the other, there are the Democrats

C
When you join this group you will have to do nothing except … in the group's aims.

G
How do we feel about Jehovah's Witnesses teaching their children that it is better to die than … a blood transfusion?

D
Maggie, honestly, it's too hot here to do anything but … in the shade and …

H
It is better to beg than …, but better to work than …
(*Russian proverb*)

For other structures where words are left out, see pages 276–281.

# verb + infinitive

Some verbs can be followed by the infinitives of other verbs.

*I **want to talk** to you for a minute.*      *We **need to change** our plans.*

**1** CHECK YOUR KNOWLEDGE. **In sentences 1–12, put in the infinitive of a verb from the boxes (nine sentences) or an *-ing* form (three sentences). Use a dictionary if necessary.**

advertise   create   establish   increase   order   reorganise

1   I've decided ............................ for a new assistant.
2   I like cooking, and I really enjoy ............................ new dishes.
3   We expect ............................ our sales by 50% in the next three years.
4   The Space Exploration Agency hopes ............................ a permanent base on the moon before 2100.
5   Our advisers suggested ............................ the whole company from top to bottom.
6   I didn't know how to get the equipment I needed, but Maggie offered ............................ it for me.

compete   convict   entertain   extend   pretend   reverse

7   We're preparing ............................ some important overseas visitors.
8   Economic growth is falling, but the new government has promised ............................ the trend.
9   The police keep arresting these well-known gangsters, but the courts never seem ............................ them.
10   The airport authorities would like ............................ Runway No 6 by 700 metres.
11   When I leave this job I won't miss ............................ to agree with everything the boss says.
12   She's strained a leg muscle, so she may not manage ............................ in the London Marathon.

**2** **Complete the sentences using verbs from the boxes. Use a dictionary if necessary.**

afford   attempt   hesitate   intend   pretend ✓

▶   I ..*pretended*.......... to understand him, but I didn't really.
1   We can't ............................ to go away on holiday this year, I'm afraid.
2   I knew she was wrong, but I ............................ to say anything.
3   I failed my driving test again, but I don't ............................ to stop trying.
4   My brother ............................ to swim across the River Severn, but the current was much too strong.

attempt   bother   choose   fail   swear   tend

5   I argued for hours, but I ............................ to convince him.
6   He's got such a bad temper, nobody ever ............................ to criticise him.
7   I had an offer of a scholarship, but I ............................ not to take it up.
8   His lectures are useful, but they ............................ to be rather boring.
9   In a court case you have to ............................ to tell the truth.
10   I spent hours helping her, and she didn't even ............................ to thank me.

For infinitives after modal verbs (e.g. *I must go*), see page 59.
For *to* used instead of a whole infinitive (e.g. *I don't play football now, but I **used to***), see page 278.

> 'What Women Want: To be loved, to be listened to, to be desired, to be respected, to be needed, to be trusted, and sometimes, just to be held. What Men Want: Tickets for the world series.'
> (*Dave Barry*)

# verb + -ing form

**Some verbs** can be followed by the *-ing* **forms** of other verbs.

*Does he ever **stop talking**?    I can't **imagine living** abroad all my life, can you?*

**1**  CHECK YOUR KNOWLEDGE. **In sentences 1–12, put in the *-ing* form of a verb from the boxes (eight sentences) or an infinitive (four sentences). Use a dictionary if necessary.**

| accept   charge   draft   polish   punish   smile |
|---|

1  The school decided ........................... the children by giving them all extra homework.
2  I dislike ........................... presents from people I don't know well.
3  Some people enjoy ........................... their cars. Not me.
4  The police expect ........................... several people with robbery.
5  'Smile!'  'I don't feel like ...........................'
6  We hope to finish ........................... the new timetable today.

| climb   reduce   juggle   replace   water   worry |
|---|

7  I've completely given up ........................... about the world's problems.
8  If we keep on ..........................., we must get to the top sooner or later.
9  I offered ........................... the vase I'd broken, but she wouldn't let me.
10  I practised ........................... for weeks, but I could only manage to keep three balls in the air.
11  My sister promised ........................... my plants while I was away, but they all died.
12  The accountants advise ........................... expenditure on staff by 25%.

**2**  **Choose the best verbs to complete the sentences.**

1  'What's your new job like?'  'Mixed. I .................. having a bit more money, but I ..................
having my own office, and I really .................. having to write a detailed report on every single job I do.'
(*admit, appreciate, deny, miss, resent*)

2  Not another meeting! I just .................. seeing all those people again. Honestly, when Peter opens his
mouth I just .................. screaming. Would you .................. going and taking notes for me? Tell
them I'm ill, or my grandmother's died, or something.
(*can't face, feel like, imagine, involve, mind*)

3  They said the job would .................. some light housework. They didn't .................. cooking,
gardening and decorating the house from top to bottom. I can't ................ staying another day – I'm off.
(*admit, imagine, involve, mention, mind*)

4  During his trial, the driver continued to .................. talking on his mobile phone at the time of the
accident, and refused to .................. driving dangerously, claiming that he was forced to accelerate in
order to .................. hitting an old lady who was crossing the road at the time.
(*admit, appreciate, avoid, deny, involve*)

'I'm thinking of leaving
his body to science.'

**prepositional verbs**  Some prepositional verbs (see page 112) can be followed by *-ing* forms.

*She insisted **on paying**.*     *I thought **of/about resigning**.*
*Vegetarians don't **believe in eating** meat.*

**3** Complete some or all of these sentences with your own ideas, using *-ing* forms.

1   I've often thought of ...................................................................................................
2   I've never thought of ...................................................................................................
3   I don't like to spend money on ...................................................................................
4   It's important to thank people for ...............................................................................
5   I don't believe in ........................................................................................................
6   I always apologise for ................................................................................................

**need -ing**  After **need**, an *-ing* form can be used in British English with a **passive** meaning.

*The car **needs washing**. (= ' ... needs to be washed.')*     *My shoes **need mending**.*

**4** Look at the pictures. What needs doing in each one? Use the words in the box.

| clean   cook   cut   make   mend   paint   re-string   service |

1   ...........................................................................................................................
2   ...........................................................................................................................
3   ...........................................................................................................................
4   ...........................................................................................................................
5   ...........................................................................................................................
6   ...........................................................................................................................
7   ...........................................................................................................................
8   ...........................................................................................................................

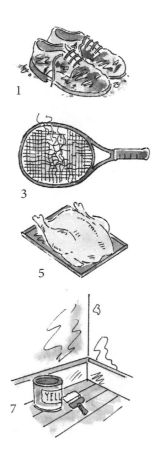

1

3

5

7

2

4

6

8

# verb + object + infinitive or *-ing* form

object + infinitive  Some verbs can be followed by **an object and an infinitive**.

*Will you **help me to pack**?     I **told them to go away**.*

This is common with some verbs expressing **wishes** and **expectations**.

*My father **wanted me to study** banking.* (NOT ~~My father wanted that I study banking.~~)
*I **would like you to come** early tomorrow.*

**1 Rewrite the sentences.**

▶ She told me the truth. (*I wanted*)
  I wanted her to tell me the truth.
  ................................................................................

▶ The library doesn't stay open late. (*I'd like*)
  I'd like the library to stay open late.
  ................................................................................

1 The visitors were early. (*We didn't expect*)
  ................................................................................

2 Alice resigned. (*Nobody wanted*)
  ................................................................................

3 People don't listen to me. (*I'd like*)
  ................................................................................

4 There's nobody to clean the office. (*We need*)
  ................................................................................

5 Everybody got upset. (*I didn't mean*)
  ................................................................................

6 Your brother could stay with us next week instead. (*I'd prefer*)
  ................................................................................

7 I applied for the job. (*Alex persuaded me*)
  ................................................................................

8 Hundreds of flights were cancelled. (*The bad weather caused*)
  ................................................................................

9 Emma became a doctor. (*Emma's parents encouraged*)
  ................................................................................

prepositions  The same structure is possible with some prepositional verbs (see page 112).

*Can you **wait for me to finish** checking my mail? I won't be long.*
*I **arranged for the students to have** meals in the canteen.*

---

### NOTES

**infinitive without *to***  Certain verbs are followed by **object + infinitive without *to***.
  *Don't **let John know** I'm here.     I **made them give** me another room.*
  *I didn't **hear you come** in last night.     I **felt the whole building shake**.*
After *help*, the structure is possible with or without *to*.
  *Can you **help me (to) get** everything ready?*
Passive versions of these structures have *to*.
  *They were made **to give** me another room.     The whole building was felt **to shake**.*

**passive infinitives**  After verbs expressing wishes and expectations, we often drop *to be* from
a passive infinitive.
  *We need this **(to be) repaired** by tomorrow.     I want that rubbish **(to be) thrown out**.*

***believe, consider* etc** Some verbs that refer to thoughts, feelings, opinions and knowledge (e.g. *believe, consider, feel, know, find, understand*) can be followed by **object + infinitive** (usually *be*) in a formal style. In a more ordinary style, *that*-clauses are more common.

*I **considered her to be** very efficient.* (Less formal: *I considered that she was …*)
*Everybody **supposed them to be** married.     We **believed her to be** reliable.*

This structure is very uncommon with *think*, and impossible with *say*.

*I **thought that** he was mistaken.* (MORE NATURAL THAN *I thought him to be mistaken.*)
*The director **said that** she was away.* (NOT … ~~said her to be away.~~)

*To be* can be dropped after *consider*.

*I considered her a first-class administrator.*

The passive version of this structure is more common than the active (see page 83).

**2** **Make these sentences more formal.**

▶ People supposed that he was an army officer. ...*People supposed him to be an army officer.*...

1 The police believe that the jewels have been stolen.
   ...............................................................................................................

2 An examination showed that the money was forged.
   ...............................................................................................................

3 Copernicus proved that Ptolemy was wrong.
   ...............................................................................................................

4 My parents considered that I was a very strange child.
   ...............................................................................................................

5 We understand that he is living in France.
   ...............................................................................................................

**object + *-ing* form** Some verbs can be followed by an object and an *–ing* form.

*I **hate people telling** me how to live my life.*

Prepositional verbs (see page 114) can be used in this structure.

*We may be ready tomorrow: it **depends on John finishing** his part of the work.*

**3** **Put in nouns and verbs from the box. Use *-ing* forms. Use a dictionary if necessary.**

customers   Mrs Jameson   people   the children ✓   them   younger people
correct   cry ✓   get   pay   talk   think

▶ Don't shout – you'll start ...*the children crying*...... again.
1 You can stop ..................... ......................, but you can't stop ..................... .....................
2 I resent ..................... ..................... the promotion – I should have had the job.
3 When they take an order, they insist on ..................... ..................... a 20% deposit.
4 I hate ..................... ..................... me, especially when they're right.

**With some verbs** (e.g. *accuse, forgive*) a preposition is necessary after the object.

**4** **Put in verbs from the box.**

accused   congratulated   forgave   prevented   talked

1 The teacher ........................... me of lying.
2 Her parents ........................... her from marrying her internet boyfriend.
3 I never ........................... Jenny for stealing from me.
4 She ........................... me into lending her my car, and then she crashed it.
5 Everybody ........................... John on getting the top job.

# infinitive and -ing form both possible

**different meanings** After some verbs, and one or two adjectives, both structures can be used with different meanings.

*Remember* and *forget* + **infinitive** refer to things that **must be done**.

*Remember to pick up the cleaning.*     *I forgot to phone Jenny – sorry.*

*Remember* and *forget* + **-ing form look back** at things that have happened.

*I still remember buying my first bicycle.*     *I'll never forget meeting the Queen.*

*Regret ...ing* also **looks back**. *Regret to ...* is used mostly to **announce bad news**.

*I'll always regret leaving school so early.*
*We regret to inform passengers that the 4.15 train has been cancelled.*

*Go on ...ing* means '**continue ...ing**'. *Go on to ...* means '**move on to** (another activity)'.

*He went on talking about himself right through the meal. Then he stopped talking about himself and went on to talk about his children.*

*Stop* is normally followed by an **-ing form**.

*I had to stop running because of knee problems.*

An **infinitive** after *stop* gives the **reason** for stopping something.

*I ran for half an hour, and then stopped to rest.*

**1** Choose the right forms of the verbs in the boxes. Use a dictionary if necessary.

| consider   force   inform   lock   marry   nag |

1  I always forget ........................... my car.
2  I regret ........................... you that your application has not been successful.
3  Relax! Why do you go on ........................... yourself to do too much?
4  I wish that woman would stop ........................... her children.
5  'Do you ever regret ........................... me?' 'Not all the time.'
6  We discussed the plans for the new building, and then went on ........................... the costs.

| believe   cancel   climb   collect   have   stretch   work |

7  After a couple of hours' driving we stopped ........................... coffee and ...........................
   our legs.
8  I'll always remember ........................... my first mountain.
9  I'll probably go on ........................... here for another couple of years.
10  I stopped ........................... in any religion in my teens.
11  'Did you remember ........................... the restaurant booking?' 'Sorry, I forgot.'
12  In an emergency, leave the building immediately. Do not stop ........................... coats
   or other possessions.

**2** Write true or false things about yourself. Use *-ing* forms.
1  I'll never forget ................................................................................................................
2  I'll always regret ..............................................................................................................
3  I hope I can go on ....................................................................... for the rest of my life.
4  I'll never stop ...................................................................................................................
5  I don't remember ..............................................................................................................

*Mean* + **infinitive** has the sense of 'intend'.

*Sorry – I didn't **mean to wake** you up.*

*Mean* + **-ing form** suggests 'involve', 'have as a result'.

*If you want to pass the exam it will **mean studying** very hard.*

*Try* can be used with both structures. To talk about doing something difficult, we more often use an infinitive.

*I **tried hard to change** the wheel, but my hands were too cold.*

We use *try* + **-ing form** to talk about trying an **experiment** (to see if something works).

*Try changing the batteries. And if that doesn't get it going, **try kicking** it.*

*Advise, allow, permit* and *forbid* are followed by **object + infinitive**, but by **-ing forms** if there is **no object**. Compare:

*John **advised us to see** a lawyer.     John **advised seeing** a lawyer.*
*They don't **allow anybody to park** here.     They don't **allow parking** here.*

After *hear, listen, see* and *watch* + **object**, we usually prefer an **infinitive** (without *to*) to talk about **complete actions**, and an **-ing** form to talk about **actions in progress**. Compare:

*I once **heard him give** a wonderful talk about women's rights.*
**Listen to Jessica singing** *in the shower!*
*The police **watched him get** out of the car and **disappear** into the bank.*
*I glanced out of the window and **saw Rob crossing** the road.*

**3** **Choose the right forms of the verbs in the boxes. Use a dictionary if necessary.**

| explode   glue   make   send   tip   train |
|---|

1  'My girlfriend won't speak to me.' 'Try ........................... her flowers.'
2  You want to do the London marathon? It will mean ........................... hard for months.
3  People heard the bomb ........................... from 50 miles away.
4  I'm sorry. We don't allow staff ........................... personal phone calls.
5  I tried ........................... the broken chair, but I couldn't make the pieces stick.
6  I meant ........................... the waiter 15%, but I gave him twice as much by mistake.

| blow   change   consult   look   tune up   visit |
|---|

7  The hospital only allows ........................... between 4.00 and 6.00.
8  The doctor advised me ........................... a heart specialist.
9  Can you hear the wind ........................... in the trees?
10  'I don't understand this word.' 'Try ........................... it up.'
11  I like to listen to the orchestra ........................... It's often better than what follows.
12  'I'm having trouble with the bank again. What do you advise?' '........................... banks.'

**4** **Write true or false things about yourself. Use infinitives or -ing forms.**

I never mean ........................................................................................... but I sometimes do.
If I was in charge of the world, I wouldn't allow people ...........................................................................
I like to watch people ...........................................................................................................................
If I'm depressed, I try ...........................................................................................................................

# infinitive and *-ing* form both possible (continued)

With *hate*, we prefer an **infinitive** when we are talking about **one present action**. Compare:

*I **hate to cook** / **cooking**.       I **hate to break** up the party, but I've got to go home.* (NOT ~~I hate breaking up...~~)

With *like*, we prefer an **infinitive** when we are talking about **choices and habits**. Compare:

*I **like to climb** / **climbing** mountains.*
*If I'm travelling, I **like to pack** the night before.* (NOT ~~I like packing the night before.~~)

After *would like/hate*, only an infinitive is possible. Compare:

*Do you like **to dance/dancing**?       Would you like **to dance**?* (NOT ~~Would you like dancing?~~)

**5** **Choose from the alternatives: A, B or both.**

1  **A** I like to start work early.    **B** I like starting work early.
2  **A** I hate to say this, but your pronunciation is terrible.
    **B** I hate saying this, but your pronunciation is terrible.
3  **A** I really like to watch old cowboy films.    **B** I really like watching old cowboy films.
4  'Can I give you a lift?'    **A** 'Thanks, I'd like walking.'    **B** 'Thanks, I'd like to walk.'
5  **A** I hate to make phone calls in a foreign language.
    **B** I hate making phone calls in a foreign language.
6  'I've written a very long poem.'    **A** 'Oh, I'd just love to see it.'    **B** 'Oh, I'd just love seeing it.'
7  **A** I like to do the most difficult jobs first.    **B** I like doing the most difficult jobs first.

*Afraid (of)* can be used with both structures.

*I'm not **afraid to tell** / **of telling** people what I think.*

But we use *afraid of ...* to talk about fear of things that happen **accidentally**.

*Let's turn the music off – I'm **afraid of waking** the baby.*

*Sure/Certain of ...ing* describe the feelings of the **person we are talking about**.

*She seems very **sure of winning**.       Are you **certain of being** ready in time?*

*Sure/certain to* ... express the **feelings of the speaker**.

*She's very confident, but I think she's **sure to lose**.       It's **certain to rain** before long.*

*Interested to ...* mostly refers to reactions to learning something.

*I was **interested to see** in the paper that they have found gold on the moon.*

*Interested in ...ing* suggests a wish to do something.

*I'm **interested in taking** a Chinese course. Do you know a good school?*

**6** **Complete some of these sentences, using *-ing* forms or infinitives.**
    **Different answers are possible.**

1  She thinks she'll pass the exam, but I think she's sure .....................................
2  'What sort of job do you want to do after you finish studying?'  'Well, I'm interested
    .....................................................
3  My father doesn't like to drive fast, because he's afraid .....................................
4  I won't wash up your glasses, because I'm afraid .....................................
5  I was really interested .....................................................
6  You seem very sure .............................................................
7  He's not that bad. I'm not afraid .............................................................

**no difference** Some verbs can be followed by infinitives or *-ing* forms with little or no difference of meaning. Common examples: *begin, can't bear, continue, intend, love, prefer, start*.

She **began to play / playing** the violin at age 4.
I **can't bear to see / seeing** animals suffer.
The members **continued to debate / debating** until midnight.
I **love to make / making** new friends.
What do you **intend to do / doing** now?
I really must **start to save / saving** money.

After *would love/prefer*, only an infinitive is possible.

I'd love to meet your friend Julia. (NOT ~~I'd love meeting~~ …)

**7** CHECK YOUR KNOWLEDGE. **Choose the best ways to complete the sentences.**

1  Did you remember … bread when you were out?  **A** *to buy*  **B** *buying*  **C** *both*
2  After she had finished her speech, the President went on … medals to the soldiers.
    **A** *to give*  **B** *giving*  **C** *both*
3  We regret … that the flight to Amsterdam will be delayed for one hour.
    **A** *to announce*  **B** *announcing*  **C** *both*
4  I like … through my lunch break so that I can leave the office early.  **A** *to work*  **B** *working*  **C** *both*
5  I don't intend … in this job for the rest of my life.  **A** *to stay*  **B** *staying*  **C** *both*
6  … you like to come out with me this evening?  **A** *Do*  **B** *Would*  **C** *both*
7  I really love … at the sea.  **A** *to look*  **B** *looking*  **C** *both*
8  We don't allow people … inside the building.  **A** *to smoke*  **B** *smoking*  **C** *both*
9  If we buy a house it will mean … a lot of money.  **A** *to borrow*  **B** *borrowing*  **C** *both*
10  'My computer won't work.' 'Try … it on.'  **A** *to switch*  **B** *switching*  **C** *both*
11  I can hear somebody … up the stairs.  **A** *come*  **B** *coming*  **C** *both*
12  I was interested … that interest rates were going up again.  **A** *to hear*  **B** *in hearing*  **C** *both*
13  Whichever party wins the election, they're sure … things even worse.
    **A** *to make*  **B** *of making*  **C** *both*
14  I hate … this, but your hair looks terrible.  **A** *to say*  **B** *saying*  **C** *both*
15  My sister can't bear … spiders.  **A** *to look at*  **B** *looking at*  **C** *both*

**8** CHECK YOUR KNOWLEDGE. **Put in five words from the box.**

| afraid | allow | forget | go on | love | regret | remember | try | try |
|---|---|---|---|---|---|---|---|---|

1  In the film *The Constant Gardener*, she plays a diplomat's wife who is murdered when she ............... to expose the illegal dealings of western drug companies.

2  I ............... once telling my father that I was bored. "BORED?" he shouted. "I wish I had the luxury of being bored. ............... working like the rest of us. Then you'll be glad of a little boredom."

3  Many doctors are ............... of being treated in their own hospitals, while a lack of support from the Government has left elderly patients at risk from hospital-acquired infections and malnourishment.

4  In a letter sent to the Queen in the 1950s, Prime Minister Harold Macmillan wrote: "After lunch, which was extremely good, Dr Adenauer delivered for an hour a lecture on the dangers of communism and the best way to deal with it in the schools, in the factories and in the homes. I ............... to inform Your Majesty that I fell asleep during the latter part of this oration."

# phone calls to make; nothing to eat

**We can use nouns or pronouns** with infinitives to say what we must or can do. The noun or pronoun is the object of the infinitive, so we don't need another object.

*I've got some **phone calls to make**.* (NOT *... to make them.*)     *I need **something to eat**.*

Relative pronouns are not used.

NOT *... calls which to make.* OR *... something which to eat.*

***enough, too*** The structure is also common after phrases with ***enough*** and ***too***.

*Have you got **enough to drink**?*     *There's **too much work to do**.*

**①** **Put in the infinitives of verbs from the box.**

> add   cross   invite   post   take   translate   wash   write

1   I'd throw a party if I could think of enough people ...........................
2   I gave Ann my blue suit ........................... to the cleaners.
3   There are three rivers ........................... before we get to the mountain.
4   I can't come out – I've got a report ...........................
5   If you've got clothes ..........................., I'll put them in with mine.
6   You've said it all. I've got nothing ...........................
7   I'm going out. Have you got any letters ...........................?
8   If there's anything ........................... into German, I always give it to Franz.

**Prepositions** can follow infinitives in this structure.

*I wish the children had a garden **to play in**.* (NOT *... a garden to play in it.*)
*I need **somebody to talk to**.*     *The floor's **clean enough to eat off**.*

In a very formal style, the preposition can be put before a relative pronoun.

*a garden **in which** to play*     *somebody **with whom** to talk*

**②** **Write descriptions of these things, beginning *something to*.**

▶  music  *something to listen to*                     ▶  a fishing rod  *something to catch fish with*
1   a sofa ...................................              6   a shelf ...................................
2   a picture ...................................          7   a purse ...................................
3   a fork ...................................             8   a bucket ...................................
4   a pen ...................................              9   a wardrobe ...................................
5   a knife ...................................            10  a notebook ...................................

**subject** We can use a structure with *for* to show the subject of the infinitive, if necessary (see page 104).

*Here are some documents **for Mary to sign**.*     *We bought a pony **for Alice to ride on**.*

**③** **Change the words *in italics*.**

▶  photos *that everybody can look at*  *for everybody to look at*
1   a ball *that the baby can play with* ...............................................
2   a lamp *that my father needs to mend* ...............................................
3   a film *that the whole family can enjoy* ...............................................
4   a problem *that the committee has to solve* ...............................................
5   a park *that everybody can walk in* ...............................................

*easy to understand* etc  After some adjectives, an infinitive can mean 'for people to …'.

*His lectures are **easy to understand**.*     *It's **too heavy to carry**.* (NOT … ~~to carry it.~~)

Prepositions can follow infinitives.

*She's nice **to talk to**.* (NOT … ~~to talk to her.~~)     *Some things are is hard **to think about**.*

**4** **Change the sentences.**

▶ This watch is very old: it can't be repaired. .....*This watch is too old to repair.*.....................

▶ It's hard to play the violin. ...*The violin is hard to play.*............................

1  The plums are ripe enough: we can eat them. ..........................................................

2  It's difficult to learn languages. ....................................................................

3  It's hard to understand her accent. ................................................................

▶ It's easy to work with Judy. ...*Judy's easy to work with.*.......................

4  It's difficult to live with Andy .....................................................................

5  It's not easy to drive on ice. .......................................................................

6  It's impossible to argue with you. ...............................................................

7  It was hard to swim across the river. ...........................................................

8  It's hard to paint with water-colours. ..........................................................

9  It's really boring to listen to Susie. ............................................................

**5** **Using this structure with prepositions, what can you say about these?**

▶ a cracked glass  ...*dangerous to drink out of*.....

1  a broken chair  ...........................................

2  a very small spoon  .......................................

3  shoes that are too small  ..............................

4  a noisy hotel room  ......................................

5  a broken pencil  ..........................................

6  a hard bed  .................................................

**6** **Correct (✓) or not (✗)?**

1  My brother is hard to learn languages.  …

2  Her pronunciation is impossible to understand it.  …

3  Pat is really interesting to talk to.  …

4  We made a tree house for the children to play in it.  …

5  This mountain is much too difficult to climb.  …

6  I'd like to go away for the weekend, but I've got nobody to go with.  …

---

**NOTES**

**passive infinitives**  After nouns and pronouns, passive infinitives may be used if we are thinking more about what has to be done, and not so much about who does it. Compare:
*I've got a pile of clothes **to wash**.*     *There's a pile of clothes **to wash / to be washed**.*

**some common expressions with passive infinitives**
(on a medicine bottle) ***to be taken*** *three times a day* (NOT ~~to take three times a day~~)
(on a parcel) ***not to be opened*** *before Christmas*
*the dog was **nowhere to be seen***     *my keys were **nowhere to be found***
*you are **to be congratulated** on your results*     *his **wife to be*** (= 'his future wife')

**Note the difference** between *nothing to do* and *nothing to be done*.
*There's **nothing to do** here. I'm bored.*     *There's **nothing to be done**. Your car is a complete wreck.*

**And note the active infinitive** in *(not) to blame*.
*Joe was **not to blame** for the accident.* (= 'The accident was not Joe's fault.')

# infinitive with its own subject: *for ... to ...*

**After an adjective or a noun**, if an **infinitive** needs **its own subject** this is introduced by *for*. Compare:

*We're ready **to start**.     We're ready **for the party to start**.*
*The plan was **to buy a bus**.     The plan was **for John to buy a bus**.*

This structure is common when we are talking about **possibility, necessity, importance** and **frequency**, and when we are **giving opinions**.

*It's **impossible for children to understand** this.     There's no **need for you to stay**.*
*I'm **anxious for everybody to have** a good time.     It was **unusual for James to swear**.*
*It was a big **mistake for the team to appoint** John as their manager.*

**1** Rewrite these sentences using *for ... to ...*

▶ They can't play tonight. (*it's impossible*)  .....It's impossible for them to play tonight..........

1 Emma shouldn't study medicine. (*It's not a good idea*)

...................................................................................................................................

2 It will be fine if you use my office. (*I'll be happy*)

...................................................................................................................................

3 I want the children to see a good dentist. (*I'm anxious*)

...................................................................................................................................

4 She's not usually ill. (*It's unusual*)

...................................................................................................................................

5 He normally plays golf at weekends. (*It's normal*)

...................................................................................................................................

6 Sue shouldn't marry Oliver. (*It would be a mistake*)

...................................................................................................................................

7 Can your brother help us? (*Is it possible*)

...................................................................................................................................

8 The meeting needn't go on for very long. (*There's no need*)

...................................................................................................................................

**for there to be**  We can use the infinitive of *there is* in this structure.

*It's important **for there to be** a fire escape at the back of the building.*

**2** Imagine you are planning a new town. Rewrite the following sentences using *for there to be*.

1 It's important that there should be public libraries.

...................................................................................................................................

2 It's vital that there should be a good public transport system.

...................................................................................................................................

3 It's important that there should be plenty of open spaces.

...................................................................................................................................

**Now write another sentence about the town using *for there to be*.**

...................................................................................................................................

**After a verb,** when an infinitive has its own subject, *for* is not normally used (see page 96).

*They **want everybody to go** home.* (NOT ~~They want for everybody to go home.~~)

However, this is possible with verbs that are normally followed by *for* (e.g. *arrange, ask*).

*I **arranged for my mother to go** to Cyprus.     Please **ask for the bill to be sent** to me.*

# to ...ing

two *to*'s   *To* can be a **preposition** (used before a noun or pronoun), or a **part of an infinitive**.

*I object **to her attitude**.* (preposition)     *We need **to talk**.* (part of infinitive)

When *to* is a **preposition**, it is followed by an *-ing* form.

*I object **to paying** so much for petrol.* (NOT ~~I object to pay so much for petrol.~~)

**1  In five of sentence-beginnings 1–10, *to* is a preposition. Which?**

▶ We need to ...No........          5  I prefer walking to ...............
▶ I object to ...Yes.......         6  We don't expect to ...............
1  I look forward to ...............   7  I usually forget to ...............
2  We hope to ...............          8  In addition to ...............
3  My brother used to ...............  9  I'll get round to ...............
4  I am used to ...............        10  My sister's planning to ...............

**2  Choose the correct way to complete each sentence.**

▶ I strongly object to *work /* (*working*) extra hours for no pay.
1  I look forward to *hear / hearing* from you soon.
2  We hope to *move / moving* to Scotland soon.
3  My brother used to *smoke / smoking*, but he stopped last winter.
4  I am used to *drive / driving* in cities, because I lived in Rome until recently.
5  I prefer walking to *cycle / cycling*.
6  We don't expect to *be / being* here at the weekend.
7  I usually forget to *book / booking* my tickets in advance.
8  In addition to *play / playing* football regularly, he's also a keen tennis player.
9  I'll get round to *weed / weeding* the garden one of these days.
10  My sister's planning to *get / getting* married in June.

*used to* and *be used to*   Don't confuse these two structures.
***I used to do** something* means 'I did it habitually, but I no longer do it'. (See page 73.)
***I am used to doing** something* means 'I've learnt to do it and it's no longer strange to me'.

*I've lived in Britain for a long time, so **I'm used to driving** on the left.*
*'Do you mind making a speech?'  'No, **I'm** quite **used to talking** to groups of people.'*

Note the common expression *get used to + -ing* form.

*When I broke my arm, I had to **get used to writing** with my left hand.*

**3  Write one thing that you're used to doing, one thing that you're not used to doing, one thing that you look forward to doing, one thing that you don't look forward to doing, and one thing that you object to doing.**

..................................................................................................................
..................................................................................................................
..................................................................................................................
..................................................................................................................
..................................................................................................................

*look forward to somebody doing something* etc   As with other prepositional verbs (see page 114), the structure can be used with an object after the preposition.

*We **look forward to John coming** back home next month.*
*I **object to people phoning** me to sell me things.*
*I'll never **get used to everybody driving** in the middle of the road in this country.*

# determiners with -ing forms: *my speaking* etc

**like nouns** When -*ing* forms are used like nouns, as subjects or objects, they can often have possessives with them.

*Do you mind **my speaking** English?*
*I understand **his wanting** a change.*
***John's agreeing** to share an office made everything much easier.*

This structure is rather formal, and ordinary non-possessive forms are common, especially with -*ing* form objects.

*Do you mind **me speaking** English?*
*I understand **him wanting** a change.*
***John agreeing** to share an office made everything much easier.*

Other determiners are also possible.

*Soldiers often say the worst thing about an attack is **the waiting**.*
***All this arguing** is getting on my nerves.*

Note that after *the ...ing*, we use *of* before an object. Compare:

***Lighting fires** is forbidden.*     ***The lighting of fires** is forbidden.* (NOT ~~The lighting fires ...~~)

**1** Rewrite these sentences to make them less formal.
▶ I'm surprised at his moving to the country. ...*I'm surprised at him moving to the country.*...
  OR ...*I'm surprised that he's moved to the country.*...
▶ Do you mind my sitting here? ...*Do you mind if I sit here?*...
1 I do not understand Maggie's wanting to go back home.
  ...........................................................................................................
2 We were surprised at Andy's being appointed District Manager.
  ...........................................................................................................
3 I hate his telling everybody what to do.
  ...........................................................................................................
4 Do you remember my telling you I knew an important secret?
  ...........................................................................................................
5 I am worried about Alice's not wanting to go with us.
  ...........................................................................................................

**nouns instead of -ing forms** When there is a noun with the same meaning as an -*ing* form, we usually prefer to use the noun after a possessive.

*His **resignation** shocked everybody.* (More natural than *His **resigning** shocked everybody.*)
*Her **decision** to speak out was very courageous.* (More natural than *Her **deciding** to speak out ...*)

**2** Do you know the right nouns to make these more natural?
1 her arriving ......................................
2 their departing ......................................
3 our preferring ......................................
4 your helping ......................................
5 his refusing ......................................
6 everybody's insisting ......................................

# more practice

**1** **Correct (✓) or not (✗)?**

1  My papers appear to have been moved.  …
2  The people next door seem to have been having parties all week.  …
3  The police believe the bank robbers still being in this country.  …
4  You were meant to have finished the work by now.  …
5  I hate the thought to get old  …
6  Who had the idea of inviting Peter's girlfriend?  …
7  What exactly needs doing to the car?  …
8  I'm not used to speaking French any more.  …
9  I don't want to do anything except sit in the sun.  …
10  I don't remember to have been here before.  …

**2** **Choose the best way to complete the sentences.**

▶  I'd like … home now.  (A) *to go*   **B**  *going*
▶  I don't like …  to places early.  (A) *to get*   (B) *getting*
1  Both the men denied … into the house.   **A** *to break*   **B**  *breaking*
2  I very much appreciate … helping me.   **A** *you*   **B**  *your*
3  Let's try … the back door.   **A** *to open*   **B**  *opening*
4  I can't afford … a new bike just now.   **A** *to get*   **B**  *getting*
5  When she moved to London, she really missed … her friends.   **A** *to see*   **B**  *seeing*
6  Do you mind … making a suggestion?   **A** *me*   **B**  *my*
7  I resent … him money when he just wastes it.   **A** *to give*   **B**  *giving*
8  Paul didn't hesitate … me when I needed it.   **A** *to help*   **B**  *helping*
9  You can't fail … their new album.   **A** *to enjoy*   **B**  *enjoying*
10  Please don't accuse me …   **A** *to lie*   **B**  *of lying*
11  His English isn't easy …   **A** *to understand*   **B**  *to be understood*
12  I've got a lot of phone calls …   **A** *to make*   **B**  *to be made*

**3** **Give your opinions about parents. Complete the first few sentences, and write some more with the same structures.**

It's important for parents to ……………………………………………………………………………………………………………………

It's very important for parents to ………………………………………………………………………………………………………

It's not important for parents to …………………………………………………………………………………………………………

It's not necessary for parents to …………………………………………………………………………………………………………

It's important for parents not to …………………………………………………………………………………………………………

……………………………………………………………………………………………………………………………………………………………………

……………………………………………………………………………………………………………………………………………………………………

……………………………………………………………………………………………………………………………………………………………………

……………………………………………………………………………………………………………………………………………………………………

……………………………………………………………………………………………………………………………………………………………………

> 'It's not that I'm afraid to die. I just don't want to be there when it happens.'
> (*Woody Allen*)

> 'If you think nobody cares if you're alive, try missing a couple of car payments.'
> (*Earl Wilson*)

> 'God in his wisdom made the fly and then forgot to tell us why.'
> (*Ogden Nash*)

**4** Put into the texts nouns that are related to the verbs in the box.

| accept   accuse   advise   agree   apologise   arrive ✓   complain   criticise   depart |
| reject   request   return   suggest |

▶ Before their ...*arrival*... at Heathrow, their passports and tickets were confiscated; when the British Airways plane landed, they were separated from the other passengers, put into a van and driven around for several hours before being forced back on the plane and sent out of the UK.

1 A punk talked about the small village in Scotland where she lives and how difficult it is to be different. Dyeing her hair blue, in the village where she lives, becomes an extremely powerful statement, saying all the things she wants to about her .............. of the local people's values.

2 I would be grateful if you could confirm your .............. of this proposal by signing the attached copy of this letter and returning it to me.

3 I am grateful to my colleagues not only for their cooperation in the study but also for their .............. to my publishing the results.

4 Mr Ellis said he first made his .............. about missing mail fifteen years ago, and was told by the post office that it would be given urgent attention.

5 My thirteenth birthday was coming up, and it seemed like a good time to make my .............. for the perfect present: a bird of prey.

6 **W**hen one quiet weekend this April Mr Parker left the country on a short trip to France, he had no idea what would await him on his ..............

7 Caroline did not seem pleased at my .............. that we should go on holiday with my mother.

8 THE PRINCE OF WALES renewed his .............. of English teaching in schools yesterday, and declared the English language had declined into a 'dismal wasteland of banality, cliché and casual obscenity'.

9 REMEMBER THE OLD .............. TO THOSE ABOUT TO GET MARRIED — DON'T.

10 On the morning of his .............. Mr Carson wandered round the offices shaking hands with everyone and everything in sight.

11 Her anger was a natural reaction to his .............. that she had been spying on him.

12 HE CAN KEEP SAYING SORRY TILL HE'S BLUE IN THE FACE, BUT I'LL NEVER BELIEVE HE MEANS IT, AND I'LL NEVER ACCEPT HIS ..............!

**5** INTERNET EXERCISE. **Use a search engine to find interesting completions for some of these sentences.**

1  It's important for politicians to ..............................................................

2  It's unusual for children to ..............................................................

3  It's good for parents to ..............................................................

4  It's valuable for people to ..............................................................

5  It's good for students to ..............................................................

**6** Choose the correct forms of the cartoon captions.

'Excuse me, but would you mind if I went and tried *to join* / *joining* another group?'

'The problem with you is that you try *to be* / *being* a lot nicer than you really are.'

# Section 8 various structures with verbs

Several different structures are introduced in this section:

- **verbs with object + complement**
  *You **make me nervous**.*
  *They **elected my sister Treasurer**.*
- **prepositional and phrasal verbs**
  *Can you **look after** the children?*
  *My car has **broken down**.*
- **verbs with two objects**
  *Can you **send me the details**?*
- **causative structures with *have* and *get***
  *I must **have my watch repaired**.*     *We need to **get the curtains cleaned**.*

Note that we discuss the grammar of phrasal verbs, but we do not give long lists of them. We think it's best to learn phrasal verbs like other words, one at a time as they are needed. In our opinion grouping them together, as some grammars do, only causes confusion.

'I'm sorry to bother you, but we've broken down. Do you happen to have a No.5 knitting needle, an empty baked-bean tin and three pints of custard?.'

'Did we have some children that grew up and went away?'

'Before you turned up I thought I was going mad.'

# verbs with object + adjective/noun complement

**adjective/noun complements** Some verbs can be followed by an object, together with an adjective or noun which gives more information about the object.

*You **make me nervous**.     Are you **calling me a liar**?*
*I **considered their request a great honour**.     They **elected my sister Treasurer**.*

**classifying verbs: complement with *as*** Verbs that say how we **classify** or **describe** something are often followed by **object + *as* + complement.**

*I **see this as** a great opportunity.     She **described her attacker as** a 'well-dressed middle-aged man'.*

**1** **Complete the sentences with words from the boxes.**

1  Let's paint the kitchen ...........................
2  I wonder why the school governors appointed Phillipson ...........................
3  I'm afraid you're not the right man to make me ...........................
4  His name's Harry, but everybody calls him ...........................
5  I consider your suggestion deeply ...........................
6  I'm going to make the small upstairs room my ...........................

| blue |
| happy |
| headmaster |
| offensive |
| Shorty |
| study |

7  We all ........................... Oscar as a sort of favourite uncle.
8  The analysts ........................... the poison as arsenic.
9  I have never ........................... Jeremy as a close friend.
10  I don't think Maggie ........................... her new job as a promotion.
11  I wouldn't ........................... him as handsome, but he's got a lot of charm.
12  This bird is now ........................... as an endangered species.

| describe |
| considered |
| identified |
| listed |
| regard |
| sees |

**thinking and feeling** Many verbs that refer to thoughts, feelings, opinions and knowledge can be followed by **object + infinitive complement** (see page 97).

*The police **believe him to have left** the country.*

This structure is formal (and more common in the passive); we often prefer *that*-clauses.

*The police **believe that** he has left the country.*

**2** **Rewrite the sentences with *that*-clauses.**

1  We feel the price to be rather high.
   ...................................................................................................................
2  I understood him to be interested in cooperating.
   ...................................................................................................................
3  An examination showed her to be seriously undernourished.
   ...................................................................................................................
4  Everybody considered Rogers to be the best candidate.
   ...................................................................................................................

---

**NOTES**

***think* and *say*** The object + infinitive structure is very uncommon with *think*, and impossible with *say*.
   *They **think that** he has arthritis.* (MORE NATURAL THAN *They think him to have …*)
   *I **said that** she was wrong.* (NOT ~~I said her to be wrong.~~)

***consider*** Note that three structures are possible with *consider*.
   *We considered **her dangerous / as dangerous / to be dangerous**.*

# revise the basics:
# verbs with prepositions and adverb particles

**preposition or particle?** The small word in a two-word verb may be a **preposition** or an **adverb particle.** (A good dictionary will tell you which.) There are some differences.

| VERB + PREPOSITION | VERB + ADVERB PARTICLE |
|---|---|
| *Look at this.* | *Look out!* |
| *Don't sit on that chair.* | *Sit down.* |
| *We ran out of the house.* | *Come back.* |
| *She climbed up the ladder.* | *She cut the wood up / cut up the wood.* |
| *I fell in the river.* | *I filled the form in. / I filled in the form.* |
| *He got off the bus.* | *Switch the light off. / Switch off the light.* |

Verbs with adverb particles are often called 'phrasal verbs'.

**1** **DO IT YOURSELF.** **Look at the examples above, and decide which three rules are correct.**

1 Verbs with prepositions are normally followed by objects. *Correct / Not*
2 Some verbs with prepositions don't have objects. *Correct / Not*
3 Verbs with adverb particles are normally followed by objects. *Correct / Not*
4 Some verbs with adverb particles don't have objects. *Correct / Not*
5 Prepositions can come before or after their objects. *Correct / Not*
6 Adverb particles can come before or after their objects. *Correct / Not*

**word order** An **adverb particle** must go **after a pronoun object** (see page 117).

*She cut **it up**.* (NOT *She cut up it.*)
*Switch **it off**.* (NOT *Switch off it.*)

Compare the word order with a **preposition** and a **pronoun object**.

*She climbed **up it**.* (NOT *She climbed it up*)     *He got **off it**.*

**2** **Preposition (PR) or adverb particle (AP)?**

▶ I fell **off** the chair. PR (You would say *I fell off it*, not *I fell it off*; so *off* is a preposition.)
1 I looked **up** the street to see if Andy was coming. …
2 I'll think **about** your suggestion. …
3 She turned **up** the next card: it was the King of Diamonds. …
4 Can you look **after** the kids for a few minutes? …
5 Nobody understood why she broke **off** their engagement. …
6 We drove **round** the town looking for a hotel. …
7 She changes **round** all her furniture every few months. …

**3** **Can you put the three prepositions and three adverb particles into the right places in the quotation?**

| around   around   into   out   through   up |
|---|

'If you run ............... a wall, don't turn
............... and give ...............
Figure ............... how to climb it,
go ............... it, or work ............... it.'
(*Michael Jordan, famous basketball player*)

**4** **Change the object to a pronoun; change the word order if necessary.**

▸ Sit on the wall. ..*Sit on it.*.....................................................................

▸ Switch on the light. ..*Switch it on.*...........................................................

1 We talked about the accident. (*preposition*) ...................................................

2 I put off the meeting. (*adverb particle*) .......................................................

3 Can you clean up the kitchen? (*adv. part.*) ..................................................

4 She put the dress on. (*adv. part.*) ..............................................................

5 I'm looking for my bag. (*prep.*) .................................................................

6 I wrote down the address. (*adv. part.*) ........................................................

7 I sent the steak back. (*adv. part.*) ..............................................................

8 I stood on the table. (*prep.*) .....................................................................

---

### NOTES

**Some verbs** have both prepositions and particles.

  I **get on with** most people.    **Look out for** potholes in the road.

**word order in passives** In passive clauses, both prepositions and particles come **after the main verb**. (See also page 79.)

  *Their wedding has been* **put off.**    *All the lights were* **switched on.**
  *She likes to be* **looked at.**    *He's already been* **spoken to.**

'No, nurse, I said switch off his mobile phone.'

'Aren't you supposed to take your trousers off?'

# more about prepositional verbs

**verb + preposition** Many verbs can be used with particular prepositions to make two-word verbs: for example *look after*, *smile at*.

I'm **looking after** the kids this evening.
Who are you **smiling at**?

The **meaning** of a prepositional verb may be **idiomatic**: different from the meanings of the two separate words. (For example, *look after* does not mean *look + after*.)
We only use a **preposition** when there is an **object**.

I don't **believe in** ghosts. BUT I don't **believe**. (NOT ~~I don't believe in.~~)

The object may be an *-ing* form (see page 95).

She insisted **on paying**.      I thought **of resigning**.

**1** CHECK YOUR KNOWLEDGE. **Choose the correct preposition. (You will need *on* five times, *into* four times, and three other prepositions once each. Use a dictionary if necessary.)**

1  It's hard for a family to live *on / from / with* one person's earnings.
2  Shall I translate this *to / in / into* English for you?
3  Dr Andrews specialises *in / for / on* dermatology.
4  I spend much too much money *for / on / at* clothes.
5  You can rely *on / at / with* me to help you.
6  The child's suffering *from / of / at* an ear infection.
7  The workforce consists mostly *from / of / in* younger people.
8  You need to focus *at / to / on* what's most important.
9  You can succeed – it just depends *from / at / on* you.
10  There are two classes of people: those who divide people *to / in / into* two classes, and those who don't.
11  He lost control of the car and crashed *against / into / on* a lamp post.
12  I ran *into / against / on* Mrs Arthur in the supermarket this morning.

**more than one preposition** Some verbs can be followed by more than one preposition, with different meanings.

**Look at** the rain!      Can you help me **look for** my glasses?
I **look after** Ellie's dogs when she's travelling.

**2** CHECK YOUR KNOWLEDGE. **Put in *of* four times, *about* five times, and *at*, *for* and *to* once each.**

1  Have you heard ........................... Mary? She's getting married in June.
2  Some English children have never heard ........................... Shakespeare.
3  Don't shout ........................... me – I don't appreciate it.
4  Could you shout ........................... Lucy and tell her lunch is ready?
5  I dreamed ........................... horses again last night.
6  I dream ........................... making enough money to stop working.
7  That boy only thinks ........................... food.
8  What do you think ........................... my new idea?
9  You remind me ........................... one of my old school friends.
10  Can you remind Sue ........................... the meeting?
11  Geriatric nurses care ........................... old people.
12  I don't think she cares ........................... anybody except herself.

**no preposition** Not all verbs have prepositions before objects, of course.

*We **considered her proposal** carefully.* (NOT ~~We considered about her proposal~~ ...)

**3** **CHECK YOUR KNOWLEDGE.** Put in a preposition (5 times) or – (5 times).

1 I think it's time to discuss ........................... our next move.
2 Joe is going to marry ........................... his boss.
3 They've just operated ........................... Andy for a stomach problem.
4 I explained ........................... her exactly how to do it, but she still got it wrong.
5 It's a nice design, but it lacks ........................... originality.
6 I really don't agree ........................... Pat's ideas.
7 She asked me to read her report and comment ........................... it.
8 How did you react ........................... Mary's news?
9 I think we're approaching ........................... the station.
10 The economy is entering ........................... a completely new phase.

---

**NOTES**

*at* With some verbs, *at* can suggest **aggressive** behaviour: for example *shout/scream/swear at,
throw (something) at, point at.*

**expressing direction** English often prefers to express direction with a preposition, rather than using the verb.
*She **went into** the room.* (Rather than *She **entered** the room.*)
*We **came down** the hill slowly.* (Rather than *We **descended** the hill slowly.*)

**word order** Prepositions often come at the ends of clauses, separate from their objects. This happens in **questions**
(see page 3), **passive structures** (see page 79), **relative structures** (see page 212) and some **infinitive structures** (see
page 102).
*What are you looking **at**?     She likes being looked **at**.     the thing that I was looking **at**     something to look **at***

**4** **GRAMMAR IN A TEXT.** Put prepositions from the box into the text.

| at | for | in | into | into | out of | out of | through | with |

Woody Allen said that he was
thrown [1].............. college for
cheating in the metaphysics
exam, because he had looked [2]..............
the soul of the boy sitting next to him.
FBI employees have other methods. An
investigation by the US Justice Department
has found that "a significant number of
FBI employees engaged [3].............. some
form of cheating or improper conduct" in
an internal exam dealing [4].............. the
FBI's policies for conducting surveillance
on Americans. The giveaway? Many of the
examinees — 200 or so — got [5]..............
a test that was expected to take them 90
minutes in fewer than 20. The agents
cheated by bringing notes [6].............. the
examination hall, by looking [7]..............
answers on computers, and by looking
[8].............. fellow examinees' answers.
Maybe what let the cat [9].............. the bag
was when one agent answered a question
with the words: "I don't know", and his
neighbour answered: "Neither do I". ◆

# more about phrasal verbs

A **phrasal verb** is made up of a **verb** and a **small adverb** ('adverb particle'). Adverb particles are not the same as prepositions (though some of them have the same form); they don't have to be followed by nouns or pronouns. The meaning of a phrasal verb may be idiomatic: different from the meanings of the two separate words. (For example, *run out* does not mean 'run' + 'out'.) Phrasal verbs are very common in an **informal** style.

---

SOME COMMON ADVERB PARTICLES
about, across, ahead, along, (a)round, aside, away, back, by, down, forward, in, off, on, out, over, past, through, up

---

*Do stop **fooling about**.*     *'Can I **look round**?'*  *'**Go ahead**.'*
*She **ran away** from home three times.*     *Do **come in**.*
***Write** this **down**, please.*     *We'll have to **put** the meeting **off** – Emma's ill.*
***Look out**!*     *Sorry to **break up** the evening, but I've got to **get back**.*

**Many phrasal verbs have one-word equivalents**; these may be a little more formal.

**1** CHECK YOUR KNOWLEDGE. **Choose the best explanations for the words *in italics*.**
▶ The secretary *passed round* the minutes of the last meeting. ( printed /(distributed)/ collected )
1 *We've run out of* coffee. ( *We've made some / We've bought some / There isn't any more* )
2 They've *called off* the strike. ( *cancelled / announced / extended* )
3 *You're breaking up.* I'll ring you back on the land line.
  ( *You're going crazy / You're unhappy / I can't hear you clearly* )
4 *You're cracking up.* ( *You're going crazy / You're unhappy / I can't hear you clearly* )
5 My application was *turned down*. ( *rejected / considered carefully / sent back* )
6 I can't *make out* what that sign says. ( *believe / see clearly / remember* )
7 You couldn't *make up* a story like that. ( *invent / improve / believe* )
8 When I walked into the classroom, the teacher was *telling off the children*.
  ( *counting them / telling them a story / criticising their behaviour* )
9 This music really *turns me on*. ( *disgusts me / excites me / surprises me* )
10 If I complain, will you *back me up*? ( *contradict me / support me / criticise me* )

**objects** Some phrasal verbs are **intransitive**: they **don't have objects** (e.g. *Look out*).
Others are **transitive** and have objects: for example, you can *turn down* a radio or a suggestion).

**2** **Choose the two best objects**
▶ turn up (a radio), a story, (a heater)
1 break up *a biscuit, a marriage, a suggestion*
2 cut up *a piece of paper, a business, an onion*
3 break off *a balloon, a relationship, a branch*
4 blow up *a bridge, a saucepan, a balloon*
5 think over *a proposal, a radio, a suggestion*
6 think up *an excuse, a business, a story*
7 wash up *an onion, a saucepan, a cup*
8 wash off *a stain, a black mark, a relationship*
9 start up *an engine, a radio, a business*

**meanings** Adverb particles can have various meanings. *Up* often means 'completely'.

*I'll cut **up** the potatoes.     Let's clean **up** the garden.     I've filled **up** my diary.*
*Why did you tear **up** my ticket?*

**3** **Look at the adverb particles in the following sentences, and choose the best meaning from the box for each one.**

> away    further    further    higher    higher    into pieces    quieter ✓    on paper
> to various people    working    not working

▶ Turn the radio **down**. ..*quieter*....           6   I wrote everything **down**. ...............
1   Go **on**. ...............                        7   Have you sent **out** the programme?. ............
2   They ran **off**. ...............                 8   Can you cut **up** the onions? ...............
3   Can you turn the air conditioning **up**? ...............   9   We walked **on** slowly. ...............
4   The electricity's **off**. ...............        10  Interest rates are going **up**. ...............
5   Is the alarm **on**? ...............

Adverb particles can usually go **before** or **after noun objects**.

*Clean up **this mess**.* OR *Clean **this mess** up.*
*I'm going to put **on a coat**.* OR *I'm going to put **a coat on**.*
*Did you throw **away the leftovers**?* OR *Did you throw **the leftovers away**?*

But an adverb particle must go **after a pronoun object**.

*Clean **it** up.* (NOT ~~Clean up it.~~)     *I threw **them** away.* (NOT ~~I threw away them.~~)

**4** **Change the sentences twice.**

▶ I couldn't put down the book. ..*I couldn't put the book down.*.....................
  ..*I couldn't put it down.*.................................................................

1   I'm going to throw out this jacket. ................................................................
    .......................................................................................................

2   Susie has broken off her engagement. ...........................................................
    .......................................................................................................

3   Could you switch on the TV? .....................................................................
    .......................................................................................................

4   Please write down these figures. .................................................................
    .......................................................................................................

5   It's time to clean out the garage. ...............................................................
    .......................................................................................................

6   I'd like to pay off the loan. ......................................................................
    .......................................................................................................

7   Do I need to fill in this form? ...................................................................
    .......................................................................................................

8   You can't turn back the clock. ...................................................................
    .......................................................................................................

9   Do you want to play back the recording? ......................................................
    .......................................................................................................

10  I'll think over your proposal. ....................................................................
    .......................................................................................................

# verbs with two objects

**direct and indirect objects**  Verbs like *give*, *bring* or *send* can have two objects: a **direct** object (what somebody gives, brings etc), and an **indirect** object (the person or thing that receives it.)

We gave **some money** to **the hospital**.      I didn't bring **the right papers** to **the boss**.
Can you describe **the driver** to **me**?

The indirect object can be a beneficiary – somebody that something is done **for**.

I'll cook **an omelette** for **you** if you like.      Shall I call **a taxi** for **Granny**?

**indirect object first**  With many of these verbs, the **indirect object** can go **first**, with **no preposition**.

We gave **the hospital** some money.      Shall I call **Granny** a taxi?

But this is not possible with certain verbs – for example *describe, explain, suggest*.

Can you describe the driver to me. BUT NOT ~~Can you describe me the driver?~~
Please explain this word to me. BUT NOT ~~Please explain me this word.~~
Let me suggest a good restaurant to you. BUT NOT ~~Let me suggest you …~~

**1**  **Eight of sentences 1–12 can be rewritten with the indirect object first.**
   **Find them and rewrite them.**

▶  I'll buy an ice cream for you.  ..*I'll buy you an ice cream.*.......................
▶  Send the bill to my wife.  ...*Send my wife the bill.*........................................
1  Can you explain this sentence to me? ..............................................................
2  Throw the ball to Sandy. ..............................................................
3  They offered a promotion to my brother. ..............................................................
4  She reads a story to her children every night. ..............................................................
5  Take this paper to the secretary, please. ..............................................................
6  Describe your dream house to us. ..............................................................
7  Shall I make a sandwich for you? ..............................................................
8  I taught the guitar to Alex's children. ..............................................................
9  Pass the salt to me, would you? ..............................................................
10  Can you suggest a cheap hotel to us? ..............................................................
11  Sing a song to me. ..............................................................
12  Could you polish these shoes for me? ..............................................................

**pronoun objects** If the **direct object** is a **pronoun**, that normally goes **first**.

*I made **them** for Mr Andrews.* (NOT ~~I made Mr Andrews them.~~)   *Pass **it** to **me**.*

**2  Change the *direct objects* to pronouns and change the sentence structure.**

▸ Could you lend Jamie *your bike*? ..*Could you lend it to Jamie?*............................................

1  Send the accountant *these figures*, please.

...................................................................................................................................

2  I offered Helen *my old car.*

...................................................................................................................................

3  Would you read us all *Amy's letter*?

...................................................................................................................................

4  I've brought Tim *these flowers.*

...................................................................................................................................

5  We gave the charity shop *a lot of old clothes.*

...................................................................................................................................

6  Why don't you send a TV company *your film script*?

...................................................................................................................................

**one object or two**  Some verbs can be followed by either a direct object, or an indirect object, or both.

*I asked **a question**.     I asked **John**.     I asked **John a question**.*

**3  In four of sentences 1–8 you can leave out the *direct object* without changing the meaning completely. Which ones?**

▸ I asked John *a question.* ...Yes.......

▸ I threw Hannah *the ball.* ..No........  ('I threw Hannah' is not at all the same.)

1  Mrs Matthews teaches children *English.* ...............

2  I cooked my wife *breakfast* this morning. ...............

3  We couldn't find the hotel, but a policeman showed us *the way.* ...............

4  I'd forgotten where she lived, but Alex told us *the address.* ...............

5  The folk group sang us *some very strange songs.* ...............

6  I bought Susie *some new shoes* yesterday. ...............

7  Can you sell me *some stamps*? ...............

8  I haven't got any money with me. Could you pay the driver *€20*? ...............

> **Note:**  When *sing, play* and *write* have no direct object, we put *to* before the indirect object.
> *Sing **her** a song.* BUT *Sing **to her**.* (NOT ~~Sing her.~~)
> *Play **us** something cheerful.* BUT *Play **to us**.* (NOT ~~Play us.~~)
> *Write **me** a letter.* BUT *Write **to me**.* (NOT USUALLY *Write me* in standard British English.)

'Why, this is so simple a five-year-old child could understand it! Go find me a five-year-old child.' (*Groucho Marx*)

'If you give me a lever and a place to stand, I can move the world.' (*Archimedes*)

'Tourists! Why don't they stay at home and just send us the money?' (*Old joke about British hotel keepers*)

'Write me a letter. Send it by mail. Send it in care of the Birmingham jail.' (*American folksong*)

'Bring me my bow of burning gold! Bring me my arrows of desire! Bring me my spear: O clouds unfold! Bring me my chariot of fire!' (*William Blake, 1757–1827*)

# some causative structures with *have*, *get* and *make*

*get somebody/something to do something* This structure often gives the idea of asking, telling or persuading somebody (or something).

*Get Louis to translate this, will you?*    *I got them to pay me in cash.*
*We tried everything, but we couldn't get the dog to stop barking.*

An *-ing* form is possible when we are talking about a **continuous** action.

*It took me all morning to get the car going.*

**1** GRAMMAR AND VOCABULARY: AIR TRAVEL. **Write some sentences about some things that they may get you to do (and not do) when you take an international flight. The words in the boxes will help.**

| arrive early ✓   fasten   fly   go through   pay extra for   show   sing |
| sit for hours   take off   wait around   wear ✓ |

▶ .....They get you to  arrive early....................................... at the airport.
▶ .....They don't get you to wear....................................... special clothing.
1 ................................................................. a metal detector.
2 ................................................................. your shoes.
3 ................................................................. your passport.
4 ................................................................. for ages.
5 ................................................................. your heavy baggage.
6 ................................................................. your seat-belt during take-off.
7 ................................................................. in a small seat.
8 ................................................................. the plane.
9 ................................................................. to the pilot.

*have/get something done* Here the focus is on the action, not the person who does it. The past participle is **passive**.

*She has her car serviced every six months.*    *I must get my watch repaired.*

**2** **Write about some of these things. Do you do them yourself, or have them done, or never have them done?**

| check blood pressure   check teeth   clean clothes   clean room   clean windows |
| do laundry   repair car/bike   put new tyres on car/bike   change watch battery |

▶ ..I have my teeth checked every six months.  ▶ I clean my windows myself...............
1 .....................................................................................................
2 .....................................................................................................
3 .....................................................................................................
4 .....................................................................................................
5 .....................................................................................................
6 .....................................................................................................
7 .....................................................................................................
8 .....................................................................................................

**experience: passive structure** We can also use *have/get* + object + past participle to talk about kinds of experience.

*Robin **had his passport stolen** in Jamaica.* (OR *Robin **got** his passport stolen …*)
*Maggie **had her roof blown off** in a storm.* (OR *Maggie **got** her roof blown off …*)

**3** **Use *have* + object + past participle to write sentences.**

▶ Joe (*leg break*) in a car crash last year.
   *Joe had his leg broken in a car crash last year.*

1 I didn't (*car steal*) but the wheels were taken off.

..........................................................................................

2 Have you ever (*letter return unopened*)?

..........................................................................................

3 Alice (*her visa application refuse*) again.

..........................................................................................

4 My sister (*short story publish*) earlier this year.

..........................................................................................

5 We (*our furniture ruin*) in the flood.

..........................................................................................

**4** **Use this structure to write about something that has (or has never) happened to you.**

..........................................................................................

---

**NOTES ON OTHER COMMON STRUCTURES**

**experience: *have* + object + infinitive / *-ing* form** This is another way of talking about experiences.
   *I **had a very strange thing happen** to me when I was in Ireland.*
   *We got home to find that we **had water coming** through the kitchen ceiling.*

**refusal: *will not / won't have …*** We can express **refusal** with ***will not have*** + object + *-ing* form.
   *The government **will not have strikers bringing** the country to a standstill.*
   *I **won't have you telling** me what to do.*

**have somebody do something** This is most common in American English.
   'The union representative is here.' '**Have him come** in, please.'

**structures with *make*** *Make* + object + infinitive (without *to*) is common.
   *They **made us open** our suitcases.*
But note that in the **passive** we use a *to*-infinitive (see page 83).
   *We **were** all **made to open** our suitcases.*
Note also the structures ***make oneself heard/understood***.
   *I had to shout to **make myself heard**.*
   *My Chinese isn't much good, but I can **make myself understood**.*

---

'I keep on having my hair cut, but it keeps on growing again.'
(*G K Chesterton*)

'He had the sort of face that makes you realise God does have a sense of humour.'
(*Bill Bryson*)

# more practice

**1** Choose the correct structures and put in words from the box.

| average   impressive   incompetent   remote   scar |

1 They should never have made that man *head / as head / to be head* of department – he's totally
   .............................
2 In view of Mrs Ellis's ........................... qualifications, we elected her *treasurer / as treasurer*.
3 Do you consider yourself *being / as being* of above ........................... intelligence?
4 Her family believe her *to be / as being* somewhere in a ........................... part of Ireland.
5 The man described his attacker *to be / as being* a tall slim teenager with dark hair and a
   ........................... on his left cheek.

**2** Put a suitable preposition (or –, for no preposition) after each verb.
   Use a dictionary if necessary.

1 live ........................... €10 a day
2 translate from German ........................... Spanish
3 specialise ........................... pharmacology
4 spend money ........................... clothes
5 rely ........................... somebody
6 suffer ........................... hay fever
7 focus ........................... the main point
8 marry ........................... somebody
9 divide ........................... three parts
10 crash ........................... a wall
11 run ........................... an old friend
12 discuss ........................... an idea
13 operate ........................... a patient
14 depend ........................... somebody
15 lack ........................... something

**3** Put a suitable adverb particle into each expression. Use a dictionary if necessary.

1 turn ........................... late for a meeting
2 think something ...........................
3 put something ........................... till later
4 send ........................... something you don't want
5 wash ........................... dirty dishes
6 pick somebody ........................... by car
7 clean ........................... a mess

**4** DO IT YOURSELF. Prepositions and adverb particles.

| at   away   back   down   off   on   round   up |

Five of the words in the box can be both prepositions and adverb particles.

**PREPOSITION**
*I looked **up** the street.* BUT NOT *I looked it up.*
Two cannot be prepositions. Which? ...........................................................
One can only be a preposition. Which? ...........................

**ADVERB PARTICLE**
*I looked **up** the word.* OR *I looked it **up**.*

**5** Correct (✓) or not (✗)?

1 Explain me what you want. ...
2 Sing me a song. ...
3 Describe me your house. ...
4 Suggest me a good restaurant. ...
5 Ask me a question. ...
6 Sing me. ...
7 Ask me. ...
8 Write me a letter. ...
9 Write me. ...
10 Give Anna it. ...

**6** Choose the right explanations.

1 We had the car taken away yesterday.
   **A** We wanted it taken away.   **B** We didn't want it taken away.   **C** Both are possible.
2 We had a policewoman come round.
   **A** We asked for her to come.   **B** We didn't ask for her to come.   **C** Both are possible.

**GRAMMAR IN A TEXT.** Complete the text with adverb particles from the box.

| down down in in in in in off out out out round up up up up |
|---|

## Moving in

When we moved ¹.............., we began by cleaning ².............. the whole place. It took days! The people who had lived there before had not been what you would call houseproud. There was rubbish everywhere that had to be collected ³.............. and thrown ⁴.............., and a whole lot of old furniture that I broke ⁵.............. and used to make a bonfire. Then we set about getting estimates for the big jobs. We weren't sure about the roof, and the first heavy rain confirmed our suspicions, as water started coming ⁶.............. and dripping ⁷.............. through our bedroom ceiling. The kitchen was in pretty poor condition, so we decided to have a complete set of new cupboards and appliances put ⁸.............. As it was the middle of winter it rapidly became clear that we would also have to put ⁹.............. a new central heating boiler. The plumbing was antique, and the electrical wiring was in bad shape, so all of that needed to be torn ¹⁰.............. and replaced. As the house was rather dark, we arranged for new bigger windows to be put ¹¹.............., and we also got some more light by cutting ¹².............. a couple of trees that were growing very close to the house. Once the electrical work was finished, we started on the redecorating, which we were doing ourselve: I went ¹³.............. scraping ¹⁴.............. all the old wallpaper, and Julie followed me room by room with the paintbrush. It was a tough period, and about twice a day I felt like giving ¹⁵.............. I was sure that we had made a bad mistake – we should have taken ¹⁶.............. a loan and bought a modern place, like all our friends. But now, two years later, it's all done, and the place is absolutely beautiful. I wouldn't change it for anything. ∎

8 **INTERNET EXERCISE.** Use a search engine to find some interesting sentences, beginning either *We cannot put off* or *They described him as.* Write them here.

.............................................................................................................
.............................................................................................................
.............................................................................................................
.............................................................................................................
.............................................................................................................

'If you don't mind, I'm going to stop this conversation right now and turn on the television. If I've got to have my intelligence insulted, then I'd rather it were done by an expert.'

## nouns

'Common nouns' can be **countable** or **uncountable**.

  *a car; three cars* (countable)    *some oil; music* (uncountable)

An important difference between the two kinds is in article use: see pages 125 and 142.

There are also so-called 'proper nouns': mainly the names of people and places.

  *Harry    President Lincoln    Piccadilly    Edinburgh    Mars*

Some grammars distinguish 'abstract' and 'concrete' nouns. However, this is not a very useful distinction, and it has no grammatical importance.

## nouns in groups

There are three common ways to put two or more nouns together:

1. **noun + noun:**

     *milk chocolate    a business administration course*

2. **possessive noun + noun:**

     *the boss's office    an hour's wait    the judge's decision    Ann's sister's husband*

3. **noun + preposition + noun:**

     *the top of the page    the rotation of the earth*

Sometimes more than one structure is possible to express a particular meaning: for example, we can say *company policy*, *the company's policy* or *the policy of the company*. More often, only one structure is correct in a particular case: we say *the end of the bed* but not ~~the bed's end~~ or ~~the bed end~~, *a garden chair* but not ~~a garden's chair~~ or ~~a chair of garden~~. The differences in use between these structures are quite complicated. There are general guidelines on pages 128–131, but it is not possible to give clear rules which will explain why one or other structure is used in every case. This is partly a matter of vocabulary rather than grammar, and it is often necessary to consult a good dictionary to be sure how a particular idea is usually expressed.

## pronouns

The word 'pronoun' is used for several kinds of word which are used when it is not necessary, or not possible, to use a more exact noun phrase. In this Section we deal with **personal pronouns** (e.g. *I*, *her*, *they*); **reflexive pronouns** (e.g. *herself*); the **indefinite personal pronouns** *one*, *you* and *they*, and the use of ***one(s)*** to substitute for countable nouns. **Relative pronouns** are covered in Section 15, and two kinds of **possessive pronoun** (*my* etc and *mine* etc) in Section 10.

'No, kickboxing is down the hall. This is box kicking.'

# countable and uncountable

**Countable nouns** like *chair*, *idea* can be used with *a/an*, and have **plurals**.

**Uncountable nouns** like *water*, *intelligence* can't be used with *a/an*, and have no plurals.
Some English nouns are uncountable, although they may have countable equivalents in other languages, e.g. *advice* (NOT NORMALLY *an advice*).

**1** CHECK YOUR KNOWLEDGE. **Choose uncountable equivalents from the box.**

| baggage evidence furniture luck money poetry progress research traffic travel ✓ weather work |

▶ a journey ...*travel*............     6 dollars and euros ...........................
1 poems ........................     7 winning the lottery ...........................
2 a rainstorm ..........................     8 getting better ...........................
3 a carry-on bag ........................     9 chairs and tables ...........................
4 cars and buses ........................     10 fingerprints on a gun ...........................
5 building a wall .........................     11 studying historical records ...........................

Some other examples: *accommodation, equipment, information, luggage, news.*
Note, however, that one or two of these words can be plural in particular expressions.

*Who did you meet **on your travels**?     She goes cycling **in all weathers**.*

**countable nouns used like uncountables** *Idea, chance, difference, point, reason, difficulty, question* and *change* can be used with *some, any* and *much*, rather like uncountables.

*Can you give us **some idea** of your plans?     I didn't have **any difficulty** finding her.*
*We haven't got **much chance** of catching the train.*

**2 Choose the best words to complete the sentences.**
1 Have you got any *point / idea / chance* what you're going to do next?
2 I can't see much *point / question / chance* in going on with this.
3 If you have any *difficulty / reason / change* getting here, give us a ring.
4 The doctor says there isn't much *difficulty / change / chance* in his condition.
5 We couldn't find any *idea / point / reason* not to pay their bill.
6 It seems there's some *point / chance / question* about her qualifications.
7 Do we have much *difference / chance / idea* of winning, do you think?
8 There's not much *point / difference / change* between 'begin' and 'start'.

## NOTES

**different meanings/uses** Some uncountable nouns can be countable with other meanings.
   *He lacks **experience**.     I had one or two strange **experiences** in Rome last year.*
   *I need more **time**.     I hope you have **a good time**.     She does good **work**.     Shakespeare's complete **works***
And some uncountable abstract nouns can be used with *a/an* when their reference is defined.
   ***an extensive experience** of tropical medicine     **a knowledge** of languages*

**making countable nouns uncountable** Countable nouns can sometimes be used like uncountables if there is an idea of **quantity** or **mass**.
   *We've got another ten metres of **wall** to paint.     I've got **too much nose** and **not enough chin**.*

**making uncountable nouns countable** With many uncountables, we use particular nouns to mean 'a piece of' or 'a certain amount of'. e.g. *a bar of soap, a flash of lightning, a stroke of luck, a grain of rice, a piece of research*. For other examples, see a good dictionary.

# mixed singular and plural

**group nouns** In British English, singular words for groups of people and organisations
(e.g. *team, family, choir, government, bank*) are often used with plural verbs and pronouns.

*My **family are** furious with me. **They** think I have let **them** down.*

This happens particularly when we are thinking about personal kinds of activity. Compare:

*The **team** really **want** to win the cup this season.*
*A rugby union **team consists** of fifteen players.*

In American English, plural verbs are uncommon with group nouns.

**1** **Choose plural verb forms and pronouns (in seven sentences) or singulars (in three sentences).**

1 The choir *has / have* thrown me out because *it says / they say* I can't sing.
2 The hospital *is / are* sending John home next week.
3 Our committee *has / have* twelve members.
4 A group of Dutch musicians *is / are* visiting Ireland.
5 The hospital *is / are* closing next month for building work.
6 Most of my family *lives / live* in Scotland.
7 The bank *closes / close* early on Fridays.
8 Our bank *is / are* always very friendly and helpful.
9 The team *is / are* getting desperate; *it hasn't / they haven't* won a game this year.
10 The golf club *is / are* putting the subscription up again.

**a number of, the majority of** etc + **plural noun** have plural verbs and pronouns.

***A number of people have** criticised our decision.*
***The majority of his students are** pleased with **their** courses.*

**plural expressions of quantity** are often treated as singular.

***Thirty miles is** a long way to run.*

**We often use** *a/an* before **adjective + plural expression of quantity**.

*I waited for **a good two hours**.     We'll need **another four tables**.*

**Common fixed expressions with** *and* are often treated like singular nouns.

***Toast and marmalade isn't** enough for breakfast, in my opinion.*

**2** **Correct the mistakes or write 'Correct'.**

▶ The majority of members ~~has~~ now voted. ...*have*...............
▶ Can you give me back that 20 euros I lent you? ...*Correct*............
1 A number of people has tried unsuccessfully to find the treasure. ...........................
2 Two hundred euros are too much to pay for an hour's consultation. ...........................
3 Can you get other three packets of butter while you're out? ...........................
4 Fish and chips are a very popular British meal. ...........................
5 A couple of unexpected problems has arisen. ...........................
6 I've had another busy few weeks. ...........................
7 Fifteen hours are a long time to drive non-stop. ...........................
8 Who are those three people? ...........................
9 The majority of the new MPs is 40 or younger. ...........................
10 £5 doesn't buy as much as it used to. ...........................

**singular noun, plural modifying expression** When a singular noun is modified by a plural expression, the verb is normally singular.

*A good knowledge of three languages is needed for the job.* (NOT *… are needed*)

**one of; more than one** Note these structures:

*One of my friends is getting married.* (NOT *One of … are …*)
*More than one person is/are going to be disappointed.*

**people doing/having the same thing** To talk about several people each doing or having the same thing, we normally use a **plural** noun for the repeated idea.

*The students can use dictionaries.* (MORE NATURAL THAN *… a dictionary.*)

We almost always use **plurals** after **possessives** in this case.

*Tell the kids to blow their noses.* (NOT *… their nose.*)     *Six people lost their lives.*

**3** **Correct or improve these sentences.**

▶  One of you ~~are~~ going to have to stand.  *is* ..................

1   Experience of working with handicapped children are an advantage. ...........................
2   I know more than one student that are certain to fail the exam. ...........................
3   Tell everybody they can leave their coat in the cloakroom. ...........................
4   I think one of my earrings have fallen off in the car. ...........................
5   John's interest in tropical animals and birds are becoming an obsession. ...........................
6   Most of the people who were at the barbecue came on a bike. ...........................
7   One of those children have gone into the wrong classroom. ...........................
8   All of my friends have got a really small room. ...........................
9   John and Henry both came with their wife. ...........................
10  Over a hundred MPs lost their seat in the last election. ...........................
11  The structure of animal societies are often very complex. ...........................

**NOTES**

After *one of the … who* etc singular and plural verbs are both common.
    *She's one of the few women who has/have climbed Everest in winter.*

After *any/none/neither/either of*, singular or plural verbs are possible (see page 169).
    *None of my friends know(s) where I am.*

**subject and complement** If a verb is a long distance from the subject, people sometimes make it agree with a following complement instead of the subject, but this is not generally considered correct. Compare:
    *The biggest problem is the holiday dates.* (NOT *… are the holiday dates.*)
    *The most interesting thing on television last week, in my own opinion, was/were the tennis championships.* (*Was* is more correct.)
A **plural** verb is, however, common in structures beginning *What*.
    *What we need is/are more people like Jeannie.*

**countries** Plural names of countries have singular verbs.
    *The United States is coming out of recession.*

**here's etc** In informal speech we often use *here's*, *there's* and *where's* before a plural noun.
    *Here's your gloves.*     *There's two policemen outside.*     *Where's those letters?*

# noun + noun or preposition structure

**Revise the basics.** A **noun + noun** phrase is often simply like a single noun which happens to have two parts. Common short combinations are often written without a space. Compare:

*light    headlight    ceiling light    cloth    washcloth    table cloth*

The first noun is often like an **object** (of a verb or preposition). It is normally **singular**, even if it has a plural meaning.

*a **shoe** shop* = 'a shop that **sells shoes**'    *a **tooth**brush* = 'a brush **for teeth**'
*a **war** film* = 'a film **about war**'

Remember: the **first** noun **describes** the **second**, not the other way round. A *race horse* is a kind of **horse**; a *horse race* is a kind of **race**. *Chocolate milk* is **milk**; *milk chocolate* is **chocolate**.

**noun + noun + noun …**   Three or more nouns can be combined. This is often done in newspaper headlines to save space.

*business administration course    DRUGS BOSS ARREST DRAMA*

**1** **Write noun + noun phrases to express the following ideas.**
1  a thief who steals bicycles ......................................
2  pots to put plants in ......................................
3  plants that grow in pots ......................................
4  lessons in music ......................................
5  a shop that sells hats ......................................
6  a bill for electricity ......................................
7  a car used by the police ......................................
8  a pond for fish ......................................
9  an engineer who works with computers ......................................
10  courses for training engineers to work with computers ......................................

**measurement expressions**   We often use **noun + noun** in expressions of measurement beginning with a number. We put a hyphen (-) between the number and the measure.

*a five-litre can* (NOT *a five-litres can*)    *a three-day course*    *eight two-hour lessons*

**2** **Write noun + noun phrases to express the following ideas.**
1  a house with four bedrooms ......................................
2  a lecture that lasts three hours ......................................
3  a note worth 100 euros ......................................
4  two notes worth 100 euros each ......................................
5  a walk ten miles long ......................................
6  a family with two cars ......................................

**3** **Can you put the words from the box into the right places in the advertisement?**

| alarm   doors   home   key   remote |
| --- |

Operate your garage ..............,
car .............. and .............. alarm
with one .............. control that fits
on your .............. ring.

**less common combinations: noun + noun not used** The **noun + noun** structure is mostly used for very **common well-known** combinations. For less common combinations, we prefer other structures – for example a preposition phrase. Compare:

*the **kitchen table*** (a common kind of table)  *a **table for the prizes*** (NOT ~~a prize table~~)
*road signs*  *signs of tiredness* (NOT ~~tiredness signs~~)
*a love letter*  *a letter from the insurance company*
*a history book*  *a book about George Washington*

**4** **Circle the correct noun group.**

▶ a beautiful princess story *or* (a story about a beautiful princess)
▶ (furniture polish) *or* polish of furniture
1  a glass factory *or* a factory of glass
2  a love story *or* a story about love
3  the garden man *or* the man in the garden
4  a night club *or* a club of night
5  dog food *or* food for dogs
6  a roof bird *or* a bird on the roof
7  a folk song *or* a song of the folk
8  a supermarket fire *or* a fire at the supermarket
9  music festivals *or* festivals of music
10  the shelf books *or* the books on the shelf

---

**NOTES**

**how much/many** We **don't** normally use **noun + noun** in expressions that say **how much/many** of something we are talking about.
   *a piece of paper* (NOT ~~a paper piece~~)   *a bunch of flowers*   *a blade of grass*
Note the difference between *a beer bottle*, *a matchbox* etc (**containers**), and *a bottle of beer*, *a box of matches* etc (**containers with their contents**).

**noun + noun or possessive structure** We **don't** normally use **noun + noun** to talk about particular people or organisations and their possessions or actions. Instead we use a possessive structure (see page 130).
   *my father's house* (NOT ~~my father house~~)
   *the President's arrival* (NOT ~~the President arrival~~)

**first noun plural** In a few **noun + noun** combinations, the first noun is **plural**.
   ***antiques** dealer*   ***sports** car*   ***drugs** problem*
This is especially the case when the first noun is mainly or only used in the plural, or has a different meaning in the singular.
   ***accounts** department*   ***customs** officer*   ***clothes** shop*
   ***glasses** case*   ***savings** account*   ***arms** trade*

Start saving from just
**£1!**
OPEN AN ONLINE SAVINGS ACCOUNT

THE ASSOCIATION OF
ART & ANTIQUES DEALERS
*Art & Antiques Fair*
Berkeley Square
22nd to 26th September
2011. Doors open from

# possessive structure or other structures

**basics: forms** Singular possessive nouns end in 's, plural possessives end in *s'*, irregular plural possessives end in *'s*.

*my **sister's** husband     my **parents'** house     my **children's** school*

Names ending in -s sometimes have a possessive in *s'*, especially in classical and literary references, but *'s* is more common.

*Sophocles' plays     Dickens' novels     James's uncle.*

A phrase of several words can have a possessive form.

*Joe and Ann's children     the man in the downstairs flat's dog*

Several nouns can be joined by possessives.

*Jane's mother's bank manager's daughter*

**1** **Correct (✓) or not (✗)?**

| | | | |
|---|---|---|---|
| 1 | Alex's brother … | 7 | womens' rights … |
| 2 | those peoples' house … | 8 | the neighbours' cats … |
| 3 | Marys' ideas … | 9 | everybody's business … |
| 4 | my mother-in-law's job … | 10 | the pilots' union … |
| 5 | my friend Jess's horse … | 11 | Emma's husband's brother's problems … |
| 6 | Pythagoras' theorem … | 12 | my fathers' handwriting … |

**belonging, characteristics: possessive or preposition structure** We use the **possessive** structure most often to talk about something that **belongs to**, or is a **characteristic of** a person, group, organisation, country or animal. The first noun is often like a **subject**.

*my **boss's** car* (My **boss has** a car.)     *Ann's idea* (**Ann had** an idea.)
*Mary's kindness* (**Mary has been** kind.)     *The **cat's** milk* (The **cat drinks** the milk.)

We don't so often use possessives to talk about characteristics or parts of **things that are not alive**. (There are some exceptions.) Instead, we use a **preposition structure**.

*the top of the page* (NOT ~~the page's top~~)     *the **bottom of** the hill* (NOT ~~the hill's bottom~~)
*the **reason for** the decision* (NOT ~~the decision's reason~~)
*the **interest on** the loan* (NOT ~~the loan's interest~~)
*the **difficulty of** the questions* (NOT ~~the questions' difficulty~~)

**2** **Circle the best expression.**

1  Peter's arm *or* the arm of Peter
2  the chair's arm *or* the arm of the chair
3  the dog's tail *or* the tail of the dog
4  the hurricane's tail *or* the tail of the hurricane
5  the investigations' results *or* the results of the investigations
6  the students' results *or* the results of the students
7  the disaster's anniversary *or* the anniversary of the disaster
8  Harry's birthday *or* the birthday of Harry
9  the clothes' price *or* the price of the clothes
10 the students' fees *or* the fees of the students
11 the house's roof *or* the roof of the house
12 Eric's family *or* the family of Eric
13 Britain's exports *or* the exports of Britain
14 bread's price *or* the price of bread

**actions** We can use the possessive structure for **actions** involving people, organisations etc.

*John's letter* (John **wrote** a letter)     *the girl's story* (the girl **told** a story)
*Malloy's arrest* (Malloy was arrested)     *the plane's arrival* (the plane arrived)

**3** **Rewrite these sentences using possessive structures.**

> | decision ✓   growth   phone call   punishment   report   success |

▶ Carl decided to go home; it surprised everybody.
   *Carl's decision to go home surprised everybody.* ................................................

1 Mary succeeded in her exams; this boosted her confidence.
   ...........................................................................................................................

2 The economy grew more slowly than expected.
   ...........................................................................................................................

3 Peter telephoned. It worried us a lot.
   ...........................................................................................................................

4 The treasurer reported on the last six months; this was encouraging.
   ...........................................................................................................................

5 The children were punished; it was very severe.
   ...........................................................................................................................

**common kinds of thing: possessive structure not used** For the names of common kinds of thing
we usually prefer **noun + noun** (see page 128), not possessive structures.

*a history book* (NOT ~~a history's book~~)     *a street lamp* (NOT ~~a street's lamp~~)

**4** **Circle the correct noun group.**

▶ a bus's station *or* (a bus station)              6  a telephone's directory *or* a telephone directory
▶ (my mother's chair) *or* my mother chair       7  a birthday's card *or* a birthday card
1  a glass's factory *or* a glass factory          8  vegetables' soup *or* vegetable soup
2  a toys' shop *or* a toy shop                     9  Andrew's plan *or* the Andrew plan
3  computer's discs *or* computer discs          10  street's lamps *or* street lamps
4  that cat's tail *or* that cat tail              11  the firm's problems *or* the firm problems
5  car's papers *or* car papers                   12  a bath's towel *or* a bath towel

Possessive structures are used for the names of a few common kinds of thing: mostly the names
of animal products, and things that are used by people.

*cow's* milk     *hen's* eggs     *a man's* sweater     *women's* magazines

**NOTES**

**Time expressions** often use possessive structures.
   *yesterday's news     last Saturday's match     this evening's programmes*
Possessives are also possible in expressions saying how long something lasts.
   *a day's journey     three weeks' holiday     four months' notice*

*at the doctor's* etc  In some common expressions, the second noun is left out.
   *I've been at the doctor's (surgery).     I'll see you at Pat's (house).*
The names of many shops and businesses have this structure, often with no apostrophe.
   *Smith's OR Smiths     Harrods     Barclays*

**Instead of a complex possessive** we may prefer a preposition structure.
   *the son of the man we met in Borneo* RATHER THAN *the man we met in Borneo's son*

For expressions like *a film of Hitchcock's*, see page 152.

# nouns for activities: using *have, make, do* etc

English often uses nouns to refer to actions. These nouns often have the same form as verbs: for example *a swim, a wash, a guess*. They are especially common in an informal style, and are often introduced by 'general-purpose' verbs like *have, take, make, give, go for*, especially when we are talking about casual or unsystematic activity.

*I like to **have a swim** every day.       I'm going to **have a wash**.*
*I don't know, but I'll **have/make a guess**.*
*I'll **have a think** and get back to you.* (informal BrE)
*Just **take a look** at yourself.       If it won't start, **give** it **a kick**.*

***Go for*** is common with nouns for **physical activity**.

*Let's **go for a walk**.       I always **go for a long run** on Sundays.*

We can use *-ing* forms in a similar way after ***do***, usually with a determiner like *some, any* etc.

*I need to **do some tidying**.       I **do a bit of painting** in my spare time.*

**1**  **Write sentences about some things you sometimes or never do at weekends, using *have, go for* and *do some/any*.**

................................................................................................................................................
................................................................................................................................................
................................................................................................................................................


# a note on gender: *he, she* or *it*?

**animals**  Pet animals are usually *he/him/his* or *she/her* and *who* rather than *it/its/which*.
*Can you find the cat and put **him** out?       She had an old dog, Susie, **who** always slept on her bed.*

**countries**  In modern English, countries are most often *it(s)*, though *she/her* is also common.
*Canada has decided to increase **its/her** trade with Russia.*

**Boats** are *it(s)* for most people, but may be *she/her* for people who work with them.
*I arrived too late for the ferry and missed **it**.       Abandon ship – **she's** sinking!*

**Cars** and other vehicles are *it(s)* except for some devoted owners.
*The man who sold **it** to me said **it** had only done 20,000 miles.*
*Now that I've put the new engine in, **she** goes like a bomb.*

**positions and jobs**  In modern usage, people often prefer to avoid specifically masculine or feminine names for positions and jobs.
*She has just been elected **chair** of the committee.* (preferred to *chairman*)
*Ann wants to work as a **flight attendant**.* (preferred to *air hostess/stewardess*)
*A **poet** I like is Wendy Cope.* (preferred to *poetess*)

***he or she***  We can use **singular *they/them/their*** (see page 139) to avoid clumsy sequences of *he or she, him or her* etc.
*If a would-be tourist wishes to apply for a visa, **they** should take **their** passport to the local consulate.*
*(Simpler than … he or she should take his or her passport …)*

# structures after nouns

**complements** Many nouns, especially abstract nouns, can have **complements** which complete their meaning. **Preposition structures, infinitives** and *that*-clauses are common.

your **criticism of the plan.**     a **desire for more involvement**
the **need to close** our Scottish branch     a **wish to change**
a **feeling that something was wrong**     his **belief that he is always right**

For the prepositions used after particular nouns, see pages 308–309.

**If an infinitive has its own subject,** we use a structure with *for* (see page 104).

There's no need **for you to stay.**     They had a plan **for me to study** medicine.

**-ing forms** Prepositional complements may include *-ing* forms.

the **advantages of being single**     their **pleasure in working together**

**kinds of complement** Some nouns can have more than one kind of complement.

the **need to find investors**     the **need for more** investment
the **reason for** the changes     no **reason to get** angry     the **reason why** I left

But not all nouns can have all kinds of complement.

the **thought of retiring** (BUT NOT ~~the thought to retire~~)
the **idea of getting** married (BUT NOT ~~the idea to get married~~)

**1** **Correct (✓) or not (✗)? (Five sentences are correct.)**

1  We have no hope of winning the match. …
2  I hate the thought to get old. …
3  Is it time for going now? …
4  We had difficulty in finding a hotel. …
5  We made a decision of going home. …
6  I've got over my fear to fly. …
7  We gave up our plan to move. …
8  There's no need to be disagreeable. …
9  She liked the idea to take a year off. …
10  I have a strong wish of being alone. …
11  Is there any need me to translate? …
12  My idea was for us to meet at 10.00. …

**2** **Write your own completions for these sentences.**

1  I hate the thought ………………………………………………………………
2  I don't like the idea ……………………………………………………………
3  I will never give up my belief …………………………………………………
4  I don't understand the reason …………………………………………………
5  There's no need ……………………………………………………………
6  I haven't much hope ……………………………………………………………

**preposition + conjunction** A preposition may be followed by a conjunction (see page 196).

We discussed the **question of whether** there was a **need for more investment**.
We had a **discussion about how** to improve communications.

But prepositions are not followed directly by *that*-clauses (see page 196).

**news of** his plans     **news that** he was leaving (NOT ~~news of that he~~ …)

Note that **related** nouns, verbs and adjectives may have **different** kinds of complement.

I have no **intention of resigning.**     I do not **intend to resign.**
a **discussion about** finance     We **discussed** finance.
**emphasis on** quality control     They **emphasised** quality control.
**pride in** his **work**     **proud of** his work

For the structures used with particular nouns, see a good dictionary.

# personal pronouns

**Revise the basics  After** *be*, we normally use object pronouns: *me, her* etc. *I, she* etc are possible, but they are very formal and unusual.

*'Hello. It's* **me.'**     *'Which is your sister?'  'That's* **her** *in the blue dress.'*

*Me, her* etc are also normal in informal **short answers** and similar structures.

*'We're going home early.'* **'Me** *too.'*     *'Who said that?'* **'Her.'**

In a more formal style, we prefer *I* **etc + auxiliary** in short answers etc.

*'I am too.' / 'So am I.'*     *'She did.'*

**1** **Make the words** *in italics* **less informal.**

▶ *'Who's got the tickets?'  'Him.'* ...He has..........................

1 *'We're going home now.'  'Us too.'* ...................................

2 *'Somebody ordered a coffee.'  'Me.'* ...................................

3 *'Who needs a taxi?'  'Them.'* ...................................

4 *'Can anybody speak Spanish?'  'Her.'* ...................................

5 *'What's the problem?'  'Him, of course.'* ...................................

*as, than, except, but* (meaning 'except')  The grammar is similar after *as* and *than*.

*You're nearly as tired* **as me.**     *I think I sing better* **than her.**
Less informal: *... as I am.     ... than she does.*

And we always use *me, her* etc after *except* and **but.**

*Everybody was in time* **except us.**     *I'll go out with anybody* **but him.**

*It was me/I that ...*   After *It is/was* etc, there are two possibilities.

*It's* **me that's** *responsible.* (informal)
*It is* **I who am** *responsible.* (very formal)

A more neutral alternative is *I am the one who/that is ...*

**2** **Change the sentences.**

▶ I speak English better than her. *(Make it less informal.)*
...I speak English better than she does....................

1 Nobody can sing better than I can. *(Make it more informal.)*

..................................................................................

2 It was she who caused the problem. *(Make it informal.)*

..................................................................................

3 Nobody understood except we. *(Correct it.)*

..................................................................................

4 It was he who discovered the solution. *(Make it neutral.)*

..................................................................................

5 It was us that got left behind. *(Make it neutral.)*

..................................................................................

6 She doesn't panic as easily as me. *(Make it less informal.)*

..................................................................................

**double subjects and objects** It is usual, and considered more polite, to mention oneself last in a double subject or object.

*You and I* *need to talk.* (more normal than *I and you …*)
*I've got tickets for* *you and me.* (more polite than *… for me and you.*)

In informal speech, *me, her* etc are often used in double subjects (especially *me*).

*John and me* *saw a great film last night.*

*I* is also used quite often in double objects.

*Between* *you and I*, *I don't think we're getting anywhere.*

These uses of *I* and *me* etc do not occur in formal writing. Many people feel they are incorrect in speech (especially *I* in double objects), though they are common in standard usage.

**3** **Normal (N), informal (I), less polite (LP) or wrong (W)?**
1  John and me are going skiing this weekend. …
2  Me and your brother spent Sunday at the swimming pool. …
3.  Between you and I, I think his marriage is in trouble. …
4  This letter is to we both. …
5  Alice is very angry with you and me. …
6  I and Maggie wanted to consult you. …
7  Harry and I are going camping. …

**4** **Very formal (F), neutral (N), very informal (I) or wrong (W)?**
1  It was James what did it. …
2  Pete and me want to talk to you. …
3  It is I who organise the timetable. …
4  She's invited the Smiths and us to dinner on Tuesday. …
5  I can run faster than he. …
6  Who would do a thing like that? Nobody but she. …
7  Will that be enough for you and me? …
8  'Who needs a lift to the station?' 'Us.' …
9  I and your mother is very worried about you. …
10  They were the ones who let everybody down. …

---

**NOTES**

**noun + pronoun** In written English and formal speech, one subject is enough: we don't repeat a noun with a pronoun.
   *My parents are retired now.* (NOT *My parents, they are retired now.*)
However, structures like this are possible in conversation.

**identifying** Remember that we use *it, this* or *that* when we name people.
   *'Who's the woman in red?' 'It's Claire Lewis.'* (NOT *She's Claire Lewis.*)
   (on the phone) *Hi, this is Mike.* (NOT *I'm Mike.*)      *Isn't that Dr Andrews?*

**Adjectives** can be used with pronouns in a few fixed expressions.
   *Clever you!* *Lucky you!*
*We, us* and *you* can be used before nouns.
   *We women* *know things that* *you men* *will never understand.*
   *What's the government doing for* *us workers*, *then?*

*He who … etc* These structures are unusual in modern English.
   *The person who takes the risk should get the profit.* (NOT *He who …*)

For singular *they* (e.g. *Somebody phoned.* *They'll call again later.*), see page 139.
For *he* or *she* used for animals, and *she* for boats, cars and countries, see page 132.

# reflexives (*myself* etc); *each other / one another*

**Revise the basics**  Reflexives have two uses:
1. for an **object** that is the same person or thing as the **subject**

*He* talks to **himself** the whole time.
*The **computer** switches **itself** off after half an hour.*

2. for emphasis: to say 'that person/thing and nobody/nothing else'.

*I got a letter from **the Minister himself**.*
*The restaurant **itself** is beautiful, but the food isn't much good.*

Remember the difference between *-selves* and *each other*.

*They write to **each other** every week.* (NOT ~~They write to themselves~~ ...)

***One another*** can be used instead of *each other*. There is no important difference.

**❶ Put in *me, her* etc, *myself, herself* etc or *each other*.**
1  We tried to paint the kitchen ...................., but it was a disaster.
2  Alice is trying to teach .................... Spanish.
3  His parents gave .................... a car when he graduated.
4  When you talk to me like that it really upsets ....................
5  Franz and Uli speak different dialects, so they sometimes misunderstand ....................
6  Jennie .................... is sweet, but I don't get on with her family.
7  If Andy ever listened to ...................., he'd realise how silly he sounds.
8  'That's a lovely necklace.' Thanks. Phil gave it to ....................'

**English and other languages**  Note that some verbs (e.g. *shave, hurry*) are reflexive in some languages, but not in English unless there is a special reason. Compare:

*I don't like **shaving**.* (NOT ... ~~shaving myself~~.)
*He can't shave **himself** now that he's broken his arm, so I have to shave him.*

**❷ Put in reflexive pronouns (twice) or – (eight times).**
1  Hurry ...........................! We're late.
2  She always takes hours to dress ...........................
3  I feel ........................... very depressed these days.
4  Little Annie can nearly dress ........................... now.
5  I hate washing ........................... in cold water.
6  I find it hard to concentrate ........................... when people are playing loud music.
7  The door slowly opened ...........................
8  The accident wasn't your fault. Don't blame ...........................
9  They married ........................... at 18 and divorced ........................... at 21.
10  His new book is selling ........................... really well.

'Suppose you were an idiot, and suppose you were a member of Congress; but I repeat myself.'
(*Mark Twain*)

'Talk to a man about himself and he will listen for hours.'
(*Benjamin Disraeli*)

'Poets have said that the reason to have children is to give yourself immortality. Immortality? Now that I have five children, my only hope is that they are all out of the house before I die.'
(*Bill Cosby*)

'The better I get to know men, the more I find myself loving dogs.'
(*Charles de Gaulle*)

'Women speak because they wish to speak, whereas a man speaks only when driven to speech by something outside himself – like, for instance, he can't find any clean socks.'
(*Jean Kerr*)

**After prepositions**, we use **personal pronouns** unless reflexives are really necessary.

*She always takes her dog **with her** when she goes out.* (NOT *... ~~with herself~~ ...*)
BUT *He's deeply in love with **himself**.*

**3** (Circle) **the right pronoun.**

1 Can you pay? I haven't got any money on *me / myself*.
2 We can't come out this evening. We've got Jane's mother staying with *us / ourselves*.
3 This isn't for you. I bought it for *me / myself*.
4 Joe has no interest in other people. He only talks about *him / himself*.
5 She walked slowly out of the room, leaving a hint of expensive perfume behind *her / herself*.
6 In her new job she's got eight people under *her / herself*.
7 He's one of those people who spend all their time having arguments with *them / themselves*.
8 I often talk to *me / myself*. It's the only way I can get intelligent conversation.

---

**NOTES**

**possessives** **Reflexives** have **no possessive** forms. Instead, we use ***my own*** etc.
*'Do you need a taxi ?' 'No, thanks, I'll use **my own** car.'* (NOT *... ~~myself's car~~.*)
But ***each other / one another*** have **possessives**.
*The twins often wear **each other's** clothes.*

**'elegant' reflexives** Sometimes reflexives are used instead of personal pronouns simply because people feel they sound good: more elegant, or important, or polite.
*This shouldn't be difficult for a clever person like **yourself**.*
*'Who's going to be there?' 'Gary, Rosanne and **myself**.'*
Some people feel this usage is incorrect; it is better to avoid it in formal writing.

***In itself*** is a useful expression for contrasting theory and practice.
*There's nothing wrong with the idea **in itself**; it just won't work in our situation.*

**subjects** *Each other / One another* are not normally used as subjects, but this sometimes happens in an informal style.
*They listened carefully to what **each other** said.*
(More normal: *They each listened carefully to what **the other** said.*)

**get** Note the use of ***get* + past participle** in some structures which have a reflexive kind of meaning, especially in an informal style.
*I can **get washed, shaved and dressed** in five minutes if I'm really in a hurry.*
*They **got married** in the village church.*
*I always **get lost** when I go walking in the mountains.*

---

## An old paradox

The village barber shaves all those people, and only those people, who don't shave themselves.

Who shaves the barber?

# one, you and they (general meaning)

*One* and *you* can mean **'people in general'** (including the **speaker** and **hearer**). *One* is more formal than *you*, and has a possessive *one's*.

*One/You* should always try to keep **one's/your** promises.
*You* need / *One* needs a visa to visit the US.

We **don't** use *one* or *you* to talk about **whole groups**.

*They speak* French in Quebec. OR French *is spoken* in Quebec.
(NOT ~~One speaks French in Quebec.~~)

And *one* and *you* are not used if they could **not apply to the speaker**.

*Where Carlos comes from, a child normally starts school at seven.*
(NOT ~~Where Carlos comes from, one/you normally ...~~)

**1** **Correct (✓) or not (✗)? Three sentences are right.**

1  In the 16th century one believed in witches.  …
2  One is knocking at the door.  …
3  You can never get everything right.  …
4  Does one accept euros in Russia?  …
5  Can one use euros in Russia?  …
6  Do you have to get a special licence to drive a lorry?  …
7  What languages does one speak in Mali?  …
8  One doesn't allow high-rise buildings in this town.  …

**2** **Complete these sentences with words from the box, and make them more or less formal.**

| adequate   avoid   direct ✓   fit   omelette   opinions   permit ✓   prepared |

▶  One can't get a … train from here to Cambridge.
    *You can't get a direct train from here to Cambridge.*
▶  You need to show your … to park here.
    *One needs to show one's permit to park here.*
1  You have to be … to do this job.
    ......................................................................
2  Sometimes one must keep one's … to oneself.
    ......................................................................
3  You need to leave early if you want to … the traffic.
    ......................................................................
4  One can't make an … without breaking eggs.
    ......................................................................
5  One can't teach people anything if one isn't … to learn from them.
    ......................................................................
6  You can't get an … knowledge of a language in a month.
    ......................................................................

*They* (informal) can mean **'the people around'** or **'the authorities'**, **'the government'**.

*They* play a lot of rugby round here.     *They* say she's back in jail.
*They're* always reorganising.     *They* don't do much for single mothers.

# singular *they*

> **singular *they*** *They/Them/Their(s)* have a common **singular indefinite** use, mostly after nouns referring to unidentified people.

*Somebody has left their car outside the office. Would they please move it?*
*I had a friend who wanted a ticket, and they had to queue for six hours.*

**1** Correct (✓) or not (✗)?

1 If anybody needs an application form, they can get it from room 6. …
2 When a student goes for their first lesson, they should sign in at the office. …
3 My sister's husband Simon is a mechanic, and they are repairing my car for me. …
4 Some fool has taken my coat and left theirs instead. …
5 Somebody said it wasn't going to rain, but they were quite wrong. …
6 I think Pete has left their umbrella behind. …
7 If anybody calls, tell them I'm out. …
8 If anybody tries to break into this house, they'll get a nasty shock. …
9 If I find out who took my bike I'll kill them. …
10 That man over there used to work with me, but they've lost their job. …

# one(s)

> **basics** We can use *one(s)* to avoid repeating a countable noun.

*'Another slice of lamb?' 'Just a small one, please.'*
*I'm going to wear my new earrings: the ones I bought in Egypt.*

> We **don't** use *one* for an **uncountable** noun.

*There isn't any brown bread. Would you like white (bread)?* (NOT … ~~white one.~~)

> If there is **no adjective**, we do **not** use *a* with *one*.

*'What sort of computer have you got?' 'One that keeps crashing.'* (NOT ~~A one~~ … ')

**1** Circle the correct answers and put in words from the box.

| buttons | goat's | olive | sea level | sharp | sun roof | throw out | transcriptions |
|---|---|---|---|---|---|---|---|

1 I'm looking for a new car. I'd like *one / a one* with a …………………………
2 Can you see my coat anywhere? It's *blue one / a blue one / a blue* with red …………………………
3 I've got too many clothes. I'm going to ………………………… *ones / the ones* I don't wear.
4 'Is that ………………………… cheese?' 'No, *sheep's / sheep's one*.'
5 I need a French dictionary – *big one / a big one* that has phonetic …………………………
6 Do you sell maps? I need *one / a one* that shows heights above …………………………
7 I want ………………………… oil, not *corn / corn one*.
8 Have you got a knife – *really / a really* ………………………… one?

**2** Give your own answers to the questions. Use *one(s)*.

1 What sort of holiday would you like this year? …………………………………………………
2 What sort of country would you like to live in? …………………………………………………
3 What sort of books do you like? …………………………………………………
4 What sort of job would you like? …………………………………………………

# more practice

**1** **Correct (✓) or not (✗)?**

1 That was a luck! …
2 Can you give me a piece of advice? …
3 I'm doing a research on Welsh history. …
4 This is a terrible weather. …
5 I had some strange experiences in Italy. …
6 It's time for a change. …
7 The detectives have found a new evidence. …
8 There's not much chance of rain. …
9 She has a good understanding of children. …
10 Have you got all the equipments you need? …

**2** **Which is/are correct – A, B or both?**

▶ Nobody .A. ready.   **A** *is*   **B** *are*   **C** both
▶ My family .C. away just now.   **A** *is*   **B** *are*   **C** both
1 The price of the rooms … ridiculous.   **A** *was*   **B** *were*   **C** both
2 The majority of the votes … now been counted.   **A** *have*   **B** *has*   **C** both
3 Emma's school … closing for a week for repairs.   **A** *is*   **B** *are*   **C** both
4 More than one house … empty in this street.   **A** *is*   **B** *are*   **C** both
5 One of my friends … on TV the other day.   **A** *was*   **B** *were*   **C** both
6 A number of viewers … complained about last night's programme.   **A** *has*   **B** *have*   **C** both
7 Julie's school … very pleased with her progress.   **A** *is*   **B** *are*   **C** both
8 42 km … too far for most people to run.   **A** *is*   **B** *are*   **C** both
9 We've had … problems with the new flat.   **A** *good few*   **B** *a good few*   **C** both
10 I need … weeks to finish the work.   **A** *another two*   **B** *two more*   **C** both
11 A good knowledge of three languages … needed for this job.   **A** *is*   **B** *are*   **C** both
12 Tell the students they can use their … in the exam.   **A** *dictionary*   **B** *dictionaries*   **C** both
13 They speak different languages, so they have trouble understanding …
    **A** *themselves*   **B** *each other*   **C** both
14 In Newcastle … a dialect called 'Geordie'.   **A** *one speaks*   **B** *they speak*   **C** both
15 Somebody has left … handbag on the bus.   **A** *her*   **B** *their*   **C** both

**3** **Correct the mistakes. (One expression is correct.)**

▶ a ~~teeth~~brush ..tooth................   |   6 the sister of Emma ...........................
1 a two-litres bottle ...........................   |   7 a factory of cars ...........................
2 a police's car ...........................   |   8 that dog tail ...........................
3 an anger scream ...........................   |   9 I'll have a think. ...........................
4 a coal miner novel ...........................   |   10 Let's make a party. ...........................
5 a club of golf ...........................

**4** **Circle the correct or most normal form.**

1 That's *she / her*.
2 *I / Me* too.
3 He's just as old as *I / me*.
4 Everybody except *we / us* was invited.
5 I always take my passport with *me / myself*.
6 I'd like *one / a one* with green stripes.
7 I *shave / shave myself* nearly every day.

**5** **Who do the pronouns *in italics* refer to?**

> A  people in general    B  certain people, not the speaker or listener(s)    C  the listener(s)
> D  the speaker and the listener(s)    E  the speaker and other people, but not the listener
> F  the authorities

▶  I think *we* both need some time to be alone.  .P.

1  If *you* really want to help someone, I think *you* have to make an effort to suffer with
   them — to see it from their point of view — and then to do something.  …

2  '*You* can't do that here, I'm afraid,' said Bramble affably.  …

3  *They* always stay till there's nothing left to eat or drink.  …

4  *They*'re always putting up taxes, but you never get anything for it.  …

5  Of course, *we* often push uncomfortable thoughts to the back of *our* minds.  …

6  Could you please at least tell *them* it's quite urgent?  …

7  Sure *we* need to talk, and *we* will also do pretty well without talking.  …

8  *We* need your help and support in this vital work.  …

**6** **Can you put the missing words into the quotations?**

> always   difficult   easiest   everything   flies   fool   impossible   never   simply

1  '*Always* and *never* are two words you should ………… remember ………… to use.' (*Wendell Johnson.*)

2  'You can't have ………… Where would you put it?' (*Steven Wright*)

3  'Why be ………… when, with a little extra effort, you can be absolutely …………?' (*Traditional*)

4  'If you can't explain it …………, you don't understand it well enough.' (*Albert Einstein*)

5  'You must not fool yourself, and you are the ………… person to …………' (*Richard Feynman*)

6  'Time ………… when you don't know what you are doing.' (*anon.*)

> coffee   diary   kitchen   mistakes   romance   sensational   shoes   thumb

7  'I never travel without my ………… One should always have something ………… to read on the train.' (*Oscar Wilde*)

8  'You must learn from the ………… of others. You cannot possibly live long enough to make them all yourself.' (*Sam Levenson*)

9  'You can never have too many …………' (*Traditional*)

10  'To love oneself is the beginning of a lifelong …………' (*Oscar Wilde*)

11  'If you can't stand the heat, get out of the …………' (*Harry S Truman*)

12  'You can always tell a logger*. Only a logger stirs his ………… with his …………' (*old Canadian saying*)

**7** **Turning verbs into nouns. You can *go for a walk* or *go for a run*. Look in a dictionary or on the internet to find six other expressions for physical activities beginning *"go for a"*.**

……………………………………    ……………………………………
……………………………………    ……………………………………
……………………………………    ……………………………………

*A man who works in forests cutting down trees.

# Section 10 determiners (1): articles, demonstratives and possessives

## what are determiners?

**Determiners** are words that come at the beginning of noun phrases, before any adjectives. They mostly show **which** or **how much/many** we are talking about.

*the manager*    *my old friend*    *that black dress*    *some oil*    *little interest*    *more time*

There are three main groups of determiners.

1. **Articles:** *a/an* and *the*.
2. **Possessives and demonstratives:** *my, your* etc and *this, that* etc. These are called 'adjectives' in some grammars, but determiners are quite different from adjectives.
3. **Quantifiers:** *all, each, every, either, some, any, no, much, many* and similar words.

Articles, possessives and demonstratives are covered in this Section, along with the possessive pronouns *mine, yours* etc. (These are not determiners, but it is convenient to deal with them here.) Quantifiers are covered in Section 11.

## articles: preliminary note

**Western European languages** such as French, German, Swedish, Greek or Spanish have articles that work more or less like English *a/an* and *the*. Speakers of these languages will have some problems with English articles, but not too many. The most important difference is the common English use of **no article** in generalisations – *the* does not mean 'all'. Compare:

*People are unpredictable.*    French  ***Les gens** sont imprévisibles.*
*I like **music**.*   German *Ich liebe **(die) Musik**.*
***Life** is a dream.*    Spanish  ***La vida** es sueño.*

Students who speak **other languages** may find correct article use difficult, even at this level. Four important things to remember are:

1. We use ***the*** when both the speaker and the hearer know **which one(s)** is/are meant.

   *Have you fed **the dogs**?* (We both know **which dogs**.)
   *Once there was a beautiful princess who lived in a big castle. One day **the princess** was out riding …* (You know **which princess** – the one I told you about in the first sentence.)
   *There's **the man** who sold me my car.* (I'm telling you **which man**.)

2. In other cases we most often use ***a/an*** with singular countable nouns; ***some*** or **no article** with uncountables and plurals.

   *My sister married **an architect**.* (not an architect that you know about)
   *I'd like to be **a dancer**.*    *We need **some pasta**.*    *There are **problems** at work.*

3. We use **no article** when we talk about people or things **in general**, using uncountable or plural nouns. (*The* does not mean 'all'.)

   *I like **music**.*    ***Food** is expensive.*    ***People** are funny.*    *I don't trust **banks**.*

4. **Singular countable nouns must** normally have an article or other determiner. We can say *the house, a house, this house, my house, every house*, but not just *house*. (There are a few exceptions in fixed expressions like *in bed, by bus*: see page 144).

Not all article uses follow these rules, but most do. For special cases, see pages 148–149.

# articles: revise the basics

**1** CHECK YOUR KNOWLEDGE. **Put in *a*, *an*, *the* or – (= no article).**

This is ¹.............. story I heard ².............. long time ago. I believe it's true. There was ³.............. little girl living in ⁴.............. small village near ⁵.............. Oxford, who was very interested in ⁶.............. history. She had learnt at ⁷.............. school about ⁸..............time when ⁹.............. Romans governed ¹⁰.............. Britain, and seen ¹¹.............. pictures of their villas with their mosaic floors, and she thought they were beautiful. So ¹².............. girl decided to discover ¹³.............. Roman villa herself. She took ¹⁴.............. her little spade, went into one of ¹⁵.............. fields near ¹⁶.............. her house and started digging. Ten minutes later she found ¹⁷.............. piece of mosaic. She ran home and showed ¹⁸.............. mosaic to her mother, who went and told ¹⁹.............. farmer who owned ²⁰.............. field.

Not surprisingly, ²¹.............. farmer was not at all pleased: he wanted ²².............. corn in ²³.............. his field, not ²⁴.............. lot of ²⁵.............. archaeologists. He told ²⁶.............. girl's mother that ²⁷.............. mosaic was not really Roman, and that anyway they were to say nothing to anybody. So ²⁸.............. little girl kept quiet, said nothing to ²⁹.............. teacher, and forgot about ³⁰.............. villa for half ³¹.............. century. But ³².............. one day, when she was ³³.............. old lady and ³⁴.............. farmer was long since dead, she was talking to ³⁵.............. friend of hers who was ³⁶.............. archaeologist, and she mentioned ³⁷.............. discovery she had made when she was ³⁸.............. little girl. He went to look, and ³⁹.............. villa was rediscovered.

**2** CHECK YOUR KNOWLEDGE. **All except two of sentences 1–10 have mistakes in. Correct the mistakes or write 'Correct'.**

▸ My mother collects ~~an old books~~. *old books* ...................

▸ Do you have a reservation? *Correct* ...........................

1  In my grandfather's time, children usually left the school at 14. ...................................

2  My youngest brother is medical student. ...................................

3  Could you close a door when you go out? ...................................

4  The most people like watching football. ...................................

5  Computers can do nearly everything. ...................................

6  I lived in the North Wales for a few years. ...................................

7  How's the Peter's new job going? ...................................

8  My boyfriend's got the very complicated personality. ...................................

9  Have you got an aspirin? I've got a headache. ...................................

10  What's most stupid thing you've ever done? ...................................

**3** **Five of these rules are good. Which are the two bad ones?**

1  *The* means something like **'We both know** which one(s) I'm talking about'.

2  We use *a/an* to talk about people and things that are **not known** to both the speaker and listener (for example, when we mention something for the first time).

3  We often put *a/an* or *the* before *my, your, his* etc.

4  We drop *the* in some common expressions like *in hospital, to bed*.

5  We use *a/an* when we say what somebody's job is.

6  We often use *a/an* before the names of countries, counties, states etc.

7  We don't usually use *the* when we are talking about people or things in general. *The* does not mean 'all'.

**Rules … and … are the bad ones.**

# articles: revise the basics (continued)

**generalising** Remember that in English, when we talk about people or things **in general,** we **don't** normally use **the**.

*People* are funny. (NOT ~~The people are funny.~~)     *I like **music**.*

For generalisations like *the telephone, the wolf*, see page 146.

**4** GRAMMAR AND VOCABULARY: SOME PROFESSIONS. **Complete the sentences with words from the box. Use a dictionary if necessary. Don't use** *the*.

> archaeologists   botanists   chefs   dermatologists   farmers   financial advisers
> florists   gynaecologists   horticulturalists   estate agents   nurses   paediatricians
> stockbrokers   surgeons   zoologists

1 ........................... specialise in women's health.
2 ........................... buy and sell property.
3 ........................... specialise in skin problems.
4 ........................... know about garden plants.
5 ........................... operate on sick people.
6 ........................... tell people what to do with their money.
7 ........................... specialise in children's health.
8 ........................... raise animals and crops for food.
9 ........................... cook food in restaurants and hotels.
10 ........................... sell flowers.
11 ........................... look after patients in hospitals.
12 ........................... buy and sell shares in companies.
13 ........................... look for the remains of past civilisations.
14 ........................... study animals.
15 ........................... study plants.

**dropping articles** In a few common kinds of expression, we drop articles after prepositions.

*She learnt about the Romans **at school**. (NOT … ~~at the school.~~)*

**5** **Four of sentences 1–10 are wrong. Correct the mistakes or write 'Correct'.**
▶ Helen's at school today. ..*Correct*.............................
▶ I'll meet you ~~outside cinema.~~ ..*outside the cinema.*.......
1 I'm going to sit in garden for a bit. ....................................
2 If you're tired, why don't you go to bed? ....................................
3 Susan's been in hospital for the last week. ....................................
4 When did your brother come out of prison? ....................................
5 Do you think everybody should go to university? ....................................
6 Let's eat in kitchen – it's more comfortable. ....................................
7 I go to gym for an hour most evenings. ....................................
8 You're not supposed to make private phone calls at work. ....................................
9 Is Henry in office yet? ....................................
10 Mary goes to church twice every Sunday. ....................................
11 I don't have to go to the work tomorrow. ....................................
12 Jessie won't start the school until she's six years old. ....................................

**6** **DO IT YOURSELF.** Decide whether the rules are right or wrong (three are wrong), and complete the examples correctly.

1  **We drop *a/an* in exclamations.**   *Right / Wrong*
   What *crazy / a crazy* idea!

2  **We often drop *a/an* after *as*.**   *Right / Wrong*
   I worked as *tourist guide / a tourist guide* last summer.

3  **We drop *the* in common expressions relating to meals.**   *Right / Wrong*
   I had *lunch / the lunch* with Pam today.   I always read the paper *at breakfast / at the breakfast*.

4  **We often drop *a/an* after *without*.**   *Right / Wrong*
   You can't drive a bus without *special licence / a special licence*.

5  **We drop *a/an* after *by* in some common expressions relating to travel.**   *Right / Wrong*
   It's quickest to go there *by car / by a car*.     And it costs more *by train / by the train*.

**geographical names**  Some place names normally have *the* (for example the names of seas and oceans, like *The Atlantic*); others do not (for example the names of countries, like *Scotland*).

**7** **INTERNET EXERCISE.** Find three more examples of each kind of geographical name.
Use the internet or a dictionary to check what the places are called in English.
Be careful to use *the* or no article as necessary.

continents .... Asia ...........   ....................   ....................   ....................

countries .... Scotland ....   ....................   ....................   ....................

counties, states etc .. Yorkshire, ....   .. Texas, ....   .... Normandy .....   ....................
.................... ....................

towns .. Belfast ....   ....................   ....................   ....................

streets .... Oxford Street ....   ....................   ....................   ....................

buildings .... The Parthenon ....   ....................
.................... ....................

seas and oceans .... The Atlantic ....   ....................
.................... ....................

lakes .... Lake Superior ....   ....................
.................... ....................

rivers .... The Thames ....   ....................
.................... 

deserts .... The Sahara Desert ....   ....................
.................... 

**countries with *the***  Note that we use *the* with the names of countries when these are **plural** or when they contain a noun like *Republic, Kingdom*.

*The* Netherlands     *The* United States     *The* Dominican Republic

**8** Write the English names of a few places in the world that you would like to see.

....................................................................................................................
....................................................................................................................
....................................................................................................................
....................................................................................................................
....................................................................................................................

# more about generalising with *a/an* and *the*

**with *a/an*** We can generalise about people or things by mentioning **one example**, with *a/an*.

*A **woman** without **a man** is like **a fish** without **a bicycle**.* (old feminist joke)
*A **baby deer** can stand as soon as it is born.     There's nothing like **a good cup of tea**.*

We can't use this structure to talk about all the members of a group together.

*Tigers are / The tiger is endangered.* (NOT ~~A tiger is endangered.~~)

**with *the*** We can generalise with *the* + **singular countable noun**.

*Schools should concentrate more on **the child**, and less on exams.*

The structure is common with the names of technological devices and musical instruments.

*The **mobile phone** has made an enormous difference to communications.*
*The **violin** is one of the hardest instruments to play.*

Remember that we do **not** normally use *the* with **plural or uncountable** nouns to generalise.

***People** are funny.* (NOT ~~The people are funny.~~)     *I like **music**.*

**1** Correct (✓) or not (✗)?

▶ A camel can go for days without water. ✓
▶ The computers do everything for us. ✗
1  Child needs to feel secure. …
2  A child needs to feel secure. …
3  The elephant is a protected species. …

4  An elephant is a protected species. …
5  Elephants are a protected species. …
6  Who invented a telephone? …
7  I love the saxophone. …
8  A picture is worth a thousand words. …

**2** Here are the names of six endangered species. If you could save just one from extinction, which one would you save?

| the African wild dog | the black rhino | the giant panda | the gorilla | the polar bear | the tiger |

I would save ………………………………

**3** INTERNET EXERCISE. **Use a search engine to find out what these people invented. Use *the* with singular countable nouns. Add an example yourself.**

| bicycle | paper clip | post-it note | postage stamp | telephone | windscreen wiper |

▶ Alexander Graham Bell invented ..the telephone.......................
1  Sir Rowland Hill invented …………………………………
2  Josephine Cochran invented …………………………………
3  Johan Vaaler invented …………………………………
4  Spencer Silver invented …………………………………
5  Nobody knows who invented …………………………………
6  Mary Anderson invented …………………………………
7  (yourexample) …………………………………………………………………………………

***the bus, the hairdresser* etc** We use *the* with a singular countable noun to talk in general about some kinds of thing that are **part of everybody's lives**, like *the bus* or *the hairdresser*. In this case *the bus*, for example, does not mean 'one bus that you know about'; we use *the* to suggest that taking a bus is a common experience that we all share.

*It's quicker to take **the bus**, but it's cheaper to walk.*
*Most people go to **the hairdresser('s)** two or three times a month.*
*It's very satisfying to sing in **the bath**.     You can't believe everything that you read in **the newspaper**.*

For similar expressions with no article (e.g. *in bed*, *by bus*), see page 144.

**physical environment: *the town, the sea* etc** We use *the* with various general expressions referring to our physical surroundings. *The* suggests 'we all know about these things'. Examples: *the town, the country, the mountains, the sea, the wind, the rain, the weather.*

*My girlfriend likes **the sea**, but I prefer **the mountains**.*
*British people talk about **the weather** a lot.     I love listening to **the wind**.*

We also talk about ***the past**, **the present*** and ***the future***.

*You can't go on living in **the past**.*

Note: **no article** is used with ***nature**, **space*** and ***society*** used in a general sense.

*We need to do more to protect **nature**. (NOT ... ~~the nature.~~)*
*I don't think it's worth spending all that money on exploring **space**.*
*We all have to live in **society**.*

**4  Correct (✓) or not (✗)?**

▶  Some men spend every evening in the pub. ✓.
▶  I'm worried about future. ✗.
1  I go to the dentist every six months. …
2  Most people like the nature. …
3  We took the children to the seaside. …
4  I like exploring the small towns. …

5  Do you take the train to work? …
6  I don't mind walking in the rain. …
7  Some people go to doctor to chat. …
8  We're off to the mountains at the weekend. …
9  Einstein said space and time are not separate. …
10  Sue lives in the country. …

***African birds / The birds of Africa*** Remember that we **don't** normally use *the* with **plural** or **uncountable** nouns to **generalise**. This is true even if there is an **adjective** which limits the meaning of the noun.

*She has written a book on **African birds**. (NOT ... ~~on the African birds.~~)*
*I like **Scottish folk music**. (NOT ... ~~the Scottish folk music.~~)*

However, if a noun is followed by an expression with *of* that limits its meaning, we **do** use *the*.

*She has written a book on **the birds of Africa**.*
*I like **the folk music of Scotland**.*

**5  Change the expressions, adding or removing *the* as necessary. The words in the box may help.**

| agricultural   economic   educational   literary   religious   society |

▶  linguistic philosophy  ..the philosophy of language..........................
▶  the history of science  ..scientific history..............................
1  the philosophy of education  ................................................
2  social psychology  ...............................................
3  French painters  ...................................................
4  art history  .....................................................
5  the development of agriculture  ....................................................
6  the study of literature  ...............................................
7  the theory of economics  ..............................................
8  the history of religion  ...............................................

For *the* + adjective in expressions like *the blind, the rich*, see page 177.

# articles: other points

Most article uses follow the simple general rules listed on page 142. Here are some examples of uses of articles (and of no article) that don't fit the general pattern.

*the* = 'the well-known' (pronounced with a strong stress, like *thee*)

*'My great-grandmother knew Winston Churchill.' 'What, not **the** Winston Churchill?'*

*the* + *job/role* used to identify

*'I met Joe Martin on holiday.' 'What, Joe Martin **the writer**?'*

*in hospital, school* etc We only drop articles when talking about the **typical use** of the places. Compare:

*John's been **in hospital** with pneumonia for the last week.     My sister works **in a hospital** for sick children.*
*I'll be **at school** all day tomorrow.     I'll meet you **at the school** at 4.30.*

Note that in American English, articles are always used with *hospital*.

*John's been **in the hospital** with pneumonia for the last week. (AmE)*

*amount, number* etc We drop *the* after *the amount/number of* and similar expressions.

*I was pleased at **the amount of money** collected. (NOT … the amount of the money …)*
*The number of unemployed** is rising steadily.*

*sort of* We usually drop *a/an* after *sort of*, *kind of* and similar expressions.

*They don't make **this sort/kind of bike** any more. (NOT … this sort of a bike …)*

*on the knee, at the side* etc We sometimes use *the* even when it is **not clear which** of several particular persons or things we are talking about. This can happen when there are several similar possibilities, and it is unnecessary to be more definite.

*She kicked him on **the knee**. (NOT … on a knee.)*
*We saw **the wheel** of a car lying by **the side** of the road,. (NOT … a wheel … a side …)*
*Peter Marsh is **the son** of an MP (who may have more than one son).*

*The* is often used in this way with *wrong*.

*He's **the wrong** man for you.     (on the phone) Sorry, you've got **the wrong** number.*

*next week* and *the next week* etc We **drop *the*** before *next* and *last* when we are talking about the time period before or after **the one when we are speaking**. Compare:

*I'll see you **next week**.     I left school **last year**.*
*The first week of the holidays was fine, but **the next week** the weather was awful.*
*1901 was **the last year** of Queen Victoria's reign.*

**1** Are the expressions *in italics* correct (✓) or not (✗)?

1  We're going to America *the next month*.  …
2  Traffic problems were caused by *the quantity of the mud* that was washed down by the storm.  …
3  There's a very strange *sort of bird* in the garden.  …
4  Harold was sent *to the prison* for three years.  …
5  I turned up at the station at *the wrong time*, and missed my train.  …
6  'My name's Bond. James Bond.' 'Not *the James Bond*?'  …
7  'This is a letter written by Livingstone.' 'What, Livingstone *the explorer*?'  …
8  What are you doing *next weekend*?  …
9  The ball hit her right in *an eye*.  …
10 I'm afraid this is *a wrong address*. Try next door.  …

***twice a week* etc**  Note the use of *a/an* to relate two different measures.

*thirty miles an hour     $1000 a day     €10 a kilo     four days a week*

**seasons**  When we talk in general about the **seasons, *the*** and **no article** are both possible.

*England is beautiful in **(the) spring**.     **(The) summer** is always a very busy time for us.*

**illnesses**  The names of illnesses and pains are usually uncountable with no article.

*They think she's got **appendicitis**.     I've got **toothache** again.*

We use *a/an* in a few cases like *a cold, a headache*.

*I've got **a terrible cold**.     Have you got **a headache**?*

In American English, words ending in *-ache* can be countable.

*I have **a toothache**.* (AmE)

**instruments**  We often drop *the* when we talk about people playing musical instruments.

*She studied **(the) oboe and (the) saxophone**.     The recording features Miles Davis **on trumpet**.*

**titles, jobs and positions**  We don't use *the* in titles like *Queen Elizabeth, President Lincoln*. And *the* is not normally used when we say that somebody has or gets a unique position (the only one in the organisation).

*John has been appointed **Sales Director**.     She was elected **President** in 2009.*

**place + building/organisation**  Names made up of **town + important building or organisation** usually have **no article**.

*She studied at **Oxford University**.     I'll be arriving at **Manchester Airport**. He plays for **Sheffield Cricket Club**.*

**mountain ranges**  have *the*; individual mountains usually have **no article.**

*the Alps     the Himalayas     the Andes     Everest     Kilimanjaro     Ben Nevis*

But *the* is used in the translations of some European mountain names.

*The Matterhorn ('**Das** Matterhorn')     The Meije ('**La** Meije')*

**radio, TV etc**  When we talk about the use of these forms of entertainment, we generally say *the radio, the cinema, the theatre*, but *television/TV* with no article.

*I always listen to **the radio** when I'm driving.     There's nothing much on **TV** tonight.*

*The* is often dropped with these words when they refer to art forms or professions.

*(The) Cinema is very different from (the) theatre.     He's worked in **radio** and **television** all his life.*

**Newspapers** usually have *the*; magazines vary.

*The Guardian     The Times     The New Yorker     New Scientist*

**2  Choose the correct way to complete each sentence.**

1  This house is really cold in …   **A** *winter*  **B** *the winter*  **C** both
2  Victoria became … in 1837.   **A** *Queen*  **B** *the Queen*  **C** both
3  My friend Greg plays … in a small orchestra.   **A** *violin*  **B** *the violin*  **C** both
4  I heard a really funny programme on … this morning.   **A** *the radio*  **B** *radio*  **C** both
5  What newspaper do you read?   **A** *Independent*  **B** *The Independent*  **C** both
6  I need a taxi to … at 5.15.   **A** *Didcot Station*  **B** *The Didcot Station*  **C** both
7  Millions of people worldwide still die of …   **A** *malaria*  **B** *the malaria*  **C** both
8  I have always wanted to work in …   **A** *theatre*  **B** *the theatre*  **C** both
9  Augustus was … of Rome from 27 BC until AD 14.   **A** *emperor*  **B** *the emperor*  **C** both

# demonstratives: *this, that, these, those*

**1** **Revise the basics. Answer the questions.**
1 Which do we use for people and things which are close to us in space?
   **A** *this/these*   **B** *that/those*
2 Perhaps we feel particularly close to things that are just going to start.
   So which do we use for things that are about to happen?
   **A** *this/these*   **B** *that/those*
3 And for things that are finished?
   **A** *this/these*   **B** *that/those*
4 We can feel emotionally close or distant to people and things.
   So which do we prefer for people and things that we don't like?
   **A** *this/these*   **B** *that/those*
5 And for people and things that we like?
   **A** *this/these*   **B** *that/those*

**2** **Revise the basics. Put in *this, these, that* or *those*.**
1 Come and look at ………………………… photo.
2 Listen to ………………………… You'll really like it.
3 ………………………… was a lovely evening. Thank you very much.
4 I don't much like ………………………… new girlfriend of yours.
5 'Would you like anything else?' 'No, …………………………'s all, thank you.
6 So tell me about ………………………… new boyfriend of yours.
7 OK! …………………………'s it! I'm not taking any more. I'm leaving you.
8 (on the phone) Hello. ………………………… is Maggie. Can I speak to Jane if she's there?
9 Tell me what you think about …………………………: I thought I'd get a job in Spain for a few months.
10 I thought I'd get a job in Spain for a few months. What do you think about …………………………?

---

**To talk about people and things,** we can use all four words as determiners with nouns.

*this woman*   *these houses*   *that solicitor*   *those clouds*

We can use also them **without nouns** to refer to **things**.

*I've read **that**.*   *Those tops aren't very nice, but I like **this**.*

But we **don't** usually use these words **without nouns** to refer to **people**.

*Tell **those people** to go away.* (BUT NOT *Tell those to go away.*)
*Ask **that woman** what she wants.* (BUT NOT *Ask that what she wants.*)

However, we use *this/that/these/those* without nouns when we are **identifying people**: saying or asking who they are.

***This** is my sister Ellen and **these** are my brothers Tony and Phil.*
***That's** Ellen's friend Sam by the door.*   *(on the phone) Hi, **this** is Mandy. Is **that** Pete?*

We also use ***those*** for people in the formal structure ***those who*** …, and similar expressions.

***Those who** cannot laugh at themselves may be missing a great joke.*
*Let us observe a moment's silence for **those who** cannot be here today.*
*Give generously for **those in need**.*

**3** Correct or not? Correct the mistakes or write 'Correct'.

▶ (on the phone) 'Hi! ~~That's~~ Mark. Who's ~~this~~?' *This is* .......... *that* ..........

▶ Pass me that spanner. .....*Correct.*.....................

1 Pass me that, would you?.....................................

2 Why's that shouting at the policeman?...................................

3 Is that your sister over there?..................................

4 Why are those shoes more expensive than these?...................................

5 This doesn't speak English – can you help?...................................

6 I'll need the names of those who missed the lesson...................................

**4** Can you complete this old joke?

................ who can, do. ................ who can't, teach. ................ who can't teach, train teachers.

---

**that/those of** In a formal style, we can use *that of* or *those of* instead of repeating a noun, in the same way as we can use a possessive.

*A dog's intelligence is much greater than **that of a cat**.* (= '... than a cat's.')
*Her novels sold much better than **those of her brother**.* (= '... than her brother's.')

---

**that clever** etc In informal speech, *this* and *that* are often used to mean 'so'.

*I've never known it **this cold** in June.     If you're **that clever**, why aren't you rich?*

This is a genuine exchange heard at a British supermarket checkout:

*'Do you mind if I go to the front of the queue? I've only got a tin of catfood.'*
*'Well, dear, if you're **that** hungry ...'*

*Not all that* can be used to mean 'not very'.

*'What was the food like?'  '**Not all that** good.'*

---

**there was this ...** *This* and *these* are often used informally to introduce elements in jokes.

*There was **this** travelling salesman who was driving to Cardiff. And he passed **these** two hitchhikers ...*

---

**that empty feeling** *That/Those* can be used in the sense of 'That/Those well-known ...'
This use is common in advertising.

*Got **that** empty feeling again? Why not open a packet of ...?*
*Tired of **those** dull weekends? Fly to Paris for only ...*

---

**5** Put in *this, that, these* or *those* and words from the box.

| bored   brilliant   computer   earn   policies   swimming pool   trip |

1 Don't throw out .......................... old ........................... It may be useful to somebody.
2 Do you know the one about .......................... two old guys who went on a..........................
   to New York?
3 'Yawwwwwwwn!' 'If you're .......................... .........................., let's go home.'
4 This Prime Minister's .......................... are little better than .......................... of
   his predecessor.
5 .......................... extra money during .......................... long winter evenings!
6 When it gets .......................... hot, I just want to live in the ..........................
7 He thinks he's a .......................... speaker, but actually he's not all .......................... good.

For *this, that* and *it* in text construction, see page 253.

---

**terminology** *This, that* etc are often called 'demonstrative adjectives' in grammars. In fact, they are not adjectives at all, but determiners (when used before nouns) or pronouns.

# possessives: *my, mine* etc

**1** CHECK YOUR KNOWLEDGE. **All except one of the following sentences have mistakes in. Correct them or write 'Correct'.**

▶ Is this bike ~~your~~? ..*yours*..........................
1 Would you mind giving me the your address? ...................................
2 I work for a man who's father once worked for my mother. ...................................
3 Their garden isn't as nice as our's. ...................................
4 Our garden involves much more work than their. ...................................
5 One's first impressions of people are usually wrong. ...................................
6 He's got a problem, but I think he's exaggerating it's importance. ...................................
7 That's not your coat – it's the mine. ...................................
8 I'd like to marry a woman whose the family have got a lot of money. ...................................

***a friend of mine*** We can't put the determiners *my, your* etc together with articles or demonstratives in English: ~~a my friend~~ or ~~that your idea~~ are impossible. Instead, we use a structure with ***of mine, of yours*** etc.

*Did you know Penny was **a friend of mine**?*
*Tell me more about **that idea of yours**.*
*She won't stop talking about **this new boyfriend of hers**.*

The structure is also possible with possessive nouns.

*Mr Hamilton is **an old school friend of my father's**.*
*What do you think of **this crazy plan of the boss's**?*
***That dog of Henry's** has dug up half my daffodils.*

Sometimes non-possessive nouns are used.

*She says she's a cousin of the **President**.*

**2** Put the expressions together.

▶ those kids + her kids ..*those kids of hers*.........................
1 a cousin + my cousin ...................................................
2 this suggestion + your suggestion ...................................................
3 a colleague + Emma's colleague ...................................................
4 that translation + Peter's translation ...................................................
5 a friend + my mother's friend ...................................................
6 these new shoes + your new shoes ...................................................
7 this latest mistake + the government's latest mistake ...................................................
8 a firm principle + my father's firm principle ...................................................
9 a strange belief + my sister's strange belief ...................................................
10 some students + my students ...................................................
11 two recent films + his recent films ...................................................
12 this wonderful girlfriend + your wonderful girlfriend ...................................................
...................................................

**3** Write sentences (true or false) about five friends of yours.

A friend of mine ...................................................
Another friend of mine ...................................................
And another friend of mine ...................................................
And another friend of mine ...................................................
And another friend of mine ...................................................

**parts of the body etc** We generally use **possessives** to talk about parts of people's **bodies** and their **clothes**.

*Alex broke **his ankle** playing football.* (NOT *Alex broke the ankle* …)
*She stood there with **her eyes** closed and **her hands** in **her coat pockets**.*
*'My exam's tomorrow.' 'I'll cross **my** fingers for you.'* (NOT … *the fingers* …)

However, we sometimes prefer *the* with words for parts of the **body** after **prepositions**, especially in some common expressions referring to **pain** and **physical contact**, and when the possessor has already been mentioned.

*I've got a pain **in the back**.     Look **me in the eye** and tell me the truth.*
*She hit **the burglar on the head** with her handbag.*

**people doing the same thing** We **don't** normally use **plural** possessives with **singular countable nouns** – for example, to talk about people doing the same thing (see page 127).

*All the children put up **their hands**.* (NOT … *put up their hand.*)
*Tell everybody they'll need **their raincoats**.*

**4** Put words from the box (singular or plural) into the sentences.
Use a dictionary if necessary.

| back   eyebrow   eyelash   lip   nostril   paw   stomach   thumb   trunk   whisker |
|---|

1  This spray is supposed to stop you getting a cold. You squirt it up both your ...........................
2  'I've got an awful pain in the ..........................' 'Too much ice cream.'
3  Why do we pat somebody on the ........................... to congratulate them?
4  I've got an .......................... in my eye.
5  I hit myself on the .......................... with a hammer when I was putting up a picture, and it hurt.
6  She thought shaving off her .......................... would make her more beautiful. I'm not so sure.
7  Elephants drink by taking up water in their .......................... and squirting it into their mouths.
8  Nobody is completely sure what cats use their .......................... for.
9  If a cat falls out of a tree, somehow it always lands on its ..........................
10  In some cultures it's normal to kiss people on the ..........................; in others not.

**NOTES**

*its*  Note that we do not usually use *its* without a noun.
> *I've had my breakfast, Jane's had hers, and the dog's had **its breakfast** too.*
> (NOT … *and the dog's had its too.*)

*one's*  The indefinite pronoun *one* (see page 138) has a possessive *one's*.
> *One should think twice before giving people **one's** address.*

*own*  We use **possessives**, not articles, with *own*.
> ***our own** home / a home of **our own*** (NOT *an own home*)

**terminology**  *My, your* etc are often called 'possessive adjectives' in grammars. In fact, they are not adjectives at all, but **determiners**.

'It is better to remain silent and be thought a fool than to open one's mouth and remove all doubt.'
(*Abraham Lincoln*)

'What's yours is mine and what's mine's my own.'
(*Old saying*)

'I believe that every human has a finite number of heartbeats. I don't intend to waste any of mine running around doing exercises.'
(*Neil Armstrong*)

'Chaos is a friend of mine.'
(*Bob Dylan*)

'I really wonder what gives us the right to wreck this poor planet of ours.'
(*Kurt Vonnegut*)

# more practice

**1** **Articles. Put in *a/an*, *the* or – (= no article).**

1 Have you got a cheaper sort of ............................. microwave?

2 What ............................. strange thing to say!

3 We all have to live in ............................. society.

4 You can't park here without ............................. permit.

5 Hawkins was appointed ............................. Defence Minister in the new government.

6 I'll be arriving at ............................. Birmingham Airport tomorrow morning.

7 Emma's in ............................. garden. I'll tell her you're here.

8 I worked as ............................. waiter for five years.

9 What do you usually have for ............................. breakfast?

10 They've got a little house overlooking ............................. Lake Windermere.

11 When was ............................. Everest first climbed?

12 How many countries are there in ............................. United Kingdom?

13 I was surprised by the amount of ............................. work that there was left to do.

14 I often buy ............................. *Times*, because I like the crossword.

15 She's a specialist in ............................. history of Morocco.

16 She's a specialist in ............................. Moroccan history

17 We usually go to ............................. mountains in July.

18 Our children are more interested in ............................. nature than ............................. sport.

19 ............................. Sahara Desert is growing steadily larger.

20 Have you noticed the number of ............................. homeless people in London?

**2** **Articles. Which is/are normal?**

1 Scotland is beautiful in … (**A** *summer* **B** *the summer* **C** both)

2 I play … in a small group. (**A** *saxophone* **B** *the saxophone* **C** both)

3 The ball hit me in … (**A** *an eye* **B** *the eye* **C** both)

4 My brother works in … (**A** *theatre* **B** *the theatre* **C** both)

5 There was a dead rabbit at … of the road. (**A** *a side* **B** *the side* **C** both)

6 I've got … (**A** *headache* **B** *a headache* **C** both)

7 I've got … (**A** *toothache* **B** *a toothache* **C** both)

8 She goes to … twice a week. (**A** *a hairdresser* **B** *the hairdresser* **C** both)

9 What are you doing at …? (**A** *weekend* **B** *the weekend* **C** both)

10 I never had the chance to go to … (**A** *university* **B** *the university* **C** both)

**3** **Demonstratives and possessives. Normal (✓) or unusual/wrong (✗)?**

1 'Can I get you anything else?' 'No, this is all, thanks.' …

2 That's it. I'm leaving! It was nice knowing you. …

3 Put those down – they're dirty. …

4 Tell those to go away. …

5 I didn't expect it to be this hot. …

6 If he's that clever, why hasn't he got a better job? …

7 Her new book isn't that good. …

8 A dog's sense of smell is far better than this of a human. …

9 She slapped him in his face. …

10 I don't like that friend of your brother's. …

4 INTERNET EXERCISE. **Use a search engine to find some sentences containing the words "surprised by the number of" or "surprised by the amount of". Write them here.**

..................................................................................................................................

..................................................................................................................................

..................................................................................................................................

..................................................................................................................................

..................................................................................................................................

5 GRAMMAR IN A TEXT. **Put *a*, *an*, *the* or – (no article) into the gaps.**

## If restaurants functioned like computer helplines

CUSTOMER: Waiter!

WAITER: Hi. My name is Bill and I'll be [1].............. your support waiter. What is [2].............. problem?

CUSTOMER: There's [3].............. fly in [4].............. my soup!

WAITER: Try again, maybe [5].............. fly won't be there [6].............. this time.

CUSTOMER: No, it's still there.

WAITER: Maybe it's [7].............. way you're using [8].............. soup. Try eating it with [9].............. fork instead.

CUSTOMER: OK. No, [10].............. fly is still there.

WAITER: Maybe [11].............. soup is incompatible with [12].............. bowl. What kind of [13].............. bowl are you using?

CUSTOMER: [14].............. soup bowl.

WAITER: OK. Maybe it's [15].............. configuration problem. How was [16].............. bowl set up?

CUSTOMER: You brought it to me in [17].............. saucer. But what has that got to do with [18]..............

fly in [19].............. my soup?

WAITER: Can you remember everything you did before you noticed [20].............. fly?

CUSTOMER: I sat down and ordered [21].............. Soup of [22].............. Day.

WAITER: Have you considered upgrading to [23].............. latest Soup of [24].............. Day?

CUSTOMER: You have more than one Soup of [25].............. Day [26].............. each day?

WAITER: Yes, [27].............. Soup of [28].............. day is changed [29].............. every hour. [30].............. current Soup of [31].............. Day is tomato.

CUSTOMER: Fine. Bring me [32].............. tomato soup and [33].............. bill. I'm running late.

WAITER: Here you are, sir. [34].............. soup and [35].............. your bill.

CUSTOMER: This is [36].............. potato soup.

WAITER: Yes, sir. [37].............. tomato soup wasn't ready.

6 **Put the correct word into the gap: *these*, *those*, *they* or *them*.**

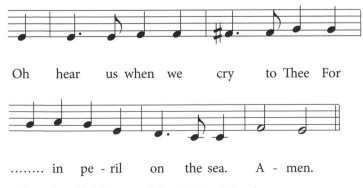

Oh   hear   us   when   we   cry   to Thee   For

........ in   pe - ril   on   the sea.   A - men.

*From the official hymn of the US Naval Academy.*

# Section 11 determiners (2): quantifiers

**Quantifiers**, like other determiners, come at the beginning of noun phrases, before any adjectives. They show **how much/many** we are talking about.

*some* strange ideas    *little* interest    *more* free time    *all* my friends
*both* hands    too *much* work    not *enough* chairs    *every* wet day

When quantifiers are used before other determiners or before pronouns, they are usually followed by *of* (see page 169).

*more of the* same    *some of his* ideas    *each of those* children    *few of them*

In this Section, we also cover **quantifying phrases** like a *great deal of, lots of*. These are not exactly determiners, but it is convenient to deal with them here.

*Every one of our cakes is special, every time*

# 50
percent more cream filling

The same great taste, but **50 percent less fat** and **33 percent fewer calories**

sweet taste and fun flavors,
with **75 percent less sugar**

Most people know that we should be eating more fruit and vegetables.

**But most of us aren't eating enough**

Less Sugar, **More Vitamins**

**MOST ADULTS EAT TOO MUCH SUGAR.**

*Up to 80 per cent of women aged 19 to 50 do not get enough vitamin D.*

Every day **26 million** adults in the UK eat **too much** salt.

# *all*

**not used for 'everybody' or 'everything'**  In modern English, we don't normally use *all* without a noun or pronoun to mean 'everybody/everyone' or 'everything'.

*All of the delegates agreed.*    *Everybody agreed.*    *We all agreed.*  (BUT NOT ~~All agreed.~~)
*I've written to all of the cousins.*    *I've written to everyone.*  (BUT NOT ~~... to all.~~)
*It all needs cleaning.*    *Everything needs cleaning.*  (BUT NOT ~~All needs cleaning.~~)

An exception: group emails often begin 'Dear All'.

*all that ...*  However, we can use *all that ...* to mean 'everything that ...'

*Tell me all (that) you can remember.*    *All (that) she earns goes to her children.*

The meaning can also be similar to 'the only thing(s) that ...'.

*All (that) I want is a place to sleep.*    *€20 is all (that) I've got till Friday.*

**leaving out** *the*  After *all*, we sometimes leave out *the* before numbers.

*She won medals in all three races.*

And we usually leave out *the* in *all day/night/week/year/winter/summer*.

*He sleeps all day and parties all night.*

Note the difference between *all day* (= 'from morning to night') and *every day* (= 'Monday, Tuesday, Wednesday, ...').

**1** **Correct (✓) or not (✗)?**

| | |
|---|---|
| 1  All I have is yours. ... | 7  She lost all she had. ... |
| 2  All of it is yours. ... | 8  She lost everything. ... |
| 3  All is yours. ... | 9  She lost all. ... |
| 4  All of the fields were under water. ... | 10  There are guests in all five rooms. ... |
| 5  All was under water. ... | 11  We did nothing all summer. ... |
| 6  Everything was under water. ... | 12  I've written to all family. ... |

**With pronoun objects** there are two possible structures.

*I've read all of them / them all.*    *She invited all of us / us all to coffee.*

**2** **Change the structure.**

▶ He's cleaned all of it.  He's cleaned it all.
▶ I love them all.  I love all of them.
1  Did you understand it all? ......................................................................
2  Do you want us all to work late? ......................................................................
3  Kara sends her regards to all of you. ......................................................................
4  I'll post all of them tomorrow. ......................................................................
5  The dog's eaten it all. ......................................................................
6  It's the same for all of us. ......................................................................

*all (of)*  After *all*, *of* is often **dropped** before **another determiner**, especially in British English.

*All (of) the trains were late.*    *All (of) my friends live a long way away.*

*all* **with the verb:**  When *all* refers to the subject it can also go in 'mid-verb' position (see page 180).

*All the children have gone home.* OR *The children have all gone home.*

# whole and all

**kinds of noun** We use *whole* mostly with **singular countable nouns**. Determiners come before *whole*. Note the difference in word order between *whole* and *all*.

*the whole* sweater – *all the* wool     *a whole* plate – *all the* food
*this whole* room – *all this* mess     *my whole* wardrobe – *all my* clothes

When there is no determiner, we use *the whole of*. This happens mostly in **generalisations**, and with **geographical names** and other proper nouns. (*All of* is also possible.)

*The whole of* science is based on observation. (OR *All of science* …)
We are expecting snow over *the whole of* Scotland. (OR … *all of Scotland*.)
She's translating *the whole of* Shakespeare into Arabic. (OR … *all of Shakespeare* …)

In other cases, we prefer *all* with uncountable nouns.

*The kids have drunk **all the juice**.* (NOT *… the whole juice.*)

**1** Write an expression with *all* or *whole* for each item in the box.

| the children   a class   a coconut   a football team ✓   the flowers ✓   China |
| the islands   the luggage   the meat   the MPs   the plan   the political party |
| the problem   the road system   the students   the traffic   the vegetables |

a whole football team     all (of) the flowers
............................................................................................
............................................................................................
............................................................................................
............................................................................................

**all with singular countable nouns** *All* is unusual with singular countable nouns, but it is possible when we are talking about things that are easily divided into parts. Compare:

*The whole knife was rusty.* (NOT *All the knife* …)     *all (of) the programme – the whole programme*
*all (of) my class – my whole class*     *all day – the whole day*

**2** Write expressions with *all* and *whole* for each item.

▸  my family  all (of) my family     my whole family
1  the country .................................................................................
2  this government .........................................................................
3  that week ...................................................................................
4  London .......................................................................................
5  the company ..............................................................................
6  our garden .................................................................................
7  South Africa ..............................................................................
8  the cake .....................................................................................

'All happy families resemble one another, but each unhappy family is unhappy in its own way.'
(*Tolstoy, Anna Karenina*)

'All the things I like to do are either illegal, immoral or fattening.'
(*Alexander Woolcott*)

'It is my ambition to say in ten sentences what others say in a whole book.'
(*Friedrich Nietzsche*)

'A man who has never gone to school may steal from a freight car; but if he has a university education, he may steal the whole railroad.'
(*Theodore Roosevelt*)

'An eye for an eye, and the whole world would be blind.'
(*Khalil Gibran*)

# both

**dropping words** After *both* we often drop *of* or *of the* in a noun phrase.

*both (of) my parents*     *both (of) these suggestions*     *both (of) the films / both films*

**With pronoun objects** there are two possible structures.

*I've seen **both of them / them both**.*     *She wrote to **both of us / us both**.*

**meaning** *Both* means 'each of two, separately'. We don't normally use *both* to refer to **one** activity done by two people together.

*My two brothers carried the piano upstairs.* (More natural than *Both my brothers carried the piano upstairs* – that would suggest that each of them did it once.)

**1** **Correct (✓) or not (✗)? (Two sentences are incorrect.)**

1  Both her sons have been to visit her  …
2  I need to talk to you both.  …
3  Both my parents first met in Paris.  …
4  Both of her sons have been to visit her  …
5  Have you got enough food for both us?  …
6  I've seen both those films already.  …

When *both* refers to the subject, it can also go with the verb in 'mid-position' (see page 180).

*Her sons **have both been** to visit her in hospital.*

# either and neither

**pronunciation** Many British people say the first syllable with the vowel /aɪ/ (as in *eye*). Many other British people, and most Americans, use the vowel /iː/ (as in *see*).

**following nouns and verbs** *Either* and *neither* are followed by **singular** nouns and verbs.

*either **hand**     neither **hand**     either **day** is OK*

With **either/neither of** + **plural noun/pronoun** we also normally use singular verbs.

***Does** either of the children **speak** French?     Neither of them **has** found a job.*

A plural verb is sometimes used in an informal style, especially after *neither*.

*Neither of the teams **were** very impressive.*

**1** **Put in *either (of)* or *neither (of)* with words from the box.**

| minister | species | child | the two star players | them | these courses | us | us |
|---|---|---|---|---|---|---|---|

1  Their meeting, so far as I could tell, did not bring …………………………………… any pleasure.
2  We're sorry, but I don't think …………………………………… can help you.
3  …………………………………… ever cleaned up his room.
4  Anyone who is interested in attending …………………………………… should contact the office.
5  …………………………………… spoke for a while, then she asked me: 'May I stay here?'
6  …………………………………………… looks likely to score in any match, ever.
7  Nobody believes that what …………………………………… says today will be policy tomorrow.
8  Both rats and humans have memory mechanisms, so we can study memory in ……………………………

***either*** **meaning 'each'** Occasionally *either* can mean *each*, especially with *side*.

*There are roses on **either side** of the door.*

# *every* and *each*

**the differences** *Every* and *each* are used with **singular** nouns and verbs. Their meaning is similar to *all (of)* + **plural noun**, but they can give more of a sense of 'separately' or 'one at a time'. They are usually both possible, but *each* can emphasise **individual differences**.

*We have now read* **all (of)** *the competition* **entries.** **Every entry** *has received careful consideration.* **Each finalist** *has produced impressive work in one way or another.*

Note that we do **not** use *every* to talk about **two** things or people.

*She can write with* **each hand.** (BUT NOT ... ~~with every hand.~~)

**1** **Circle** the correct or best answer.

1  The team have lost *each / every* match they've played this season.
2  *Each / Every* player has had a personal interview with the manager.
3  Every *player / players* would like to do better.
4  But *each match / each the match* brings new problems.
5  Higgins kicks equally badly with *each / every* foot.
6  Lucas falls over *each / every* time he tries a header.
7  Every player *has / have* tried to join another team
8  But each manager in turn *say / says* 'Sorry, no room'.

**every/each one of** Before a determiner with a plural noun, we use **every one of.** A following verb is **singular.** *Each (one) of* is used in the same way, but *one* is often dropped.

**Every one of** *his books* **is** *worth reading.*      **Each (one) of** *his plots* **has** *a new twist.*

The same structure is used before a **pronoun**.

*I've read* **every one of them.**      *I* **buy each (one) of them** *as soon as it comes out.*

**2** Correct (✓) or not (✗)?

1  Every of my friends lives in London.  …
2  I remember each one of my teachers.  …
3  Each of the rooms are painted in a different colour.  …
4  She's broken every one of her arms.  …
5  Every one of you needs to be here tomorrow at six o'clock.  …
6  Each one my brothers is strange in his own way.  …

**every two weeks etc** We can use a plural numerical expression after *every*.

*every two weeks*      *every three months*      *every ten years*

**3** Write a sentence with *every* to say how often you do something.

.......I buy a new coat every five years........................................................................

.................................................................................................................................

---

**NOTES**

**position of *each*** When *each* refers to the subject, it can be put either with the noun  or in 'mid-verb' position (see page 180).

> **Each suspect** *was seen separately.* OR *The suspects* **were each seen** *separately.*

**almost** We can say **almost every**, but not ~~almost each~~.

> *I like almost every one of Mozart's operas.* (BUT NOT ... ~~almost each one~~ ...)

# some, any, no, none: revise the basics

*some* and *any*: **the difference** *Some* most often means 'a (not large) number or amount of'.
It is rather like the article *a/an*, but is used with uncountable and plural nouns.
We use *some* most often in **affirmative (+)** sentences.
*Any* can have a similar meaning, but is used in **negative** sentences and in most **questions.**

*We've got **some** problems at work.     Barbara has made **some** mushroom soup.*
*There aren't **any** shops in our village.     Do you speak **any** German?*

We prefer *some* in **questions** when we **expect** or **invite** people to say **'Yes'** (for example, in **requests** and **offers**).

*Can I make some suggestions?     Would you like some more coffee?*

We use *any* in affirmative sentences with words that add a **negative** meaning.

*She **hardly** does **any** work.     I've **never** had **any** trouble with this car.*
*They **refused** to accept **any** help.     He **denied any** knowledge of the theft.*

**1**  **CHECK YOUR KNOWLEDGE.** (Circle) the correct form.
1  I've bought *some / any* new jeans.
2  Can I get you *some / any* water?
3  I've got hardly *some / any* clothes.
4  We don't need *some / any* help.
5  I scarcely speak *some / any* Arabic.
6  Here are *some / any* of my photos.
7  *Some / Any* people are really crazy.
8  May I use *some / any* of your coffee?

*any* **not negative**  Remember: *any* is not negative. For a **negative** meaning we use ***not any***.

*'Can I borrow some sugar?'  'Sorry, I have**n't** got **any**.'* (NOT ~~'Sorry, I've got any.'~~)

We don't normally use *not any* with singular countable nouns.

*We have**n't** got **a car**.* (NOT ~~We haven't got any car.~~)

*no* and *none*  *No* is a more emphatic way of saying '**not any**'.

*Sorry, we've got **no** milk.* (NOT ... ~~We haven't got no milk.~~)
*There were **no** newspapers this morning.*

At the beginning of a sentence, ***no*** is almost always used.

***No** children are allowed here.* (NOT ~~Not any children~~ ...)     ***No** buses run on Sundays.*

Before *of*, and without a noun, we use *none*.

***None** of us knew where he was.* (NOT ~~No of us~~ ...)     *'Any problems?'  '**None**.'*

To talk about **two** people or things, we use ***neither***, not *none*.

*Neither of my parents has written to me.* (NOT ~~None of my parents~~ ...)

**2**  **CHECK YOUR KNOWLEDGE.** Correct (✓) or not (✗)?
1  I haven't got any ideas. ...
2  I've got no ideas. ...
3  I've got any. ...
4  I've got none. ...
5  Not any dogs can speak. ...
6  No dogs can speak. ...
7  No of them were ever seen again. ...
8  None of her letters arrived. ...
9  None of my arms is very strong. ...

***somebody, anybody* etc**  The differences between *somebody* and *someone*, *somewhere* and *anywhere* etc are similar to the differences between *some* and *any*.

> 'Can you imagine a world without men?
> No crime and lots of happy, fat women.'
> (*Nicole Hollander*)

# *some/any* or no quantifier

> **limited numbers/quantities** We prefer *some* and *any* to talk about **limited numbers or quantities**. We don't use *some/any* to talk about **unlimited numbers or quantities**, or when we are not thinking about numbers or quantities at all. Compare:
>
> *Can you buy **some eggs**?* (perhaps a dozen)    *I don't eat **eggs**.* (in general)
> *Is there **any petrol** in the car?*    ***Petrol** is really expensive.*
> *Put **some wood** on the fire.*    *Most paper is made from **wood**.*

> We **don't** use *some* to talk about **exact numbers or quantities**.

> *Dachshunds have **very short legs**.* (NOT *… some very short legs.*)

> We **don't** normally use *some* in **descriptions** or **definitions**.

> *He's got **long hair**.* (NOT *He's got some long hair.*)
> *Both my brothers are **lawyers**.* (NOT *Both my brothers are some lawyers.*)

**1** Put in *some, any* or nothing (–).

1  Bring ........................... water in case we get thirsty.
2  The President appealed for ........................... medicine for the refugees.
3  The baby has ........................... beautiful little toes.
4  You have ........................... great ideas.
5  I don't think the people next door are ........................... students.
6  I got talking to ........................... students in the pub.
7  Scientists say there is mostly ........................... iron at the centre of the earth.
8  The human body consists mainly of ........................... water.
9  Have you got ........................... music that's good for dancing?
10  Polar bears have ........................... thick fur because of the cold.

**2** Put in *some water* (three times), *any water* (twice) and *water* (three times).

1  … We came across a natural well, completely still, reflecting the sky and the rocks. I knelt down, scooped ................................... into my palms, and began to drink. The water tasted wonderfully sweet. I felt completely satisfied.

2  they will not be allowed to dig holes for ................................... on their traditional land. Tribal leaders protested that

3  Add the garlic and chilli and some peeled tomatoes. Sprinkle the tomatoes with salt and pepper, pour on ................................... and put the lid on.

4  My last request was "Do you have ...................................?" He brought me a jug with clean water. It was the cleanest water I had seen for years.

5  ................................... has disappeared from supermarket shelves after the discovery of dangerous chemicals in several samples of bottled mineral water. Analysts say

6  We got ................................... and red cabbage and put them into a beaker and heated it. When the water went purple we mixed some of it with acid, alkalis and washing powder. The test tube with acid turned pink, the alkalis turned yellow and the washing powder turned green.

7  We attempted to boil the kettle for a nice cup of tea. This took ages, and when the kettle had boiled, there was hardly ................................... in it – the kettle was leaking badly. It was the worst hotel I have ever stayed in.

8  Scientists may have solved the longstanding mystery surrounding the origin of ................................... on earth. It is now believed that comets and asteroids

# more about *some*

**contrastive use of *some*** We can use *some* (pronounced /sʌm/) to make a **contrast**.

***Some** people like her, but I don't.*     ***Some** say this, others say that.*
***Some** children learn to read very early.* (But others don't.)

***some* meaning 'unknown'** *Some* (pronounced /sʌm/) can refer to an unknown person or thing.
It often suggests lack of interest, or a low opinion of somebody/something.

*'Where's Harry?' 'I don't know. Out at **some** meeting.'*
*She married **some** furniture salesman, I think.*

**enthusiastic *some*** Another informal use of *some* is to express enthusiastic approval.

*Boy, that was **some** party! It went on for three days!*

***some* meaning 'an impressive number'** *Some* can suggest that a number is impressive.

*Our products are exported to **some** sixteen countries.*
*The letter was signed by **some** eighty distinguished scientists.*

**1** **How is *some* pronounced in these sentences? Say them.**

▶ We need some bread. /sm/     ▶ I'll buy some. /sʌm/
1  There are some children at the door. …
2  Some of us are worried about the future. …
3  Shall I put on some music? …
4  His work has won some eight international awards. …
5  She's gone to live in some village near Cambridge. …
6  I've got some work to do this evening. …
7  Some people believe him. I can't think why. …
8  We're out of coffee. Can you get some on your way home? …

**2** **Put the letters of the expressions from the box into the texts.**

> A  some 3,000   B  some five months   C  some of *(twice)*
> D  some people *(twice)*   E  some stupid law   F  some two million

1  … need less sleep than others. Margaret Thatcher famously got by on four hours a night as Prime Minister, while George W. Bush wanted at least eight. Scientists may now be able to explain why: new research suggests that … us are genetically programmed to spend longer in bed than others.

2  Why are … us such bad timekeepers? Sometimes it is a matter of personality. … are simply arrogant. They think 'My time is more valuable than yours'.

3  "I have a wonderful piano back home that I can't bring because … says you can't take a piano on a plane," he says.

4  The ship will carry … passengers, and will be like a floating luxury hotel.

5  Yesterday, … users of the city's underground railway tried to board packed buses, sat in long traffic jams or walked to work after strikes stopped trains running.

6  Her journey started in Venezuela, and ended … and 4,500 miles later in the deep south of Chile. The journey in between, by plane, bus, car, on foot and horse, was not always easy.

# more about *any* and *no*

*if any*  We often use *any* with *if*.

*If you have **any** difficulty, let me know.*

We can also use *any* **without** *if* to mean 'if there is/are any'.

*Any fog will disappear by midday.*      *Let me know about **any** problems.*

We prefer *some* to suggest a **positive** expectation.

*If you want **some** really good advice, go and talk to Dan.*

*any* **for free choice**  We can use *any* to give the idea of **free choice**, with the meaning of 'it doesn't matter who/which/what'. With this meaning, *any* is common in affirmative sentences as well as questions and negatives, and can be used with singular countable nouns.

*Smoking kills – ask **any** doctor.*      *Come **any** day you like.*
*She goes out with **any** boy who asks her.*

In **negative** sentences, we often use *just any* for this meaning to avoid confusion. Compare:

*He doesn't work for **anybody**.* (This could mean 'He works for nobody.')
*He doesn't work for **just anybody**.* (He only works for certain people.)

*no problem* **etc**  We can use *no* with **singular countable nouns**, but only when the meaning is **emphatic**.

*That's **no problem**.*      *He found himself with no money, **no house** and **no job**.*
*George is **no fool**.*      (BUT *A whale is **not a** fish*. NOT ~~A whale is no fish.~~ – not emphatic)

**1**  **Put in words from the box with *any*, *no* or *not a*.**

| bird   charity   complaints   driver   help   leftover food   passport   post office   questions   thief |

1   If you need ....................................., just phone me.
2   How can I go to America with ...................................?
3   Ann didn't take the money. She's a strange person, but she's ...................................!
4   ................................... should be addressed to the manager.
5   I don't give money to just ...................................
6   A platypus lays eggs, but it's ...................................
7   'Where can I pay my car tax?' 'At ...................................
8   If there are ..................................., I'll answer them after the talk.
9   The train couldn't leave because there was ...................................
10  Can you put ................................... in the fridge?

## NOTES

*none*  Before *of*, or with no noun, we use *none* instead of *no*.
   *None of the letters arrived.*      *I wanted coffee, but there was **none** left.*

**singular or plural**  After *any/none of* with a plural noun, we can use a singular verb (more formal) or a plural verb (informal and common).
   *If **any of the new students needs** information, he or she should ask at the office.*
   ***None of my friends** really **understand** me.*

For *any* and *no* as adverbs (e.g. *any better, no different*), see page 186.

# much, many, more and most

*much* and *many* not used  In **informal** speech, *much* and *many* are used in questions and negatives, but they are **unusual** in **affirmative (+)** sentences (especially *much*).

*Have you got **much** work just now?* BUT NOT ~~I've got much work just now.~~
*There aren't **many** cinemas here.* BUT NOT USUALLY *There are many cinemas here.*

Instead, we use expressions like *a lot of*, *plenty of* etc in informal speech.

*I've got **a lot of** work just now.*     *There are **plenty of** cinemas here.*

However, *much* and *many* are common after *too*, *so* and *as*, even in affirmative sentences.

*We've had **too much** rain this month.*     *There are **so many** people who need help.*
*Help yourself – take **as much** as you like.*

formal style  In **formal** speech or writing, *much* and *many* are more **normal** in **affirmative** sentences.

*There has been **much** discussion about the causes of the recent crisis.*
***Many** of you are wondering why I have called you here today.*

**1**  **Make these sentences more formal (>F) or more informal (>I).**

▶  Much time has been spent on this. (>I)  *A lot / Lots / Plenty of time has been spent on this.*
▶  We've received plenty of suggestions. (>F)  *We have received many suggestions.*

1  Dr Andrews speaks many languages. (>I)
   ................................................................................................................

2  There has been much discussion about the results. (>I)
   ................................................................................................................

3  The staff have got a lot of reasons for striking. (>F)
   ................................................................................................................

4  The new regulations have caused much confusion. (>I)
   ................................................................................................................

5  Plenty of voters stayed at home on election day. (>F)
   ................................................................................................................

6  Many English children have difficulty learning to spell. (>I)
   ................................................................................................................

*many a*  This structure is not very common in modern English.

*There is a house in New Orleans; it's called the Rising Sun.*
*It's been the ruin of **many a** poor boy; and I, oh God, am one.*
(American folk song)

*More* and *most* are the comparative and superlative of both *much* and *many*.

***more** time     **more** problems     **most** modern art     **most** cars*

We normally use ***most***, not *the most*, to mean 'the majority of'.

*I dislike **most** pop music.* (NOT ~~I dislike the most pop music.~~)
***Most** children like junk food.* (NOT ~~The most children like junk food.~~)
***Most** of us were really tired.* (NOT ~~The most of us~~ ...)

But *the most* is possible when we are directly comparing one situation with another.

*Lucy found **(the) most** blackberries, but she also ate **(the) most**.*
*Which of your parents earns **(the) most** money?*

For expressions like *far more, a lot more*, see page 186.

# little, few, less, fewer, least and fewest

**(a) little and (a) few** *Little* and *few* are rather **negative**: they mean '**not much/many**'.
*A little* and *a few* are more **positive**: their meaning is more like '**some**'.

*Shakespeare knew **little** Latin and less Greek.*
*I know **a little** French – enough to get by in France.*
***Few** people today believe that the earth is flat.*
*I'm still in contact with **a few** of my old school friends.*

**1** *Little* **or** *a little*? *Few* **or** *a few*?
1  I'm sorry, but there is ........................... point in further discussion.
2  I can finish this in ........................... hours – no problem.
3  He explained everything several times, but ........................... of us understood him.
4  The refugees had ........................... water and no food.
5  Most people went home at the interval, but ........................... of us stayed till the end.
6  We all need ........................... encouragement from time to time.

**formality** *Little* and *few* (without *a*) are rather **formal**; in a **conversational** style we prefer
***not much/many*** or ***only a little/few***.

*Shakespeare didn't know **much** Latin.*   ***Only a few** people think the earth is flat.*

**2** **Make these expressions more informal.**
▶  little time *..not much time..*
    OR *..only a little time..*
1  few friends ...................................
2  little milk ...................................
3  little hope ...................................
4  few answers ...................................
5  little work ...................................
6  few cities ...................................

**Less etc** *Less* and *fewer* are **comparative**: they are the opposite of *more*.
*Least* and *fewest* are **superlative**: they are the opposite of *most*.
*Less* and *least* are used with **singular** (uncountable) nouns.
*Fewer* and *fewest* are used with **plural** nouns.

*less* time    *less* money    *fewer* jobs    *fewer* houses

*Less* is also common with plurals (e.g. **less jobs**, **less houses**). However, some people believe that
this is incorrect, including many teachers and examiners, so be careful!

**3** **Write** *less / the least / fewer / the fewest*.
1  I spend ................................... money on clothes in the whole family.
2  As the years go by, I seem to read ................................... books.
3  ................................... boys than girls study languages.
4  I have much ................................... interest in politics than most people.
5  Which class has ................................... students in it?
6  John does ................................... practice than anybody, but he usually wins.
7  The people who do the most talking sometimes talk ................................... sense.
8  And the people who say nothing at all make ................................... mistakes.
9  Our team has won ................................... matches in the group.
10  There were ................................... people at the meeting than usual.

For expressions like *much less, far fewer*, see page 186.

# enough

word order  Remember that *enough* comes **after adjectives** but **before nouns**.

*Is your room **warm enough**? Have you got **enough blankets**?*

Note the different possibilities when *enough* comes with **adjective + noun**.

*We haven't got **enough cold beer**. (We've got some cold beer, but not enough.)*
*We haven't got **cold enough beer**. (We've got some beer, but it's not cold enough.)*

**1** Write sentences for the situations, using *We haven't got* and *enough*.

▶ The room is too small. ..*We haven't got a big enough room.*............
▶ We need more sweet biscuits. ..*We haven't got enough sweet biscuits.*............
1 The ladder is too short. We haven't got ............
2 The knives are too blunt ............
3 The car is too slow. ............
4 We need more fresh bread. ............
5 The lights are too dim. ............
6 We need more hot water. ............
7 The screws are too big. ............
8 You need more green paint. ............
9 Your handwriting's very unclear. ............
10 I need more white T-shirts. ............

enough … (for) … to …  An infinitive structure is common after *enough*.

*Have you got **enough** paint **to finish** the wall?*
*I don't think there are **enough** of us **to make up** a football team.*
*We do not have **enough** empirical data **to come** to a firm conclusion.*

If the infinitive needs another subject, we introduce it with **for**.

*Is there **enough** hot water **for me to have** a bath?*

**2** Make questions beginning *Is/Are there …?*

▶ time / me / shower  ..*Is there enough time for me to have a shower?*............
1 eggs / me / make omelette ............
2 chairs / us all / sit down ............
3 coffee / everybody / have some ............
4 time / me / make a phone call ............
5 petrol / us / get home ............
6 money / both of us / get tickets ............
7 computers / John / use one ............
8 copies of the book / me / take three ............

adverbs with *enough*  Before *enough*, we can use *(not) nearly, just, quite* or *more than*.

*There's **not nearly enough** milk.*     *I've done **quite enough work** for one day.*

**3** Write about a country, city or other place using these structures.

▶ ..*In my town, there are not nearly enough open spaces.*............
............
............
............
............
............
............

# quantifying phrases

***deal, amount, number*** *etc **A great deal** and expressions with **amount** are most common with uncountable nouns. With plurals, we usually prefer expressions like **a large/small number**.*

***a great deal*** *of trouble*     ***a small amount*** *of money*
***a large number*** *of complaints* (MORE NORMAL THAN *a large amount of complaints* or *a great deal of complaints*).

*When singular quantifying expressions are used with nouns, a following verb is singular after uncountable nouns, plural after plural nouns (see page 126).*

*A large amount of **money has** been stolen.*
*A large number of **books have** been stolen.* (NOT USUALLY *A large number of books has …*)
*The majority of the **prisoners have** been recaptured.*
*A couple of their **friends have** found them a place to live.*

***a lot of*** *and **lots of** Remember that both of these informal expressions can be used with singular or plural nouns. A following verb is singular after singular nouns, plural after plural nouns.*

*A lot of **money has** been spent … / Lots of **money has** been spent …*
*A lot of **students think** … / Lots of **students think** …*

**1 Choose the best form.**

1   The majority of people *believe / believes* things are getting worse.
2   Only a small *number / amount* of voting papers *was / were* spoiled.
3   Lots of time *is / are* wasted in committee meetings.
4   A lot of us *is / are* worried about the future.
5   A large *number / amount* of money will be needed for the repairs.
6   The majority of criminals *is / are* non-violent.
7   A *great deal / large number* of my friends are mad about football.
8   A large proportion of school-leavers *has / have* trouble finding jobs.

**2 Put the letters of the expressions from the box into the texts.**

| A a great deal of pleasure    B a great deal of research    C a great deal of sympathy |
| D a large amount of ammunition    E a large amount of money    F a large amount of tax |
| G a large number of shops    H a large number of people    I a large number of frozen meals |

1   He was a loving husband and father, a great actor and a real gentleman in the true sense of the word. He gave … to many people by his acting, and I know that I will be only one of many who will miss him.

2   In the story, Shirley decides to fulfil an old dream and go to Greece. Leaving her husband a note to explain where she has gone, and …, she just takes off.

3   Armed police were called to the area in an effort to find him this afternoon. It is feared that he may have slipped into nearby woodland, armed with two shotguns and ….

4   I have … for those who are genuinely unable to work through illness.

5   Someone told me that if I bought a property with cash I would be hit for …. Is this true?

6   The city centre manager admitted that because of the financial crisis, … in the city are lying empty.

7   There is now … to suggest that it is not teachers' subject knowledge that determines how well their pupils achieve, but how they use their assessment of pupils' progress to plan and shape succeeding lessons.

8   I've bought myself a piggy bank into which I put a pound daily. It's not …, but it becomes reassuringly heavy, and there's a certain childish enjoyment in piling the money into towers in order to count it.

9   The study shows that for the first time in history … of all incomes cannot cook.

# *of* with quantifiers

*some of, any of, much of* etc  Before **another determiner** (e.g. *a, the, this, my*), and before *it/us/you/them*, we use **quantifiers with *of*.** Compare:

*some* friends (NOT ~~*some of friends*~~)     *some of my* friends (NOT ~~*some my friends*~~)
*any* boots     *any of these* boots     *any of them*
not *much* information     not *much of the* information     not *much of it*

Before *of*, we use *every one* and *none*, not *every* and *no*.

*every branch*     *every one of* our branches     *no ring*     *none of* these rings

We use **quantifier + *of*** before geographical and personal names and similar words.

*He travelled through **most of** Europe before he was 20.     I've seen too **much of** Susan this week.*

**1**  **Put in the quantifiers with or without *of*. Make any other changes that are necessary.**
   1  Here are ..................................... my photos. (*some*)
   2  ..................................... people are really crazy. (*some*)
   3  I don't want ....................................., thanks. (*any*)
   4  You can see ..................................... films without going to the cinema. (*most*)
   5  .............. the trains were on time. (*no*)
   6  .............. the lectures were at all interesting. (*few*)
   7  They didn't eat ..................................... it. (*much*)
   8  ..................................... them had a different solution. (*every*)
   9  There was very ..................................... discussion of the plans. (*little*)
  10  ..................................... the farm was flooded. (*most*)

*all (of), both (of)*  After *all* and *both*, we often **drop *of*** before another determiner.

*all (of) her* friends     *both (of) my* knees

*a lot of, the majority of* etc  After **longer quantifying expressions** (see page 168), we always use *of* before nouns, even if there is no other determiner.

*a lot of* people (NOT ~~*a lot people*~~)     *a great deal of* trouble     *the majority of* voters

**verb after *any of* etc**  With *any, none, neither* and *either of* + **plural noun/pronoun**, singular and plural verbs are both possible. **Plural** verbs are usually more **informal**.

*Do/Does* any of these lights work?     None of my friends *speak(s)* Italian.
Neither of his parents *was/were* at home.

**2**  **Correct (✓) or not (✗)?**

  1  I've lost all my papers. ...
  2  'Coffee?' 'Yes, a lot of, please.' ...
  3  Neither of my sisters is married. ...
  4  I've lost most my money. ...
  5  The majority of us disagree. ...
  6  Wait a couple minutes, please. ...
  7  None of my friends were interested. ...
  8  I've seen most Europe and some America. ...
  9  She's got pain in both her legs. ...
 10  None of my friends was interested. ...
 11  We've had a great deal of trouble. ...
 12  I doubt if any of them understand you. ...

*us all* etc  Instead of *all of it/us/you/them*, we can use *it all, us all* etc (see page 157.) This structure is also possible with *both* (see page 159).

# more practice

**① Which is/are correct?**

1 I've told him ... **A** *all* **B** *everything* **C** both
2 ... music. **A** *Everybody likes* **B** *All like* **C** both
3 They explained their plans to ... **A** *all of us* **B** *us all* **C** both
4 He's drunk ... **A** *all the milk* **B** *the whole milk* **C** both
5 I like ... **A** *both them* **B** *both of them* **C** both
6 A lot of people ... she's right **A** *think* **B** *thinks* **C** both
7 Lots of people ... she's right. **A** *think* **B** *thinks* **C** both
8 There isn't much to eat, but we've got ... eggs. **A** *few* **B** *a few* **C** both
9 ... any of your friends speak French? **A** *Do* **B** *Does* **C** both
10 We haven't got ... glasses. **A** *big enough* **B** *enough big* **C** both

**② Correct the mistakes or write Correct.**

▶ ~~Each them~~ got a present. ...Each of them............... OR ...They each..............
▶ I've been waiting all day. ...Correct.......................
1 Jamie has passed all five exams. .......................................
2 Write down all you can remember. .......................................
3 I've written to every of my cousins. .......................................
4 They collect our rubbish every two weeks .......................................
5 Some salesman came to the door today. I told him to go away. .......................................
6 Let me know about any problems you have. .......................................
7 Is there enough for everybody to have some? .......................................
8 You can have either room – they're all free. .......................................
9 The men both picked the bed up and threw it out of the window. .......................................
10 Water is composed of some hydrogen and some oxygen. .......................................

**③ Which of these is most formal?**

> A Plenty of people are worried about rising prices.  B Many people are worried about rising prices.
> C A lot of people are worried about rising prices.

... is most formal.

**④ Which person is probably in more of a hurry?**

> A Sorry, I can't stop. I haven't got any time to talk.
> B Sorry, I can't stop. I've got no time to talk.

... is probably in more of a hurry.

**⑤ What does this mean?**

> I don't read just any book.

**A** I don't read any books at all.  **B** I only read books that interest me.
**C** I read more than one book at a time.

**⑥ Does the speaker have a bicycle or a car?**

> I had to put new tyres on every wheel.

.......................................

**7** Look at these statistics, taken from the internet. (They are not necessarily all accurate!) Then complete some of the sentences.

89% of British people live in towns or cities.
0.8% of British people work in agriculture.
70% of people in India work in agriculture.
Les than 9% of people in the world own a car.
63% of American people have a pet.
80–90% of American adults say they believe in God.
Over 50% of British adults are married.
Over 10% of British adults are separated or divorced.
Nearly 20% of British adults have a university degree.
Nearly 30% of British adults have no educational qualifications.
60,000 Scottish people speak Scots Gaelic.
29% of British people aged 16–18 wear glasses or contact lenses.
Around two million adult Americans are in prison.

**According to the statistics:**

The majority of ....................................................................

The majority of ....................................................................

Nearly all .......................................................................

Most .........................................................................

A large proportion of ..............................................................

A surprising number of ...............................................................

A large number of ..............................................................

Surprisingly many ................................................................

Not many ...................................................................

Surprisingly few ...............................................................

A minority of ..............................................................

Only a few .................................................................

Very few ................................................................

Hardly any ...............................................................

**8** INTERNET EXERCISE. Use a search engine to find a few interesting statistics about another country, and write some sentences like the ones in Exercise 7.

.................................................................................................................

.................................................................................................................

.................................................................................................................

.................................................................................................................

.................................................................................................................

'We have lots of information technology. We just don't have any information.'

# Section 12  adjectives, adverbs and comparison

## adjectives and adverbs

The grammar of adjectives and adverbs should mostly be well known at this level. A few more problematic points are revised or introduced in the following pages. Some specific adjectives and adverbs are dealt with in Appendix 10, page 309. For the spelling of adverbs ending in *-ly*, see page 296.

## comparison

We often express the idea of 'how much' by comparing one thing (or event or quality) with others, or with some standard. Common ways of doing this are:

**comparative structures**

*old**er** than*    ***more*** *reliable than*    *the **biggest***    ***most*** *unusual*    *as much **as***
*less interesting than*    *the **least** effective*    ***more** and **more***

**conjunctions, prepositions,  adjectives and adverbs**

***as** everybody expected*    ***like** a bird*    ***different** from*    *the **same** as*    *so easy*
***such** a fool*    ***rather** poor*    ***quite** remarkable*    ***very** late*    ***too** early*    *cool **enough***
***a lot***    *not **much***    ***how** fast?*

Most of these structures should be well known to advanced students. This Section revises some points that may still cause difficulty, and introduces some new material.

Imperial

world's smallest!
**real!**
natural!
world's biggest!
healthy!
**tasty!**
IRRESISTIBLY CRUNCHY!
*faster!*  **cooler!**
SAFER!
S T Y L I S H !
luxurious
super tough!  **FREE!**
organic!
essential!

**Imperial** thick double cream has a unique, fresh taste and texture. Beautifully firm and silky rather than thin and watery, it stays in shape and stands on top of fruit or pastries without soaking in.

That's why **Imperial** is the deliciously different and exceptionally versatile natural thick double cream.

# adjective or adverb?

*friendly* etc  A few words ending in *-ly* are normally **adjectives**, not adverbs. Examples: *costly, cowardly, deadly, friendly, likely, lively, lonely, lovely, silly, ugly, unlikely.*

*a **cowardly** decision*    *a **deadly** poison*    ***friendly** people*    *a **silly** idea*

There are no adverbs *friendly/friendlily* etc; the ideas have to be expressed differently.

*She smiled **in a friendly way**.* OR *She gave **a friendly smile**.* (NOT ~~She smiled friendly.~~)

***Daily**, weekly, monthly, yearly* and *early* can be **both adjectives and adverbs**.

*It's a **daily** paper.*    *It comes out **daily**.*    *I got up **early** to catch the **early** train.*

**1** **Put in some of the adjectives from the box (different answers are possible).**

> costly  cowardly  deadly  early  friendly  likely  lively  lonely  lovely
> monthly  silly  ugly  unlikely

1  a(n) ........................... weapon
2  a(n) ........................... attack
3  a(n) ........................... mistake
4  Cinderella's ........................... sisters
5  in the ........................... event of a crash
6  a long and ........................... wait
7  ........................... flowers
8  ........................... music
9  very ........................... people
10 ........................... letters

**adjective complements**  **Adjectives** are used after **link verbs** (e.g. *be, seem, sound, feel*), because they describe the **subject** rather than an action.

*That sounds **right**.* (NOT ~~That sounds rightly.~~)    *I felt **angry**.* (NOT ~~I felt angrily.~~)

This can happen after other verbs, when we describe the subject or object, not the action. Compare:

*He fell **awkwardly** and twisted his shoulder.*
*He fell **unconscious** on the floor.* (NOT ~~He fell unconsciously.~~)
*I painted the wall **badly**.* (NOT ~~I painted the wall bad.~~)
*I painted the wall **white**.* (NOT ~~I painted the wall whitely.~~)

**2** **Put in adjectives from the box (but make one of them an adverb).**

> careful  clean  quiet  short  small  tight

1  As the plane approached the runway, I pulled my seatbelt ...........................
2  SUPER BLANCO gets your clothes ........................... every time!
3  I thought if I stayed really ..........................., nobody would notice me.
4  Chop the onions up really ..........................., can you?
5  Please handle this box ...........................; the contents are fragile.
6  Don't cut my hair so ........................... this time, please.

**special cases.**  Some adjective forms are used informally as adverbs, and some common adverbs have two forms with different uses.

*He talks **real funny**.*    *How **high** can you jump?*    *We think very **highly** of her.*

> 'Don't wait for people to be friendly, show them how.'
> (*Unknown author*)

> 'There are times when it is more courageous to be cowardly.'
> (*Norman Reilly Raine*)

> 'Being the boss anywhere is lonely. Being a female boss in a world of mostly men is especially so.'
> (*Robert Frost*)

> 'Don't be afraid to look silly.'
> (*Tara Strong*)

# adjectives: order

This is a complicated (and not very important) point. There is a lot of variation in usage; general tendencies are as follows. For fuller information, consult a comprehensive grammar.

> **Adjectives (and nouns used like adjectives)** for **colour, origin/place, material** and **purpose** go in that order before nouns. Other words come before these.

|  | OTHER | COLOUR | ORIGIN/PLACE | MATERIAL | PURPOSE |  |
|---|---|---|---|---|---|---|
| a | big | green | Italian | glass | flower | vase |
|  | cheap | brown |  | leather | football | boots |

> **Opinions** often come **before descriptions**.

*boring* old books      a *sweet* little girl      *cool* new clothes

**1** **Here are descriptions from newspapers and magazines. Rewrite each description in the right order.**

  ▶  group: *drama / college*  ..college drama group.................................... (place before purpose)
  1  eyes: *wide / blue* .........................................................................................
  2  pants: *nylon / ski / black* ...............................................................................
  3  cap: *red / woollen* .......................................................................................
  4  boots: *German / climbing* ...............................................................................
  5  town: *northern / charming / little* ....................................................................
  6  jacket: *long / cotton* ....................................................................................
  7  glasses: *steel-framed / dark / heavy* .................................................................
  8  house: *old / lovely* .......................................................................................
  9  student: *American / strange / new* ....................................................................
  10  university: *modern, concrete and glass, impressive* ...............................................

> ***First**, **next** and **last** usually come before numbers and *few*.
>
> the ***first three*** weeks (MORE NORMAL THAN *the three first weeks*)
> the ***first few*** miles      the ***next six*** lessons      my ***last two*** holidays

**2** **How have you spent the last few days? What are you going to do in the next three or four days/weeks/months/years? Write a few sentences.**

  In the last few days ..............................................................................................
  ...........................................................................................................................
  ...........................................................................................................................
  ...........................................................................................................................
  ...........................................................................................................................

> **Note:** *And* is used with adjectives before a noun if we are talking about **different parts** of something, or if we are saying that something belongs to **different categories**.
>   *a green and black dress      a national and international problem*
>   (BUT NOT ~~a nice and old woman~~)
> After a noun, *and* is normal before the last of two or more adjectives.
>   *He was like a winter's day: **short, dark and dirty**.*

For commas with adjectives, see page 301.

# position of adjectives

Most adjectives can go **either before a noun or after a link verb** like *be, seem, look*. But some usually only go in one of these places.

**mainly before nouns** *elder* and *eldest, old* (= 'having lasted a long time'), *little* (especially in British English) and *live* (= 'not dead'). Compare:

*My **elder** sister is a pilot.     She's three years **older** than me. (NOT ~~She's three years elder~~ ...)*
*She's a very **old** friend. (NOT THE SAME AS She's very **old**. She might be quite young.)*

**Intensifying** (emphasising) adjectives *complete, mere, sheer, total* etc normally only go before nouns.

*He's a **mere** child. (BUT NOT ~~That child is mere.~~)     It was a total failure.*

**mainly after link verbs** *afloat, afraid, alight, alike, alive, alone, asleep, awake.* Compare:

*The baby's **asleep**.     A **sleeping** baby. (NOT ~~an asleep baby~~)*
*She was **afraid**.     A **frightened** woman. (NOT ~~an afraid woman~~)*

*Well* and *ill* are most common after link verbs. Compare:

*I'm not feeling **well**.     He's a very **healthy** man. (LESS COMMON ... a well man)*
*Her mother's **ill**.     It must be hard to spend your life looking after a **sick** person.*

**1** **Put one word into each sentence.**

1  It's a nice ..................... flat.     The flat is very ..................... (*little, small*)
2  The cat keeps bringing in ..................... mice.     My grandfather is still ..................... (*alive, live*)
3  His idea is ..................... madness.     That kind of madness is ..................... (*sheer, worrying*)
4  I like being ......................     Annie's a very..................... woman. (*lonely, alone*)
5  The days feel like ..................... dreams.     Is Emma ..................... yet? (*awake, waking*)
6  The pool is full of ..................... leaves.     The boat won't stay ..................... for long. (*floating, afloat*)

**Complex adjective phrases** usually come after nouns, most often in relative clauses.

*We need people (who are) **prepared to travel**. (NOT ... ~~prepared to travel people~~)*

But we can split expressions beginning with *different, similar, the same, next, last, first, second* etc, *difficult, easy* and comparatives and superlatives.

***different** ideas **from yours**     the **next** train **to arrive**     an **easy** problem **to solve***

**2** **Put together the two groups of words in each case (without adding any) to make one correct expression.**

▶  a religion / different from hers  *a different religion from hers* ...........................
1  a life / different from this one .................................................................
2  the item / first on the agenda .................................................................
3  a dialect / difficult to understand ...............................................................
4  singers / better than you .......................................................................
5  the delegate / last to speak .....................................................................

---

**NOTES**

**fixed phrases** In a few fixed phrases (mostly titles) the adjective follows the noun.
   *Secretary **General**     court **martial** (= 'military court')     Poet **Laureate***
   *President **Elect**     Attorney **General**     God **Almighty**!*

**Note also the order in** *six feet tall, two years old* etc; *something nice, nothing new* etc.

For *available, possible, present* and *proper* before or after nouns, see pages 306–307.

# participles used as adjectives

**When we use *-ing* forms** as **adjectives**, they are called 'present participles'. We can also use past participles (e.g. *closed, broken*) as adjectives. (The names 'present' and 'past' participle are misleading; the forms have no particular time reference.)

*I imagined that I was a **falling** leaf.*    *Will you glue this **broken** chair?*

**Compound adjectives** can be made with participles. We use hyphens (-) before nouns.

*quick-growing trees*    *home-made cake*    *a recently-built house*

Note the word order in these compound adjectives when the participle has an object.

*French-speaking Canadians* (NOT ~~speaking-French Canadians~~)

**1  Make compound adjectives.**

▶ birds that eat seeds  ..*seed-eating birds*..
1  Finns who speak Swedish ........................
2  bats that eat fruit ........................
3  people who love music ........................
4  traffic that moves fast ........................

5  people who work hard ........................
6  a story that never ends ........................
7  headphones that reduce noise ........................
8  equipment that moves earth ........................

***very* or *(very) much*** When a past participle is used as an **adjective** (often to talk about feelings and reactions), we can emphasise it with ***very***.

*a **very frightened** animal*    *She looked **very surprised**.*

When the word is part of a **passive verb**, we prefer ***much*** or ***very much***.

*He's **much imitated** by other writers.* (NOT *... ~~very imitated~~ ...*)
*Britain's trade position has been **very much weakened** by inflation.*

The difference between the two structures is not always clear, and it is often necessary to consult a good dictionary to see how particular past participles are used.

**2  Put in *very* (four times) and *very much* (four times).**

1  ........................ shocked
2  ........................ improved
3  ........................ impressed
4  ........................ pleased

5  ........................ changed
6  ........................ enlarged
7  ........................ upset
8  ........................ misunderstood

## NOTES

***the problems discussed* etc**  Not all past participles can be used as adjectives. But note the common use of a past participle after a noun (rather like a relative clause: see page 211).

> *I didn't understand the **problems discussed**.* (= '... the problems that were discussed')
> *The **people questioned** were all released.* (NOT ~~The questioned people~~ ...)

**active past participles**  Past participles used as adjectives normally have a passive meaning. A ***broken*** *chair* is a chair that **has been broken.** But there are some exceptions – for example, an *escaped prisoner* is a prisoner who **has escaped.** Other exceptions:

> *a **retired** general/teacher* etc    *a **fallen** leaf/tree* etc    *a **vanished** civilisation* etc
> *a **collapsed** building/lung* etc    ***developed** countries* etc    ***advanced** students* etc
> *a **grown-up** son* etc    ***faded** colours* etc    ***increased** activity* etc    ***swollen** ankles* etc

Some active past participles are only used in compounds, or after *be*. Examples:

> *the **recently-arrived** train* (BUT NOT ~~the arrived train~~)    *a **well-read** woman*
> *a **much-travelled** man*    *Where are you **camped**?*    *Those days are **gone**.*

***short-haired* etc**  *-ed* can also be added to **nouns** to make compound adjectives like *short-**haired**, long-**sighted**.*

# adjectives without nouns

**well-known social groups**  We can use *the* + **adjective** to talk in general about some commonly-recognised **groups of people**.

*the young    the old    the rich    the poor    the sick    the disabled    the blind    the deaf*
*the mentally ill    the homeless    the unemployed    the dead*

These expressions are **plural**: *the blind* means 'blind people **in general**'. Compare:

*Perhaps **the deaf have** more problems in mainstream education than **the blind**.*
***Some blind people** have guide dogs.* (NOT *Some blind have*…)
*I read to **the blind woman** upstairs most evenings.* (NOT … *the blind upstairs*.)
*I was at school with **a blind boy**.* (NOT… *a blind* …)

The expressions don't have possessives.

*In the country **of the blind**, the one-eyed man is king.* (NOT … *the blind's country* …)

We can't use all adjectives like this: we don't say *the selfish* or *the mean*, for example.

**1** **Correct (✓) or not (✗)?**
1   The mentally ill has rights, just like the rest of us.  …
2   200 years ago the sick were entirely dependent on charity.  …
3   The problems of the poor are often serious.  …
4   The unemployed's numbers are rising.  …
5   Under this government the poor is getting poorer.  …
6   Some homeless sell magazines in the street for a living.  …
7   I'm getting really fed up with that young next door.  …

The structure is also used with **nationality words** ending in *-ch, -sh* and *-ese*.

*The Irish have a great musical tradition.*
BUT *The Brazilians speak Portuguese.* (NOT *The Brazilian* …)

**2** **Can you answer these questions?**
▶  Who have their capital in Hanoi?  *the Vietnamese* …………
1   Who invented gunpowder? ………………………………
2   Who invented cricket? ………………………………
3   Who had a revolution in 1789? ………………………………
4   Who are part of the UK in the north, and a Republic in the south? ………………………………………
5   Who have their capital in Cardiff? ………………………………
6   Who live in a country which is partly reclaimed from the sea? ………………………………………
7   Who have a great reverence for a mountain called Fuji? ………………………………………
8   Who have a national dish called 'paella'? ………………………………

Note:  **A very few singular adjectives** are used without nouns to talk about individuals.
   *The body of **the deceased** (= 'the dead person') was found in the river.*
   ***The accused** refused to answer questions.*
   *Smith and Jewell jointly received the prize, though in fact **the former** did the majority of the work and **the latter** contributed very little.*

> 'I think you'll find the only difference between the rich and other people is that the rich have more money.'
>
> (*Mary Calum*)

# structures after adjectives

**complements**  Many adjectives can have **complements** which complete their meaning. Preposition structures, infinitives and *that*-clauses are common.

*critical **of** the plan.*     *anxious **to** succeed*     *sure **that** she was right*

**-ing forms**  Prepositional complements may include *-ing* forms.

*angry **about having** to stop*

**kinds of complement**  Some adjectives can have more than one kind of complement.

*happy **about** the decision*     *happy **to** be home*
*proud **of** being Scottish*     *proud **to** know you*     *ready **for** breakfast*     *ready **to** stop*

For the prepositions used after particular adjectives, see pages 308–309.

**1  Change the structure. The words in the brackets may help.**

▶  I was pleased to get promoted. (*about*)  ..I was pleased about the promotion. ..........

1  We were sorry to miss the concert. (*that*)
   ...............................................................................................................

2  I was surprised at your remembering me. (*that*)
   ...............................................................................................................

3  We're ready to have a holiday. (*for*)
   ...............................................................................................................

4  He was aware of having made a mistake. (*that*)
   ...............................................................................................................

5  We're happy that we are here. (*infinitive*)
   ...............................................................................................................

6  I was furious that the plane was delayed. (*about*)
   ...............................................................................................................

7  They were not prepared for a long wait. (*infinitive*)
   ...............................................................................................................

8  I was anxious for a better job. (*infinitive*)
   ...............................................................................................................

**Too and enough + adjective** often have infinitive complements.

*He's too old **to change**.*     *Andy's not good enough **to play in goal**.*

**2  Put in the infinitives of words from the box.**

| accommodate   concentrate   make   manage   play   reach   sleep |
| --- |

1  I was too tired ..................................... on the lesson.
2  The children were much too excited .....................................
3  I don't think Mary's tall enough ..................................... basketball.
4  Is the hotel big enough ..................................... all the conference delegates?
5  Johnson's too inexperienced ..................................... a multinational company.
6  The hose isn't long enough ..................................... from here to the pond.
7  I'm much too upset ..................................... a sensible decision right now.

**If an infinitive has its own subject,** we use a structure with *for* (see page 104).

*I'm ready **for Mr Ellis to give** me his report.*     *This is too heavy **for one person to lift**.*

For structures like *easy to please*, see page 103.   For infinitives and *-ing* forms after *sure*, *certain* and *interested*, see page 100.
For adjective + preposition + conjunction (e.g. *uncertain about where we were*), see page 196.

# adverb position (1)

Adverb position depends on the type of adverb, and some adverbs can go in more than one position. Usage in this area is complicated; general tendencies are as follows. For fuller information, consult a comprehensive reference grammar or usage guide.

**Connecting adverbs and comment adverbs** usually come at the beginning of a clause. Connecting adverbs join a clause to what came before; comment adverbs give the speaker's opinion.

*Then* they went home.     *Next*, we need to look at costs.     *However*, James disagreed.
*Stupidly*, I forgot to thank Maggie.     *Fortunately* nobody noticed the mistake.

*Maybe* and *perhaps* also usually come at the beginning.

*Maybe* you're right.     *Perhaps* we should think again.

**Focusing (emphasising) adverbs** most often go with the verb if they emphasise words later in the sentence.

*They're **even** open **today**.*     *I've **only** been here **a month**.*

But they can also go **before** the words that they emphasise.

*They're open **even today**.*     *I've been here **only a month**.*

**1** **Rewrite the sentences with a more normal order.**

▶ We play only on Saturdays. .....*We only play on Saturdays.*.............
1  He wears a hat even in bed. ....................................................................
2  I wanted only to help you. ....................................................................
3  He believes even in ghosts. ....................................................................
4  My French is worse even than yours. ....................................................................
5  It's open only to members. ....................................................................
6  I forgot even to phone home. ....................................................................
7  I sing only on special occasions. ....................................................................
8  He's there only in office hours. ....................................................................

**Expressions that say how**, **where** and **when** most often go at the end; usually in that order.

*They played **brilliantly in Coventry on Saturday**.*
*Pam works **in London on Wednesdays**. (NOT ~~Pam works on Wednesdays in London.~~)*
*I'm going **to bed early**. (NOT ~~I'm going early to bed.~~)*

We do **not** normally put these adverbs **between a verb and its object**.

*You speak **Japanese very well**. (NOT ~~You speak very well Japanese.~~)*
*Let's discuss the budget **now**. (NOT ~~Let's discuss now the budget.~~)*

**2** **Show where the adverbs should go.**

▶ They were talking/in the corner. (*quietly*)
1  I think in the bath. (*best*)
2  I never worked at university. (*very hard*)
3  He wrote his best novels. (*in the 1960s*)
4  We're having a meeting on Tuesday. (*here*)
5  Please put these on the top shelf. (*carefully*)
6  I'm playing golf in Scotland. (*at the weekend*)
7  Please take the cat out of here. (*at once*)
8  Jennie sang at Harry's wedding. (*beautifully*)

**NOTES**

**Adverbs of place and time** can go at the beginning for emphasis.
   *In Germany they do things quite differently.*     *On Monday I'll be back home.*
**After verbs of movement**, we often put an **expression of place first**.
   *They went outside slowly.*

# adverb position (2): with the verb

Adverbs that go in mid-position, with the verb, mostly express **indefinite frequency**
(e.g. *always, often*), **certainty** (e.g. *definitely, probably*) or **completeness** (e.g. *partly, completely*).
Their exact position is usually:
– **before** one-word verbs      – **after** the first auxiliary in more complex verbs
– **after** *am, are, is, was* and *were* even if these are not auxiliaries.

I **completely forgot** to phone Maggie.      Annie **has definitely decided** to leave.
They **should never have been** invited.      John **is usually** at home in the evenings.

**1** ▐ CHECK YOUR KNOWLEDGE. ▌ **Show where the adverbs should go.**

▶ I have ⁄admired Joe's self-confidence. (*always*)
1 People like Joe know best. (*always*)
2 They have made a mistake in their lives, it seems. (*never*)
3 Or at least, they will admit that they have made one. (*never*)
4 They are calm and happy. (*usually*)
5 They tell us, very kindly, how to run our lives. (*often*)
6 Because they know better than we do. (*invariably*)
7 This is because they are right. (*always*)
8 The only trouble is, they are wrong. (*nearly always*)

**with *not*** Adverbs can come before or after *not*, depending on the meaning. Compare:

I **don't really like** her. (mild dislike)      I **really don't like** her. (strong dislike)
She does **not always** welcome visitors.      He's **probably not** at home.

**emphatic position** These adverbs can often be put earlier when verbs are emphasised.

He **has certainly** forgotten. (normal)      He **certainly HAS** forgotten. (emphatic)

**2** Ⓒircle **the expression that has the most normal order.**

1 I *will probably not / will not probably* be in the office tomorrow.
2 The train *is certainly / certainly is* going to be late.
3 We *can definitely / definitely can* give you some help.
4 Tina's *always not / not always* so bad-tempered.
5 I'm sorry, but I'm *definitely not / not definitely* interested in your proposition.
6 Don't worry – it doesn't matter. Honestly, it *really doesn't / doesn't really* matter.
7 The building work is *completely not / not completely* finished, I'm afraid.
8 Emily is *often not / not often* depressed, but she's having a bad week.

## NOTES

**American English** Earlier positions are common in American English.
> He **probably has** arrived by now. (BrE emphatic; AmE normal)

**other positions** Some adverbs of indefinite frequency can also go at the beginning of sentences
(e.g. *often, occasionally, sometimes*).
> **Sometimes** I wonder what it's all about.      **Occasionally** we have a weekend at home.

This is not possible with *always* and *never* except in imperatives. (See page 10.)
> He **always** forgets. (NOT ~~Always he~~ …) BUT **Always think**. (NOT ~~Think always~~ …)

**Adverbs never** normally separate the verb from the object.
> We **often speak Spanish** at home. (NOT ~~We speak often Spanish at home.~~)

# comparison: *as ... as*

**1** CHECK YOUR KNOWLEDGE. **Which words can complete the sentence?**

He's .............. friendly as she is.  **A** *as*  **B** *so*  **C** *not as*  **D** *not so*

---

**adverbs with *as ... as*** We can use various adverbial expressions before *as ... as* and *not as/so ... as*.

**just** as happy    **nearly** as big    **not nearly** as/so intelligent    **not quite** as/so cheap
**nothing like** as/so interesting    **every bit** as good    **almost** as bad
**almost exactly** as cold    **half** as wide    **twice** as long    **three times** as heavy

**2** Use adverbs with *as ... as* or *not so/as ... as* to compare these.

▶ Europe – big – Siberia  .....*Europe is not nearly as big as Siberia.*..........
1 France – big – Texas  ...............................................................
2 the United States – big – Canada  ...............................................................
3 the Eiffel Tower – tall – the Petronas Twin Towers  ...............................................................
4 a koala bear – dangerous – a grizzly bear  ...............................................................
5 Mars – distant – Jupiter  ...............................................................
6 Minus 40° Fahrenheit – cold – minus 40° Celsius  ...............................................................

**3** Use adverbs with *as ... as* to compare people or things that you know with each other, or with yourself.

▶ .....*My brother is not nearly as patient as me.*..........
...............................................................
...............................................................
...............................................................
...............................................................

---

**dropping *as*** The first *as* is sometimes dropped, especially in a poetic style.

*When thus he had spoken, the hot sun was setting,*
*The streets of Laredo grew* **cold as the clay**. (American folk song)

**4** See if you can decide which adjectives go into these traditional Texan comparisons.
(Note: no first *as*.)

| big | busy | cold | deaf | fast | happy | pretty | slow | useless |
|-----|------|------|------|------|-------|--------|------|---------|

................ a baby's smile    ................ as a banker's heart    ................ as a fence post
................ as small town gossip    ................ as grass growin'    ................ as ice trays in hell
................ as ants at a picnic    ................ as a pig in a peach orchard    ................ as West Texas

---

## NOTES

*As much/many as* can suggest a large amount or number.
   *His paintings can sell for* **as much as** *half a million dollars.*
   *There are* **as many as** *50 students in some of the classes.*

*Not so much as* can be used when we say what is the real point.
   *It was* **not so much** *his appearance that I liked* **as** *his personality.*
*Not so much as* can also be used critically in the sense of 'not even'.
   *She did**n't so much as** say 'Thank you'.*

**infinitives** When we use *as ... as* with infinitives, we sometimes drop *to* from the second.
   *It's as easy to do it now as* **(to) leave** *it till tomorrow.*

# -er and -est or more and most?

**Two-syllable adjectives** ending in *-y* have comparatives and superlatives in *-ier, -est*.

*happy – happier – happiest      easy – easier – easiest*

Some others can also have *-er* and *-est*, especially those ending with unstressed syllables.

*narrow – narrower – narrowest      simple – simpler – simplest*
*clever – cleverer – cleverest      quiet – quieter – quietest*

With adjectives ending in *-ing, -ful, -ed* and *-less*, and some others, the structure with *more* and *most* is the usual or only possibility.

*tiring – more tiring – most tiring      hopeful – more hopeful – most hopeful*

To find the normal forms for a particular two-syllable adjective, check in a good dictionary.

**longer adjectives with -er, -est** Common adjectives like *unhappy, untidy* (the opposites of two-syllable adjectives ending in *-y*) can have forms in *-er, -est*.

*She's looking **unhappier / more unhappy**.      He's **the untidiest / most untidy** child!*

Some compound adjectives can also have two forms.

*more good-looking* OR *better-looking      most well-known* OR *best-known*

**1** **Put in the comparatives or superlatives of words in the boxes. Use a dictionary if necessary.**

> dim   efficient   imaginative   infuriating   peaceful   smooth   unhappy

1  You really are the ..................................................... person I know. You drive me mad!
2  This new production process is really much ..................................................... than the old one.
3  Artists are ..................................................... than other people – at least, they think so.
4  95% of users say our soap gives them a softer, ..................................................... skin.
5  Relations between the two countries are the ..................................................... for 20 years.
6  This has been the ..................................................... year of my life.
7  These new energy-efficient lights seem ..................................................... than the old ones.

> clever   dense   discouraging   lazy   shocking   silky   useful

8  'I've bought an electric corkscrew.' 'I hope it's ..................................................... than the last one.'
9  Dream Caress Shampoo gives you the ..................................................... hair ever.
10  Darren is the ..................................................... person in the family – according to Darren.
11  Have you seen the front page? It's the ..................................................... report I've ever seen.
12  Nobody's ..................................................... than Jessica. She thinks work is a disease.
13  He's the ..................................................... teacher – nothing we do is right.
14  Sea water is ..................................................... than fresh water, so it's easy to float on it.

> **Note:** **One-syllable adjectives** sometimes have *more* and *most*: for example, when a comparative
> is not followed directly by *than*.
>       *The road's getting steadily steeper / **more steep**.*
> And when we say that one description is more accurate than another, we use *more*.
>       *It's **more red** than orange.* (NOT *It's redder than orange.*)
> ***Most*** is sometimes used in a formal style with long or short adjectives to mean 'very'.
>       *That's **most kind** of you.*
> ***Real, right, wrong*** and ***like*** always have *more* and *most*.
>       *You couldn't be **more right**.      He's **more like** his mother than his father.*
> Comparative **adverbs** normally have *more* and *most*, except for one-syllable adverbs like *fast, soon,* and *early*.
>       *more slowly* (NOT *slowlier*)   BUT   *faster, sooner, earlier.*

# double comparative structures

*more and more*  We can use **double comparatives** to say that something is changing.

*It's getting **darker and darker**.*
*She drove **more and more slowly**.* (NOT ... ~~more slowly and more slowly.~~)

**1** Put in double comparatives of the words in the box. More than one answer may be possible.

| authoritarian   quiet   irresponsible   polluted   smelly   strongly   uncomfortable   unpredictable |
|---|

1  The seats got ................................................................. as the evening went on.
2  Rulers become .................................................. as they continue in power.
3  The weather's getting ..................................................
4  This cheese is getting ..................................................
5  At the end of the piece the music gets .............................................................,
    until it dies away completely.
6  The beaches are becoming ..................................................
7  I'm afraid your brother is getting ..................................................
8  The wind's blowing ..................................................

*the ... the*  We use this structure with comparatives to say that things change or vary together.
Note the word order (in both halves): *the* + **comparative** + **subject** + **verb**.

*The older I get, the happier I am.* (NOT ~~Older I get~~ ...)
*The more dangerous it is, the more I like it.* (NOT ~~More it is dangerous~~ ...)
*The more money he makes, the more he spends.*     *The more I study, the less I learn.*

In longer sentences, *that* is sometimes put before the first verb.

*The more information **that** comes in, the more confused the picture is.*

**2** Make chains with *the ... the*.

▶  they open factories – manufacture cars – make money
    *The more factories they open, the more cars they manufacture. The more cars they manufacture, the more money they make. The more money they make, the more factories they open.*

1  he wins races – he gains confidence
    ..................................................................................................

2  he loves her – she ignores him
    ..................................................................................................

3  she works – she is successful – she gets responsibility
    ..................................................................................................
    ..................................................................................................

4  I cook  – you eat
    ..................................................................................................

5  I go to the gym – I take exercise – I get fit
    ..................................................................................................
    ..................................................................................................

6  *(your example)* ..................................................................................
    ..................................................................................................

# more about comparatives

***the cleverer students*** We sometimes use comparatives to mean 'relatively', 'more than the average'. Comparatives make a less clear and narrow selection than superlatives. Compare:

*We've started a special class for the **cleverer** students.*
*The **cleverest** students are two girls from York.*

This use is common in advertising to make things sound less definite or more subtle.

***Less expensive*** *clothes for the **fuller** figure.* (nicer than 'cheap clothes for fat people')

***the faster of the two*** When a group has only two members, we sometimes use a comparative with a superlative meaning.

*Both cars perform well, but the XG2SL is the **faster** of the two.*

Some people feel that a superlative is incorrect in this case.

**1 Correct (✓) or not (✗)?**

1 These books are designed for younger readers.  …
2 Alice is by far the more sociable of the three girls.  …
3 Only the most determined students finished the course.  …
4 I'm right-handed, but my left arm is the stronger one.  …
5 This music probably won't appeal to oldest people.  …
6 Some of the newer fashions really make you look weird.  …
7 I'm going to try one of the easier exams.  …
8 The older woman in Cambridge is 103 today.  …
9 The harder instrument to learn is probably the violin.  …

**2 Complete the texts with words from the box.**

| fuller   older   richer   shorter   slower   smaller   taller   younger |

1 **Are ............... men more desirable and successful?**

2 **Lingerie for the ............... figure.** Special offers, lower prices.

3 For the handsome ............... man, 5′8″ or under, a great fit and a great look.

4 Never allow the smarter child to laugh at the ............... child.

5 It's now the ............... people, like pop musicians or sports stars, who make fortunes and set the standards.

6 In these villages, researchers found in the 1950s that nearly all the ............... people were still at work.

7 The ............... people, who could afford it, built large houses surrounded by gardens.

8 His previous experience had been as assistant boss of one of the ............... London museums.

**Note: *all the* etc with comparatives** In some fixed expressions, *all the* + comparative means 'even more because of that'.
    *'We can stay an extra three days.'  '**All the better**.'*
    *'Susie isn't eating this evening.'  'Good. **All the more** for us.'*
*Any the, none the* and *so much the* are used in similar ways.
    *I listened to everything he said, but ended up **none the wiser**.*
    *'Jake doesn't want to go on holiday with us.'  '**So much the worse** for him.'*

# more about superlatives

**superlatives without *the*** We sometimes drop *the* when superlative adjectives and determiners are used without nouns, and before superlative adverbs.

*Which of you three is (the) strongest?     The person who eats (the) fastest gets (the) most.*

And we don't use *the* when we are contrasting somebody or something with him/her/itself in other situations. Compare:

*He's **the nicest** of my three uncles.     He's **nicest** when he's had a few drinks. (NOT He's the nicest when …)*
*England is **most beautiful** in spring.*

**1 Correct (✓) or not (✗)?**

1  John's is best plan.  …
2  It's coldest here in January.  …
3  What's the earliest day you can manage?  …
4  The nights are the longest in December.  …

5  It's best if we go away this weekend.  …
6  That's most exciting suggestion I've heard all day.  …
7  Jamie talked most, but Louise said most.  …
8  You're least attractive when you laugh.  …

**Note the use of infinitives** after superlatives.

*the **youngest** person **to climb** Everest     the **first** man **to run** a mile in four minutes*

**2 Can you find some examples of the first/oldest/youngest/etc people to do things?**

▸  Marconi was the first person to communicate by radio.
............................................................................................................................
............................................................................................................................
............................................................................................................................
............................................................................................................................
............................................................................................................................

**3  GRAMMAR IN TEXTS.** Complete the texts with the infinitives of the verbs in the box.

| complete   eat   graduate   obtain   swim |

**1**
SOME PEOPLE feel they have to walk to the North Pole; others try to climb the world's highest mountains. Andy Hayler has fulfilled a much more pleasant ambition. He thinks he has become the first person ........................... in every three Michelin-star restaurant in the world.

**3**
A 36-year-old lawyer today set off in an attempt to become the first person ........................... the 203-mile length of the River Thames. But first, he had to run 19 miles in the summer heat before the river becomes deep enough to swim in, at Lechlade, Gloucestershire. In January he became the first person ........................... a long-distance swim in all five oceans.

**2**
The Australian Aboriginal leader Charlie Perkins was the first indigenous person ........................... from an Australian university in 1965, and went on to become a prominent indigenous leader who campaigned for civil rights reform.

**4**
A year ago Sally Cluley became the youngest person ........................... a British pilot's licence, which she did in just four weeks. After turning 17, she was allowed to fly herself and three passengers anywhere in Europe.

# *much, far* etc with comparatives and superlatives

To say *how much* better, older, bigger, more etc, we can use for example *much, far, very much, any, no, rather, a little, even, a bit* (informal), *a lot* (informal), *lots,* (informal).

Jamie is **much/far older** than me.     Greek is **very much more difficult** than Spanish.
We'll need **rather more** money than that.     Can you speak **a bit more slowly**?
Today's **even hotter** than yesterday.     This car uses **a lot less** petrol than the old one.
Is your mother **any better**?     I'll be **no longer** than five minutes.
We've had **far fewer** accidents since they lowered the speed limit.

Before a plural noun, we use *many more*, not *much more*.

You'll have **many more opportunities** in the future.

**1** **Correct the mistakes or write 'Correct'.**
- ▶ It's getting much darker. ....*Correct*....................
- ▶ I'm ~~quite older~~ than you. ....*much / far / a lot older*....
- 1 Can you walk a bit faster, please? ...................................
- 2 She's very less shy than she used to be. ...................................
- 3 It'll be much hotter tomorrow. ...................................
- 4 The economy is growing far slowly than last year. ...................................
- 5 The trains are any cleaner than they used to be. ...................................
- 6 English is difficult, but Russian is even difficult. ...................................
- 7 His cooking is no better than it used to be. ...................................
- 8 I'm very much happier these days. ...................................
- 9 There are a lot fewer butterflies this year. ...................................
- 10 We sold much more tickets than we expected. ...................................

**2** **Compare two people you know, using *far / much / very much* with a comparative (2 sentences ) and with *less* (2 sentences).**

...................................................................................................................
...................................................................................................................
...................................................................................................................
...................................................................................................................

Before superlatives, we can use for example *much, by far, quite* (meaning 'absolutely'), *almost, practically, nearly* and *easily*.

This is **much the most expensive** of them all.     She's **by far the youngest**.
He's **quite the most stupid** man I've ever met.     I'm **nearly the oldest** in the firm.
This is **easily the worst** film I've seen in my life.

Note also *very* + **superlative**.

Their house **is the very nicest** in the street.     300g of **your very best** butter, please.

**3** **Write about people or things that you know, using these superlative structures.**
- ▶ ....*My mother is by far the most interesting person I know.*....................
- 1 ...................................................................................................................
- 2 ...................................................................................................................
- 3 ...................................................................................................................
- 4 ...................................................................................................................

# *much* in affirmative sentences?

**much as quantifier** *Much* can be a quantifier before a noun (see page 165). In this case, *much* is **unusual** in **affirmative** sentences except in a formal style. Compare:

We haven't had **much** rain recently.     Do you get **much** junk mail?
**Much** time has been spent discussing these questions. (formal)
BUT We've got **a lot of** milk to use up. (NOT ~~We've got much milk~~ …)

However, *much* is normal in affirmative sentences after *so*, *too* and *as*.

She's caused **so much** trouble.     Those kids get **too much** money.
You can take **as much** as you want.

**much as adverb** As an adverb, *much* is also **unusual** in **affirmative** sentences. Compare:

I didn't enjoy the film **much**.     How **much** do you worry about the future?
We walked **a lot** when we were on holiday. (NOT ~~We walked much~~ …)

However, **very much** is common in affirmative sentences, particularly when expressing personal reactions.

I **very much** like your new hairstyle.     You've helped us **very much**.
Thank you **very much**. (BUT NOT ~~Thank you much.~~)

Note that *very much* never normally separates the **verb** from the **object**.

We very much **appreciate your help**. OR We **appreciate your help** very much.
BUT NOT ~~We appreciate very much your help.~~

**Before comparatives and superlatives**, *much* is **normal** in **affirmative** sentences.

I'm feeling **much better** today.     This is **much the worst** book I've read all year.

**1** **In three of sentences 1–8, *much* is unnatural. Correct them.**

▶ She's got ~~much~~ money.   She's got a lot of / plenty of money.
▶ He talks too much.   OK.
1  He talks much. ………………………………………………………
2  We very much enjoyed the film. ……………………………………
3  People haven't talked much about what happened. ………………………………
4  I feel much happier after our discussion. ……………………………………
5  I much like your new flat. ……………………………………………
6  I've eaten as much as I want. ………………………………………
7  I get much less freedom in the new job. …………………………………
8  There was much rain in the night. …………………………………………

For the use of *much* or *very* before past participles (e.g. *much changed, very surprised*), see page 176.

---

'Some people think that football is a matter of life and death. I can assure them that it is much more serious than that.'
(*Bill Shankly*)

'Too much of a good thing can be wonderful.'
(*Mae West*)

'Alone we can do so little; together we can do so much.'
(*Helen Keller*)

'The researches of many commentators have already thrown much darkness on this subject, and it is probable that if they continue we shall soon know nothing at all about it.'
(*Mark Twain*)

'If you believe in what you are doing, then let nothing hold you up in your work. Much of the best work of the world has been done against seeming impossibilities. The thing is to get the work done.'
(*Dale Carnegie*)

'My reading of history convinces me that most bad government results from too much government.'
(*Thomas Jefferson*)

'The years teach much which the days never know.'
(*Ralph Waldo Emerson*)

# *such* and *so*

*Such* is used before (**adjective +**) **noun**. *A/An* comes after *such*.

**such an** idiot   **such a** long way   **such** good food   **such** boring lectures

*So* is used before an adjective alone, an adverb or a quantifier.

They're **so stupid**.   I'm glad you're doing **so well**.   She's got **so many** shoes!

We can't put *such* or *so* after a determiner.

We stayed in their house, which is so beautiful. (NOT … ~~their such/so beautiful house.~~)

**1  Correct the mistakes or write 'Correct'.**

▶ It's so warm! ..*Correct*..............

▶ It's ~~a so warm~~ day! ..*such a warm*......

1 They're so kind people. ..........................

2 He's a such nice boy! ..........................

3 I've had so many problems!
    ...........................

4 This is a so good hotel. ..........................

5 They're such careless. ..........................

6 She's such a professional. ..........................

7 Don't talk so nonsense! ..........................

8 Please don't drive so fast. ..........................

*so long a wait* etc  In a formal style, we can use *so* before **adjective** + *a/an* + **noun**.

I was not expecting **so long a wait**. (Less formal: … *such a long wait*.)

The same structure is possible with *as*, *too* and *how*.

They gave us **as nice a time** as they could.   It was **too difficult a question**.
**How big a budget** does your department need?

This structure is only possible with noun phrases beginning *a/an*.

(NOT ~~so perfect performances~~ OR ~~too cold soup~~ OR ~~how regular support~~)

**2  Complete the sentences with *so*, *as*, *how* or *too* + adjective + *a/an*.**

▶ We do not usually get ..*so good a result.*.......................... (*good result*)

1 It was.......................... to be true. (*good story*)

2 I've never had .......................... as this one. (*exciting year*)

3 .......................... do you need for the job? (*big budget*)

4 It was .......................... – I felt really embarrassed. (*stupid mistake*)

5 She's much .......................... to criticise you. (*polite person*)

6 .......................... did you have to wait? (*long time*)

7 It was .......................... to disagree about. (*small thing*)

8 I will do .......................... as I can. (*good job*)

'He was such a lovely baby.'

# *like* and *as*

similarity: *like* or *as* We can use both words to say that things are **similar**.
*Like* is a **preposition**, uscd bcforc a **noun** or **pronoun**.

*The whole experience was **like a dream**.*    *They're not **like us**.*

*As* is a **conjunction**, used before **subject** + verb or a **prepositional expression**.

*They left **as they came**, without a word.*    *In Britain, **as in many countries**, ...*

Note the common expressions **as I said**, **as you know**, **as you see**, **as usual**, **as before**.
In informal speech (but less often in writing), many people use *like* as a conjunction.

*Nobody knows him **like I do**.*    ***Like I said**, everything's OK.*

Also in informal speech, *like* is now commonly used to mean 'as if'.

*She was eating fudge **like** her life depended on it.*

jobs and functions: *as* We use *as*, not *like*, to talk about jobs, functions and roles.

*I'm working **as a driver**.* (NOT ... ~~like a driver.~~)    *Don't use your plate **as an ashtray**.*
Compare: ***As your boss**, I must congratulate you.* (I am your boss.)
          ***Like your boss**, I must congratulate you.* (We both congratulate you.)

**1** *Like*, *as* or both (in informal speech)?

1  My sister isn't very much ........................... me.
2  ........................... I said, I can't help you.
3  The journey was ........................... a nightmare.
4  He sleeps ........................... he eats, noisily.
5  ........................... Chairman, it was my job to open the meeting.
6  Your writing is ........................... your father's, unreadable.
7  The rain stopped ........................... it started, suddenly.
8  Molly's late, ........................... I expected.
9  I used my coat ........................... a pillow.
10  In Paris, ........................... in Rome, traffic is heavy.

**2** Can you put the words into the right quotations?

| a train   car alarms   flutter   looks   looks   thoughts |

1  'Scientists have proved that it's impossible to long-jump 30 feet, but I don't listen to that kind of talk.
........................... like that have a way of sinking into your feet.'
*(Carl Lewis, winner of 9 Olympic gold medals)*

2  "What are you drawing?"
"God."
"But nobody knows what God ........................... like."
"They will in a minute."
*(Conversation between English primary-school child and her teacher)*

3  'My eyelids ........................... like the wings of a butterfly being born from its chrysalis.'
*(From a poem by a truly terrible poet)*

4  'My face ........................... like a wedding cake left out in the rain.' *(W H Auden)*

5  'She had a penetrating sort of laugh. Rather like ........................... going into a tunnel.'
*(P G Wodehouse)*

6  'Men are like ........................... – they both make a lot of noise no one listens to.' *(Diane Jordan)*

# more practice

**1** **Correct the mistakes (one sentence is correct).**
▸ Today is ~~hoter~~ than yesterday. ...**hotter**...................
1 Marquez is the younger president for the last 70 years. .........................
2 Her budget is twice bigger than mine. .........................
3 I didn't expect the analysis to be such accurate. .........................
4 Is karate more easy than other martial arts? .........................
5 He's a great trumpet player, but I improvise better as him. .........................
6 The snake was terrifying – it was so long as my arm. .........................
7 Japanese writing is not quite the same like Chinese. .........................
8 Please put both hands on the wheel and drive slowlier. .........................
9 Your American colleagues are so nice people! .........................
10 Alice is looking progressively unhappier – what's the matter? .........................
11 What's the best exercise routine for a guy as me? .........................
12 What's the less expensive way to get to France? .........................
13 The more I break cups, the less I have to wash up. .........................
14 My work's getting more interesting and more interesting. .........................

**2** **Which of these are not adverbs?**

| easily   early   friendly   lately   quickly   silly   slowly   ugly   weekly |

................................................................. are not adverbs.

**3** **Which is/are correct? (Circle) A, B or both.**
1 **A** the last to arrive guest    **B** the last guest to arrive
2 **A** insect-eating birds    **B** eating-insect birds
3 **A** the deaf next door    **B** the deaf man next door
4 **A** The Austrian speak German.    **B** The Austrians speak German.
5 **A** one of his more interesting books    **B** one of his most interesting books
6 **A** He's nicest when he's asleep.    **B** He's the nicest when he's asleep.
7 **A** your so beautiful country    **B** your country, which is so beautiful
8 **A** so gifted a child    **B** such a gifted child
9 **A** I wiped the table clean.    **B** I wiped the table cleanly.
10 **A** Do it as I do.    **B** Do it like I do.

**4** **Correct (✓) or not (✗)?**
1 Thank you much. ...
2 Thank you very much. ...
3 I like very much your hairstyle. ...
4 I very much like your hairstyle. ...
5 I like your hairstyle very much. ...
6 This jacket is much the best. ...
7 I'm much happier now. ...
8 I'm far happier now. ...
9 I'm a lot happier now. ...
10 I'm very happier now. ...
11 I'm very tired. ...
12 I'm much tired. ...
13 I'm far tired. ...
14 His singing is very imitated. ...
15 His singing is much imitated. ...

# Woolly mammoth extinction probably not due to humans

20,000 years ago woolly mammoths were found all over Europe. But as time went on, their populations became [1]............................, and they occupied [2]............................ of the continent, until a few thousand years ago they became extinct. Why did this happen? The reasons are not altogether [3]............................ Some scientists argue that it was because they were killed off by hunting, as the human population in Europe grew [4]............................ However, [5]............................ research suggests that the cause was [6]............................ climate change.

| |
|---|
| clear |
| larger |
| less and less |
| more probably |
| more recent |
| smaller |

During the last ice age in Europe the climate was [7]............................, there was [8]............................ in the atmosphere, and conditions were [9]............................ to grassland than to trees. There were [10]............................ forests, and vast areas of pasture which provided an ideal environment for [11]............................ herbivores (grass-eating animals) such as woolly mammoths.

| |
|---|
| cold and dry |
| few |
| large |
| less CO2 |
| more favourable |

However, around 20,000 years ago the Northern European ice cover began to retreat, the climate became [12]............................, and there was more $CO_2$ in the atmosphere. The new conditions favoured the growth of trees, so that forests began to cover [13]............................ of the land, while grasslands were [14]............................ reduced.

This meant that ultimately there was [15]............................ food to sustain the European woolly mammoth populations. 14,000 years ago they were [16]............................ found only in Northern Siberia. As conditions became more and more [17]............................ their numbers were further reduced, until around 4000 years ago they died out [18]............................ .

| |
|---|
| completely |
| greatly |
| mainly |
| more and more |
| not enough |
| unfavourable |
| warmer and wetter |

# Section 13 prepositions

Prepositions are words that express relationships in space and time, as well as other more abstract relationships: cause, purpose, possession, exception and many others. Prepositions are difficult to use correctly: a small number of words cover a very wide range of concrete and abstract meanings, and the differences between them are not always very clear or systematic. Also, one language does not always use the 'same' preposition as another to express a particular meaning. Their correct use is mainly a question of vocabulary rather than grammar, but they are usually included in grammar books. This Section deals with some of the more important points which can still cause problems at this level.

For common **verb + preposition**, **noun + preposition** and **adjective + preposition** combinations, see pages 308–309.

## time: revise the basics

**1** DO IT YOURSELF. **Look at the examples in the box and complete the rule for the use of** *at, in* **and** *on* **to talk about time.**

> in March    in 1988    at Easter    in the evening    on Tuesday    on Friday morning
> at the weekend    at midday    we got there in two hours    at 10.25

RULE:  ..*at*.......... + clock time or particular time            ............... + part of a particular day
       ............... + part of a day                        ............... + weekend, public holiday
       ............... + particular day                       ............... to say how long something takes
       ............... + longer period

**2** DO IT YOURSELF. **Look at the examples in the box and complete the rule.**

> See you next week.    I'm away this Saturday.    I play every evening.    What time does it finish?
> The meeting's on Tuesday.    You'll be sorry one day.    Ollie phoned this morning.

RULE:  Before expressions of time beginning *this, next, every, one* and *what*,
       we usually ...................................................................

**3** **Put in** *at, in, on* **or – (= no preposition).**
1   I'll never forget ............... that week.
2   Candy's birthday was ............... Sunday.
3   My parents got married ............... 1994.
4   We usually go skiing ............... January.
5   I'll be back home ............... this evening.
6   Do you know ............... what time it starts?
7   I swim ............... every Friday evening.
8   Can we talk about this ............... supper?
9   Let's go sailing ............... one weekend.
10  Is Luke free ............... Monday afternoon?
11  We're seeing the family ............... Christmas.
12  Can you learn a language ............... six weeks?
13  ............... what day are we going to Pat's?
14  I always get hay fever ............... June.
15  I hate to work ............... the evening.
16  What are you doing ............... your birthday?

# *in* and *on* (place): revise the basics

**1** **DO IT YOURSELF.** **Choose the right answers.**
1  We use *in / on* with two-dimensional spaces like floors, tables, walls or ceilings.
2  We use *in / on* with three-dimensional spaces like boxes, rooms, towns or countries.

**clothes and jewellery**  Remember: people are **in** clothes, and jewellery is **on** people.

*Who's the man **in** the dark coat?*    *She's got three lovely bracelets **on** her arm.*

**islands**  We often use *on* before the names of islands unless they are very big. Compare:

*I know a really good hotel **on/in Skye**.*    *We spent a week **in Iceland**.*

**2** **Put in *in* or *on* (or both).**
1  She had rings ............... every finger.
2  The hotel has even got a helipad ...............
   the roof.
3  Put the salad ............... a bowl, not
   ............... a plate.
4  Who put that poster ............... the wall?

5  We met ............... the Isle of Wight.
6  I was sitting behind a woman ...............
   a big hat.
7  His office is down at the end – it's got his
   name ............... the door.
8  There's a spider ............... the ceiling.

# *at* (place and movement): revise the basics

**where things happen**  We often use *at* to talk about where something **happens** – for example,
a meeting place, a point on a journey, somebody's workplace.

*I'll meet you **at the cinema**.*    *We stopped for an hour **at Chester**.*
*Turn left **at the traffic lights**.*    *Alice works **at the British Consulate**.*

And we often use *at* with words for things that people **do**, or the places where they do them.

*at* a concert    *at* breakfast, lunch etc    *at* a party    *at* a restaurant    *at* work
*at* the office    *at* the theatre/cinema    *at* the station    *at* (the) school/university

*At* and *in* are often **both possible**. We prefer *in* when we are thinking more about the **place itself**,
and not just the activity. Compare:

*He gave the talk **at Central College**.*    *There were over 800 people **in the hall**.*

**big places**  We don't use *at* with the names of very big places. Compare:

*We rented a car **at Heathrow**.*    *We rented a car **in London**.* (NOT ... ~~at London~~.)
*He arrived **at work** late.*    *He arrived **in England** last week.*

**1** **Put in *in* or *at*.**
1  I always read the paper ............... breakfast.
2  You change trains ............... Carlisle.
3  I once spent a week ............... Berlin.
4  Let's meet ............... Jessie's.
5  Can you pick me up ............... the station?

6  There was a bird ............... my room.
7  Sue wasn't ............... the meeting.
8  How many people live ............ your village?
9  There's a strike ............... the factory.
10  James works ............... Universal Export.

**Note:  targets**  We use *at* in some cases to talk about the target of a perception, reaction or movement (sometimes
aggressive). This happens, for example, after *look, stare, smile, laugh, shout, arrive,*
*throw, shoot.* See pages 308–309.

# prepositions with -*ing* forms

**Remember** that we use -*ing* forms after prepositions.

*We'd better think **about going** home.     I drove 300 miles **without stopping**.*

When *to* is a preposition, it is also followed by -*ing* forms (see page 105).

*I look forward **to seeing** you soon.     You'll soon get used **to working** here.*

We use *by ... ing* to say what **method** or **means** we use to do something.

*You can find out almost anything **by looking** on the internet.*
*You won't get rich **by writing** poetry.*

**1  Write your own answers to these questions. Use *by ... ing*.**

1  How can you make a lot of money quickly? ....................................
2  How can you learn a new language successfully? ....................................
3  How can you annoy the neighbours? ....................................
4  How can you make a small child happy? ....................................
5  How can you make a cat happy? ....................................
6  How can you impress your family? ....................................
7  How can you get to sleep easily? ....................................
8  How can you make everybody love you? ....................................

We use *for ... ing* to give the **purpose** of something – to say what it is used for.

*Have you got anything **for getting** fruit juice off clothes?*
*'What's that thing **for**?'  '**Crushing** garlic.'*

**2  What are these for? Use a dictionary if necessary.**

1  a kettle ....................................
2  a saw ....................................
3  a crane ....................................
4  a fire extinguisher ....................................
5  a safe ....................................
6  a paper-clip ....................................
7  a drill ....................................
8  a saucepan ....................................
9  a corkscrew ....................................
10  a pair of pliers ....................................

*Before, after* and *since* can be used as **prepositions** (and can be followed by -*ing* **forms**) or as **conjunctions** (followed by **subject + verb**). Both structures are common.

*Check the mirror **before driving off** / **before you drive off**.*
*I never want to work **after going out** for lunch / **after I've been out** for lunch.*
*I've learnt a lot **since coming** here / **since I came** here.*

'Either you let your life slip away by not doing the things you want to do, or you get up and do them.'
(*Roger von Oech*)

'I succeeded by saying what everyone else is thinking.'
(*Joan Rivers*)

# end-position of prepositions

**Prepositions often go together** with particular verbs, nouns and adjectives (see pages 308–309).

*look at    listen to    a need for    the thought of    anxious about    proud of*

In structures where a verb, noun or adjective is moved to the end of a clause, the preposition may stay with it, especially in an informal style. As a result, the preposition is separated from its object. This happens in questions (see page 3), relatives (see page 212), passives (see page 79), and some infinitive structures (see page 102).

*Who did she **travel with**?    What's the **meeting about**?    What are you **waiting for**?*
*That's the course that I'm **interested in**.    She's somebody that I've got no **time for**.*
*The plan needs to be **thought about**.    I don't like being **stared at**.*
*I'll need a quiet room to **work in**. (NOT … a quiet room to work in it.)*
*The chair's too fragile to **sit on**.    This is not important enough to **worry about**.*

**In a very formal style**, the preposition can go earlier in most of these structures.

***With** whom did she travel?    That is the course **in** which I am interested.*
*I will need a quiet room **in** which to work.*

This is not possible with passives, or with infinitive structures after *too* and *enough*.

**① Formal (F), informal (I) or wrong (W)?**

1   Who's the book by?  …
2   She is a woman for whom I have considerable respect.  …
3   From him has not been heard for weeks.  …
4   The children need friends to play with.  …
5   The ice was much too thin to skate on.  …
6   This is the restaurant I told you about.  …
7   I cannot think of anything about which to write.  …
8   John simply can't be relied on.  …
9   There isn't enough light by which to read.  …
10   On what are your suspicions based?  …

---

**NOTES**

**non-identifying relatives**  Non-identifying relative structures (see pages 210 and 215) are mostly rather formal, and it is normal to put a preposition earlier, before the relative pronoun.

> *I had a visit from Paul Barton, **for whom** I was working at that time.*
> *I sent her a bouquet of orchids, **with which** she was absolutely delighted.*

**during etc**  A few prepositions do not normally come at the end of sentences. They include *during, since, above, below, before, because of, besides.*

> ***During** whose lesson did you fall asleep? (NOT Whose lesson … during?)*
> ***Since** when have you been a golfer? (NOT When have you been a golfer since?)*
> *There's a meeting at twelve, **before** which we need to talk to Lonnie.*
> *(NOT … which we need to talk to Lonnie before.)*

---

'I feel about aeroplanes the way I feel about diets. It seems to me they are wonderful things for other people to go on.'
(*Jean Kerr*)

'A door is what a dog is perpetually on the wrong side of.'
(*Ogden Nash*)

# prepositions before conjunctions

**before *that*** We don't use prepositions directly before the conjunction *that*.
In indirect speech, prepositions are usually dropped. Compare:

*I **knew about** his illness.     I **knew that** he was ill.* (NOT ~~I know about that he was ill.~~)

We also drop prepositions before *that* in common expressions referring to emotional reactions.

***Sorry about*** *the delay.     **Sorry that** I can't help.* (NOT ~~Sorry about that I can't help.~~)

***the fact that*** In other cases, we more often use the expression ***the fact that*** instead of dropping
a preposition.

*The judge referred **to the fact that** the child was unhappy at home.*
(NOT ~~The judge referred (to) that the child~~ …)
*He said the parents were responsible **for the fact that** the child had run away.*
(NOT … ~~responsible (for) that the child had run away.~~)

**1** **Choose the best ways of completing the sentences.**

1  I had an idea *that / of that* she was mistaken.
2  We apologise *for that / for the fact that* there were no announcements.
3  Everybody was surprised *that / at that* the baby was so strong.
4  They were in good shape, in spite *that / of that / of the fact that* they had to spend the night
   in freezing conditions.
5  They paid no attention *that / to that / to the fact that* the prisoner was seriously ill.
6  Everybody was responsible *for that / for the fact that* the company was losing money.
7  Somebody complained *that / about that* there was nowhere to sit down.

**question words** After some very common words like *tell, ask, depend, sure, idea, look,* prepositions
can be dropped before *who, which, what* and other question words.

*Tell me **(about) where** you went.     It depends **(on) what** Jamie thinks.*
*I've no **idea (about) how** it works.     Nobody's sure **(of) when** it will stop.*

In other cases it is unusual or impossible to drop the preposition.

*I'm worried **about where** she is.* (NOT ~~I'm worried where she is.~~)
*I'll base my decision **on how** much free time I can get.*

***If*** does not normally follow prepositions; we use *whether* instead.

*I'm concerned **about whether** she has a place to live.* (NOT ~~I'm concerned about if~~ …)

**2** **Cross out the preposition where it's possible to drop it (in four sentences)**

▶  Ask him ~~about~~ what he wants. …………………………
▶  I'm confused about where he's gone. ..*can't drop*………..
1  Tell us about what you did. …………………………
2  Are you sure of where we are? …………………………
3  I have a proposal about what to do. …………………………
4  Have you heard Jan's theory about why cats have tails? ……………………………
5  It all depends on what you mean by 'mean'. …………………………
6  She had no explanation for how the crash had happened. ……………………………
7  Look at what the kids have done. …………………………
8  The police are asking questions about where everybody was. ……………………………

# six confusable prepositions

## *between* and *among*

**1** DO IT YOURSELF. **Look at the examples and complete the rules.**

*I was sitting **between** Jodie and Phil.     His house is hidden **among** the trees.*
*Luxembourg is situated **between** Belgium, France and Germany.*
*The licence is somewhere **among** my papers.*

RULES:  1.  We say ........................ things on two sides
            2.  We say ........................ two or more clearly separate people or things.
            3.  We say ........................ a group, crowd or mass of things that are not seen separately.

## *by* and *until*

**2** DO IT YOURSELF. **Look at the examples and complete the rules.**

*'How soon can you fix the car?'  '**By** Tuesday at the latest.'*
*You can have the room **until** tomorrow. But you must be out **by** 12.00.*
*She'll be gone **by the time** we get there.     I'm staying **till** Saturday.*

RULES:  1.  To say that **a situation will continue up to** a certain moment, we use ........................
            2.  To say that **something will happen at or before** a certain moment, we use ........................
            3.  Before a subject and verb, we use ...................................................... not *by*.
            4.  In an informal style, we can use ........................ instead of ........................

## *during* and *for*

**3** DO IT YOURSELF. **Look at the examples and complete the rules.**

*I was in Japan **for** two months **during** the winter.*
*I was awake **during** the night, so I read **for** a couple of hours.*

RULES:  1. ........................ tells you **when**.     2. ........................ tells you **how long**.

**4** **Put in suitable prepositions and words from the boxes.**

| attractive   evils   habits   realises   tomorrow |

1  Thirty-five is a very ........................ age. London society is full of women who have remained thirty-five ........................ years. (Oscar Wilde)
2  ........................ the time a man ........................ that maybe his father was right, he usually has a son who thinks he's wrong. (Charles Wadsworth)
3  The second half of a man's life is made up of nothing but the ........................ he acquired ........................ the first half. (Fyodor Dostoevsky)
4  Never put off ........................ ........................ what you can do the day after tomorrow .(Mark Twain)
5  ........................ two ........................ I always pick the one I never tried before. (Mae West)

| advice   interval   love   strange   surprised   war |

6  The ........................ will be over ........................ Christmas. (Popular belief in 1914)
7  When I was born I was so .................... I didn't talk .................... a year and a half. (Gracie Allen)
8  If you haven't found something ........................ ........................ the day, it hasn't been much of a day. (John A Wheeler)
9  ........................ is the delightful interval ........................ meeting a beautiful girl and discovering that she looks like a haddock. (John Barrymore)
10  It is very difficult to live ........................ people you love and hold back from offering them ........................ (Anne Tyler)
11  I got to the theatre late, and they wouldn't let me in ........................ the ........................ They should have kept me out longer. (Evan Stabetsi)

# six more confusable prepositions

## with and by

**1** DO IT YOURSELF. **Look at the examples and complete the rules.**

'He got where he is **by** hard work.' 'No, he got there **with** his wife's money.'
I killed the rat **by** hitting it **with** a shoe.

RULES: 1. We use ........................ to say what somebody **does** to get a result.
2. We use ........................ to say what somebody **uses** to get a result.

## with and by in passive clauses

**2** DO IT YOURSELF. **Look at the examples and complete the rules.**

The window was broken **with** a hammer.     The car was damaged **by** a falling rock.
I was interviewed by three directors.

RULES: 1. In passive clauses, we use ........................ for the **agent** – the person or thing that does something.
2. In passive clauses, we use ........................ for a **tool** or instrument that the agent uses.

## besides and except

**3** DO IT YOURSELF. **Look at the examples and complete the rules.**

I like all musical instruments **except** the organ.
**Besides** the piano, he also plays the accordion and the organ.

RULES: 1. ........................ **adds**: it's like saying 'with' or 'plus' (+).
2. ........................ **subtracts**: it's like saying 'without' or 'minus' (–).

## opposite and in front of

**4** DO IT YOURSELF.

**Look at the diagram and complete the captions.**

1. A is ........................ B.
2. A is ........................ B.

1  [A][B]     2  [A][B]

**5** Put in suitable prepositions and words from the box.

| boss   criminals   government   gun   help   not   rain   taxes |

1  You can get farther ........................ a kind word and a ........................ than you can ........................ just a kind word. (*Al Capone*)

2  In this world nothing can be said to be certain ........................ death and ........................ (*Benjamin Franklin*)

3  ........................ the noble art of getting things done, there is the noble art of ........................ getting things done. (*Lin Yutang*)

4  I get by, ........................ a little ........................ from my friends. (*John Lennon*)

5  ........................ working faithfully eight hours a day, you may eventually get to be a ........................ and work twelve hours a day. (*Robert Frost*)

6  Democracy is the worst form of ........................ ........................ all the others. (*Winston Churchill*)

7  A poet is someone who stands outside in the ........................ hoping to be struck ........................ lightning. (*James Dickey*)

8  There are people in the country ........................ politicians, entertainers and ........................ (*Charles Kuralt*)

# more practice

**1** Put suitable prepositions or – (= no preposition) into the texts.

 **How we met:** our love stories

### A Judy and Luke

Luke was a motorbike-riding pizza deliverer. I watched him pull up ¹............... front ²............... my house ³............... a warm spring day ⁴............... last year ⁵............... his motorbike. I peeped ⁶............... the window to get a good look ⁷............... him — love ⁸............... first sight!

### B Don and Beth

Originally classmates ¹............... Stockport Grammar School, leaving ²............... 1964, we lost contact ³............... 40 years. ⁴............... a school reunion, we met again. So how is romance ⁵............... age 62? It's beautiful.

### C Chris and Emma

We met ¹............... the train to Bristol ²............... St Patrick's Day ³............... 2000. We got talking, and realised we lived only a few miles ⁴............... each other and took the same trains ⁵............... and ⁶............... Bristol ⁷............... every day. We are now married and live ⁸............... Bath ⁹............... our daughter, Cara.

### D Lisa and Bill

We met ¹............... a mutual friend ²............... one night ³............... a party ⁴............... a football match. Bill was ⁵............... the dance floor and I was so amazed ⁶............... his dance moves that I couldn't take my eyes ⁷............... him. ⁸............... the next week ⁹............... a group dinner ¹⁰............... a restaurant ¹¹............... Brighton, we got talking again, and one thing led ¹²............... another. We have been engaged ¹³............... a year and plan to get married ¹⁴............... July 18.

**2** Write a few lines about how you first met somebody. (It doesn't have to be a love story!) Put in plenty of prepositions.

...................................................................................................................................
...................................................................................................................................
...................................................................................................................................
...................................................................................................................................
...................................................................................................................................

'Gerald, I don't think our both being left-handed is enough.'

'"I would be happy to marry you for money," she sighed ...'

## sentences and clauses

A sentence can have more than one clause, usually joined by a conjunction which shows the relationship between them (e.g. *when, because, if, that, and, but*).

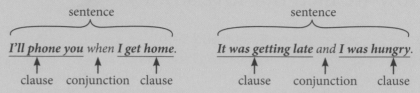

**noun, adverb and adjective clauses** A clause with its conjunction can act as part of another clause – for instance, it can be like a **noun** object or an **adverb**.

| | |
|---|---|
| *I told them* | ***a lie.*** <br> ***that I knew nothing about it.*** |
| *We stopped* | ***immediately.*** <br> ***as soon as we could.*** |

Relative clauses are rather like **adjectives**.

| | | | | |
|---|---|---|---|---|
| *She told me* | *a* | ***funny*** | *story.* | |
| | *a* | | *story* | ***that made me laugh out loud.*** |

**equal-weight clauses** In other cases, two clauses may have equal weight – neither is part of the other.
> ***Joe cooked supper*** *and* ***Pete washed up.***
> ***She was poor*** *but* ***she was honest.***

**terminology** If one clause is part of another, it is called a 'subordinate clause'; the other is the 'main clause'. Clauses with equal weight are called 'co-ordinate clauses'.
Sentences containing subordinate clauses are called 'complex sentences' in grammars; sentences made up of co-ordinate clauses are called 'compound sentences'.

**no conjunction Participles** and **infinitives** can begin clauses. These are normally joined to other clauses with no conjunction.
> *I rushed out of the house,* ***slamming the door behind me.***
> *He went up to his room,* ***to find a dog asleep on his bed.***

This Section deals with some general questions to do with co-ordinate and subordinate clauses. Sections 15–17 deal with adjective (relative) clauses, noun clauses (e.g. indirect speech structures) and adverb clauses (e.g. clauses beginning *if*, *when*, *after*, *as*, *because*). For punctuation between clauses, and differences between conjunctions and adverbs, see pages 254–256.

# conjunctions: revise the basics

**position:** A conjunction **joins** two clauses, but it does not always come between them. A conjunction together with an adverb clause may **begin** a sentence.

*When I get home,* I put on the TV. (OR *I put on the TV when I get home.*)

When an **adverb clause begins** a sentence, it is more often separated by a comma, even if it is short. Compare:

*When she had time,* she practised the piano.
She practised the piano *when she had time.*

**One conjunction** is enough to join two clauses.

*Although* she was tired, she went to work. OR *She was tired,* **but** she went to work.
(BUT NOT *Although she was tired, but she went to work.*)

However, two subordinate clauses may be joined by ***and*** or ***or*** as well as their own conjunctions.

*We came back* **because** *we ran out of money* **and because** *Ann was ill.*
*She didn't write* **when** *I got married* **or when** *we had our first child.*

## 1 Correct (✓) or not (✗)?

1  Because he was a cruel and vicious tyrant, so people hated him.  …
2  I'll help you if I have time and if I feel like it.  …
3  We encouraged him, although he didn't have much chance of winning.  …
4  As the book was really boring, so I stopped reading it.  …
5  Although I disagree with everything you say, and although I think your views are dangerous, you have the right to free expression.  …
6  Although only a minority voted for him, but somehow he was elected.  …
7  I don't play golf when it's raining or when it's too cold.  …
8  I felt lazy, and because I didn't have any real work to do, I took the afternoon off.  …

## 2 Here are some sentences taken from books and magazines. Complete them with conjunctions from the box.

| after  after  after  although  although  and because  because  so  when |
| when  where  where |

1  ………………… they had reached that decision she began to cry and would not be consoled.
2  'There's not a lot you can do ………………… you come across someone like that,' she said.
3  A man who hired two youths to fire-bomb his neighbours ………………… they complained about his loud music was jailed for 12 years yesterday.
4  They believed they had created a society ………………… people could develop free of exploitation.
5  First thing in the morning ………………… we were all trying to get ready, we constantly got in each other's way.
6  Membership dropped by 23,000 last year, ………………… officials say additional members attracted this year have almost offset that loss.
7  ………………… Carter broke his leg in midweek, he could be back in training in November.
8  Put the bowls in a dark place ………………… the temperature does not exceed 45°F (°C).
9  Riot police fired tear gas and chased students across the campus ………………… they boycotted classes.
10  Snow is more dangerous for a pilot than rain ………………… it reduces visibility more.
11  The money from the fund never got to the people who needed it, because it wasn't publicised enough, ………………… the charity administrators were inefficient.
12  There was nothing to do all day ………………… we just lay about drinking coffee and talking about life.

# *and* and *or*

*My brother works in a bank **and** his wife's an accountant.*
*It was pitch dark **and** bitterly cold.     He doesn't like rock music **or** jazz.*

In a list, we usually put *and* or *or* before the last item.

*We need eggs, butter, cheese, milk **and** coffee. We don't need bread, rice **or** pasta.*

We don't normally repeat unnecessary words after *and* and *or*.

*I've studied pure (maths) and (I've studied) applied maths.*

**1** **Cross out the unnecessary words and add commas (,) where needed.**
- ▶ I've been to Brazil and ~~I've been~~ to Argentina.
- 1 Should I wash this jacket or should I dry-clean this jacket?
- 2 You can come with me or you can wait here.
- 3 Do you speak English or do you speak German or do you speak Chinese?
- 4 I've written six letters and I've posted six letters this morning.
- 5 I'm depressed because I've worked all day and because I've achieved nothing.
- 6 These people will service your car and these people will clean your car and these people will polish your car.

*or* **or** *nor* We normally add a second negative idea with *or*.

*He doesn't smoke **or** drink.     I've never played football **or** rugby.*

*Nor* can be used to give extra emphasis. *Neither* cannot be used like this.

*She didn't phone that day, **nor** the next day. **Nor** the next.* (NOT *… neither the next.*)
Note that inversion is used after *nor* (see page 258).
*I don't smoke or drink. **Nor do I** gamble.*

**2** **Complete these sentences in any way you like.**
I can't ………………………………… or …………………………………
I don't like ………………………………… or …………………………………
I've never ………………………………… or ………………………………… nor …………………………………

*Try and* **…** is often used in an informal style instead of *try to* …

***Try and** eat something – you'll feel better if you do.     I'll **try and** call you tomorrow.*

This only happens with the base form *try*, not with *tries*, *tried* etc.

*I tried to explain what I wanted.* (NOT *I tried and explained* …)

**3** **Complete one or more of these sentences in any way you like.**
Next year I'm going to try and …………………………………………………………………………
I think people should try and …………………………………………………………………………
The government should try and …………………………………………………………………………

For *and* with adjectives, see page 174. For *both …and* and *either … or*, see page 203.

# double conjunctions: *both … and; (n)either … (n)or*

**balance** In a formal style, when we use these expressions we prefer to balance the structures, so that a similar expression comes after each conjunction.

*She **both dances and sings**.* (Better than *She **both dances and** she **sings**.*)
*John works **both with children and with animals**.*
OR *John works with **both children and animals**.*
(Better than *John **both works with children and animals**.*)
*They decided that they could **either stay in or go for a walk**.*
(Better than *…they could **either stay in or** they could **go for a walk**.*)
***Either the Director had missed the train or he had forgotten the appointment**.*
(Better than ***Either the Director had missed the train or forgotten the appointment**.*)

In an informal style, unbalanced structures are quite common.

**1** **Make these sentences more balanced.**

1  This drug can both reduce inflammation and pain.
......................................................................................................

2  You'll either leave this house or I'll call the police.
......................................................................................................

3  He either didn't hear me or he deliberately ignored me.
......................................................................................................

4  He both writes teaching materials and computer manuals.
......................................................................................................

5  They have either gone to bed or there's nobody at home.
......................................................................................................

6  Conrad either commutes to London or he lives there; I forget which.
......................................................................................................

7  Both your car needs a service and it needs some urgent repairs.
......................................................................................................

8  He either lied to me or he lied to Jenny.
......................................................................................................

**2** **Write some sentences about yourself (true or not).**

1  I will either ...................................................................................
2  Either I will ...................................................................................
3  Both I and ......................................................................................
4  I can both ......................................................................................
5  I can neither ..................................................................................

**Note:** We don't normally join clauses with *both … as well as*.
*I play both the guitar and the trumpet.* OR *I play the guitar as well as the trumpet.*
BUT NOT ~~*I play both the guitar as well as the trumpet.*~~

'Neither a borrower nor a lender be.'
(*William Shakespeare*)

'Neither a man nor a crowd nor a nation can be trusted to act humanely.'
(*Bertrand Russell*)

# tense simplification after conjunctions

**present for future** If the time is shown clearly once in a sentence, this may be enough.
So **tenses** are **simplified** in subordinate clauses **after** time **conjunctions** and many others.
For example, we often use **present tenses** instead of *will* …

*I'll be glad **when** we **arrive**.     We will all be delighted **if** he **wins**.*
*This discovery will mean **that** we **spend** less on food.*

**1** Complete the sentences using *will* once and a present tense once.

1  You ........................... hamburgers wherever you ........................... (*find, go*)
2  When I ........................... time, I ........................... to her. (*have, write*)
3  ........................... here until the plane ........................... off? (*you stay, take*)
4  It ........................... interesting to see whether he ........................... you. (*be, recognise*)
5  I ........................... where you ........................... (*go, go*)
6  He ........................... a reward to anybody who ........................... his pen. (*give, find*)
7  One day the government ........................... people what they ........................... (*ask, want*)
8  You ........................... all the shops ........................... closed tomorrow. (*find, be*)
9  Whether I ........................... or not, I ........................... a good time. (*win, have*)
10  As soon as I ........................... I ........................... you. (*arrive, phone*)

**We use a present perfect** (instead of a future perfect) after many conjunctions to express
**completion** in the future.

*I'll tell you **when I've finished**.* (NOT … *when I'll have finished.*)
*After **we've sold** the house we're going to spend three months travelling.*

**2** Complete the sentences in any way you like.

I'll ..................................................... when I've .....................................................
I won't ..................................................... until I've .....................................................

**past for would** After conjunctions, we often use **simple past** tenses instead of *would* ….

*In a really free country, you could say anything **that** you **wanted** to.* (NOT … *that you would want to.*)
*He would never do anything **that made** her unhappy.*
*It would be nice **if** she **asked before** she **borrowed** things.*

**3** Complete these sentences, using *would* … once in each.

1  In a perfect world, you ........................... to say exactly what you
   ........................... (*be able, think*)
2  I ........................... to help anybody who ........................... in trouble,
   whether I ........................... them or not. (*always try, be, know*)
3  He ........................... anything that ........................... against his conscience.
   (*never do, go*)
4  It ........................... nice if everybody ........................... what they
   ........................... (*be, have, want*)
5  I ........................... anybody who ........................... to me like that. (*hit, talk*)
6  In your position, I ........................... the boss what I ...........................
   (*tell, think*)
7  I ........................... happier if I ........................... live where I
   ........................... (*be, can, like*)
8  I knew he ........................... me what I ........................... for. (*not give, ask*)
9  If we lived in London, it ........................... that we ...........................
   less time travelling. (*mean, spend*)

> **Instead of progressive or perfect forms,** we sometimes use simple tenses.

*He's working. But at the same time as he **works**, he's exercising.* (OR *... as he's working ...*)
*I couldn't get in, because I had forgotten where I **put** the keys.* (OR *... I had put ...*)

**4  Complete these sentences.**

1  I ..................................... sorry that I ..................................... her when she
   ..................................... it. (*be, not help, need*: past perfect once)

2  It ..................................... a good time while it ..................................... (*be, last*: present
   perfect once)

3  I ..................................... the people I ..................................... with. (*usually like, work*:
   present perfect once)

4  For the previous thirty years, he ..................................... no more than he
   ..................................... to. (*do, need*: past perfect once)

5  Usually when she ..................................... to you she ..................................... about
   something else. (*talk, think*: present progressive once)

**5  Complete some of these sentences in any way you like.**

I would never ..................................... a person who .....................................
.....................................

It would be nice if .....................................

In a perfect world, you would be able to ..................................... when .....................................
.....................................

I would be happier if ..................................... what .....................................
.....................................

I wouldn't want to live in a country where .....................................
.....................................

I couldn't love anybody who .....................................

I couldn't work in a job where I had to .....................................

> **dropping *be*** After some conjunctions we can drop pronouns and forms of *be*.

*If in doubt, ask.* (= 'If you are in doubt.')

**6  Cross out words to make the sentences shorter.**

▶  I'll pay for you if ~~it is~~ necessary.

1  Cook the meat slowly until it is tender.

2  Once I was in bed I went straight to sleep.

3  Climb when you are ready.

4  A student, however clever he or she is, needs to work hard.

5  Apply the ointment liberally where it is required.

> **We don't drop *be*** after *because*, *before* or *after*.

*I stayed at home because I was ill.* (NOT *... ~~because ill.~~*)
*He worked as a driver before he was promoted.* (NOT *... ~~before promoted.~~*)

# past tense with present or future meaning

After *I'd rather* and *it's time*, a **past verb** has a **present** or **future** meaning.

*I'm busy today.* ***I'd rather we had*** *the meeting tomorrow.* (NOT ~~I'd rather we have~~ …)
***It's time you went*** *to the dentist.* (NOT ~~It's time you go~~ …)

**1** Write sentences using *It's time you/he/etc.*
- ▶ You ought to change your shirt. *It's time you changed your shirt.*
- 1 We ought to take a break.
  ......................................................................................................................
- 2 You need to water the garden.
  ......................................................................................................................
- 3 You should wash the car.
  ......................................................................................................................
- 4 Jenny ought to get up.
  ......................................................................................................................
- 5 We haven't been to the theatre for ages.
  ......................................................................................................................
- 6 We need to clean the windows.
  ......................................................................................................................

**2** Rewrite the replies, using *I'd rather we/you/etc.*
- ▶ 'Will you buy the tickets?' 'You buy them.' *'I'd rather you bought them.'*
- 1 'Let's talk.' 'Tomorrow.' ...............................................................................
- 2 'Shall I come at nine?' 'Ten.' ......................................................................
- 3 'I'll ask Harry.' 'No, don't.' ......................................................................
- 4 'I'll phone Jill tomorrow.' 'Tonight.' .........................................................
- 5 'Let's play bridge.' 'Poker.' .......................................................................
- 6 'Let's speak English.' 'Spanish.' ................................................................

After *wish* and *if only*, **past tenses** express a **present** meaning.
These structures express **regrets,** and wishes for **unlikely** or **impossible** things. *Were* is possible instead of *was*, especially in a formal style.

*I* ***wish*** *I* ***was/were*** *a long way away from here.*     ***If only*** *I* ***had*** *a bit more money!*

We use ***would*** … to say what we **would like people or things (not) to do.** This can sound dissatisfied, annoyed or critical.

*I wish this computer* ***would stop crashing***.     *If only he* ***would turn down*** *his radio!*

We use a **past perfect** to express **regrets about the past**.

*I wish I* ***had looked after*** *my teeth.*     *If only we'****d started*** *earlier, we'd be there now.*

**3** Complete these sentences in any way you like.
- 1 I wish I was .................................................................................
- 2 I wish I wasn't ............................................................................
- 3 I wish I could .............................................................................
- 4 I wish I knew .............................................................................
- 5 I wish I didn't ...........................................................................
- 6 I wish I had ...............................................................................
- 7 I wish I had never ......................................................................
- 8 I wish people wouldn't ...............................................................
- 9 I wish the government would .......................................................

For tenses with *if*, see pages 232–234. For the use of past tenses for politeness, see page 290.

# more practice

**1** **Read the text, and then complete some of the sentences about yourself.**
**Be careful with the tenses.**

---
**IF I HAD A FREE YEAR, AND ENOUGH MONEY TO DO WHAT I WANTED:**
I'd get up when I felt like it and go to bed when I felt like it. I'd eat and drink what I
wanted, when I wanted. I'd watch thousands of films – especially old Westerns. People
would always be welcome at my house, provided they phoned first – I don't like being
interrupted. If I got an invitation from somebody boring I'd just ignore it. I'd spend a lot of
time seeing my real friends – and then I'd disappear for weeks, and nobody would know
where I'd gone. I'd read all the books I'd never had time to read. I'd fulfil a lifelong ambition
by taking singing lessons. And I'd give money and help to people who really needed it.

---

If I had a free year, and enough money to do what I wanted:

1  I'd ................................................................................................. people who
....................................................................................................................

2  I'd ..................................................................................................... when
....................................................................................................................

3  I'd ..................................................................................................... what
....................................................................................................................

4  I'd ................................................................................................ whenever
....................................................................................................................

5  I'd ................................................................................................ whatever
....................................................................................................................

6  I'd ..................................................................................................... where
....................................................................................................................

**2** **Complete the cartoon captions with some of the words from the box.**

| as   come up with   fills up   moves   understand   until   when   while |
| --- |

'We can't say "new and improved" ..........................
we ..................................... a product.'

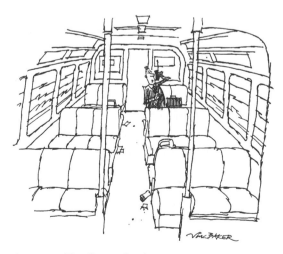

'Listen, I'll call you back ..........................
the carriage ..................................... a bit'

CONJUNCTIONS, CLAUSES AND TENSES **207**

Relative pronouns are *who*, *whom*, *which* and *that*, used to join clauses to nouns.

Relative clauses are parts of sentences that begin with relative pronouns.

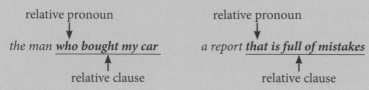

relative pronoun                    relative pronoun

*the man* **who bought my car**        *a report* **that is full of mistakes**

relative clause                    relative clause

Relative clauses are often called **adjective clauses**, because they add to the meanings of nouns, rather like adjectives. Compare:

   *ripe* plums     plums **that are ready to eat**

There are **two kinds** of relative clause (see page 210): those that say **who or what** we are talking about ('identifying clauses**\***') and those that just give **extra information** ('non-identifying clauses**\*\***').
   *the man* **who bought my car** (identifying: says **which man**)
   *Joe Smith*, **who bought my car**, (non-identifying: just says more about Joe Smith)
Non-identifying clauses are mostly rather formal, and more common in writing than in speech.

# relatives: revise the basics

This unit revises the grammar of 'identifying' relative clauses (the most common kind).

**1** CHECK YOUR KNOWLEDGE. **Six of sentences 1–10 are wrong. Correct the mistakes or write 'Correct'.**
   ▶ I don't enjoy films that I can't understand ~~them~~. ....*that I can't understand.*....
   ▶ What's the name of the man who just came in? ....*Correct*................
   1  I like people which smile a lot. ....................................
   2  This is a book will interest children of all ages. ..........................
   3  Is there anything I can do for you? ...........................
   4  Motor racing is a sport who doesn't excite me at all. .....................
   5  We've lost the key that it opens the cellar. ........................
   6  I forget everything what I read. .........................
   7  They made me an offer which I couldn't refuse. .......................
   8  They made me an offer that I couldn't refuse. .......................
   9  They made me an offer I couldn't refuse. .......................
   10 They made me an offer that I couldn't refuse it. ......................

**2** DO IT YOURSELF. **Here are five simple rules about relative structures. Four are correct. Circle the number of the bad one.**

   1  We use *who(m)* for people and *which* for things.
   2  We can often use *that* instead of *who(m)* or *which*.
   3  We can often drop *that*.
   4  After *everything*, *anything* or *nothing*, we use *what*, not *that*.
   5  *Who* and *which* **replace** *he*, *she*, *it* etc: we don't use both kinds of pronoun together.

\* also called 'defining' or 'restrictive' clauses.    \*\* also called 'non-defining' or 'non-restrictive' clauses.

**dropping relative pronouns** We can drop *who*, *which* or *that* when it is the **object** of the following verb; **not** when it is the **subject**.

*I found the key (**that**) I had lost. (**that** = the key = the **object** of lost)*
*This is the key **that** opens the front door. (**that** = the key = the **subject** of opens)*

**3** **Cross out *that* if it can be dropped from the descriptions.**

- ▶ the people ~~that~~ I work with ...........................
- ▶ the people that live at No 6 ...*Cannot be dropped*...
- 1 a bird that catches fish ...........................
- 2 some girls that I know ...........................
- 3 three films that I like ...........................
- 4 a pill that cures headaches ...........................
- 5 something that made me laugh ...........................
- 6 something that you must remember ...........................

**4** **Complete the definitions with the words in the box. Drop *that*.**
**Use a dictionary if necessary.**

| avoid   believe ✓   do without   forgive   read   satisfy   see coming   solve   understand |
| --- |

- ▶ An incredible story is one ...*you can't believe.*..............................................
- 1 An illegible letter is one you ...............................................................
- 2 An incomprehensible book is ...............................................................
- 3 An insoluble problem is ...............................................................
- 4 An insatiable desire is ...............................................................
- 5 An unpardonable insult is ...............................................................
- 6 Something inevitable is something you ...............................................................
- 7 Something unpredictable is something ...............................................................
- 8 Something indispensable is ...............................................................

**which, that and what** We don't use *what* in the same way as *which* or *that*. **What** replaces **noun + which/that**: it means something like 'the thing(s) that'. Compare:

*I gave them **the money that** they wanted.*     *I gave them **what** they wanted.*
(NOT *~~I gave them the money what~~ ...*)

We normally prefer **that**, not *which*, after **all, everything, nothing, the only** ... and **superlatives.**
**What** is **not correct** in these cases.

*I've told you **everything that** matters.* (NOT ... *~~everything what matters.~~*)
*Is this the **only song (that)** you can sing?* (NOT ... *~~what you can sing?~~*)

**5** ***What* or *that*?**

- 1 ..................... she did was very upsetting.
- 2 The things ..................... you said made Ellie cry.
- 3 Why don't you tell me ..................... I need to know?
- 4 I've told you ..................... I remember.
- 5 The only thing ..................... I forgot to buy was rice.
- 6 I understood nothing ..................... she said.

For more about *whom*, see page 307.

# identifying and non-identifying relative clauses*

**identifying relative clauses** say **who or what** we are talking about.

The US President **who followed Abraham Lincoln** was Andrew Johnson.
The only person **that supported my idea** was Hilary Mason.
The book **that got the prize for best first novel** was written by my landlady.
The flowers **Lucy bought yesterday** are all dead.

**non-identifying relative clauses** do not say who or what we are talking about, because this is already clear. They just give **more information**.

President Andrew Johnson, **who followed Lincoln**, was extremely unpopular.
(President Andrew Johnson alone tells us who.)
Hilary Mason, **who supported my idea**, didn't manage to convince the others.
'Wild cherries', **which got the prize for best first novel**, was written by my landlady.
The roses in the living room, **which Lucy bought only yesterday**, are all dead.

**1** **DO IT YOURSELF.** **Look at the examples above and think about the questions.**

1 Without the relative clauses, which make more sense – the first four examples or the others?
............................

2 In which kind of clause can we use *that* instead of *who(m)* or *which*? ............................

3 In which kind of clause can we leave out a relative pronoun when it is the object? ............................

4 Which kind of clause is separated by commas in writing? ............................

**2** **Put in one or two commas if necessary.**

▶ The doctor who saw my mother says she is very fit.  (no commas)

▶ Dr Harrison, who saw my mother, says she is very fit.

1 The people who borrowed our flat left it in a shocking condition.

2 I am sorry for people who cannot laugh at themselves.

3 She spent her childhood in Warwick which is a long way from the sea.

4 My cousin Julie who is a fashion designer has gone to work in New York.

5 The address that she had given him did not exist.

6 We went to see a film called 'Black Island' which was really good.

**3** **Change *who/whom/which* to *that*, or leave it out if possible.**

▶ This is Emma, who lives next door. ...No change...........

▶ I don't like people ~~who~~ can't say 'Thank you'. ...that.................

▶ She didn't reply to any of the letters ~~which~~ I sent her.

1 This house, which is now a museum, belonged to a famous artist. ............................

2 He moved to a town called Northbury, which is close to the mountains. ............................

3 I will never forget the things which happened on my 16th birthday. ............................

4 What happened to the papers which Anthony gave you? ............................

5 He wrote a book called 'Under the Rainbow', which got terrible reviews. ............................

6 I had good advice from Keith, whom I consulted about the situation. ............................

7 Do you know Philip Sanders, who lives downstairs? ............................

8 The man who looks after our garden has had an accident. ............................

9 They wanted €600, which was far too much. ............................

10 Nobody believed the stories which my brother told. ............................

* Also called 'defining and non-defining' or 'restrictive and non-restrictive'.

# reduced relative clauses

We sometimes **leave out** *who/which/that* + *is/are/was/were* before **participles** (-*ing* and -*ed* forms).

*Who is that child* **throwing** *stones at our house?* (= '... **who is** throwing ...')
*Most of the people* **invited** *did not even reply.* (= '... **who were** invited ...')
*Books* **printed** *before 1600 are rare and valuable.* (= '... **that were** printed ...')

This also happens with prepositional phrases and some adjectives (e.g. *possible, available*).

*Can you pass me the papers* **on that table?** (= ' ... that are on that table?')
*Tuesday is the only date* **possible** *for the meeting.* (= '... that is possible.')

Note that *who/which/that* + *have* **cannot** be left out in the same way.

*We need to talk about some problems* **that have arisen** *during the operation.*
(NOT *... ~~some problems arisen during the operation.~~*)

**1** **Change the words in italics.**

▶ Ann can't eat *dishes that are made with milk*. dishes made with milk

1 *The students who were taught by Oliver* all got excellent results.
...........................................................

2 *Cars that are parked in this street* will be towed away.
...........................................................

3 I thought that *the girl who was talking to Patrick* looked really nice.
...........................................................

4 Whose are *those books that are piled up* on the stairs?
...........................................................

5 I can't hear myself think because of *the birds that are singing* outside.
...........................................................

6 We need to reduce the amount of *plastic that is used for packaging*.
...........................................................

7 There is a special price for *people who are studying full-time*.
...........................................................

8 A letter *that was posted in 1986* has just been delivered to my sister.
...........................................................

9 We do not have all *the books that were requested*; we are sending *those that are in stock*.
...........................................................

10 Please let me have all *the tickets that are available*.
...........................................................

**2** **Put the letters of eight of the participles into the texts.**

| A applying | B applied | C hoping | D hoped | E interviewing | F interviewed | G planning |
|---|---|---|---|---|---|---|
| H planned | I printing | J printed | K showing | L shown | M teaching | N taught | O using | P used |

1 Almost half of the young people ... said that they were or had been gang members

2 Books ... in the late 19th century are particularly at risk because of weaknesses in the paper

3 There is a particular emphasis on encouraging women into the traditionally male-dominated subjects ... here.

4 a business adviser, trainer and mentor for people ... to set up businesses in creative industries, such as film, art and design

5 When ... pictures of leaves, 94 per cent were unable to identify the common native trees from which they fell.

6 the amount of plastic ... in supermarket packaging

7 None of the people ... for the job had any relevant experience.

8 The place is full of rich beautiful girls ... that they might bump into a footballer

# prepositions in relative clauses

identifying relative clauses  In identifying clauses, verb, adjective or noun + preposition combinations usually stay close together. This means that prepositions can be separated from their relative pronoun objects.

|  | OBJECT |  | V/A/N + PREPOSITION |
|---|---|---|---|
| *something* | *(that/which)* | *we* | *talked about* |
| *the girl* | *(who/that)* | *you were* | *interested in* |
| *a change* | *(that/which)* | *there is* | *no good reason for* |

**1** Correct the confusions and write proper definitions for the different things, ending in prepositions.

▶ You carry water in a basket. *No. A basket is something you carry shopping in.*

1 You keep yourself dry with an extinguisher.
No. An extinguisher is something you ...................................................................

2 You play music on an umbrella.
..............................................................................................................

3 You keep things cold in a bucket.
..............................................................................................................

4 You stick things together with an axe.
..............................................................................................................

5 You cut wood with a saucepan.
..............................................................................................................

6 You put out a fire with a piano.
..............................................................................................................

7 You carry shopping in a freezer.
..............................................................................................................

8 You cook soup with glue.
..............................................................................................................

Prepositions can also go before their objects, but this is rather formal.
After prepositions, we normally use *whom*, not *who*.

*something about which we talked*     *the people to whom I applied*

**2** Rewrite three of your answers from Ex. 1 in a more formal style.

▶ *A basket is something in which you carry shopping.* ................................................
..............................................................................................................
..............................................................................................................
..............................................................................................................

**3** Write definitions ending in prepositions for three or more of these words.

▶ bedroom *a room you sleep in* ...........................................
1 birthplace .............................................................................
2 home .................................................................................
3 library ...............................................................................
4 colleague ...........................................................................
5 employer ............................................................................
6 wife or husband ...................................................................

*There will be a short speech from the President, **after which** drinks will be served.*
*In 1956 she met Andrew Carstairs, **with whom** she later made several films.*

4 **Join the sentences in the places marked \*, to create more formal sentences
using prepositions with *whom* or *which*.**

▶ His grandfather gave him a new bicycle\*. He was absolutely delighted with it.
   *His grandfather gave him a new bicycle, with which he was absolutely delighted.*

1 Joe Peters\* has just opened a restaurant. My father plays golf with him.
   ........................................................................................................................

2 This bracelet\* is apparently very valuable. I paid £5 for it.
   ........................................................................................................................

3 Martin Oliver\* is a very successful farmer. I am working for him at the moment.
   ........................................................................................................................

4 Our little village school\* has been turned into a museum. I learnt to read and write in it.
   ........................................................................................................................

5 The committee have appointed a new treasurer, Peter Barnes\*. I have no confidence in him.
   ........................................................................................................................

6 Hutchins had an operation on his knee\*. He was unable to play for three months after that.
   ........................................................................................................................

*She called me a liar, **at which point** I decided to end the conversation.*
*They may wish to spend the night, **in which case** we will have to find them a room.*

5 **Complete each sentence with a preposition, *which* and an expression from the box.
Different answers may be possible.**

| case   disturbing experience   point   pleasant post   time   unexciting work ✓ |
|---|

▶ I washed dishes from morning to night, ..*for which unexciting work*............... I was paid
   £3 an hour.
1 We arrived at midnight, ...................................................... all the restaurants were closed.
2 The office may be closed, ...................................................... we will have to come back
   tomorrow.
3 Her handbag was stolen on a day-trip to Calais, ...................................................... she
   never travelled abroad again.
4 John's heart started beating extremely fast, ...................................................... we decided
   to call the doctor.
5 In 1956 he was appointed Ambassador to Uruguay, ...................................................... he
   spent the next five years.

# relatives: other points

**more about *who*, *which* and *that*** While we often use *that* instead of *who* in identifying relative clauses, it is rather informal, especially as a subject in writing. Compare:

*The people **who** live next door have got eight cats.* (normal)
*The people **that** live next door have got eight cats.* (informal)

Remember that we don't normally use *that* in non-identifying clauses.

*Mr and Mrs Harris, who live next door, …* (NOT ~~Mr and Mrs Harris, that live~~ …)

In both formal and informal styles, *that* is more common than *which* after indefinite subjects like *everything, something, anything*, and *nothing*.

***Everything that** he said was crazy.* (More normal than *Everything which he said* …)

***Whom*** is quite formal, and is dying out in informal speech. It is still common in non-identifying clauses, but it is rare in identifying clauses except after prepositions. Compare:

*She was surprised to see Laura, **whom** she had last met at Andrew's wedding.*
*Look! There's the man **(who)** we saw climbing on the bridge!*
(More natural than *There's the man whom we saw* …)

**whose** Relative ***whose*** is used before nouns, and can refer back to both **people** and **things**.

*He was a man **whose face** was on posters everywhere.*
*We bought a TV, **whose main function** was to keep the children quiet.*

We can use a structure with *of which* to express the same kind of meaning.

*… a TV, **the main function of which** was to keep the children quiet.*

These are rather formal structures; in informal speech they are less often used.

*I've got some friends **with a house that** looks over a river.* (More natural in conversation than *I've got some friends **whose house** looks over a river.*)

**1** **Circle the letter of the most informal sentence in each group.**

1  A  The person that told you that was mistaken.
   B  The person who told you that was mistaken.

2  A  I have had a card from those French people whom we met in Moscow.
   B  I have had a card from those French people we met in Moscow.
   C  I have had a card from those French people that we met in Moscow.

3  A  He made a speech whose purpose was completely unclear.
   B  He made a speech the purpose of which was completely unclear.
   C  He made a speech; its purpose was completely unclear.

**2** **Complete these sentences in any way you like, using *whose*.**

▶  An unsuccessful builder is one  *whose houses fall down.* ......................................

1  An unsuccessful gardener is one .................................................................

2  An unsuccessful parent is one .................................................................

3  An unsuccessful doctor is one .................................................................

4  An unsuccessful writer is one .................................................................

5  An unsuccessful teacher is one .................................................................

6  An unsuccessful tourist guide is one .................................................................

7  An unsuccessful cook is one .................................................................

8  An unsuccessful lion tamer is one .................................................................

**which = whole clause** *Which can refer back not just to a noun, but also to a **whole clause**.*

*We replaced **the pump, which** wasn't working properly.* (*which* = 'the pump')
***We replaced the pump, which** took two days.* (*which* = 'We replaced the pump')

Note that *what* cannot be used in this way.

*He got the job, **which** surprised us all.* (NOT ... ~~what surprised us all.~~)

**3** **Put in *which* or *what*.**

1 He lent me his car, ........................... was very kind of him.
2 I very much liked ........................... you wrote about me.
3 The shop was closed, ........................... was a nuisance.
4 Nobody had ........................... I wanted.
5 He runs three miles a day, ........................... keeps him fit.
6 This is not ........................... I asked for.
7 We're going to redecorate the house, ........................... will keep us all busy.
8 They made Alex Managing Director, ........................... pleased everybody.

**when, where etc** *After words for **time** and **place**, we can **use *when*** and ***where*** as relatives.*

*I'll never forget **the day (when)** I arrived in Athens.* (= '... the day **on which** ... ')
*Do you know **a garage where** I can get cheap tyres?* (= '... a garage **at which** ...')

We can **drop *when*** after common words for time, and we can **drop *where*** after *somewhere, anywhere, everywhere, nowhere* and *place*.

*the day I arrived      that time we went down to Exeter      the year I worked in Egypt
somewhere we can get a drink      everywhere she goes      a place I can sleep*

We use ***why*** as a relative after ***reason***. It can be **dropped**.

*I never found out the **reason (why)** she left.* (= '... the reason **for which** ...')

Note also that ***in which*** is often **dropped** after ***way***.

*I didn't like the **way (in which)** he spoke to me.*

**4** **Finish the sentences as you like, using *when*, *where* or *why*.**

1 Your birthday is the anniversary of the day .................................................................................
2 A supermarket is a place ...........................................................................................................
3 A church is a place ...................................................................................................................
4 Sunday is a day .......................................................................................................................
5 I'll never forget the day ...........................................................................................................
6 I know a place .........................................................................................................................
7 I'll never know the reason .........................................................................................................

**indefinite expressions** After indefinite expressions like *a man* or *some books*, there is not always a clear difference between 'identifying' and 'non-identifying' clauses. The choice of structure may simply depend on whether the information in the relative clause is an important part of the meaning or not.

*My sister married **a famous architect (that) she met** in Australia.* OR
*My sister married **a famous architect, whom she met** in Australia.*
*I've got **a new car that goes** like a bomb.* OR
*I've got **a new car, which goes** like a bomb.*

**dropping subject pronouns** In **informal speech**, subject pronouns are sometimes dropped.

*Is there **anybody here drives** a white Ford van? It's blocking the entrance.*
*There's **a guy works** in my office **thinks** he can read minds.*

# more practice

**1** **Which is/are correct? Choose one or more.**

1 Is that the flat … you used to live in? (**A** *that*   **B** *what*   **C** *which*)

2 I know a man … can do the repair for you. (**A** *that*   **B** *who*   **C** *which*)

3 Here's the bus … need to catch. (**A** *that you*   **B** *which you*   **C** *you*)

4 This is the file … (**A** *you wanted*   **B** *that you wanted it*   **C** *that you wanted*)

5 I've spoken to Mr … says he can help you. (**A** *Hawkins, who*   **B** *Hawkins who*)

6 Did you see the children … stones? (**A** *who throwing*   **B** *who were throwing*   **C** *throwing*)

7 The company made a large profit, … was a pleasant surprise. (**A** *which*   **B** *which it*   **C** *what*)

**2** **Read the sentences and answer the questions.**

> She threw a party for all the people in the office who had visited her in hospital.

1 Were all the people in the office invited to the party? ...............

> Congratulations to the three Greek students, who passed the exam.

2 Did any Greek students not pass? ...............

> My school! I still have nightmares about the teachers, whom I hated.

3 Did I hate all the teachers? ...............

**3** **Rewrite these sentences more formally with *whose*.**

▶ He was a man with a name that was on everybody's lips.
  *He was a man whose name was on everybody's lips.* ..............................

1 They showed me some shoes with a price tag that made me go pale.
  ........................................................................................

2 I once had a friend from Norway. His grandfather had been a famous explorer.
  ........................................................................................

3 We had a dog. Its main interests were sleeping and eating.
  ........................................................................................

4 We stayed in a lovely hotel. Its dining room had a view of the Grand Canyon.
  ........................................................................................

5 I once lived next door to a woman with a son who is now a famous rock star.
  ........................................................................................

**4** **Make the sentences more formal or more informal, and put in the names of the tools from the box. Use a dictionary if necessary.**

> bottle-opener   drill   file   pair of pliers   saw   spanner ✓

▶ A tool that you tighten nuts with is called a ...............
  *A tool with which you tighten nuts is called a spanner.* ...............

1 A tool that you make holes with is called a ...............
  ........................................................................................

2 A tool with which you make metal smooth is called a ...............
  ........................................................................................

3 A tool that you take the tops off bottles with is called a ...............
  ........................................................................................

4 A tool with which you grip things is called a ...............
  ........................................................................................

**Take expressions from the box and put them together in the right order, adding _who_, _whose_ or _where_ where necessary, to complete one or more of the newspaper reports.**

....................  accompanied him on his travels.        ....................  left Venice in 1269,
....................  army defeated the English forces at the Battle of Hastings on October 14th,
had become dissatisfied with Caesar's assumption of absolute power.        Marco Polo,
has returned together with his father Niccolò and his uncle Maffeo Polo,
....................  , like many of the Roman population,        ....................  was killed in the battle.
has been killed in a battle on the Little Bighorn River,        The Emperor Julius Caesar,
....................  his troops were outnumbered and wiped out.        led by Marcus Junius Brutus,
....................  Marco served as adviser to Kublai Khan,
News has just reached us that General George Armstrong Custer,
The Polos claim to have spent over 20 years in China,
travelling extensively through his empire as an ambassador.
was assassinated earlier today by a group of conspirators
....................  was attempting to put down a revolt by a coalition of Indian tribes,
was crowned King of England today in Westminster Abbey,
....................  was on his way to the Senate for an important meeting,        William of Normandy,

---

## AUC 709
### IDIBUS MARTIIS
# CAESAR ASSASSINATED

...............................................................
...............................................................
...............................................................
...............................................................
...............................................................
...............................................................
...............................................................
...............................................................
...............................................................
...............................................................
...............................................................
...............................................................

---

## Venetian Daily Courier
### May 17 1295
# THE POLOS ARE BACK!

...............................................................
...............................................................
...............................................................
...............................................................
...............................................................
...............................................................
...............................................................
...............................................................
...............................................................
...............................................................
...............................................................
...............................................................

---

## LONDON GAZETTE
### 25 DECEMBER 1066
# WILLIAM CROWNED

...............................................................
...............................................................
...............................................................
...............................................................
...............................................................
...............................................................
...............................................................
...............................................................
...............................................................
...............................................................
...............................................................
...............................................................

---

## DENVER POST
### June 28 1876
# CUSTER DEAD

...............................................................
...............................................................
...............................................................
...............................................................
...............................................................
...............................................................
...............................................................
...............................................................
...............................................................
...............................................................
...............................................................
...............................................................

## subjects and objects

Clauses can act as subjects or objects in other clauses, rather like nouns. These **noun clauses** usually begin with *that* or a **question word**. Compare:

*I forgot **our appointment**.     I forgot **that I was supposed to see John**.*
***Her method** is a secret.     **How she does it** is a secret.*

Note that we don't separate a clause object from its verb with a comma.

*He insisted that he was in the right.* (NOT ~~He insisted, that he was in the right.~~)
*I did not understand what they wanted.* (NOT ~~I did not understand, what they wanted.~~)

## introductory *it*

We often put heavy subjects like noun clauses later in a sentence (see page 228).
Instead of the clause, we put *it* in the subject position.

*It's odd **that he hasn't phoned**.     It was amazing **how many languages she spoke**.*

## indirect speech

A common use of noun clauses is in indirect speech.

*Everybody said **that he would lose**.     I asked **where I should pay**.*

# indirect speech: revise the basics

**In the structure called 'indirect speech',** we report other people's words, thoughts, beliefs etc by making them part of our own sentence.

*He said **he was tired**.     They thought **Don understood everything**.     Everybody wondered **where she was.***

**The tenses** in indirect speech are generally the normal ones for the situation. Compare:

*Lucy **was** cross.     Lucy **told** me she **was** cross.*
*I was sad because she **hadn't written**.     I **asked** why she **hadn't written**.*
*It **will rain** tomorrow.     The forecast **says** it **will rain** tomorrow.*

**tense changes**  But the tenses in indirect speech may be different from those originally used (because the original words may be reported at a later time).

*Yesterday Lucy **told** me she **was** cross.* (Reporting '*I'm cross!*')
*I **asked** why she **hadn't written**.* (Reporting '*Why **haven't** you **written?***')

**Other words** may also be different (because of the change of place and person).

*She said **she** didn't like it **there**.* (Reporting '***I** don't like it **here**.*')

***would** for future*  After **past** reporting verbs, we use **would** to talk about the **future**. This is an example of 'future in the past' (see page 37).

*I phoned to **say** I **would** be home after midnight again.*
*(Compare: The train was late as usual, so we **would** be home after midnight again.)*

**questions**  In indirect questions, the **subject** usually comes **before the verb**. *Do* is **not** used, and there are **no question marks**.

*She asked where **I had** been.* (NOT ~~She asked where had I been?~~)
*They want to know where **you live**.* (NOT ~~They want to know where do you live.~~)

*Yes/No* questions are reported with *if* or **whether**.

*Do you know **if/whether** Pete's in the office today?*

*say* and *tell*  *Say* is most often used **without a personal object**. If a personal object is necessary, we use *to*.

*Katy said she would be late.* (NOT ~~Katy said me that~~ …)
*And I say **to all the people** of this great country* …

*Tell* normally has a **personal object**.

*Katy told me she would be late.* (NOT ~~Katy told she would~~ …)

**1** CHECK YOUR KNOWLEDGE. **Choose the correct form.**

1 My teachers always said I *need / needed* to concentrate more.
2 I don't know where I *have / had* put my glasses.
3 In those days, people believed the earth *is / was* flat.
4 Lucy wasn't happy in *this / that* job, so she went back to college.
5 I took Sylvia some flowers, but she said *I / she* didn't want them.
6 Everybody knew that Emma *will / would* make a lot of money.
7 Do you know *where the police station is? / where is the police station?*
8 I can't tell *is she awake. / if she's awake.*
9 The children *said / said us* they wanted to go home.

**2** CHECK YOUR KNOWLEDGE. **Correct (✓) or not (✗)?**

1 The children told they didn't like school dinners.  …
2 Andrew thinks he would move to Ireland soon.  …
3 Nobody could understand why did she marry him.  …
4 I have no idea what I'm going to do tomorrow.  …
5 We were surprised because we hadn't heard from Josie.  …
6 Oliver said he doesn't come to see us yesterday because he's tired.  …
7 I asked Henry what he wanted for his birthday?  …
8 Did you ask Claire if she needs the car today?  …

**3** GRAMMAR IN A TEXT. **We have corrected one mistake in the following text. Can you find the other ten and correct them?**

I went over to Sheffield to see Sam the other week. When I turned up at his place,

                                                      *was*

he was obviously in a funny mood. I asked him what the problem is, but he doesn't

want to tell me very much. He did say he was fed up with living here, and that

perhaps he will start looking for a job somewhere else in the next few days. I asked

if everything was OK with your girlfriend? He told everything was fine, but I didn't

really believe him. I asked what did he think about taking a day off and going

fishing, but he said he was much too busy this week. I decided there wasn't much I

can do for him, so I said goodbye and came back home. I don't think I would see

him again soon.

# indirect speech: more about tenses

**situations that have not changed**  If the original speaker was talking about a **present or future situation that is still present or future** when the words are reported, the tenses are sometimes **not changed** after a **past** reporting verb.

'The earth **is** round.' ➔ He **proved** that the earth **is/was** round.
'It **will** be cold tonight.' ➔ The forecast **said** it **will/would** be cold tonight.
'How old **are** you?' ➔ Didn't you hear me? I **asked** how old you **are/were**.

A **past tense** is preferred in this situation if the speaker is reporting something that is not true, or that he/she does **not take responsibility for**.

Ptolemy believed that the sun **went** round the earth.
(Compare: Copernicus proved that the earth **goes/went** round the sun.)
The company's report for this year claimed that business **was** continuing to improve.

**1** Choose the correct verb forms (one or both in each case), and put in suitable words from the box. Use a dictionary if necessary.

| afterlife  authority ✓  contemporaries  continent  independent  microscopic  planet |
| possessions  preserve  reincarnation  sacrifice  soul |

▶  The Greeks believed that there *are* /*(were)* many gods. Zeus had ..*authority*........... over the sky, his brother Poseidon over the seas, and his brother Hades over the underworld.

1  The Aztecs believed that human ........................... *is / was* necessary in order to protect humanity from the anger of the gods.

2  Eratosthenes proved that the world *is/was* round, but most of his ......................... believed that it *is / was* flat.

3  The ancient Egyptians believed that the body *contains / contained* a ..........................., the 'ka', which *continues / continued* to exist after death but which *can / could* not exist without the body. So they did their best to .......................... the body.

4  Many ancient civilisations believed that it *is / was* important to bury dead people's .......................... with them for use in the ...........................

5  Many Indian religions teach ..........................: the belief that people *are / were* born again after they die.

6  Galileo proved that the .......................... Jupiter *has / had* four moons.

7  Columbus thought that the American .......................... *is / was* India.

8  Louis Pasteur proved that many illnesses *are/were* caused by .......................... bacteria.

9  Einstein proved that time and space *are / were* not .......................... of each other.

**past and past perfect**  We use a past perfect tense (in indirect speech and other structures) when it is necessary to **make it clear** that something happened **earlier** than another past event.

He **told** them that he **had been** in prison. (NOT ... ~~that he was in prison.~~)
They **didn't give** him the job because he **had been** in prison.

But when the time relations are clear from the situation, a past perfect is not always necessary.

We **were** glad to hear that you **(had) won** first prize.
The teacher **explained** that dinosaurs **dominated** the earth for 250 million years.
(More natural than ... had dominated ...)

A past perfect in direct speech will be unchanged in indirect speech.

I recognised her: we **had met** before. ➔ ... He said they **had met** before.

**reporting modal verbs** The modals *could*, *would*, *should*, *might*, *ought* and *must* are usually **unchanged** after past reporting verbs. This is also true of *needn't* and *had better*.

'It **would** be nice if you **could** come.' → He **said** it **would** be nice if I **could** come.
'You **must** apply in writing.' → They told me I **must** apply in writing.
'We**'d better** stop.' → I thought we**'d better** stop.
'You **needn't** stay.' → I told her she **needn't** stay.

*Shall* and *should* (conditional) may be reported as *would* because of the change of person.

We **shall/should** be delighted to come. → They said they **would** be delighted …

But *shall* in **offers** is reported as *should*.

'**Shall** I carry that bag?' → He wants to know if he **should** carry that bag.

**conditionals** Sentences with *if* that refer to **unreal present situations** can often be reported in two ways.

'If I **had** any money, I **would buy** you a drink.'
→ He said if he **had** any money he **would buy** me a drink.
OR → He said if he **had had** any money he **would have bought** me a drink.

**②** **Put in suitable verbs. (Different answers may be possible.)**

1  I looked at the weather forecast, and decided I ........................... put on a raincoat when I went out.
2  They said the train was usually half empty, and that I ........................... reserve a seat.
3  The driving instructor told me I ........................... always check the mirror before driving off.
4  She looked very worried; I wondered if I ........................... offer to help her.
5  John told us that if he had more time he ........................... liked to stay an extra day, but he had to get back to Scotland.
6  I told my mother that I ........................... taken her shopping if my car hadn't been off the road.
7  The regulations made it clear that all students ........................... pay their fees in advance.
8  The exam was in three days, so I thought I ........................... do a bit of studying.

**③** **Complete one or more of these sentences in any way you like.**

When I got up today I thought I ..................................................................................................................
When I left school I decided I ..................................................................................................................
My teachers often said I ..................................................................................................................
My parents told me I ..................................................................................................................

**④** **GRAMMAR IN TEXTS.** **Put in the letters of seven of the expressions in the box.**

| A had better   B had better start   C must be   D must go   E must have |
| F must start   G should get   H should have   I should move   J should wait |

1  My father owned a small business near London, and when the manager had a heart attack, he told me I … and run it. I was just 21 and it was a hell of a learning curve.

2  I realised the other day that I … spent more hours of my life watching Doctor Who than any other TV programme.

3  "Let me bring you breakfast in bed," he said. I thought I … dreaming. Then I remembered: my birthday. Well, once a year is better than nothing.

4  Six months after the baby was born, I decided that we … cats. "We will be a proper family then," I said. "I hate cats," she said. Oh, well.

5  We'd been thinking for a while that we … a party. We thought June 18th would be a good date.

6  Six months into our relationship I suggested that we … in together.

7  We had been joking about getting married for ages and I had said to him that we … do it before I was 30.

# indirect speech: other points

*If* and *whether* are both used to report *yes/no* questions.

*They wouldn't tell me **if/whether** I had passed.*

After verbs that are more common in a **formal** style, ***whether*** is preferred.

*We **discussed whether** we should lower the prices.*

In a two-part structure with ***or***, ***whether*** is preferred in a formal style.

*They have not said **whether** they will close the Birmingham branch **or** keep it open.*

We use ***whether***, not *if*, after **prepositions**.

*We were talking **about whether** it was worth going out.* (NOT … ~~about if~~ …)

***how to* etc**  The structure **question word + infinitive** is common. It often corresponds to a direct question with *should*.

*She asked me **how to address** the letter.* ('How **should** I address the letter?')
*I don't know **where to go**.*      *Tell me **what to play**.*      *I don't know **when to start**.*

**dropping *that***  In an informal style, we often drop *that* after some common reporting verbs.

*We **said (that)** we had had enough.*      *I **knew (that)** you were going to be late.*
*The teacher **suggested (that)** I should apply for a university place.*

But *that* cannot be dropped after certain verbs, especially intransitive verbs – for example *reply, shout, email.*

*Alice **replied that** she had not made up her mind.* (NOT ~~Alice replied she had~~ …)
*He **shouted that** he wanted to be left alone.* (NOT ~~He shouted he wanted~~ …)

**infinitives**  Speech relating to **actions** (e.g. promises, agreements, orders, offers, requests, advice, suggestions) is often reported with **infinitives**.

*'I'll write every day.'* → *He **promised to write** every day.*
*'OK. I'll wait.'* → *She **agreed to wait**.*
*'Would you like me to babysit?'* → *Ann has **offered to babysit**.*

Note that *suggest* is not used in this way.

*'Why don't we take a day off?'* → *He **suggested taking** a day off.* OR *He **suggested that** we should take a day off.* BUT NOT ~~He suggested to take a day off.~~

**1** **Correct or improve five of sentences 1–9.**

▶ I didn't know ~~how interpret~~ her reply. ..*how to interpret*..........
▶ I knew I had made a mistake. ..*Correct*.................
1  The insurance company emailed me they accepted my claim. ....................................
2  There was a lot of disagreement about if we should work on Saturdays. ..............................
3  Carl suggested to have further discussions before making a decision. ..................................
4  Can you show me where to sign? ...................................
5  They wanted to start, but I objected I wasn't ready. ..................................
6  Nobody could decide what to do next ...................................
7  It is uncertain if the food supplies will last or not. ..................................
8  We need a discussion soon about whether to reorganise the whole business. .................................
9  Eric suggested we should check the wiring to see if that would solve the problem.
   ...................................

**2** **Choose the best words to complete the sentences. Use a dictionary if necessary.**

1  (*evidence, proof*) There's a lot of ........................ that our distant ancestors came from Africa, but it's not absolutely certain.

2  (*evidence, proof*) The police claim to have absolute ........................ that the crime was committed by Hawkins.

3  (*agreement, discussion*) Do we have Emma's ........................ to continue as Treasurer for another year?

4  (*lie, claim*) Nobody could decide whether it was a deliberate ........................ or simply a mistake.

5  (*confusion, exaggeration*) He said he earned $500,000 a year, but that was certainly a(n) ........................

6  (*discussion, refusal*) It was difficult to know how to express my ........................ politely.

7  (*confusion, disagreement*) I shouted to Amy that the train was coming in, but she didn't hear me in the ........................

8  (*agreement, claim*) What do you think about Paul's ........................ that he's related to the royal family?

---

**NOTES**

**informal questions** In informal speech, reported questions sometimes have the same word order as direct questions.

'*What **is the time?**'* ➔ *She asked me what **was the time**.*
'*Where **is the nearest chemist's?**'* ➔ *I didn't know where **was the nearest chemist's**.*

**long reports** In long reports (for example of speeches), indirect speech structures may be used with very few reporting verbs.

*The Prime Minister **explained that** he was acting in the best interests of the country. He had been faced with a difficult choice, and he had thought long and hard about how to proceed. He had consulted the Cabinet about whether to take public opinion into account, and had finally decided against it. The reason for this, **he said**, was …*

**real indirect speech** Exercises in books like this are useful for practising the grammar of indirect speech, but they are necessarily rather artificial. In real life, when we report what people say, we re-express their meaning, but we don't necessarily keep very close to the original words. The sentence 'I think your hair looks great', for example, might be reported as 'She said she liked my hair' or 'She thought my hair was terrific' or in many other ways. And it would be strange to report 'Isn't she beautiful!' as 'He asked if she wasn't beautiful'. Indirect speech in English is mostly a matter of common sense: saying what is natural in the situation. The notes and exercises in this Section may be useful, but there is no need to learn a lot of complicated rules.

# verbs in *that*-clauses: subjunctives

**subjunctives** Many languages have special verb forms that are used to talk about possibilities rather than facts. In European languages these are often called 'subjunctives'.

The older English subjunctives have mostly disappeared; in their place, we mostly use ordinary verb forms or modal verbs. However, subjunctives survive in a few cases.

*that he go, that she be* etc  A **third-person** singular present form **without -s** can be used after *that* in a formal style, when we say that things are (un)important or (un)desirable. The same forms are used in both present and past sentences.

*It is important that the child **go** to a first-class school.*
*We were anxious that everyone **receive** the information as soon as possible.*

With verbs that are not third-person singular, the forms are the same as ordinary present-tense verbs (but they may refer to the past).

*He suggested that I **move** to another office.*

*Do* is not used in negative subjunctives.

*The committee was concerned that the club **not overspend** its budget.*

*Be* is used as a subjunctive instead of *am/are/is*, often in passives.

*The doctor recommends that she **be** allowed to sit up out of bed for an hour a day.*

**1** **Here are some sentences from reports of meetings. Put in the subjunctives of verbs from the box.**

| be   clarify   consider   direct   not be   provide   put   realise   take on |
|---|

1  The committee also recommended that the government ......................... the complicated rules regarding the supply of heat and energy.
2  May I suggest that the College ......................... its attention to providing adequate parking facilities?
3  The secretary insisted that the gentleman ......................... his name and address.
4  It is important that the public ......................... the danger and ......................... pressure on all governments to agree to large arms cuts.
5  We recommend that the subscription ......................... increased during the current year.
6  It is essential that the club ......................... extra staff for the Christmas period.
7  Do members consider it desirable that the Newsletter ......................... published on line?
8  The Chairman asked that the committee ......................... his suggestion at the next meeting.

**The old past subjunctive *were*** can be used instead of *was* after *if* (see page 233), and *wish* (see page 206), and in the expression *as it were*. These uses are mostly formal  (but *If I were you* is also common in informal speech).

*It would be better **if** the meeting **were** postponed until Tuesday.*
*She walked very slowly, **as though** she **were** tired or ill.*
*I **wish** I **were** somewhere else.     **If I were you** I'd go home.*
*She's a second mother to me, **as it were**.*

**NOTES**
**In British English**, subjunctives are not very common; we more often use ordinary verb forms or *should ...* (see page 225). In American English subjunctives are more frequent.

**Past tenses** are used in some cases with present or future meanings to talk about possibilities rather than facts – for instance after *if* (see page 233), *wish* (see page 206) and *it's time* (see page 206). These were originally subjunctives.

# verbs in *that*-clauses: *should*

**importance, necessity etc** In a formal style, *should* is often used in *that*-clauses after words expressing the **importance** of an action, especially in British English.

*It is **important** that somebody **should** talk to the police.*
*It was his **wish** that the money **should** go to charity.*
*I **insisted** that the contract **should** be read aloud.*

**1** Put in adjectives from the box to show your own opinion.

| desirable   essential   not essential   important   quite important   not important |
| necessary   not necessary   vital |

It is ..................................... that everybody should go to university.
It is ..................................... that all children should learn foreign languages.
It is ..................................... that more houses should be built.
It is ..................................... that more roads should be built.
It is ..................................... that everybody should speak English.
It is ..................................... that rich people should pay higher taxes.

**2** Complete one or more of these sentences in any way you like, using *should*.

I am anxious that people ...............................................................................................
My parents always insisted that .....................................................................................
My teachers always insisted that ....................................................................................
I suggest that everybody ................................................................................................
It is really important that nobody ..................................................................................

**reactions** We can also use ***that … should*** after words expressing **personal reactions** and **judgements**.

*It's surprising **that** she **should** say that to you.*
*It was odd **that** she **shouldn't** have invited Emma.*

**3** Complete the sentences with *should* and words from the box.

| be   forget   lose   not care   think   want |

1  I'm sorry you ..................................... that I did it on purpose.
2  Do you think it's normal that the child ..................................... so tired?
3  It was natural that they ..................................... him to go to a good school.
4  I was upset that she ..................................... my birthday.
5  I'm surprised that you ..................................... what people say about you.
6  It's silly that he ..................................... sleep over such a small problem.

**Note:** sentences like these are also possible without *should*.
   *It's important that somebody **talks** to the police.* OR *… that somebody **talk** to the police.*
   *It was odd that she **didn't invite** Emma.*
A structure with *for* + subject + infinitive is often also possible (see pages 102 and 104).
   *It's important **for somebody to talk** to the police.*      *It was odd **for her not to invite** Emma.*

# more about *that*-clauses

**Some nouns, verbs and adjectives** can be followed by *that*-clauses; some cannot.

his **wish** that we should agree     the **importance** of our agreeing (NOT ~~the importance that we should agree~~)
I **hope** that you'll be happy.     I **want** you to be happy. (NOT ~~I want that you'll ...~~)
It's **essential** that you come.     It's **worth** your coming. (NOT ~~It's worth that you come.~~)

Unfortunately there is no easy way to decide which nouns, verbs or adjectives can be followed by *that*-clauses. It is best to check in a good dictionary.

**That** can sometimes be dropped informally in indirect speech (see page 222), and in other cases after some common verbs, adjectives and conjunctions; not usually after nouns.

Luke **said** (that) he was feeling better.     I'm **glad** (that) you can stay.
Can you move over **so (that)** I can sit down?     (BUT NOT ~~the news she had gone~~)

**1** **In six of sentences 1–10, *that* can be dropped. Cross it out.**

▶   I thought ~~that~~ I was going to fall.
▶   Nobody believed his insistence that he was innocent. (*Can't drop 'that'*)
1   We were really surprised that she didn't want to go.
2   It's funny that Maggie hasn't phoned.
3   I simply don't agree with your view that a boarding school is the right place for Harry.
4   We were having such a good time that we didn't want to go home.
5   Now that we're all here, perhaps we can start.
6   Jason's report indicates that we need to reduce expenditure on advertising.
7   You can take my bike provided that you bring it back this evening.
8   Do you believe her claim that she used to run a big company?
9   Supposing that you had to go into hospital, who would look after the kids?
10   Nobody paid any attention when he screamed that there was a ghost in the room.

***the fact that*** As subjects, *that*-clauses are usually introduced by the expression *the fact*.

**The fact that** she was foreign made it difficult for her to get a job.
(NOT ~~That she was foreign made it difficult ...~~)

**2** **Put the sentences together using *the fact that*.**

▶   The company was losing money. This caused our partners concern.
    *The fact that the company was losing money caused our partners concern.*

1   Nobody would tell me anything. This added to my difficulties.
    ..................................................................................................

2   We had comprehensive insurance. This made things much easier.
    ..................................................................................................

3   His father knew the President. This helped to keep him out of jail.
    ..................................................................................................

4   I spoke three languages. This helped me to work abroad.
    ..................................................................................................

5   She had a small child. This was taken into account at her interview.
    ..................................................................................................

For *the fact that* ... after prepositions, see page 196.
For prepositions dropped before *that*-clauses, see page 196. For *it* as introductory subject/object for *that*-clauses, see pages 228–229.

# more about question-word clauses

Clauses beginning with question-words can act as subjects, objects or complements in sentences, rather like nouns.

*Who you invite* is your business.     Do you see *how he treats me?*
I often think about *where I met you.*     A hot bath is *what I need.*

This is common in indirect speech (see page 218).

He didn't tell us *where he was going.*     Ask her *when she'll be ready.*

Question-word clauses beginning with *how* are often rather informal. Compare:

I'm surprised at *how fast she can run.* (informal)     I'm surprised at *her speed.*

Subject clauses often come later, with *it* as an introductory subject (see page 228).

*It's* your business *who you invite.*     *It* doesn't matter *where we stay.*

At the beginning of a sentence we use *whether*, not *if*.

*Whether* we can stay here isn't yet certain. (NOT ~~If we can stay here isn't yet certain.~~)

**1  Rewrite these sentences with question-word clauses.**

▶  This is the amount that I've done. (*how*)  *This is how much I've done.*

1  Her address is not important. (*where*)

.......................................................................................

2  You can do the job in any way you like. (*how*)

.......................................................................................

3  Our arrangements will depend on her time of arrival. (*what time*)

.......................................................................................

4  I don't know his date of birth. (*when*)

.......................................................................................

5  Can you ask about their wishes? (*what*)

.......................................................................................

6  Their reason for being here is not at all clear. (*why*)

.......................................................................................

7  I'll spend my money in any way I choose. (*how*)

.......................................................................................

8  His knowledge of French doesn't matter. (*whether*)

.......................................................................................

---

*whoever, whatever, whichever*  These three words can begin subject and object clauses.

*Whoever* phoned just now was very polite.     Use *whichever* room you like.
*Whatever* is in that box is making a funny noise.

**2  Rewrite the words in italics with *whoever*, *whatever* or *whichever*.**

▶  I'll marry *the person I choose.*  *whoever I choose.*
1  Send it to *the person who pays the bills.* ....................................................
2  This is for *anybody who wants it.* .............................................................
3  Take *anything that you want.* .................................................................
4  I'll agree to *anything that you say.* ..........................................................
5  *The person who gets this job* will have a difficult time. ...................................
6  *The team that wins* will play United in the next round. ....................................

For prepositions dropped before clauses (e.g. *Look (at) what you've done*), see page 196.
For *whoever, whatever* etc in adverb clauses, see page 243.

# preparatory *it*

**preparatory subject** When the subject of a sentence is a **clause**, we generally use *it* as a **preparatory subject**, and put the **clause later**.

*It's odd **that he hasn't phoned**.* (More natural than *That he hasn't phoned is odd*.)
*It was amazing **how many languages she spoke**.*    *It doesn't matter **who knows**.*

The same thing happens when the subject is a clause beginning with an infinitive (or an infinitive alone).

*It's important **to read page 12**.* (More natural than *To read page 12 is important*.)
*It was good **to relax**.*

In an informal style, we sometimes use the same structure with *-ing* form subjects.

*It's boring **listening to him**.*    *It was nice **seeing you**.*

**1** Use *It's* and the expressions in the box to complete the sentences. Different answers may be possible.

> a pity   amazing   doesn't interest me   exciting   nice   probable   strange   surprising
> typical of him   upset everybody   your task

▶ how many unhappy marriages there are
   *It's surprising how many unhappy marriages there are.*

1  to steal the secret formula
   ......................................................................................

2  what she can do with a few leftovers out of the fridge
   ......................................................................................

3  how they all disappear when it's time to do some work
   ......................................................................................

4  that he kept swearing at the referee
   ......................................................................................

5  what you think
   ......................................................................................

6  that so few people came
   ......................................................................................

7  to forget to buy the tickets
   ......................................................................................

8  when a baby starts talking
   ......................................................................................

9  that we'll be a little late
   ......................................................................................

10  being back home
   ......................................................................................

Note also the structure *It looks as if/though …*

*It looks as if she's going to win.*    *It looks as though we'll miss the train.*

**2** Write a sentence about tomorrow's weather.
   ▶ *It looks as if it's going to snow / it might be extremely hot / …*
   ......................................................................................

**Note:** We don't normally use preparatory *it* for a noun subject.
   *The new concert hall is wonderful.* (NOT USUALLY *It's wonderful the new concert hall.*)

**preparatory object**  In some cases, we can use *it* as a **preparatory object**. This happens when a clause or infinitive object has a **complement**.

*I find **it odd** that Andy's away.* (More natural than *I find that Andy's away odd.*)
*My blister made **it a problem** to walk.*

BUT *I can't bear to upset him.* (NOT ~~I can't bear it to upset him.~~ The infinitive clause *to upset him* has no complement.)
Note the use of *as* after *regard, see* and *view*.

*I regard it **as** thoroughly bad manners that they never thanked us.*

**③** **Put in *it* or nothing (–) to make correct sentences.**

1  She made ........................... clear that she disagreed.
2  We found ........................... tiring to listen to him.
3  Oliver can't bear ........................... to be alone for long periods.
4  I consider ........................... a crime that they've put up VAT again.
5  Do you think ........................... right that Nicole didn't get the job?
6  I forgot ........................... that I had promised to phone Josie.
7  Everybody knew ........................... that there was something wrong.
8  The friendly atmosphere of the school made ........................... a pleasure to study there.
9  I always find ........................... a strain to pack when I'm going away.
10  I regard ........................... as really irritating to have to carry identification everywhere.

**other cases**  We also use preparatory *it* in some cases when there is no complement. This happens: in the structures *owe it to …* and *leave it to …*

*We **owe it to** society to help those who need help.*      *I'll **leave it to** you to inform the other members.*

in the structures *like/love/hate it* + clause

*We **love it** when you sing.*

in the structure *take it that …*

*I **take it that** you won't be working tomorrow.* (= 'I assume/suppose that …')

in the structure *would appreciate it if …*

*We **would appreciate it if** you would keep us informed.*

**④** **Complete the sentences with words from the box and *it***

| appreciate   hate   leave   take   owe |

1  Children often ................................... when you treat them like children.
2  We ................................... to our parents to keep them young by constantly surprising them.
3  I would ...................................if you would turn down your radio a little.
4  Can we ................................... to Alison to book the hotel?
5  You're looking depressed. I ................................... you didn't get the job.

'It would have been cheaper to lower the Atlantic.'
(*Lew Grade, talking about the film 'Raise the Titanic'*)

'I love it when someone insults me. That means that I don't have to be nice.'
(*Billy Idol*)

'We owe it to each other - and to our children and grandchildren - to leave our planet in a better state than when we found it.'
(*Christopher Dodd*)

'I find it very offensive when the government tells me what I can and cannot watch.'
(*Michael Badnarik*)

'It is not good to be too free. It is not good to have everything one wants.'
(*Blaise Pascal*)

# more practice

**1** **Which is/are correct? Circle A, B or both.**

▶ I said I ... understand.   **A** *don't*   **(B)** *didn't*

▶ Everybody thinks ... are special.   **(A)** *they*   **(B)** *that they*

1 A man just phoned to ask if we ... any jewellery to sell.   **A** *have*   **B** *had*

2 Jamie wanted to know if you ... him some advice.   **A** *could give*   **B** *could have given*

3 There was a big discussion about ... we should buy a car.   **A** *if*   **B** *whether*

4 I knew I ... leave that beautiful place.   **A** *must*   **B** *had to*

5 We were wondering how old you ...   **A** *are*   **B** *were*

6 The Minister replied ... had no comment.   **A** *he*   **B** *that he*

7 I don't know what ... say to my parents.   **A** *to*   **B** *I should*

8 It is essential that the police ... informed.   **A** *not be*   **B** *should not be*

9 I suggested that he ... for another job.   **A** *look*   **B** *looks*

10 It's not worth ... back tomorrow.   **A** *your coming*   **B** *that you come*

11 ... he can stay in the country depends on the kind of visa he has.   **A** *If*   **B** *whether*

12 I find ... that Anna hasn't been to see us.   **A** *strange*   **B** *it strange*

13 I can't bear ... spiders.   **A** *to look at*   **B** *it to look at*

14 We regarded ... a good sign that we hadn't heard from Maggie.   **A** *it*   **B** *it as*

15 **A** *What he thinks doesn't matter.*   **B** *It doesn't matter what he thinks.*

**2** **Read the conversation. Imagine that Emma talks to a friend some weeks later and tells her about the conversation, using indirect speech structures (*I said/told him that ... ; I asked him if ...; so he said ...* etc). Write Emma's report. (Different answers are possible.)**

EMMA:   Carl, we need to talk.

CARL:   I can't talk just now, Emma.

EMMA:   Well, we'd better talk soon. Would this afternoon be OK?

CARL:   No, it wouldn't.

EMMA:   What are you so busy with?

CARL:   I've got a lot of urgent work.

EMMA:   Come on, Carl, you can't keep avoiding things!

CARL:   You're in a bad temper today.

EMMA:   Do you want to know why?

CARL:   I don't think so.

EMMA:   Well, Carl, you can either listen to me or find another girlfriend.

CARL:   Wow! That's a really difficult choice.

EMMA:   OK. I'm not taking any more of this nonsense.

CARL:   Could you close the door on your way out?

.... *I told Carl that we needed to talk, but he said* ....................................................................

................................................................................................................................................

................................................................................................................................................

................................................................................................................................................

................................................................................................................................................

................................................................................................................................................

................................................................................................................................................

Here are some beliefs from the mythologies of four civilisations: the Sumerians (Middle east, 6,000–2,000 BC), the Norse people of ancient Scandinavia, the Zulus of southern Africa, and the Navajo of the western United States. Can you guess which people believe(d) what?

**1** According to their traditional beliefs, there is a creator god (*Unkulunkulu*), who does not concern himself with ordinary human affairs. It is the ancestor spirits (*Amatongo* or *Amadhlozi*) who have the power to intervene in people's lives for good or bad. People believe that it is possible to make contact with the spirit world and influence the ancestors, for instance by consuming a special drink, *muthi*, made from a mixture of herbs. White *muthi* can cause healing or prevent misfortune. Black *muthi* can bring illness or death to others, or riches to the user. Users of black *muthi* are considered witches, and rejected by society. Many of these traditional beliefs are still widespread among the modern population.
**Which civilisation?**
......................................

**2** They believed that the universe was a closed dome surrounded by a saltwater sea. The earth was the base of the dome; below it was an underworld and a freshwater ocean. There were many gods. The chief god of the dome-shaped universe was named An, but there were as many as 60 x 60 (3600) gods altogether, many of whom represented the natural forces of the world. According to these people's mythology, the gods originally created human beings as servants for themselves, but freed them when they became too difficult to control.
**Which civilisation?**
......................................

**3** In their mythology, there are Holy People or gods, and Earth Surface People. They believe that the Holy People passed through a succession of underworlds, each of which was destroyed by a flood, until they arrived in the present world and created First Man and First Woman. The Holy People gave the Earth Surface People all they needed to survive, and then moved away to live above the earth. The gods include Changing Woman or Spider Woman, the wife of the Sun God, and her twin sons the Monster Killers. Other gods include a joker god Kokopelli, as well as animal, bird and reptile spirits, and natural phenomena such as wind, weather, light, darkness, and the moon, stars and planets. Gods can be helpful or harmful to humans, depending on their moods and how they are approached. Constant attention to ceremonies and taboos is necessary in order to keep in harmony with the supernatural powers. **Which civilisation?**
......................................

**4** They believed there were nine worlds, including the human world Midgard. The worlds were connected by Yggdrasil, the world tree, with Asgard at its top and Niflheim at the bottom. Asgard contained Valhalla, where the souls of the greatest fighters lived. Living in the ice world Niflheim was a dragon who chewed at the roots of Yggdrasil. Asgard could also be reached by Bifrost, a rainbow bridge guarded by Heimdall, a god who could see and hear for a thousand miles. Other gods included nature spirits: for example two ravens representing thought and memory, a gigantic wolf, an eight-legged horse, and a sea-serpent that was coiled round Midgard. According to their myths, at the beginning there were just two worlds of fire and ice: Muspelheim and Niflheim. When the warm air of Muspelheim hit the cold ice of Niflheim, creation began, and the other worlds and gods came into existence. One day when the gods were walking they found two tree trunks. They changed them into humans, whom they named Ask and Embla, and built Midgard for them. **Which civilisation?**
......................................

▲ Sumerian gods

▲ Kokopelli

◀ a Norse carving

a Zulu mask ▶

# Section 17 adverb clauses

A clause with its conjunction (if it has one) can act like an **adverb** in another clause. Adverb clauses, like adverbs, can express a number of different ideas: for example condition, time, place, cause and contrast.

> *If I feel like it*, *I'll watch a film.* (Compare ***Perhaps*** *I'll watch a film.*)
> *We stopped* ***as soon as we could***. (Compare *We stopped* ***immediately***.)
> *I camped* ***where there was running water***. (Compare *I camped* ***there***.)
> *She left home* ***because she wanted to travel***. (Compare *She* ***therefore*** *left home.*)
> *Although I was furious*, *I said nothing.* (Compare ***However***, *I said nothing.*)

In this Section we look at sentences with conditional clauses, and some other kinds of adverb clauses (including clauses beginning with participles and infinitives).

# *if*: how many 'conditionals'?

**not just three or four structures** Many students' grammars and course books suggest that there are three possible structures in sentences with *if*: the so-called 'first', 'second' and 'third' conditionals. Some add a fourth: the 'zero conditional'. This is rather misleading. In fact, any normal combination of tenses is possible with *if*. A few examples:

> *If your mother* ***phones***, *I'll take* *a message.* ('first conditional'.)
> *If Susan* ***won't be*** *at the party tonight, I'm not going*.
> *If Andy only* ***started*** *the job yesterday, he* ***won't finish*** *it this week.*
> *If I* ***knew*** *the answer, I* ***would tell*** *you.* ('second conditional')
> *If I ever* ***knew*** *the answer, I* ***forgot*** *it again a long time ago.*
> *If that* ***was*** *Lucy, she* ***has put on*** *a lot of weight.*
> *If you* ***throw*** *something away, you always* ***find*** *you need it soon after.* ('zero conditional')
> *If you* ***would take*** *the trouble to listen you* ***would understand*** *what she means.*
> *If I* ***had known*** *what was going to happen I* ***wouldn't be*** *here now.*
> *If God* ***had wanted*** *us to fly, He* ***would have given*** *us wings.* ('third conditional')

**a more simple and sensible way to look at *if*** There are **two** main kinds of structure with *if*.

1. **ORDINARY TENSES** We can use the same structures with *if* as we do with other conjunctions, choosing the normal tense for the meaning that we want to express, as in most of the examples above. Compare:

   - *If Andy only* ***started*** *the job yesterday, he* ***won't finish*** *it this week.*
     *Because Andy only* ***started*** *the job yesterday, he* ***won't finish*** *it this week.*
   - *Oil* ***floats if*** *you* ***pour*** *it on water.*
     *Oil* ***floats when*** *you* ***pour*** *it on water.*

   After most conjunctions, we generally use a **present tense** to talk about the **future** (see page 204); this happens with *if* as well.

   > *I'll tell you* ***what*** *I* ***hear***.       *I'll tell you* ***as soon as*** *I* ***hear***.       *I'll tell you* ***if*** *I* ***hear***.

2. **SPECIAL TENSES FOR 'UNREAL' SITUATIONS** We often use **past** or **past perfect** tenses to suggest that we are talking about an **unreal**, improbable or imagined situation. This happens after various conjunctions, including *if*, and is common in sentences with *would*. Compare:

   > *I* ***would*** *give you anything* ***that*** *you* ***asked*** *for,* ***whenever*** *you* ***asked*** *for it.*
   > *I* ***would*** *give you money* ***if*** *you* ***asked*** *for it.*
   > *I wish* ***that*** *I* ***had studied*** *economics.*
   > *I* ***would*** *have found a better job* ***if*** *I* ***had studied*** *economics.*

# *if*: revise the basics

**ordinary tenses with *if*** We can use the **same tenses** after *if* as after **other conjunctions** – whatever are the normal tenses for the meanings we want to express.

*If John **didn't** come in this morning, he's probably ill.* (Compare: *As John **didn't** come in this morning, he's probably ill.*)

Remember that we use a **present** tense after most conjunctions to talk about the **future**.

*I'll phone you **if** I **have** time.* (Compare: *I'll phone you **when** I **have** time.*)

**1** (Circle) the correct tense and put in a suitable word from the box.
**Use a dictionary if necessary.**

| election estimate expenditure factory form pass reservation shares |

1 If anybody *stops / stopped / will stop* you, show them this ...........................
2 If you *fill / filled* in the ........................... last week, you *don't / didn't* need to do it again now.
3 I'll be really upset if the New Reactionary Party *wins / will win* the ...........................
4 What will you do if the ........................... *closes down / will close down* ?
5 If I *sell / will sell* my car, it *reduces / will reduce* my ........................... a good deal.
6 If we *buy / will buy* ........................... in United Projects Limited, will we make a lot of money?
7 We *decide / will decide* whether to repair the roof when we *get / will get* the builder's ...........................
8 If Andy *has / had* forgotten to make a ..........................., we probably *don't / won't* get a table at the restaurant.

**'unreal' situations** We often use a **past** tense with *if* to talk about things that are **not real** or **not probable now**. This is common in sentences with ***would* + infinitive**.

*If I **had** a free year, I **would travel** round the world.*
*It **would be** great if Lucy **got** the job, but I don't suppose she will.*

After *if*, we often use ***were* instead of *was*.** In a formal style, *were* is considered more correct.

*If I **was/were** fitter, I would play football every weekend.*
*If he **were/was** more honest, more people would vote for him.*

**2** Put in words from the box in the correct form (past tense or *would* + infinitive).
**Use a dictionary if necessary.**

| bake care about convert go sailing join not be redecorate tidy up |

1 If I had more energy, I ....................................... the garden.
2 If I could find the recipe, I ....................................... you a beautiful cake.
3 I'd read more poetry if most of it ....................................... so boring.
4 We ....................................... the kitchen if we didn't disagree passionately about the colour.
5 If you really ....................................... me, you would talk to me instead of watching football on TV.
6 If I were free on Saturdays, I ....................................... at weekends.
7 If we ....................................... the attic, it would make a nice playroom for the children.
8 Would you laugh at me if I ....................................... the navy?

***should*** After *I* and *we*, ***should*** is possible instead of *would*. (*Would* is more common.)

*If I had time, I **would/should** learn the guitar.*

→

# *if*: revise the basics (continued)

*could* and *might* in sentences with *if* As well as *would*, we can use **could** (= 'would be able to')
and **might** (= 'would perhaps').

*I could lend you my car if you wanted.*     *He might agree if we talked to him.*

**3** Complete these sentences using *could* or *might*.

1 If it wasn't raining, we ..................................... tennis. (*play*)
2 If she asked me politely, I ..................................... like helping her. (*feel*)
3 If he wasn't so bad-tempered. I ..................................... out with him. (*go*)
4 If I had more money, I ..................................... a small flat. (*get*)
5 If you spoke more slowly, I ..................................... you better. (*understand*)
6 If you cooked it in butter, it ..................................... better. (*taste*)

*unreal past* We can use a **past perfect** with *if* to talk about an **unreal situation in the past** –
to imagine the results of something that didn't happen. This is common in sentences with
*would have* + past participle.

*If they had played a bit harder, I think they would have won.*
*If you hadn't said that to Mary, everything would have been all right.*

**4** These are some sentences taken from real conversations about the past. Put in the verb forms.

1 If I ......................................, I .....................................
   somebody else. (*realise; send*)
2 It ..................................... nice if he .....................................
   me out. (*be; ask*)
3 This ..................................... if they .....................................
   things through. (*not happen; think*)
4 If she ..................................... to the eye hospital, she
   ..................................... two years for an operation. (*go; wait*)
5 It ..................................... a fortune if we .....................................
   (*cost; carry on*)
6 If she ..................................... at Christmas, she .....................................
   ..................................... crazy. (*not go away; go*)
7 If I ..................................... it, somebody else .....................................
   ..................................... it. (*not do; do*)
8 But the river was in flood. If he ....................................., he .....................................
   ..................................... washed out to sea. (*fall in; be*)
9 If she ..................................... before she died, her sister .....................................
   .....................................
   nothing. (*marry; get*)
10 If we ..................................... what to do, we .....................................
   ..................................... it. (*know; do*)

*would have been* etc with present or future meaning We can also use *would have* + past participle
to talk about **present and future situations** which are **no longer possible** because of the way things
have turned out.

*If she hadn't crossed the road without looking, she would have been alive today.*
(OR ... *she would be alive today.*)
*If my mother hadn't met my father thirty years ago, I wouldn't have been here now.*
(OR ... *I wouldn't be here now.*)

# unless

*I'll be here tomorrow* **unless** *there's a train strike.*
*Let's go and see a film –* **unless** *you're too tired.*

**1** Change *if not* to *unless*, or vice versa.

1 You can have the car tonight if Harry doesn't need it.

   ................................................................................................................

2 I'll do some gardening if it doesn't rain.

   ................................................................................................................

3 He'll pass the exam unless they ask him about Shakespeare.

   ................................................................................................................

4 He's usually pretty good-tempered, unless people ask him for money.

   ................................................................................................................

5 I can't understand Spanish if you don't speak very slowly.

   ................................................................................................................

6 If they don't mend the road soon, there's going to be an accident.

   ................................................................................................................

*I'll be surprised* **if** *she doesn't phone.* (BUT NOT *I'll be surprised unless she phones.* The meaning is not 'I'll be surprised except if she phones'.)

# *if* and *in case*

*I'll get some meat out of the freezer now,* **in case** *the boys come for lunch.*
*I'll cook it* **if** *they come; if they don't, we can have it this evening.* (NOT *I'll cook it in case they come* …)
*People insure their houses* **in case** *there's a fire.* (NOT *… if there's a fire.*)
**If** *there's a fire, the insurance company pays for the damage.* (NOT *In case there's a fire* …)

*I've made up a bed in the spare room* **in case** *William* **should** *stay the night.*
*I wrote down his name in case I* **should** *forget it.*

**1** ⃝Circle *if* or *in case* and put in words from the box.

| automatically brand-new message mobile rusty sprinklers |

1 I've bought some ........................... skis *if* / *in case* we get some snow.
2 *If* / *In case* we go to France, I hope my French isn't too ...........................
3 Most hotels these days have ........................... in all the rooms *if* / *in case* there's a fire.
4 The system turns on ........................... *if* / *in case* there's a fire.
5 Give me your ........................... number *if* / *in case* I need to get in touch.
6 *If* / *In case* I'm not there when you ring, just leave a ...........................

# *if*: more advanced points

**will in polite requests** We can use *will* (meaning 'are willing to') after *if* in **polite requests**.

*If you **will** follow me, I'll show you to the waiting room.*

*Would* is also possible in this structure.

*If you **would** just wait here for a moment, I'll see if she's free.*

**if … will: results** We can use *if … will* to mean 'if this will happen as a **result**'.

*We can come tomorrow evening instead **if it will make things easier**.*
*All right. I'll give up smoking **if it will make you happy**.*
(BUT NOT ~~I'll feel better if I will give up smoking.~~ Giving up smoking is not the result.)

**if … will in indirect speech** *Will* is also used after *if* in **indirect questions** (see page 218).

*I don't know **if** Ellie **will** be home for supper.*

**1** **Put in *will* with verbs from the box. Use a dictionary if necessary.**

| accept   agree   check   cure   improve   sign   solve   write down |

1  If you .................................... the visitors' book, I'll take you upstairs.
2  We'll get a new engine. It's expensive, but if it .................................... the problem, it's worth it.
3  I don't know if she .................................... to see you without an appointment.
4  I don't want an operation, but I'll have one if it .................................... my stomach trouble.
5  If you .................................... the wording, I'll print out the letter.
6  Let's get a private teacher for him, if it .................................... his exam results.
7  I doubt if he .................................... any money for the work.
8  If you .................................... your name, I'll see if the manager is free.

**if it wasn't for / hadn't been for … etc** This is a way of saying 'without this fact, person etc …, things would be / have been different'. In a formal style we can use *weren't* instead of *wasn't*.

*If it **wasn't for** your help, I'd be in trouble.*     *If it **were not for** modern medicine, I would be dead.*
*If it **had not been for** Tom, it is difficult to know what they would have done.*

We can express these ideas with **but for** (a little more formal).

*But for your help …*     *But for Tom …*

**2** **Rewrite the sentences using *if it wasn't / hadn't been for* ….**
▶  We have a dog, so I get some exercise.  *If it wasn't for the dog, I wouldn't get any exercise.*
▶  Because of Annie's brilliant idea, we found a place to stay.  *If it hadn't been for Annie's brilliant idea, we wouldn't have found a place to stay.*
1  I have a cat, so I have somebody to talk to.
....................................................................................................
2  Because I had a mobile phone, I was able to get help.
....................................................................................................
3  Because of your mother, things weren't OK.
....................................................................................................
4  Because of chocolate, I eat too much.
....................................................................................................
5  Because of old Mrs Perkins, the bank robbers didn't get away.
....................................................................................................

*if necessary* etc  We sometimes leave out **subject** + *be* after *if*. Note the common fixed expressions ***if necessary***, ***if any***, ***if anything***, ***if ever***, ***if in doubt***, ***if possible***.

**3 Choose the best expression.**

1  I'll work late tonight *if in doubt / if necessary*.
2  *If ever / If in doubt,* ask someone to explain.
3  He rarely *if ever / if anything* smiles.
4  We get few tourists here, *if ever / if any*.
5  'How's your leg?' '*If anything / If in doubt,* it's a little better, thank you.'

*if … should; if … happen to*  We can suggest that something is unlikely, or not particularly probable, by using ***should*** (not *would*) with *if*.

*If you **should** find yourself in Edinburgh, come and see us.*

***If … happen to*** is similar.

*If you **happen to** pass a paper shop, can you get me* The Times?

The two structures can be used together.

*If you **should happen to** see Tom, tell him I need those papers.*

**4 Use *should* and/or *happen to* with verbs from the box to complete the sentences.**

| feel like   have   run into   run out of   turn up |

1  If you .......................................................................... Emma, give her my love.
2  If Oliver ...................................................................., tell him I'm out.
3  If you .......................................................... a spare hour or two, come and see our new boat.
4  If I ................................................................. money, I've got some jewellery I can sell.
5  If you .......................................................... changing your job, have a word with my father.

*if … was/were to*  This structure emphasises that we are talking about something imaginary – just playing with an idea, so to speak.

*If the boss **were to** come in now, we'd be in real trouble.*
*What would you say if I **were to** ask you out for a drink?*

This can be a way of making a request less direct (see also page 291).

*If you **were to** move your chair a bit, we could all sit down.*

**5 Write a sentence beginning 'If I were to win the lottery …'**

.......................................................................................................................

**inversion**  In a very formal or literary style, conditional clauses can begin with **auxiliary** (especially *had*, *were* or *should*) + **subject**, instead of using *if*. This is not very common in modern English.

***Had I realised*** *the situation, I would have informed the police.*
***Were she*** *my daughter, I would insist that she behave properly.*
***Should anyone*** *object, they must be told to put their complaint in writing.*

**6 Rewrite these sentence beginnings using inversion.**

1  If she had asked, .............................................................................
2  If we were to close the department, ....................................................
3  If the soldiers had invaded, ..............................................................
4  If you had waited another week, .........................................................
5  If our finances were in better order, ....................................................
6  If the tax inspector should enquire, .....................................................

→

# *if*: more advanced points (continued)

**if for definite situations**  The most common use of *if* is to talk about **possible** or **uncertain** situations: the basic idea is 'If A happens, B will happen; if A doesn't happen, B won't happen'. But *if* can also be used to talk about what happens in **definite situations**, in sentences like the following. Note that *will* is possible with *if* in this case.

*'I'm not enjoying this.'  '**If** that's how you feel, why don't you go home?'*
*'Peter won't be there this evening.'  'Well, **if** he won't be there, it's not worth going.'*
*That's bad news. **If** they're going to close the factory, we're all in trouble.*
***If** I'm angry, it's because you lied to me.*

**if meaning 'although'**  In a formal style, *if* can be used to admit something before making a contrasting point. The meaning is rather like *although*. This is common in the structure **if + adjective** (with no verb).

*His style, **if simple**, is pleasant to read. (= 'Although his style is simple, it's …')*
*Their income, **if lower** than last year's, is enough for them to live on.*

**if meaning 'even if'**  We can use *if* to mean 'even if'.

*I'll finish this report **if** it takes me all night.     I'll learn to drive **if** it kills me.*

**7** **Complete the sentences using *if* and expressions from the box.**

| Jones has dropped out    stylish    that's your idea    tedious    I have to knit it |
|---|

1  Her singing, ...................................................................., has no real feeling.
2  .................................................................... of a joke, it's not mine.
3  ...................................................................., that's great – I've got a chance of winning.
4  The lecture, ...................................................................., was quite informative.
5  You'll have a new sweater for your birthday ....................................................................myself.

**8** **Write your own beginning for this sentence.**
.................................................................... if it kills me.

**other words and expressions**  A number of other words and expressions have similar meanings to *if* and are used in similar structures.

***Supposing** I went away for a week – would that be OK?*
*She says she'll lend us the flat **on condition that** we keep it clean.*

'California is a fine place to live, if you happen to be an orange.'
(*Fred Allen*)

'If I were your wife I would put poison in your coffee.' 'And if I were your husband I would drink it.'
(*Nancy Astor and Winston Churchill*)

'An Englishman, even if he is alone, forms an orderly queue of one.'
(*George Mikes*)

# *if*: informal structures

Some conditional structures are found mostly or only in informal speech.

**if I were you, I should/would ...**  This is a common way of giving advice.

*If I were you*, *I should sell that car.*     *I wouldn't take the job if I were you.*
*If I were you*, *I'd tell him to go somewhere else.*

We often drop *If I were you.*

*I should take an aspirin.* (= 'I suggest you take an aspirin.')
*I shouldn't worry.* (= 'Don't worry.')     *I wouldn't do that.*

**extra *not***  An extra *not* is sometimes put into *if*-clauses in sentences expressing doubt or uncertainty.

*I wonder if we **shouldn't** call the doctor.* (= '... if we should call the doctor.')
*I wouldn't be surprised if we **didn't** get some snow.* (= '... if we got some snow.')

**parallel verb forms**  In informal speech, (but rarely in writing) conditional sentences may have *would* or *'d* in both parts.

*How **would** we feel if this **would** happen in our family?*
*If I'd have known, I'd have told you.*

In past sentences of this kind, full forms (*had* or *would*) are sometimes used instead of *'d*, for emphasis or in negatives. The following are genuine examples taken from conversation.

*I didn't know. But if I **had've** known ...*
*If I **would've** had a gun, somebody might have got hurt.*
*If we **hadn't've** checked the opening times, I don't know what would have happened.*

**no *if***  In very informal speech (not in writing), *if* is sometimes **dropped**.

*You're not hungry, I won't bother to cook.*

This can sound aggressive.

*You want to get in, you pay like everybody else.*
*They don't like it here, they can go somewhere else.*

**❶ Rewrite these sentences so as to make them less informal.**

▶  I'd get that coat cleaned.  *If I were you, I would get that coat cleaned.*

1  I wonder if it wouldn't be better to wait till tomorrow.
   ....................................................................................

2  If she'd have asked me I'd have told her to go home
   ....................................................................................

3  What would you have said if one of your children would have done that?
   ....................................................................................

4  You need a drink, there's some beer in the fridge.
   ....................................................................................

5  I shouldn't park there.
   ....................................................................................

6  I wouldn't be surprised if she didn't just go just back home one of these days.
   ....................................................................................

# notes on some conjunctions

*as, since* and *because* (**reasons**) We prefer *as* and *since* to give a reason which is already known, or which is not the most important part of what we are saying. *As-* and *since*-clauses often come at the beginnings of sentences, leaving the more important information for later.

*As/Since you couldn't get here, we postponed the party till next weekend.*

We use *because* when the reason is new, or gives more important information.

*Why am I angry? I'm angry **because** you're acting like a spoilt child, that's why.*

**1** Is one better than the other or not? (Circle) A, B or both.

1  The parcel got there late … I forgot to post it.  **A** *as*  **B** *because*
2  … you wouldn't listen to me, I went and talked to the manager.  **A** *As*  **B** *Since*
3  … everybody's on holiday, all the offices are closed.  **A** *As*  **B** *Since*
4  I went to sleep in the lecture … it was so boring.  **A** *because*  **B** *as*
5  'Why are you so late?' '… the buses weren't running, I had to walk.'  **A** *Because*  **B** *Since*
6  … I was ill for six months, I lost my job.  **A** *As*  **B** *Because*

*when, as* and *while* (**things happening at the same time**) All three of these can be used for a longer 'background' situation which is going on when something else happens.

*The doorbell always rings **when you're having a bath**.*
***As I was walking down the street**, I saw Joe coming out of a bookshop.*
***While they were playing cards**, somebody broke into the house.*

*As* and *while* can also be used with simple tenses in this case, especially with 'state' verbs like *sit* or *lie*.

***As** I sat reading the paper, the door burst open.*

For simultaneous long actions, we generally use *while*, with simple or progressive verbs.

***While** you **were reading** the paper, I **was working**.*
*Pete **cooked** supper while I **watched / was watching** TV.*

**2** Choose the best verb form or conjunction.

1  She always interrupts me when I *try / am trying* to work.
2  The electricity went off while I *watched / was watching* the football.
3  *As / When* I lay on the beach, I got more and more sleepy.
4  Andy *packed / was packing* the suitcases while I got the children ready.
5  *As* I *got / was getting* up, I heard a noise in the kitchen.

'I'm sorry, but as your account's not with us
you'll have to show me a cheque card.'

*while* and *whereas* (**contrast**) Both of these are rather formal, particularly *whereas*.

*Ann is a gifted pianist, **while** her husband is an excellent violinist.*
*The north of the country is heavily wooded, **whereas** the south is semi-desert.*

**3** **Compare yourself with some other people.**

I'm ...................................................................., while

....................................................................

I'm ...................................................................,

....................................................................

I'm ...................................................................,

....................................................................

**4** **Compare two places.**

.................................... is ...................................., while

....................................................................

*as if* and *as though* After these, a past tense can suggest **unreality** in the present.

*Carol looks as if she **is** rich, and Harry talks as if he **was** rich.*
(Carol is probably rich; Harry probably isn't.)
*He always walks into a room as though he **owned** the place.*

*Like* is often used informally instead of *as if/though*. Some people consider this incorrect.

*You look **like** you've had bad news.*

**5** **Which is better?** (Circle) **A, B or both.**

1  You look as if you … had a shock.   **A** *have*   **B** *had*
2  His voice sounds as if he … talking under water.   **A** *is*   **B** *was*
3  The heating's off. It seems as though the thermostat … faulty.   **A** *is*   **B** *was*
4  She talks to people as if she … a senior member of the royal family.   **A** *is*   **B** *was*
5  Her French is as good as if she … grown up in France, but she's never been there.   **A** *has*   **B** *had*

**6** **Complete the sentence in any way you like.**

I sometimes feel as if ...............................................................................

*whether … or…* can be used to mean 'It doesn't matter whether … or …'.
Different structures are possible.

***Whether** you like swimming **or** climbing **or** walking, you'll find something to enjoy.*
***Whether** you like it **or not**, I'm going to Ireland.*
***Whether or not** you agree, we're having a party here next weekend.*
***Whether** he stays **or whether** he goes, I'm not having any more to do with him.*

**7** (Circle) **A, B or both.**

1  …, it's a wonderful story.   **A** *Whether or not he's lying*   **B** *Whether he's lying or not*
2  Whether we go out … stay in, we'll need to have something to eat.   **A** *or*   **B** *or whether*
3  … it rains at the weekend, we're going camping.   **A** *Whether or not*   **B** *Whether or doesn't*
4  I'm leaving this job next month, … they can find a replacement for me.   **A** *Whether*   **B** *Whether or not*
5  I'll enjoy the match, whether we win …   **A** *or not*   **B** *or whether not*

→

# notes on some conjunctions (continued)

**five time conjunctions** *Now (that)* is used when we talk about new circumstances.

*Now the exams are over, I can enjoy myself.*

*Once* expresses a necessary starting point for a situation. It is not followed by *that*.

*Once Phil gets here we can start.*     *Once I've found a job I'll feel better.*

*The moment (that)* and (in British English) *immediately* and *directly* are similar to *as soon as*.

*I loved you the moment I saw you.*     *Tell me immediately you have any news.*
*Directly I walked in the door, I smelt smoke.*

**8** **Is one better than the other or not?** (Circle) A, B or both.

1   … you've tasted their ice cream, you won't be satisfied with anything else.   **A** *Once*   **B** *Once that*
2   What are you going to do … you've got all this free time?   **A** *now*   **B** *now that*
3   … I saw what was happening in the bathroom, I phoned a plumber.   **A** *Now*   **B** *Immediately*
4   … Alex walked in, I knew there was going to be trouble.   **A** *The moment*   **B** *The moment that*
5   Give me a ring … you arrive.   **A** *directly*   **B** *now that*

**9** **Complete these sentences in any way you like.**

Once I've ......................................................................................................................................,
I'll ...........................................................................................................................................
The moment I saw ..................................................................................................................

**After *so that*, *as … as* and *than*, present** and **future** tenses are often both possible.

*She's going to start out early so that she doesn't/won't get stuck in rush-hour traffic.*
*I'll get there as early as you do/will.*
*I'll probably have more trouble than you do/will.*

**After *because* and *although*,** tense simplification (see pages 204–205) does not usually happen:
we use *will* and *would*, not present or past tenses.

*I'll be OK because Andy will go with me.* (NOT … ~~because Andy goes with me.~~)
*I'd be happy to help you, although I wouldn't be free in the evenings.*
(NOT … ~~although I wasn't free in the evenings.~~)

**10** **Is one better than the other or not?** (Circle) A, B or both.

1   I don't think I'll stay in this job as long as you …   **A** *will*   **B** *do*
2   I'll pass your message to Maggie, although I … see her until Sunday.   **A** *don't*   **B** *won't*
3   I'm going to stop work early so that we … time for a proper talk.   **A** *have*   **B** *will have*
4   You'll certainly get better exam results than I …   **A** *do*   **B** *will*
5   We can't go on holiday next week, because the car … ready in time.   **A** *isn't*   **B** *won't be*

For tenses in subordinate clauses, see also pages 204–205. For tenses with *since*, see page 49. For tenses after *bet* and *hope*, see page 307.

'Once the toothpaste is out of the tube,
it's hard to get it back in.'
(*H R Haldeman*)

# whoever, whatever, wherever etc

> **Whoever, whatever, wherever etc** (meaning 'It doesn't matter who/what/where/etc') can introduce adverb clauses. Present tenses are used for the future.

**Whoever** *comes to the door, tell them I'm out.*
**Whatever** *you do, I'll always love you.* (NOT ~~Whatever you'll do~~ …)
**Wherever** *he goes, he'll find friends.*
**Whichever** *of them you marry, you'll have problems.*
*I try to see Vicky* **whenever** *I go to London.*
**However** *much he eats, he never gets fat.*

**1** Put in *whoever, whatever* etc.

1 ......................... you marry, make sure he can cook.
2 Keep calm, ......................... happens.
3 You'll be very welcome, ......................... day you come.
4 The people in Canada were friendly ......................... we went.
5 You can stay with us ......................... you like.
6 ......................... many times you say that, I won't believe you.
7 ......................... you explain it to her, she's still going to be angry.
8 It's certain to be a good game, ......................... wins.
9 ......................... I try to talk to her she goes out of the room.

**2** Rewrite the words *in italics*.

▶ *I don't know who directed this film*, but it's not much good.
  .Whoever directed this film ...............................................

1 People always want more, *it doesn't matter how rich they are.*
  ................................................................................

2 *It doesn't matter how you travel*, it'll take you at least three days.
  ................................................................................

3 *You can say what you like*, I don't think he's the right man for you.
  ................................................................................

4 *It doesn't matter what problems you have*, you can always come to me for advice.
  ................................................................................

5 *Any time I see you* I feel nervous.
  ................................................................................

6 *It doesn't matter what time you turn up*, we'll be glad to see you.
  ................................................................................

> We can use **no matter who/what/where** etc in the same way as *whoever* etc.

**No matter who** *comes to the door, tell them I'm out.*

**3** Put in *no matter who/what/etc.*

1 ......................... you do, I'll always believe in you.
2 ......................... train we take, we can't get there before 10.00
3 ......................... hard he tries, he always gets everything wrong.
4 ......................... you say, I know I'm right.
5 ......................... we go away, Paul won't be able to come with us.
6 ......................... many times I tell them, they forget.

For *whoever, whatever* and *whichever* in noun clauses, see page 227.

# participle clauses

Participles (*-ing* and *-ed* forms) can introduce clauses (without conjunctions).
This is rather formal, and is more common in writing than in speech.

*Looking out of the window*, Harry saw that it was snowing again.
*Knowing what he was like*, I was careful to be polite.
*Not being a very sociable person*, he found a seat where he could be by himself.
Alice had a violent row with Peter, *completely ruining the evening*.
*Having found what I was looking for*, I went back home.
*Stored in a cool place*, this bread will last for weeks.

**1  Rewrite the sentences with participle clauses.**

1  *As I didn't want* to upset everybody, I said nothing.

......................................................................................................................................

2  On Friday George arrived, *and brought* news from the Irish cousins.

......................................................................................................................................

3  The dog rushed round the room, *and broke* one priceless ornament after another.

......................................................................................................................................

4  *As I knew* what he liked, I sent him a large bouquet of orchids.

......................................................................................................................................

5  *If it is fried in butter,* it should taste delicious.

......................................................................................................................................

6  A train caught fire near Oxford, *and caused* long delays.

......................................................................................................................................

7  *As I was not in a hurry,* I stopped for a coffee and a sandwich.

......................................................................................................................................

8  *As he had lost* all his money, he had no way of getting home.
   Having ...............................................................................................................................

**2  GRAMMAR IN A TEXT.  Put the participles from the box into the text.**

belonging   checking   getting   protected   provided   satisfied   shooting
sipping   stolen   stopping   walking   watching

Carson was sitting comfortably in the deep leather armchair that had
belonged to his father, [1].................... his drink and [2].................... a
rather bad comedy programme. As he relaxed into the evening, a black saloon,
[3].................... earlier from outside a hotel in Kensington and immediately
[4].................... with new licence plates, drifted slowly down the street outside
his house. It was a street of big houses, [5].................... by tall hedges and
well-kept gardens, and obviously [6].................... to people with few money
worries. This was the driver's third time round, [7].................... for pedestrians,
people in parked cars, or any other possible witnesses. Finally [8]....................
, he pulled over to the side of the road, [9].................... just outside Carson's
driveway, and switched off the engine. The doors opened at once, all four
of them [10].................... out, Henry [11].................... out the nearest street
light with a silenced .22 as they did so. They moved quickly into the driveway,
Marco first, Pepe last, [12].................... backwards to make sure no one was
watching, and went quietly up to the front door.

**'misrelated' participles** The subject of a participle clause is normally the same as the subject of the main clause, and it is generally considered incorrect to mix subjects, at least in formal writing. Compare:

*Standing by the window*, Sue gazed at the mountains. (Sue stood; Sue gazed)
*Standing by the window*, *the mountains seemed very close.*
(This sounds as if the mountains were standing by the window.)

However, mixed subjects are common when one of them is *it* or *there.*

*Being French, **it** is surprising that she is such a terrible cook.*
*Having so little time, **there** was not much that I could do.*

This also happens with some fixed expressions describing the speaker's attitude (e.g. *generally speaking, judging from …, considering …, taking everything into consideration.*)

*Generally speaking*, *men can run faster than women.*
*Judging from his expression*, *he was in a bad mood.*

**3** (Circle) the best continuation.

1 Getting out of the car, *Mrs Perkins / the pavement* …
2 Working late at night, *a noise / Josie* …
3 Starting German lessons, *the verbs / I* …
4 Looking out of the window, *Sandra / a taxi* …
5 Sitting in the front row at the circus, *an elephant / the children* …
6 Waking up suddenly, *I / a smell of burning* …

'Standing by the window, the mountains seem very close.'

**4** Correct (✓) or not (✗)?

1 Considering everything, the holiday was a success. …
2 Running up the stairs, my wallet fell out of my pocket. …
3 Brushing her teeth, a thought suddenly occurred to her. …
4 Generally speaking, children don't like green vegetables. …
5 Looking under the bed, I found a book that I'd lost. …
6 Being short of time, the housework didn't get done. …

**own subject** If necessary, a participle clause can have its own subject.

*Nobody having anything more to say, **the meeting** broke up.*
*Hands held high, **the dancers** circle to the left.*

**5** Add subjects from the box.

| her doll | her smile | smoke | the fire | the school hall | the treasurer |
|----------|-----------|-------|----------|-----------------|---------------|

1 ………………………………… having gone out, the room began to feel quite cold.
2 A little girl walked past, ………………………………… dragging behind her on the pavement.
3 A car roared round the corner, ………………………………… pouring from the exhaust.
4 ………………………………… being much too small, the concert was held outside.
5 ………………………………… fixed in place as if with glue, the Princess distributed the prizes.
6 ………………………………… having finished his report, questions were invited from the members.

# after ...ing, on ...ing etc

**Some conjunctions and prepositions** can introduce participle clauses.

*After waiting for two hours I gave up and went home.*
*Check the mirror before driving off.*
*I've learnt a lot since coming here.*
*Always wear gloves when working with chemicals.*
*I find it difficult to read while travelling.*
*In deciding to spend a year studying Arabic, I made a very wise decision.*

*On doing* something (formal) means '**when/as soon as** you do something.'

*On hearing the fire alarm, go straight to the nearest exit.*

**1** Complete the sentences with *before, after* or *since* and words from the box.
Use *-ing* forms.

| abandon | analyse | apply | qualify | rearrange | sign |
|---------|---------|-------|---------|-----------|------|

1 ............................................................. the powder, Dr Fisher reported that it was poisonous.
2 ........................ spending hours ........................ the furniture, I put it all back where it was before.
3 ................................................................ for that job, take a careful look at the conditions of work.
4 ................................................................ as an accountant, Rachel hasn't actually done a day's work.
5 ................................................................. a contract, always look carefully at the small print.
6 ................................................................ the ship, the crew spent three days in an open boat.

**2** Put in words from the box. (Different answers may be possible.)

| after | before | before | besides | in | on | on | since | when | while |
|-------|--------|--------|---------|----|----|----|-------|------|-------|

1 I've heard nothing ........................... sending in the application.
2 ........................... arriving at the airport, you should go directly to the check-in desk.
3 They met ........................... studying in Germany.
4 ........................... twisting his ankle, he also cracked a rib.
5 Please check the lights ........................... locking up.
6 Keep the room well ventilated ........................... using this product.
7 ........................... being introduced, British people often shake hands.
8 I usually read in bed for a bit ........................... putting the light out.
9 I never want to work ........................... going out for lunch.
10 ........................... agreeing to sign a three-year contract, Patrick made a serious mistake.

**3** Complete this sentence about yourself.

After finishing my studies, I ...................................................................................................................

**Note:** A few conjunctions (e.g. *until, when, if*) can introduce clauses with past participles.
*Keep stirring until cooked.*     *When arrested, he confessed at once.*
*If asked, say nothing.*     *Once deprived of oxygen, they die within minutes.*

For *by ...ing* used to talk about methods (e.g. *You won't get rich by writing poetry*), see page 194.

'On first entering an underground train,
it is customary to shake hands with
every passenger.'
(*R J Phillips: misleading advice for tourists*)

# infinitive clauses

**infinitive clauses of purpose** are often constructed with *in order* and *so as* in a formal style. Compare:

*I moved house to be nearer to my work.* (normal)
*I moved house **in order to be** / **so as to be** nearer my work.* (more formal)

These structures are very common with negative infinitives of purpose.

*I moved house **so as not to be** too far from my work.*
(more normal than *I moved house not to be too far from my work.*)

1  **Why might you do the following? Give possible reasons, using *so as (not) to* or *in order (not) to*.**

▶  lock your house  *so as not to be burgled* ...........................................
1  wear a raincoat  ...............................................................
2  put an extra blanket on your bed  .................................................
3  get a dog  ....................................................................
4  buy a map  ....................................................................
5  write down a phone number  ......................................................
6  set your alarm clock  ..........................................................
7  join a club  ..................................................................
8  go to a gym  ..................................................................
9  stop eating chocolate  .........................................................
10  buy a bicycle  ...............................................................

**(only) to find …**  Infinitive clauses can be used to say what somebody **learnt** or **found out** at the end of a journey or task.

*I arrived home **to find** that the house had been burgled.*

The idea of surprise can be emphasised with *only*.

*He spent four years studying geology, **only to discover** that there were no jobs.*

2  **Write your own continuation for one or more of these sentences, using (only) to find/discover/learn/realise.**

He arrived at his girlfriend's house, ...............................................................
I spoke to them carefully in French, ...............................................................
She opened the parcel with great excitement, .......................................................
We arrived at the address on the invitation, ......................................................
I opened the door of my room, ......................................................................

**To see/hear …**  can be used to give the reason for a false impression.

***To hear** her talk, you'd think she was made of money.*
***To see** her look at him, you'd never realise that she hates him.*

3  **Write your own continuation for one or more of these sentences.**

To see them together, you'd think ...................................................................
To read the advertisement, you'd think ..............................................................
To see him playing tennis, you'd never guess ........................................................
To hear him talk, ...................................................................................

# more practice

**1** **Correct or not? Correct the mistakes or write 'Correct'.**

▶ I'll see you tomorrow if I'll have time. ..*have*..................

▶ You look as though you've got toothache. ..*Correct*.....................

1 If I had finished my studies I would have been a dentist now. .....................................

2 The way he drives, I'll be surprised unless he has an accident soon. .....................................

3 In case Sally comes this weekend, we'll take her ice-skating. .....................................

4 If you would wait here for a moment, I'll see if the manager is free. .....................................

5 Let's get a new computer, if it will speed things up. .....................................

6 If it hadn't been for Joe we'd have been in bad trouble. .....................................

7 If you in doubt, just ask somebody what to do. .....................................

8 If you should happen to see Carl, give him my best wishes. .....................................

9 I don't know what we'd do if the boss were to walk in now. .....................................

10 I'll finish this race, even it kills me. .....................................

**2** **Which is/are correct? Circle A, B or both.**

1 Our train was delayed … there was an accident.   **A** *as*   **B** *because*

2 I'm tall and fair, … the rest of my family are short and dark.   **A** *while*   **B** *whereas*

3 Whether you like it or …, I'm coming with you.   **A** *not*   **B** *don't*

4 … we're all here, perhaps we can start.   **A** *Now*   **B** *Now that*

5 … the toothpaste is out of the tube, you can't put it back.   **A** *Once*   **B** *Once that*

6 You will have to wait in the queue, … you are.   **A** *whoever*   **B** *whoever that*

7 Looking out of the window, … a wedding procession.   **A** *there was*   **B** *I saw*

8 Nobody … any better ideas, we spent the evening at home.   **A** *having*   **B** *had*

9 On … the room, please switch off all the lights.   **A** *leaving*   **B** *you leave*

10 … at him, you would never dream he was a billionaire.   **A** *Looking*   **B** *To look*

**3** **Very formal (F), very informal (I) or normal (N)?**

1 Had she known what he was really like, she would never have married him. …

2 I've got a sore throat. I wonder if I haven't got flu. …

3 I don't know what I would have done if it hadn't been for your help. …

4 If I'd have been there, I'd have said something to her. …

5 Once the flood waters had gone, people began to return to their homes. …

6 Were we to open a new branch, what would be the expected costs? …

7 If necessary, you can get help from a customer service officer. …

8 You want a licence, you fill in this form. …

**4** **Complete some of these sentences any way you like.**

Whenever ................................................................................................, I feel nervous.

Wherever you go, ...........................................................................................................

However much ..................................................., I always ...............................................

Whatever happens, I .......................................................................................................

**GRAMMAR IN A TEXT.** A few years ago, Kipling's 'If' was voted Britain's favourite poem. **You may like to read it with a dictionary.**

# IF

If you can keep your head when all about you
Are losing theirs and blaming it on you,
If you can trust yourself when all men doubt you,
But make allowance for their doubting too;

If you can wait and not be tired by waiting,
Or being lied about, don't deal in lies,
Or being hated, don't give way to hating,
And yet don't look too good, nor talk too wise:

If you can dream - and not make dreams
    your master;
If you can think - and not make thoughts
    your aim;
If you can meet with Triumph and Disaster
And treat those two impostors just the same;

If you can bear to hear the truth you've spoken
Twisted by knaves to make a trap for fools,
Or watch the things you gave your life to, broken,
And stoop and build 'em up with worn-out tools:

If you can make one heap of all your winnings
And risk it on one turn of pitch-and-toss,
And lose, and start again at your beginnings
And never breathe a word about your loss;

If you can force your heart and nerve and sinew
To serve your turn long after they are gone,
And so hold on when there is nothing in you
Except the Will which says to them: 'Hold on!'

If you can talk with crowds and keep your virtue,
Or walk with kings - nor lose the common touch,
if neither foes nor loving friends can hurt you,
If all men count with you, but none too much;

If you can fill the unforgiving minute
With sixty seconds' worth of distance run,
Yours is the Earth and everything that's in it,
And - which is more - you'll be a Man, my son!

*(Rudyard Kipling, 1865–1936)*

'Well, wherever he is, he's just
dug up two dozen snowdrops!'

**INTERNET EXERCISE.** Use a search engine to find some interesting sentences with *unless*,
and some with *in case*. Write them here. Does *unless* always mean 'except if'?
And is *in case* nearly always used for precautions?

................................................................................................................................
................................................................................................................................
................................................................................................................................
................................................................................................................................

# Part 2 grammar beyond the sentence

It is not possible to make a clear division between 'sentence grammar' and 'text grammar': many aspects of language structure are important in both areas. However, the following sections deal particularly with grammar that is useful for producing and understanding written and spoken texts.

## Contents of part 2

'I miss the good old days when all
we had to worry about was nouns and verbs.'

# information structure: what comes first?

**important new information last** When we communicate about a situation, we can organise the information in different ways. Most often, a clause or sentence moves from 'known' to 'new'; from low to high information value. So we often start with something that has already been mentioned, or that is already familiar, or that is not the main point.

*'How's Joe these days?' 'Oh, fine.* **He's** *just got married to a very nice girl.'*
(more natural than '... **A very nice girl's** *just got married to him.'*)
*Then* **she** *met another rich man.* (more natural than *Then* **another rich man** *met her.*)
**Sally** *was bitten by a dog.* (more natural than **A dog** *bit Sally.*)
**Our dog** *bit the postman.* (more natural than **The postman** *was bitten by our dog.*)

**1** **Which is most natural? Circle A or B.**

1  **A** I've got a few pounds in the bank.    **B** The bank is holding a few pounds of mine.
2  'Where does Angela live?'    **A** 'The bank is opposite her flat.'    **B** 'Her flat is opposite the bank.'
3  **A** Then he had another operation.    **B** Then the surgeons operated on him again.
4  'Where are my keys?'    **A** 'They're by the phone.'    **B** 'The phone is by them.'

**order of clauses** An adverb clause can go before or after a main clause. The clause with the newer or more important information usually goes last.

*Sonia screamed* **when she saw the monster**. (gives her reason for screaming)
**When she saw the monster**, *Sonia screamed*. (gives her reaction to the monster)

**2** **Choose explanations from the box for the main point of each sentence, and write the letters.**

> A cause of destruction   B consequence of earthquake   C reaction to rising costs
> D reason for abandonment   E reason for building   F solution to space problem

1  The company abandoned the project because costs had tripled.  …
2  Because costs had tripled, the company abandoned the project.  …
3  When the 1986 earthquake struck the town, the cathedral was destroyed.  …
4  The cathedral was destroyed when the 1986 earthquake struck the town.  …
5  So that Andy could have his own room, we built an extension onto the house.  …
6  We built an extension onto the house, so that Andy could have his own room.  …

**Note: end-weight** Longer and heavier structures normally come last in a clause or sentence. (They usually have the highest information value in any case.)

> *I was astonished at* **the time it took him to get dressed in the morning**. (more natural than *The time it took him to get dressed in the morning astonished me.*)

Because of this, we often use a structure with preparatory *it*, in order to move a clause or infinitive subject to the end of a sentence (see page 228).

> *It worried me that she hadn't been in touch for so long.* (more natural than *That she hadn't been in touch for so long worried me.*)
> *I consider it important to read all the small print before signing a contract.*

Adverbs do not normally separate a verb from its object. However, an adverb may come before a very long and heavy object. Compare:

> *She plays tennis* **very well**. (NOT *She plays very well tennis.*)
> *She plays* **very well** *every game that you can think of, and several that you cannot.*

For special structures used for emphasis, and other kinds of special word order, see pages 257–261.

# information structure: getting the right subject

**choosing the structure** English clauses usually begin with the grammatical subject; so speakers and writers choose structures that will put 'known' or less important information in the subject position (depending on what they want to highlight).

*(That storm!)* **It** *damaged Margaret's roof pretty badly.*
*(Look at Margaret's roof!)* **It** *got damaged in the storm.*
*(Poor old Margaret!)* **She** *had her roof damaged in the storm.*

In these examples, an active structure makes it possible to start with the storm, a passive makes it possible to start with the roof, and the structure with *have* makes it possible to start with Margaret. (For more about choosing between actives and passives, see pages 80–81.)

**1** **Rewrite the sentences twice.**

1 Burglars stole all Sandra's jewellery.
All ....................................................................................................................................
Sandra ...............................................................................................................................

2 My palm was read by a fortune-teller.
I ........................................................................................................................................
A .......................................................................................................................................

3 We had the central heating put in by Jenkins and Fowler.
The central heating ...........................................................................................................
Jenkins and Fowler ...........................................................................................................

4 The doctor checked my blood pressure.
My blood pressure .............................................................................................................
I ........................................................................................................................................

5 The car was serviced by my neighbour, who's a mechanic.
My ....................................................................................................................................
I ........................................................................................................................................

6 I had the house looked at by a qualified surveyor.
The ....................................................................................................................................
A .......................................................................................................................................

**choosing the verb** We can often get the right element in the subject position by choosing the right verb. Compare:

- *The biscuit factory* **employs** *7,000 people.* (in an article about local industry)
  *7,000 people* **work for** *the biscuit factory.* (in an article about the local population)
- *Paul* **led** *the children outside.* (giving information about Paul)
  *The children* **followed** *Paul outside.* (giving information about the children)

**2** **Rewrite the sentences with different verbs.**

1 Oliver impresses everybody. (*admire*)
..............................................................................................................................................

2 I bought a faulty hair dryer from a man in the market. (*sell*)
..............................................................................................................................................

3 I learnt Spanish from Mrs Lopez. (*teach*)
..............................................................................................................................................

4 I borrowed the money I needed from my sister. (*lend*)
..............................................................................................................................................

5 Joe's stories amuse everybody. (*laugh*)
..............................................................................................................................................

6 The flu epidemic in 1918–19 killed over 20 million people. (*die*)
..............................................................................................................................................

*It, this* and *that* can all be used in a text to refer back to something. There are sometimes differences. *It* usually refers to something that is already being discussed.

*As the cleaner was moving the computer, he dropped **it** onto the table. **It** was badly damaged.*
(The computer was damaged.)

*This* refers to something new that is just being brought to somebody's attention.

*As the cleaner was moving the computer, he dropped it onto the table. **This** was badly damaged.*
(The table was damaged.)

**1  Choose the best pronoun.**

1  The house that she bought was in the centre of the village, near the church. *It / This* had four rooms and a pleasant garden.
2  THE OLD SCHOOL HOUSE, BARTON. *It / This* is an attractive 19th-century house, recently restored and in excellent condition, with a mature garden …
3  After she had lived there for a time, she decided to paint the house pink. *It / This* upset the neighbours a bit.
4  I saw a really good film yesterday. I think you'll like *it / this*.
5  VAMPIRES FROM SPACE: *It / This* is a film for all the family …
6  Scientists have now decided that chocolate is good for you. *It / This* is welcome news for my wife.
7  He put the chocolate in his pocket and forgot about *it / this*. *It / This* melted.

*This* is also used to refer forward to something new that is going to happen or be said.
*That* refers back to what has already happened or been said, with more emphasis than *it*. Compare:

*Tell me what you think about **this**: I thought I'd get a job in Spain for a few months.*
*I thought I'd get a job in Spain for a few months. Tell me what you think about **that**.*

**2  Choose the best pronoun.**

1  So you think your French is good? OK, see if you can translate *this / that*.
2  'Where's the hair dryer?'  'I put *it / this* in the top cupboard.'
3  So then I told her exactly what I thought of her kids. *It / That* really got her jumping up and down.
4  *That / This* was a lovely meal. Thank you very much.
5  Now what about *this / that / it*? Suppose we go camping in Scotland in July, and then in August we …
6  In the middle of the service a dog came into the church. Mrs Perkins got up and took *it / that* out again.

When *he, she* and *it* are used, it is important to make sure the reference is clear. Here is a note from the *Independent* newspaper, apologising for confusing readers the day before.

## Pronoun soup again on Wednesday.

Christina Patterson commented on a row between Iain Duncan Smith and George Osborne: 'But he did, according to one source, tell the Chancellor that he was 'not prepared to tolerate' the 'appalling' way he treated his department, and that he should 'show more respect.'

His staff, he said, 'did not deserve to be treated in such an arrogant way'.'

The words "he" and 'his' appear seven times. The first, second, fourth, sixth and seventh times, they mean Mr Duncan Smith; the third and fifth times, they mean Mr Osborne. More than once, the reader pauses to work out who "he" is.

Guy Keleny, *The Independent* (adapted)

# conjunctions and adverbs: structure and punctuation

**Conjunctions** (see pages 200–206) make **grammatical** and **meaning** connections – they join clauses into sentences, and show the relationship between them. Some conjunctions:

*and, but, or, so, before, after, when, as soon as, because, since, although, if, that*

When a conjunction comes between two clauses, there is normally either **no punctuation** (especially if the clauses are short) or a **comma (,)** before it in writing.

*I had supper **before** I phoned Jean.     I was very unhappy**, so** I decided to change my job.*

**Adverbs** can make **meaning** connections, but they do **not** make **grammatical** connections: they do not join clauses into sentences. Some adverbs:

*however, then, therefore, meanwhile, consequently, in fact, also, as a result, on the other hand, indeed*

When an **adverb** comes between two clauses, there is normally either a **full stop (.)** or a **semi-colon (;)** before it in careful writing, because the clauses are still separate.

*I had supper**; then** I phoned Jean.* OR *I had supper**. Then** I phoned Jean.*
(better than *I had supper, then I phoned Jean.*)
*I was unhappy**; therefore** I moved away.* OR *I was unhappy**. Therefore** I moved away.*

**1** **Put a comma, a semi-colon or nothing between the words in italics.**

1 One person asked a *question   then* there was a long silence.
2 We will ship your *order   as soon as* we have received supplies from the manufacturer.
3 The brakes need *attention   also*, there is a problem with the steering.
4 It was bitterly *cold   and* snow was forecast.
5 It was not possible to make a *decision   because* the necessary information was not available.
6 A is greater than B, and B is greater than C *therefore* A is greater than C.
7 Not enough people bought *tickets   so* the concert was cancelled.

***but*** **and** ***however*** **But** is a **conjunction**; ***however*** is an **adverb**. Note the difference in punctuation **before** these words.

*It was cold**, but** it was pleasant.*
*It was cold**. However,** it was pleasant.* OR *It was cold**; however,** it was pleasant.*
(better than *It was cold, however …*)

Note that we also put a comma **after** *however*.

**2** **Rewrite the sentences, changing *but* to *however* or vice versa.**

▸ Alice was clearly the best candidate, but she did not get the job.
  *Alice was clearly the best candidate; however, she did not get the job.*
▸ The audience was small; however, they were clearly appreciative.
  *The audience was small, but they were clearly appreciative.*
1 She has considerable musical ability; however, her technique is poor.

2 Nobody liked him, but everybody agreed that he was a good manager.

3 It is a reliable and economical car, but its performance is disappointing.

4 Simpson was not playing at his best; however, he managed to win the match.

5 The house is in reasonable condition, but the roof will need some repairs.

**3** Rewrite the sentences using the adverbs and adverbial expressions in the box.
Be careful with the punctuation.

> also   consequently   on the other hand   then   there

1   The bank is very inefficient, and the staff are remarkably rude.

    ......................................................................................................................................................

2   We bought a map before we set off to explore the town.

    ......................................................................................................................................................

3   There had been no investment for years, so the railways were in a terrible state.

    ......................................................................................................................................................

4   The people are friendly, but it is difficult to get to know them really well.

    ......................................................................................................................................................

5   We walked down to the beach area, where we found the men we were looking for.

    ......................................................................................................................................................

**4** Complete these sentences any way you like.

1   I like ...................................................; however, ..............................................................

2   ................................................ can be useful; on the other hand, ......................................

3   ................................................ is ......................; in addition, ..........................................

> **position**   Conjunctions always begin clauses. Adverbs can often go in different places in a clause
> (but not between the verb and the object). If an adverb interrupts the normal word order of a clause,
> it may be separated by two commas.

*He confessed to 114 murders, but the police did not believe his story.*
(BUT NOT … ~~the police but did not believe his story.~~)
*He confessed to 114 murders; **however**, the police did not believe his story.*
*He confessed to 114 murders; the police, **however**, did not believe his story.*
*He confessed to 114 murders; the police did not, **however**, believe his story.*
*He confessed to 114 murders; the police did not believe his story, **however**.*
(BUT NOT … ~~the police did not believe, however, his story.~~)

**5** Rewrite the sentences, putting the expressions *in italics* in other places.

1   He had little talent; *on the other hand*, his sister was a brilliant musician.

    ......................................................................................................................................................

2   The hospital was seriously understaffed; *in spite of that*, the standard of care was excellent.

    ......................................................................................................................................................

3   Andrew overslept; *as a result*, the whole family missed the plane.

    ......................................................................................................................................................

> 'The past is not dead.
> In fact, it's not even past.'
> (*William Faulkner*)

> 'It is forbidden to kill;
> therefore all murderers are
> punished unless they kill in
> large numbers and to the
> sound of trumpets.'
> (*Voltaire*)

> 'The reasonable man adapts
> himself to the world; the
> unreasonable one persists
> in trying to adapt the world
> to himself. Therefore all
> progress depends on the
> unreasonable man.'
> (*G B Shaw*)

> 'Never doubt that a small group
> of thoughtful, committed citizens
> can change the world. Indeed, it
> is the only thing that ever has.'
> (*Margaret Mead*)

# linking clauses with conjunctions and adverbs (continued)

**6** **GRAMMAR IN A TEXT.** Put commas (,,) or semi-colons (;;) before the numbered words.

In the early years we were breaking new ground ¹and there were naturally a number of difficulties ²however, business was for the most part excellent. Credit was easily available ³indeed, the banks were only too anxious to offer loans to new companies ⁴in addition, interest rates rarely went above 4% through the whole of the period. Costs were low ⁵also, there was an almost inexhaustible demand for our product. Staffing was sometimes problematic ⁶since a large proportion of the labour force was semi-skilled at best ⁷and experienced and well-qualified managers were by no means easy to find. This meant that there was a rapid turnover of employees ⁸consequently quality sometimes suffered ⁹although customers were not in general highly critical. Now, twenty years later, conditions have changed dramatically ¹⁰and the overall picture is very different indeed ¹¹however, I am happy to say that despite everything we are still managing to remain profitable.

---

**NOTES**

**Commas are often used before conjunctions** to separate longer or more complicated clauses (see page 254). Shorter pairs of clauses are often connected without commas. Compare:

*Joseph went home because he was tired.*
*Joseph decided to go home earlier than he had planned, because he was beginning to have trouble keeping his eyes open.*

**contrast** Commas are particularly common before conjunctions expressing contrast.

*Ann is very sociable, **while** her sister is quite shy.*
*He kept shivering, **although** it was a warm day.*

And **adverbs** expressing contrast often have commas **after** them.

*They were becoming increasingly discouraged. **However,** they continued walking.*
*Income is satisfactory; **on the other hand,** expenditure has increased alarmingly.*
***Yet,** at the beginning of a clause, is a **conjunction**, and is not followed by a comma.*
*It was cold, yet it was pleasant.* (NOT ... *yet, it was pleasant.*)

**clause position** Clauses that begin sentences are usually separated by commas. Compare:

***As soon as it boils,** turn down the heat.*     *Turn down the heat **as soon as it boils**.*

**punctuation with no conjunction** When two main clauses are joined without a conjunction, they can be punctuated with a semi-colon, a colon or a dash, but not a comma.

*We had no idea where he was; he had completely disappeared.*
(NOT *We had no idea where he was, he had completely disappeared.*)
*She had one basic principle: she was always right.*
*We will send your order as soon as possible – this will probably be in early July.*

**one-clause sentences** Sometimes a single clause with a conjunction is written as a separate sentence. Some people feel this is incorrect, but it is normal in question-and-answer sequences, or when a writer wishes to give extra emphasis to a clause.

*Why are we in financial trouble? **Because** the banks lent money to the wrong people.*
*He was charming. **But** he was totally without a conscience.*

---

For *however* as a conjunction (e.g. ***However** we travel, we have to go through London*), see page 243.

# special word order: fronting

**fronting and topicalisation** Affirmative sentences usually begin with a grammatical subject.

*We have already discussed that question at some length.*
*My father just can't stand people like that.*

If we begin a sentence with something else ('fronting') this is often to give it **emphasis**, and to make it the **topic** – the thing we are talking about – even though it is not the grammatical subject. This can also move the main new information to the end – the most natural position (see page 251).

*That question we have already discussed at some length.*

Fronting is not particularly common in written English – we generally prefer to find ways of making the topic the grammatical subject (see page 252).

*That question has already been discussed at some length.*
*That question has already received lengthy discussion.*

But fronting something that is not the subject is very common in speech (see pages 282–283).

*That question – well, look, we've already gone over it again and again, haven't we?*
*People like that my father just can't stand.*

Question-word clauses are often fronted.

*What I'm going to do next I just don't know.*

**1  Rewrite these sentences, fronting the words *in italics*.**

1  I am putting *all the information you need* in the post today.

.............................................................................................................................

2  We can supply and deliver *any item in our catalogue.*

.............................................................................................................................

3  They never found out *how she got the gun through customs.*

.............................................................................................................................

4  We are planning to redecorate *the kitchen* in the autumn.

.............................................................................................................................

5  These shoes will *last for ever.*

.............................................................................................................................

6  We had *a very good lesson* this morning.

.............................................................................................................................

7  That does me *a fat lot of good*!

.............................................................................................................................

## NOTES

*As* and *though* can be used in a rather formal structure after a fronted adjective or adverb. In this case they both mean 'although', and suggest an emphatic contrast.

> *Cold as/though it was, we went out.*
> *Bravely as/though they fought, they had no chance of winning.*
> *Much as/though I respect your point of view, I can't agree.*

In American English, *though* is unusual in this structure, and *as … as* is common.

> *As cold as it was, we went out.*

*He's gone I don't know how far.* In informal speech, part of an indirect question can be fronted, as in the following examples.

> *He's been talking for I don't know how long.*
> *We spent I can't tell you how much money on the holiday.*
> *Andy gave me you'll never guess what for my birthday.*

# special word order: inversion

**We put auxiliary verbs before subjects** ('inversion') in several structures – most commonly in questions and in clauses beginning *so/nor/neither.*

What time *is it*?     Tired? So *am I*.     She can't swim, and nor/neither *can I*.

**after fronted negative expressions**  If we put certain negative adverbs and adverbial expressions at the beginning of a clause for emphasis, they are followed by **auxiliary verb + subject.** This structure is usually rather formal.

*Under no circumstances* **can we** *cash cheques.*
(NOT ~~Under no circumstances we can cash cheques.~~)
*Not until much later* **did we** *learn the truth.*

The same thing happens with *seldom, little, never, hardly (… when), scarcely (… when), no sooner (… than), not only* and *only* + time expression. These structures are formal and literary.

**1** **Normal (N), formal/literary (F) or wrong (W)?**
▸ Seldom had she felt such terror.  F.
1 Hardly had I arrived when the problems began.  …
2 I had no sooner unpacked than the telephone rang.  …
3 Not only they refuse to pay taxes; they also reject the authority of the state.  …
4 Little did they know what was to happen.  …
5 At no time did she contact the police.  …
6 I did not try to influence him in any way.  …
7 Under no circumstances I will apologise.  …
8 Never again would he believe a politician's promises.  …
9 Sometimes had I felt so frightened before.  …

**2** **Rewrite these sentences in a more normal style.**
▸ Under no circumstances would I ask her for help.
  *I would not ask her for help under any circumstances.*
1 Not until July was he able to start walking again.
  ...............................................................................................
2 Hardly had I got into the house when he started shouting at me.
  ...............................................................................................
3 Never has the world faced a crisis of this order.
  ...............................................................................................
4 Only later did I find out where they had gone.
  ...............................................................................................
5 Not only did we lose our money; we also wasted our time.
  ...............................................................................................

**after so, as, than**  In a literary style, inversion is possible after *so* + **adjective/adverb**, and in clauses beginning *such, as* or *than*. These structures are not very common.

*So rapidly* **did they** *advance that the enemy were taken by surprise.* (more normal: *They advanced so rapidly that …*)
*Such* **was his reputation** *that few people dared to question his judgement.*
*She was politically quite naive,* **as were** *most of her friends.*
*Country people tend to speak more slowly* **than do** *city-dwellers.*

**3** **Rewrite these sentences in a more normal style.**

1 So friendly were the people in the village that we soon felt completely at home.

..................................................................................................................................

2 Harold went into the civil service, as did most of the students in his year.

..................................................................................................................................

3 Emma learnt much more quickly than did the other children.

..................................................................................................................................

**after expressions of place and direction** In literary and descriptive writing, structures like the following are common when sentences begin with expressions of **place** or **direction**.

*In front of the door **stood a man** in naval uniform.*
*Round the corner **came three women** on horseback.*
*Above the town **stands a Norman castle**.*

This structure is also common in informal speech with **here**, **there** and other short adverbs.

*Here **comes the bus**.     There **goes your sister**.*
*Up **walked a policeman**.     Out **came Mrs Potter**.*

We do not use inversion when the subject is a pronoun.

*Out **she came**.* (NOT ~~Out came she.~~)

**4** **Complete these sentences in any way you like.**

1 Into the kitchen rushed .........................
2 Out of the cupboard fell .........................
3 Over the wall flew .........................
4 Through the door came .........................

5 On the table sat .........................
6 Away ran .........................
7 In walked .........................
8 Here comes .........................

**reporting** In written story-telling, direct speech can be followed by **reporting verb + subject**.

*'It's getting late,' **said Mary** / Mary said.*
*'Go away!' **shouted the shopkeeper** / the shopkeeper shouted.*

This does not happen if the subject is a **pronoun**.

*'Come in,' **she said**.* (NOT ... ~~said she.~~)

**5** **Add reporting verbs and subjects (from the box, or from your imagination), using inversion.**

> added   explained   growled   howled   said   screamed   shouted   whispered
> beautiful Melanie   Mrs Carter   my father   the bank manager   the general
> the ghost   the President   the teacher

1 'Go away,' .........................
2 'I love you,' .........................
3 'No,' .........................
4 'Yes,' .........................

5 'I hate you,' .........................
6 'Never,' .........................
7 'It's Tuesday.' .........................
8 'Come here,' .........................

**Note:** *May* can come before the subject in **wishes**.
   *May all your dreams come true!*     *May that man rot in hell!*

For inversion in conditional structures (e.g. *Had I known, I would have …*), see page 237.

# emphasis: *it ... that*

*It is/was ... that* We can use *It is/was* to highlight an expression that we want to emphasise; we put the rest of the sentence into a *that*-clause.

*James crashed the car last week.*
- → *It was James* that crashed the car last week. (not Peter)
- → *It was the car* that James crashed last week. (not the motorbike)
- → *It was last week* that James crashed the car. (not this week)

We can also use a *who*-clause to emphasise a personal subject.

*It was James **who** crashed the car ...*

**1** **Change these sentences to emphasise each part in turn.**

1  Mary was supposed to interview the new students today.

.............................................................................................................................
.............................................................................................................................
.............................................................................................................................

2  Paul met his bank manager in prison.

.............................................................................................................................
.............................................................................................................................
.............................................................................................................................

3  Henry's dog dug up Philip's roses yesterday evening.

.............................................................................................................................
.............................................................................................................................
.............................................................................................................................

4  Mrs Hawkins lost an earring in the supermarket.

.............................................................................................................................
.............................................................................................................................
.............................................................................................................................

**Contrast** We can emphasise a contrast with *It's not / It wasn't ...* OR *It's / It was ... not ...*

*It's not the children* that need help, *it's their parents*.
*It was her beauty* that he noticed, *not her personality*.

**2** **Change these sentences, beginning *It's not / It wasn't ...***

1  We don't need butter, we need sugar. ...........................................................................
2  I bought a van, not a car. ...........................................................................................
3  Joseph isn't the Director, Maggie is. .............................................................................
4  I forgot her address, not her name. ...............................................................................
5  He doesn't collect stamps, he collects coins. ...............................................................
6  I love Sam, not you. ....................................................................................................

**Note** the use of pronouns and verbs in this structure in different styles.

| INFORMAL | FORMAL |
|---|---|
| *It's **me that's** right.* | *It is **I who am** right.* |
| *It's **you that** will pay the fine.* | *It is **you who will** pay the fine.* |

# emphasis: *what ... is/was*

*What ... is/was* We can use a structure with *what* (= 'the thing(s) that'), to put the words that we want to emphasise at the end of a sentence.

*His voice irritates me.* → *What irritates me **is his voice**.*
*I saw a white bear.* → *What I saw was **a white bear**.*

This structure (unlike the one with *it*) can emphasise a **verb**. We use *What ... do/does/did*.

*I switched off all the lights.* → *What I did was **(to) switch off** all the lights.*
*It searches the whole internet.* → *What it does is **(to) search** the whole internet.*

**1** Change the sentences so as to emphasise the words in *italics*. Begin *What ....*

▶ She broke *her ankle*.  *What she broke was her ankle.* ................................................

1 I want *more time to think*.

    ...........................................................................................................

2 I need *something to eat*.

    ...........................................................................................................

3 She hated *his possessiveness*.

    ...........................................................................................................

4 I have never understood *how aeroplanes stay up*.

    ...........................................................................................................

5 I *called the police at once*.

    ...........................................................................................................

6 She *teaches English in prisons*.

    ...........................................................................................................

We can use *all* (*that*) (meaning '**the only thing that**') in the same way as *what*.

*All* (*that*) he needs is a bit of sympathy.     *All* (*that*) you do is press this button.

**2** Complete these sentences about people you know.

1 All he/she is interested in is ...................................................................................
2 All he/she wants is ...............................................................................................
3 What he/she really likes is .....................................................................................
4 What he/she really hates is ....................................................................................
5 What he/she mostly does at weekends is ................................................................

---

**NOTES**

Instead of *what*, we can use *the person/people who...*, *the thing that ...* and similar structures.
    *Louise phoned.* → *The person who phoned* was Louise. (NOT ~~Who phoned was Louise.~~)
    *His stupid laugh annoyed me.* → *The thing that annoyed me* was his stupid laugh.

*where/when/why ...* Expressions of place, time, manner and reason can be emphasised with *where/when/how/why* instead of *what*. This is rather informal.
    *Where you pay is in Room 24 on the first floor.*     *When we met was last January.*
    *How I did it was by using a mirror.*     *Why I'm here is to talk about my plans.*

# discourse markers: introduction

**Discourse markers** are words and expressions which help to structure spoken exchanges and written text. They can communicate several things:

- **'What are we talking about?'** Discourse markers can introduce or clarify a topic.
- **'Where are we?'** They can show divisions and changes of topic.
- **'What are we doing?'** They can show the type of communication that is going on.
- **'How do I feel about this?'** They can show one's attitude to what one is saying.
- **'What about you?'** They can show one's attitude to the reader or listener.

English has a very large number of discourse markers. Some are used in all kinds of discourse, some mostly in formal writing, and others mainly in informal speech. The most common are discussed briefly in the following pages. Examples and practice are given for those whose function may not be clear. Note that some discourse markers, especially in speech, have several uses.

Most discourse markers are adverbs or adverbial expressions. Some are conjunctions. For differences in punctuation and other points, see pages 254–256.

It is only possible to give a very limited amount of information about discourse markers in a book of this kind. For more details, see the section on discourse markers in the *Cambridge Grammar of English* by Carter and McCarthy (Cambridge University Press 2006), and the entries on particular words and expressions in the *Oxford Advanced Learner's Dictionary*.

*And speaking of Australia, one of the strangest films*

*My name's Katrina by the way.*

On the other hand, you'll never know if you can do it till you try.

QUITE FRANKLY, WE ARE HAVING A BAD YEAR.

As regards the concept of time, the poem is remarkable

As for that business of going to the police, I am sorry I mentioned it.

On the whole he had a poor opinion of human nature

As far as age is concerned, a person who has reached 18 can

As a result, they were transferred to different prisons.

Though he lives on its doorstep, so to speak, Vic has never been inside the place.

**To begin with, let me remind you**

BORED AND LONELY, YES, BUT I HAD A REASONABLY PLEASANT TIME ALL THE SAME.

Turning now to benefit payments,

Er, right, as I was saying, there's two types of iron oxide

BEFORE TURNING TO THESE QUESTIONS, THOUGH, I'D LIKE TO GET SOME REACTIONS TO THE CURRENT SITUATION,

I GUESS, LOOKING BACK ON IT, I WAS HER TOY BOY.

In conclusion, the main findings from the project can be summarised as

# discourse markers: linking and structuring

(*Items in red:* formal, most common in writing; **in green:** informal, most common in speech; others: common in both speech and writing.)

**What are we talking about?'** Some discourse markers say what a speaker or writer is going to focus on, and may show a link with previous discussion.

> talking/speaking of/about; regarding; as regards; as far as … is concerned; as for

*'I saw Max and Sue today. You know she –' 'Talking of Max, you know he's leaving?'*
**Regarding** *that car you were thinking of selling – how much do you want for it?*
**As far as** *your transfer request is concerned, we'll be discussing it at the next meeting.*
*I've invited Andy and Bob.* **As for** *Stephen, I never want to see him again.*

**'Where are we?'** Some discourse markers show subdivisions and changes of topic.

> **STRUCTURING:** first of all; firstly, secondly etc; to begin with; to start with; in the first place; before turning to; for one thing; for another (thing); lastly; finally
> **NEW SUBJECT:** turning now to … ; now; all right; right; OK
> **BRIEF CHANGE OF SUBJECT:** incidentally; by the way
> **RETURNING TO PREVIOUS SUBJECT:** to return to the previous point; as I was saying
> **SUMMING UP:** in conclusion; to sum up; briefly; in short

**1  Choose the best discourse markers.**

1  *First of all, / Incidentally,* let me welcome everybody to our annual conference.
2  *For one thing, / Regarding* those reports we were talking about …
3  *Now, / To begin with,* the other main problem is organisational.
4  *By the way, / Right,* let's move on to look at the post-war years.
5  *In conclusion, / Firstly,* it seems clear that none of the factors we have discussed contributed to the spread of the epidemic.
6  I was talking to Annie yesterday. *By the way, / As I was saying,* did you know she's got a new job? And she told me …
7  I don't think I can help you. *Incidentally, / For one thing,* I haven't got the time. And then I'm going to be away all next week.
8  *As far as the repairs are concerned, / In the first place, the repairs,* I think the best thing is to leave them until the new year.
9  Our room was dirty, the food was poor, and the promised 'view of the sea' required a powerful telescope. *As for / Talking about* the service, it was appalling. And *right, / finally,* the bill contained a large number of errors. *In short, / For one thing,* the entire holiday was a disaster.

**2  Here are some sentences from books and magazines. Complete them with expressions from the box.**

> as far as   as for   first of all   for one thing   speaking of

1  ....................................., I was genuinely upset by what had happened; for another, I knew it was pointless expecting him to change his mind.
2  ....................................., he knew how to listen — which is very rare.
3  And .................................... you, Fiona, words fail me.'
4  But .................................... efficiency is concerned the work could be done without nearly so many.
5  ....................................the wind, it was getting stronger and I was getting colder.

# discourse markers: showing what is going on

*(**Items in red:** formal, most common in writing; **in green:** informal, most common in speech; others: common in both speech and writing.)*

**'What are we doing?'** Some discourse markers make it clear what kind of communication is going on: information, explanation, argument, persuasion, …

> **GENERALISING; EXCEPTIONS:** on the whole; to a great extent; to some extent; in general; in all/most/many/some cases; broadly speaking; apart from; except for
> **SHOWING A LOGICAL CONNECTION:** consequently; therefore; as a result; so; then
> **SHOWING SIMILARITY:** similarly; in the same way; just as

### 1 Choose the best discourse markers.

1  *On the whole, / Then,* people like to help others.
2  Central European languages, *in the same way as / apart from Hungarian*, are related to each other.
3  Atmospheric pressure is lower at altitude. *Consequently, / Similarly,* climbers can find it difficult to get enough oxygen.
4  Russia relies on its grain harvests to feed its population. *Similarly, / As a result*, India and China are dependent on rice.
5  *In general, / In some cases*, an unhappy childhood leads to criminal behaviour.
6  *Broadly speaking, / Consequently*, if you're nice to people, they'll be nice to you.
7  Losses have been heavy this year. *As a result, / On the whole*, we are cutting back investment.

> **SHOWING A CONTRAST:** nevertheless; nonetheless; despite this/that; yet; however; in spite of this/that; still; mind you
> **BALANCING CONTRASTING POINTS:** on the one hand; whereas; while; on the other hand
> **PERSUADING:** after all; look; look here
> **CONTRADICTING:** on the contrary; quite the opposite

*The Greeks and Romans had no symbol for zero.* **Nevertheless/Nonetheless,** *they made remarkable progress in mathematics.*
*Arranged marriages are common in many Middle Eastern countries. In the West,* **on the other hand,** *they are unusual.*
*Some people think Wales is in England.* **On the contrary,** *they are different countries.*
*The weather here is pretty depressing.* **Mind you,** *it's beautiful in spring.*
*I like the mountains,* **whereas/while** *my wife prefers the seaside.*
*Why shouldn't she buy a horse if she wants to?* **After all,** *it's her money.*

**Note the difference** between *on the other hand* (contrast) and *on the contrary* (contradiction).
For more about *on the other hand* and *however*, see page 307. For more about *after all*, see page 306.

### 2 Choose the best discourse markers.

1  She does badly at school. *On the contrary, / On the other hand,* she's a brilliant musician.
2  Their father died when they were small. *Despite that, / On the one hand,* they had a happy childhood.
3  Bankers are generally nice people. *Mind you, / After all,* I wouldn't want my daughter to marry one.
4  Let's give them some money. *On the other hand, / Look,* they really deserve it.
5  I don't dislike him at all. *On the contrary / However,* I think he's a great guy.
6  I think we should forget what she did. *After all, / Nonetheless,* she has apologised.
7  I don't think it's the right job for her. *On the other hand, / Still,* it's her decision.
8  *Mind you, / look here,* what are you doing in my room?

> **CONCESSION:** it is true (that); certainly; granted; if; may; of course; stressed auxiliaries …
> **COUNTER-ARGUMENT:** … nevertheless; nonetheless; however; even so; but; still; all the same

**These expressions are used** in a three-stage argument structure
1  We say something that points in a certain direction.
2  We agree (the concession) that there are facts that point in the other direction.
3  But we finish (the counter-argument) by going back to the original position.

*… cannot agree with colonialism.* **It is true** *that the British* **may** *have done some good in India.*
**Even so,** *colonialism is basically evil.*
*He was incapable of lasting relationships with women.* **Certainly,** *several women loved him, and*
*he was married twice.* **All the same,** *the women closest to him were invariably deeply unhappy.*
*Very few people understood Einstein's theory.* **Of course,** *everybody had heard of him, and a fair number*
*of people knew the word 'relativity'.* **But** *hardly anybody could tell you what he had actually said.*
*His poetry,* **if** *difficult to understand,* **nonetheless** *has a good deal of charm.*

**Note the use of** *it is true, certainly* **and** *of course* in the examples above. When they are used in this way, a
reader knows that they will be followed by *but, all the same* or a similar expression.

**3** **Put discourse markers from the box in the right places. (Different answers are possible.)**

> but   certainly   even so   granted   it is true   still   nonetheless   of course

1  I am not impressed by her work. …………………………, she writes like an angel. …………………………
   she has nothing to say of any interest.
2  It was a successful party. The Scottish cousins were ………………….……… a little surprised by the
   family's behaviour. …………………………, they were impressed by the friendly welcome they received.
3  I'm glad to have a place of my own. …………………………, it's a long way from the centre, and it needs
   redecorating. …………………………, it's home.
4  It's quite a big job. …………………………, Alice will be helping with the deliveries. …………………………,
   it'll take a couple weeks.
5  We are still a long way from economic recovery. ………………….……, unemployment figures are going
   down. …………………………, there is little genuine improvement in the overall situation.

> **ADDING:** moreover; furthermore; further; in addition; what is more; also; as well as that;
> on top of that; another thing is; besides; I mean
> **GIVING EXAMPLES:** e.g.; in particular; for instance; for example
> **MAKING THINGS CLEAR; GIVING DETAILS:** that is to say; in other words; actually; I mean

**4** **Cross out the one discourse marker that is wrong.**
▶  I prefer to go by train when possible. Air travel is tiring.
   *Furthermore,* / *Moreover,* / ~~*For instance,*~~ it is expensive.
1  I dislike a lot of modern music. *In particular,* / *Also,* / *For example,* I hate hard rock.
2  I've got a funny feeling about him. *For example,* / *That is to say,* / *I mean,* I don't trust him.
3  I don't like her going out alone at night. You don't know what sort of people she's going to meet.
   And *besides,* / *another thing is,* / *in other words,* she's far too young.
4  He disliked arguing about money. *Indeed,* / *That is to say,* / *For instance,* it made him feel quite ill.
5  It's a difficult climb. *In particular,* / *Actually,* / *I mean,* / it's pretty nearly impossible.

# discourse markers: *you* and *I*

(*Items in red: formal, most common in writing;* **in green:** *informal, most common in speech; others: common in both speech and writing.*)

**How do I feel about this? And what about you?** Some discourse markers address the hearer or reader. For example, they express the speaker's or writer's attitude to what he/she is saying, or modify what is being said to make the communication more effective.

> **SHOWING SPEAKER'S/WRITER'S ATTITUDE:** no doubt; honestly; frankly
> **SOFTENING AND CORRECTING:** in my view/opinion; apparently; so to speak; that is to say; more or less; I think; I feel; I suppose; really; I reckon; I guess; sort of; kind of; well; at least; I'm afraid; or rather; actually; I mean
> **GAINING TIME:** let me see; let's see; let me think; well; you know; I don't know; I mean; kind of; sort of

The government, **no doubt** for excellent reasons, has reduced unemployment benefit.
(*No doubt* is often ironic: the writer may not be at all sure that the reasons are good.)
'What do you think of my hair?' '**Frankly**, darling, it's a disaster.'
Jamie isn't really very efficient, is he? **That is to say**, he's not always very good at organising his work.
**At least**, that's my impression.
'I **sort of** wondered if you could help me with this.' 'Sorry, **I'm afraid** I'm not free.'
She lives at 19 Gordon Terrace – **or rather**, Gordon Close. (NOT ... *or better* ...)
I can't get to the hospital to see Julie. **I mean**, not this week, anyway.
'How much is it going to cost?' '**Let me see**. There's materials. And customs. And...'

**1** Put in discourse markers from the box.

> apparently   at least   frankly   honestly   I'm afraid   I suppose   let me see
> no doubt   or rather   so to speak

1 This student has worked hard, but I ........................... do not feel able to recommend her for a scholarship.
2 ........................... you will be paying your rent by the end of the week, Mr Jenkins?
3 She doesn't keep her promises. ..........................., not always.
4 'How did the team do?' '........................... they lost.'
5 There's a meeting on Tuesday – ........................... Thursday.
6 'When are you going to be ready?' '........................... I've got to make a couple of phone calls ...'
7 ........................... we can travel half-price at the weekend.
8 'Do you like my poetry?' '..........................., no.'
9 That child is a one person crime wave, ...........................
10 I don't have much time to help you with the decoration. ........................... I could come in on Saturday for an hour.

> **DISMISSING WHAT WAS SAID BEFORE:** in any case; anyhow; anyway; at any rate

**These expressions mean** 'What was said before doesn't matter – this is the real point.'

*I'm not sure what time I'll arrive, maybe seven or eight.* **In any case / Anyhow / Anyway / At any rate**, *I'll certainly be there before 8.30.*

**2** Complete the sentences with expressions from the box.

> He wouldn't listen to me   I'm really not hungry   it was one of them   it's better than sleeping in the car

1 Maybe it was Peter, or maybe it was Joe. Or Jack. Anyway, ...........................
2 I don't really feel like eating out tonight. I'm tired, and it's raining. In any case, ...........................
3 The hotel's probably OK. It's cheap, and the place seems clean. At any rate, ...........................
4 I can't be bothered to tell him what I think. ..........................., anyhow.

> **REFERRING TO THE HEARER'S/READER'S EXPECTATIONS:** in fact; as a matter of fact; to tell the truth; well; actually

**These expressions** introduce information that will contradict (usually), modify or perhaps confirm what the hearer or reader thinks.

*It is generally believed that Marquez died in the civil war.* **In fact**, *recent research shows that he survived and fled to Bolivia, where …*
*'How are your medical studies going?'* '**To tell the truth**, *I've decided to drop out for a year and get a job.'*
*'Hello, Adrian.'* '**Actually**, *my name's Richard.'*
*'Was the skiing good?'* '*Yes,* **actually**, *it was wonderful.'*
*'Let's catch the 4.30.'* '**Well**, *I'm afraid it doesn't run on Thursdays.'*

**3** **Put in suitable discourse markers (different answers are possible).**
1 'Happy birthday.' '……………………………, my birthday's next week.'
2 The Nobel Prize was awarded to Wilson, Crick and Watson. But …………………………… an important part of the work was done by Rosalind Franklin, whose contribution was largely ignored.
3 'How's your novel going?' '……………………………, I haven't started it yet.'
4 'Have you tried that new Italian restaurant?' 'Yes, ……………………………, we went there last night. It's very good.'
5 Most people think a tomato is a vegetable. ……………………………, it is really a fruit.
6 'I'm not going to tell him.' 'Nor am I.' '……………………………, somebody will have to tell him.'

> **CHECKING COMMON GROUND:** you know; you see: (you) know what I mean?

**A speaker says 'you know'** to tell the hearer (or to pretend) that they share the same piece of information.

*I was talking to Marty –* **you know**, *the guy who works with Alex – and he said …*
*We were in Haworth –* **you know**, *the village where the Brontës lived. And …*
*You can get really cheap computers if you know who to ask.* **You know what I mean?**

**You see** introduces information that the speaker thinks the hearer does not share.

*It's no good using this battery charger.* **You see**, *it's 12 volts, and your battery is 6 volts.*

**4** **Choose the best discourse markers.**
1 Try to speak slowly and clearly. *You see / You know*, she's a bit deaf.
2 We could get lunch at La Cantina – *you see, / you know*, that place opposite the station.
3 I've had a letter from Phil – *you see / you know*, Jan's brother-in-law.
4 I'm sorry, but you can't come in here. *You see, / You know*, it's for members only.
5 We've got a plague of greenfly. *You see / You know*, those little bugs that eat roses.

**NOTES**

**Some reporting verbs** can show the speaker's or writer's attitude to what is being reported.
**Suggest** and **imply** make it clear that he/she is not reporting definite facts. **Claim** often throws doubt on what follows.
   *These findings* **suggest** *that a cure for the common cold may be close.*
   *The Minister* **claims** *that the new working practices will increase efficiency by 35%.*
**Allege** is common in reports of unproved criminal accusations.
   *It is* **alleged** *that, during the night of June 17th, Hawkins broke into the factory …*

**I mean** usually has very little meaning! It is often just a signal (pronounced very quickly and unclearly) that something more is going to be said.
   *We had a great time at Andy's.* **I mean**, *he's a really nice guy, and* **I mean**, *we played football all afternoon …*

# discourse markers: more practice

**1** **Discourse markers in formal texts. Choose the best expressions from the boxes to complete the sentences.**

| as far as | as regards | in conclusion | in general | to a great extent | turning now |
|---|---|---|---|---|---|

1 ....................................., though there is no denying the seriousness of the problem, many questions still remain unanswered.

2 ..................................... age is concerned, a person who has reached 18 has the legal capacity to contract as an individual.

3 It is an old maxim but it is true: ....................................., you are what you eat.

4 ..................................... to consider the other main group of younger household carers, there are an increasing number, currently about 11 per cent, of elderly people living with younger people, usually daughters and sons-in-law.

5 ..................................... export credit, two types are available from most banks.

6 ....................................., women are healthier and live longer than ever before; indeed on average they can expect to live 5 years longer than men.

| briefly | broadly speaking | it is true that | on the contrary | or rather | what is more |
|---|---|---|---|---|---|

7 Do not be afraid that people will look down on you because of your regional accent — ....................................., your accent may in all probability be your most interesting and valuable possession.

8 ....................................., if the referee points his fingers this indicates that someone has done something wrong.

9 For the Third World, ..................................... the underdeveloped world, these questions have existed for the greater part of this century.

10 ....................................., the higher an individual is in the social strata the less likely he or she is to be arrested, prosecuted and (if prosecuted) found guilty.

11 ..................................... three senators have been accused of fraud, bribery and tax evasion in the past three years, but they have all been cleared of these charges by other senators.

12 The difference is that I have been fortunate to find a career that I love and, ..................................... get paid reasonably for it.

**2** **INTERNET EXERCISE.** **Use a search engine to find ten or more sentences beginning with some of the above discourse markers, and write them here.**

.............................................................................................................................

.............................................................................................................................

.............................................................................................................................

.............................................................................................................................

.............................................................................................................................

.............................................................................................................................

.............................................................................................................................

.............................................................................................................................

.............................................................................................................................

.............................................................................................................................

.............................................................................................................................

.............................................................................................................................

**❸ Some informal discourse markers. Choose the best expressions from the boxes to complete the texts.**

| all the same    frankly    incidentally    sort of    to tell the truth    you know |

1 ................................., have you been to the local library yet?

2 ................................., I wasn't really listening to what everyone was saying.

3 ................................., Dorothy, you and I will just have to go out together more often.

4 I felt so ashamed because I didn't recognise her and she was ...............................talking to me as if she knew me, and I thought oh very friendly person, you know?

5 ................................., what you're saying is absolute rubbish.

6 You can't expect a reference book to be quite as gripping as an adventure novel, but ...............................I read it cover to cover.

| anyway    as for    as I was saying    by the way    mind you    you see |

7 He never called her. Because unattractive men don't want unattractive girls, ...................................

8 We're getting closer. Not much closer, ..................................., but certainly closer.'

9 Maggie paused, then went on, '..................................., my own mother used to make steak-and-kidney pudding.'

10 ................................., while I think of it, Anne was just about to leave the country when you rang, but she says when she gets back in September you're to give her a call.

11 ................................. you, you're not only poor, you're stupid.

12 I don't know who was in charge, maybe the fat man. ..................................., he was the one who did the talking.

'Mind you, this is a rough area to bring a kid up in.'

'It sort of makes you stop and think, doesn't it.'

'Frankly, Wallace, I think you'd better stop telling it. If no one laughs, it may not be a joke.'

# understanding complicated sentences

**When clauses are made part of others ('embedded'),** this can make sentences harder to understand, causing problems for readers or listeners, especially if the natural flow of the 'outside' clause is interrupted.

*The government, **if recent reports can be trusted**, has decided to raise interest rates.*
*The strikes **which have caused serious disruption to travellers on a number of airlines in recent months** are likely to continue if agreement is not reached.*
*A bus **which ran downhill out of control after its brakes failed** crashed into a factory wall, damaging the premises and slightly injuring several passengers.*

**1** DO IT YOURSELF. **Why do the embedded clauses make the above sentences harder to read? Circle the letter of the best explanation.**

   **A** They separate the subject from the object.    **B** They separate the subject from the verb.
   **C** They separate the verb from the object.

**Embedded clauses can separate** words which belong together, and put together words that don't.

*Mr Andrews, **when he saw the policeman, started** running as fast as he could.*
(It was not the policeman who started running.)
*A Liverpool man **who lives alone except for his cat has just won** the lottery.*
(The cat has not won the lottery.)
*Pasteur's discovery **that microscopic bacteria caused diseases revolutionised** medicine.*
(It was not the diseases that revolutionised medicine.)

**Descriptive phrases** can have the same effect.

*The woman **in the blue dress over there by the parking meter looks very like Susie.***
(The parking meter doesn't look like Susie.)
*That picture **of the children standing in front of the palace talking to the Prime Minister is wonderful**.*
(It is not the Prime Minister that is wonderful.)

**2 Underline the embedded clause or phrase.**

   ▶  The dog <u>that Harry gave as a birthday present to his Aunt Elizabeth</u> was hideously ugly.

   1  The car that was parked outside the front gate needed cleaning.

   2  Mr Fisher, after he had completed his discussions with the bank manager, drew a large sum of money out of the bank and caught the next plane.

   3  One way of deciding what to do if you have difficulty in deciding your next course of action is to toss a coin.

   4  The people in the enquiry office on the second floor of Robinsons don't know anything.

**When *that* is left out**, this can cause difficulty.

*Several **people Martin** knew well when he was at university years before had now become prominent members of the government. (= '… people **that** Martin knew …')*
*A man who **claimed he was** an experienced surgeon, and carried out several operations, had no medical training whatever. (= '… claimed **that** he was …')*

Extra difficulty can be caused when relative clauses end in **prepositions**.

*The spanner **Oliver was trying to get the wheel-nuts off with** was the wrong size.*

**3** Make these sentences easier to read by adding *that*.

▶ The car he was driving must have cost a fortune.
 *The car that he was driving* …
 ........................................................................................................................

1 Some papers a dustman found lying in the street were secret government documents.
 ........................................................................................................................

2 A picture a schoolboy bought for £5 has turned out to be worth £10,000.
 ........................................................................................................................

3 She insisted she thought he knew she was on the train.
 ........................................................................................................................

4 If the details you provided were correct, a new password will have been emailed to you.
 ........................................................................................................................

5 The man the terrorists bought the guns from was an undercover policeman.
 ........................................................................................................................

6 MPs are demanding an investigation over claims reporters hacked into their phones.
 ........................................................................................................................

7 A girl Helen was at school with is now a very successful TV producer.
 ........................................................................................................................

8 The ladies men admire, I've heard, would shudder at a wicked word. (*Dorothy Parker*)
 ........................................................................................................................

9 Money makes money, and the money money makes makes money. (*Benjamin Franklin*)
 ........................................................................................................................

**4** Find the beginnings of sentences 1–5 in the box.

▶ *C.* his brother was a beautiful green colour.
1 … the Prime Minister had the whole country crying with laughter.
2 … baby elephants would look wonderful in the living room.
3 … the number 10 bus had just flown in from Iceland.
4 … her father smelt very strange.
5 … my wife blew up in Austria.

| A Margaret insisted that the picture her daughter had painted of |
|---|
| B A story that was published in yesterday's paper about |
| C The toy train Harry bought for ✓ |
| D The car I bought to go to Greece with |
| E The sinister-looking man who was sitting alone on |
| F The aftershave Sue gave |

**5** Can you write beginnings for these endings?

1 ................................................................................. her sister was much too small.
2 ................................................................................. the garden was very nervous.
3 ................................................................................. me were not true.

**6** Can you make complete sentences including these groups of words? (Don't separate them.)

1 the food they ..............................................................................................................
2 a thing people use ......................................................................................................
3 a thing children ..........................................................................................................
4 the man the police ......................................................................................................
5 she bought didn't ........................................................................................................
6 saw wasn't ..................................................................................................................

→

# understanding complicated sentences (continued)

Reduced relative clauses (see page 211) can make sentences particularly hard to read.

*Many of the objects recovered by the police were found to have been stolen from homes in the neighbourhood.. (= '… the objects that were recovered …')*
*The majority of those interviewed were opposed to the recommendations. (= '… those who were interviewed … ')*
*Two wolves seen roaming in the New Forest are believed to have escaped from a nearby private zoo. (= '… wolves that have been seen …')*
*Most of the great museums built in the 19th century were partly financed by donations from wealthy philanthropists. (= … museums that were built …)*

**7** **Put in words from the box to make the sentence easier to read.**

> are   are   were   which   which   who

Many of the gold and silver objects excavated from the 3000-year-old royal tombs resemble items of jewellery still made today by craftsmen trained in the traditional skills.

.................................................................................................................................................
.................................................................................................................................................
.................................................................................................................................................

Regular past participles look like past tenses, and this can cause confusion.

*A number of the children asked for comments on the proposals to expel some immigrants told the police they disagreed. (The children didn't ask for comments: the meaning is '… the children who were asked …'.)*

**8** **Rewrite the words in *italics* to make the meaning clearer.**

▶ A young *civil servant arrested* after shootings on Tyneside left one person dead is to be
  charged with murder.  *civil servant who was arrested*..............................................................

1 A *separatist accused* of leading an attack on a French police barracks in which four gendarmes
  died has been arrested.....................................................................................................

2 *Police called* to a house in Hampshire after neighbours reported cries for help found
  18-year-old M F stuck in a small toilet window after being locked out of his home.

  .................................................................................................................................................

3 *Three immigrants returned* to their countries by the authorities are to appeal against
  their deportation.............................................................................................................

**9** INTERNET EXERCISE. **Use a search engine to find sentences containing the following:**

"a woman arrested" (meaning 'a woman who was arrested')
.................................................................................................................................................

"the people the police" (meaning 'the people that the police')
.................................................................................................................................................

"the money the family" (meaning 'the money that the family')
.................................................................................................................................................

Complicated negative structures can cause confusion.

*It was not that Mary didn't believe that John had not been telling the truth.* (Did she think he had or not?)

**10** **Read the sentences and answer the questions.**

1 There is no sound basis for denying reports that no members of the expedition failed to reach their goal. *Did they all get there?* ...............

2 It is not unlikely that the ongoing investigation will show that the allegations of corruption against the President are not without foundation. *Is the President probably corrupt?* ...............

3 She didn't not want to go to the party; she just didn't want to go unless Harry wasn't going. *Did she want to see Harry at the party?* ...............

**11** GRAMMAR IN A TEXT. **Here are some more extracts from news reports and other sources, to give additional practice in reading complicated sentences.**

A 24-year-old labourer who was arrested in Trafalgar Square when he allegedly attempted to knife a traffic warden is said to have injured three policemen.

The rebel leader found out that although the soldiers he bought the guns from had taken careful precautions the police had planted an informer among them.

PICTURES of the baby the judge ordered should not be identified by reporters appeared in a Sunday newspaper.

POLICE HUNTING thieves who dumped a ten-month-old baby in an alley after finding him inside a car they stole have charged two teenage boys.

The head doorman at a nightclub where the ecstasy pill which killed P L was sold has admitted he knew drugs were sold at the club.

The report will look into claims the design of the courthouse the men escaped from was at fault.

**Statements reassuring the public people needing intensive care are getting it are total nonsense.**

It is understood a taxi driver was forced to bring the bomb to Strand Road police station early on Tuesday by two men armed with a gun.

IF PREDICTIONS that the British National Party will gain at least one seat when the European Parliament election results are announced tonight are accurate, many Labour MPs will see it as a political disaster grave enough to spark a major revolt.

**The thick blanket of smog that has shrouded Moscow as peat fires continue to burn just outside the city has worsened.**

It is not impossible that X will turn out, taking everything into account, to have been the most unmemorable Prime Minister in recent history.

# complex noun phrases in writing

**premodification** In speech, noun phrases are usually simple. Before the noun, there may be a determiner and an adjective, or perhaps another noun; not usually very much more.

*his blue jeans     a broken window     the kitchen table     Andy's sister*

In formal writing, a lot of information may be packed into complex structures before the noun.

*his badly faded, torn blue jeans     Andy's rather eccentric football-playing sister*

**postmodification** Noun phrases may also be extended by structures that follow the noun.

prepositional phrases
*the girl **in the green dress**     a hotel **near the river***

**participle phrases**
*a factory **making parts for aero engines**     the people **invited to meet the President***

relative clauses
*ideas **that changed the world**     his coach, **with whom he has been for five years***

**other descriptive phrases**
*an influential woman, **greatly admired by her contemporaries***
*the first violinist, **so-called leader of the orchestra***

**1** **Use words from the boxes (and others if necessary) to turn the nouns into complex noun phrases. Different answers are possible.**

| beautifully   built   happy   maintained   situated   solidly   spent most of her childhood   well |
| --- |

▶ the house *...the solidly built, well maintained, beautifully situated house where she spent most of her happy childhood.*

| awfully   badly   boring   delivered   long   terribly   sent me to sleep |
| --- |

1 a lecture ..................................................................

| balding   highly   motor   really   skilled   slightly   tall   worked on my car |
| --- |

2 the mechanic ..................................................................

| badly   brought up   extremely   irritating   next door   noisy   terribly |
| --- |

3 the children ..................................................................

| commanded   caused massive loss of life   hastily   incompetently   planned   unnecessary |
| --- |

4 an invasion ..................................................................

| furnished   light and airy   pleasantly   splendid view of the sea   within easy reach of the town centre |
| --- |

5 an apartment ..................................................................

## For Sale

Ref no: 18211

An extended and improved three-bedroom semi-detached house situated in this popular and convenient seaside village location

# mixed structures

*Where did you say you were going?* Question words and relative pronouns usually refer to the clause that immediately follows them.

*They asked **what I wanted**.*      *There's the man **who bought my car**.*

But a question word or relative can sometimes refer to a *that*-clause that follows a verb like *say*, *think* or *wish*.

*Where did you say **(that) you were going for Christmas**?*
*This is the room **that** I thought **(that) we could use for the meeting**.*

**1 Put together the beginnings and ends.**

|   |   |   |   |
|---|---|---|---|
| ▶ | Who did you say (that) you wish | A | Davy would like. … |
| 1 | Here's a book that I think (that) | B | I could possibly work with. … |
| 2 | Is this the bracelet that you said (that) | C | nobody will get on with. … |
| 3 | Jamie's somebody that I don't think (that) | D | we couldn't cross. … |
| 4 | We got to a river that we knew (that) | E | you had married? ▶ |
| 5 | We've got a new manager that I'm sure (that) | F | you wanted to give to Jenny? … |
| 6 | When do you suppose (that) | G | you'll be able to pay me? … |

We usually drop *that* after *say* etc in this structure. When the question word or relative refers to the **subject** of the *that*-clause, we **always** drop *that* after *say* etc.

*Who did you **say was** coming round this evening?*
(NOT ~~Who did you say that was coming round this evening?~~)
*Here's the woman that Ann **said would** show us round the church.*
(NOT ~~Here's the woman that Ann said that would show us~~ …)
*Classical music is the kind that we keep **thinking will** turn into a tune.* (Fred McKinney Hubbard)

**2 Is it possible to put in *that*?**

▶ Who did you say ………………………… you met in Sheffield? …Yes:…..

▶ Who did you say ………………………… phoned? ..No:……

1 We're going to meet somebody ………………………… I know that you'll like. ………….

2 It's a house that we feel ………………………… we might want to buy. ………….

3 Can you suggest somebody that you think ………………………… might be able to help us? ………….

4 The police have arrested a man that they believe ………………………… is responsible for the burglaries. ………….

5 She's found a hairdresser that she says ………………………… does a wonderful job. ………….

6 Here are the papers that I thought ………………………… I'd lost. ………….

*a car that I didn't know how fast it would go* In speech (but not in writing), it is quite common to mix a relative structure with an indirect question, as in the following genuine examples.

*I was driving a car that I didn't know how fast it would go.*
*I don't like singing songs that I don't know what they mean.*
*There's still one piece of the puzzle that I can't work out where it goes.*

*… which I should be grateful if …* In this structure, a relative pronoun refers to an if-clause after *I should be grateful* and similar expressions.

*I am enclosing a form **which** I should be grateful **if you would complete and return**.*
*Please find attached an information sheet **which** we would be **pleased if you would pass on to anyone interested**.*

# ellipsis after auxiliaries

**avoidance of repetition** We often use just the first part of a verb phrase, instead of repeating words which have already been said or written, or which can be understood from the context.

*They have promised to compensate the villagers, and we believe that they will.*
(more natural than … *that they will compensate the villagers.*)
*'Is she happy?' 'I think she is [happy].'*

**ellipsis first** Normally words are dropped **after** they have been used once, but it can happen the other way round if a sentence starts with a conjunction.

*When you **can** [send us a postcard], please send us a postcard.*
*If I **may** [explain something to you], I'd like to explain something to you.*

**do in place of auxiliary** When there is no auxiliary, *do* is used in ellipsis.

*Does the dog eat cornflakes? He certainly **does** [eat cornflakes].*
*They wanted me to tell them the truth, so I **did** [tell them the truth]in the end.*

**1** Make these sentences and exchanges more natural by cutting out unnecessary expressions after auxiliaries.

▶ 'Have you got their address?' 'I'm sure I have ~~got their address~~.'
1  'Get up.' 'I am getting up.'
2  I didn't talk to him yesterday, but I did talk to him today.
3  'If I hadn't been there, you'd have been in trouble.' 'You're right, I would have been in trouble.'
4  They think I don't care, but I do care.
5  'The bedroom needs painting.' 'It certainly does need painting.'
6  If you can have a word with Phil, please have a word with Phil.
7  'The car's running badly.' 'Yes, it is running badly.'
8  Lucy doesn't go out much, and Sue doesn't go out much either.

**2** GRAMMAR IN A TEXT. **Read the text. What words have been dropped or replaced?**

## Nobody wants to quarrel less than I do

'I came round because I really think the whole thing is too absurd.'
'So do I. I always did (▶).'
'You can't have (1) half as much as I did (2). I mean really, when one comes to think of it. And after all these years.'
'Oh, I know, And I dare say if you hadn't (3), I should have (4) myself. I'm sure the last thing I want is to go on like this. Because, really, it's too absurd.'
'And if there's one thing I'm not, it's ready to take offence. I never have been (5), and I never shall be (6).'

'Very well, dear. Nobody wants to quarrel less than I do (7).'
'When a thing is over, let it be over, is what I always say. I don't want to say any more about anything at all. The only thing I must say is that when you say I said that everybody said that about your spoiling that child, it simply isn't what I said. That's all. And I don't want to say another thing about it.'
'Well, certainly I don't (8). There's only one thing I simply can't help saying … '

(Adapted from a piece by *E M Delafield*)

▶  think the whole thing was too absurd.
1  ..................................................................................................................................
2  ..................................................................................................................................
3  ..................................................................................................................................
4  ..................................................................................................................................
5  ..................................................................................................................................
6  ..................................................................................................................................
7  ..................................................................................................................................
8  ..................................................................................................................................

*do so*  The slightly formal expression **do so** can replace a repeated verb phrase.

*The government has agreed to raise the retirement pension, and will **do so** as soon as the financial situation has improved.*
*I need to speak to Anna. I'll try to **do so** tomorrow.*
*He promised to paint the staircase, but he hasn't **done so**.*

We don't normally use *do so* if we are not talking about deliberate actions by the same person.

*I love the saxophone, and I always **have**.* (NOT ... ~~I have always done so.~~ Not a deliberate action.)
*Angela's taken her pilot's licence, and I'd like to **do that** too.* (NOT ... ~~and I'd like to do so.~~ Not the same person.)

**3** **GRAMMAR IN A TEXT.** **Put the letters of the boxed expressions into the right texts.**

A  did so   B  done so   C  has already done so   D  shall do so again   E  will do so

1
The employers of both parents are expected to contribute to childcare. Ask your employer for information on the child care scheme. If the employer does not contribute to the costs, the government ... .

(*Government publication*)

2
In case none of your friends or family ..., let me be the first to wish you a very happy new year!  Now before you ask whether the spring sunshine has gone to my head, I must tell you tell that I am referring to the tax year which began on April 6th.

(*British MP*)

3
I ALWAYS WRITE to my sister on Ada's birthday. I ... last year; and what was very remarkable, my letter reached her on her wedding day, and her letter reached me at Ravenna on my birthday.

(*Article in Literary Gazette, November 1824*)

4
I remain confident in the future of South Africa, provided we continue to adhere to the great constitutional compromise that we initiated 20 years ago. South Africans have a special ability to overcome problems. We astounded the world in 1990 and in 1994, and .... With all its faults and challenges, the South Africa of 2010 is a far better place than the South Africa of 1990.

(*F W de Klerk, Sunday Times February 13 2010*)

5
I always eat peas with honey
I've ... all my life.
They do taste kind of funny
But it keeps them on the knife.

(*anonymous*)

**NOTES**

***might do* etc**  In British English, *do* can be used after another auxiliary.
   '*Are you going to Helen's party?*' '*We might **do**.*' (OR '*We might.*')
   '*Close the door.*' '*I have (**done**).*' (OR '*I have.*')

***could be*, *might have* etc**  We don't always drop *be* or *have* after a modal.
   '*Could they be talking about us?*' '*I suppose they **could (be)**.*'
   '*Do you think she might have forgotten?*' '*Yes, she **might (have)**.*'
And we can't normally drop *be* or *have* if the modal is used for the first time.
   '*Are they French?*' '*They **may be**.*' (NOT '*~~They may.~~*')
   *I'm not sure if she has forgotten, but she **might have**.* (NOT ... ~~she might.~~)

# ellipsis with infinitives

**to for whole infinitive**  We often use *to* instead of repeating a whole infinitive phrase.

*'We can't guarantee that we'll make a profit, but we expect **to** [make a profit].'*
*'Are you and Gillian getting married?'  'We hope **to** [get married].'*
*'Let's go for a walk this afternoon.'  'I don't want **to** [go for a walk this afternoon].'*
*'Sorry I shouted at you. I didn't mean **to** [shout at you].'*

**Be and have** are not usually dropped after *to*.

*There aren't so many butterflies as there used **to be**. (NOT … as there used to.)*
*I haven't got all the papers that I expected **to have**. (NOT … that I expected to.)*

**1**  **Complete the sentences with verbs from the boxes, followed by *to*.**

| afford  hope  intend  mean  need  seems  used  was going |

1  We'd like to get a new car, but we can't …………………………
2  I don't play much football now, but I ………………………… when I was at school.
3  I'm sorry I woke you up – I didn't …………………………
4  'Why didn't you phone?'  'Sorry. I …………………………, but I ran out of time.
5  'Are you seeing Peter tomorrow?'  'No, I don't ………………………… We've already talked things over.'
6  'Does Emma like her new job?'  'She …………………………'
7  'Don't lend him any money, will you?'  'I don't …………………………'
8  We're not making a profit, but we ………………………… soon.

**dropping *to***  *To* is used like this particularly after **verbs that don't usually stand alone**, but need to be followed by an infinitive (as in the above examples). In other cases, we may drop *to* as well as the infinitive.

*'Did you get the eggs?'  'Sorry, I forgot / I forgot to.' (Forget often stands alone)*
*'See if you can cheer Maggie up.'  'I'll try / I'll try to.' (Try often stands alone.)*
*He'll never leave home. He hasn't got the courage / the courage to. (after a noun)*
*I'm not going to do the exam. I'm not ready / not ready to. (after an adjective)*

And note the common use of *like* without *to* after a conjunction.

*Use my car **if** you **like**.     Pay **when** you **like**.     Park **where** you **like**.*

**2**  **Put in *to* if it is necessary, *(to)* if it is optional, and – (nothing) if it is impossible.**

▶  I don't know if I can get here tomorrow, but I hope ..*to*.………
▶  It would be good if you could cheer Helen up. Please try ..*(to)*.……
▶  Stay the night if you like –.……………
1  'Are you coming swimming?'  'No, I don't want ……………
2  'Would you like to be on TV?'  'No, I'd hate ……………'
3  He doesn't work. He's got so much money he doesn't need ……………
4  You were going to buy something for supper. Did you remember ……………?
5  Come round when you like ……………
6  She could get into the national team. She's got the talent ……………
7  I'm not going to say anything to her. I'm afraid ……………
8  I may pass the exam, but I don't really expect ……………

# ellipsis with *so* and *not*

**We can use** *so* instead of repeating words in a *that*-clause. This happens after *believe, hope, expect, imagine, suppose, guess, reckon, think, be afraid.*

*'Are you ready?' 'I think **so**.'* (= *'I think that I'm ready.'*)     *'Shall we go to the party?' 'I suppose **so**.'*

**negative structures**  We can make these structures negative in two ways.

*'Will it rain?' 'I **don't** expect **so**.'* OR *'I expect **not**.'*
*'We won't have enough money for a holiday.' 'I **don't** suppose **so**.'* OR *'I suppose **not**.'*

**Hope** and **be afraid** are normally used with **not**. **Think** is more common with **don't ... so**.

*I may have to work this weekend. I **hope not**.* (NOT ~~I don't hope so.~~)     *'Is the bank open?' 'I'm afraid **not**.'*
*'Have you got a cold?' 'I **don't** think **so**.'* (more natural than *I think not.*)

**1** **Add affirmative (+) or negative (–) answers.**

▶  'Is she French?' (*think* +) …*I think so.*…………………………
▶  'Can we get tickets? (*expect* –) …*I don't expect so.*……… OR …*I expect not.*…………………
1  'Has she got flu?' (*afraid* +) ……………………………………………
2  'Do we need to go shopping?' (*think* –) ……………………………………………
3  'It doesn't matter, does it?' (*suppose* –) ……………………………………………
4  'Do you think you'll get the job?' (*hope* +) ……………………………………………
5  'Is the building finished?' (*believe* +) ……………………………………………
6  'Are we working tomorrow?' (*hope* –) ……………………………………………
7  'Did Joe pass the driving test?' (*afraid* –) ……………………………………………

**after *say* and *tell***  We can use *so* after *say* and *tell* to avoid repeating information. We use this structure mostly to justify statements – to say why they should be believed. Compare:

*'Julie's crazy.' 'Who **says so**?' 'Dr Cameron.'*     *'You're crazy.' 'Who **said that**?' 'I did.'*

***so I hear* etc**  We can use *so* at the beginning of a clause with *say, see, hear, understand, tell, believe* and a number of other verbs. A present tense is common.

*It's going to be a cold winter, or **so** the newspaper **says**.*

**2** **Put in expressions from the box.**

| says so   says so?   So I hear – that's terrible   So I see   So I understand   so it said on the news   told me so |
|---|

1  'I've just had my hair done.' '……………………………………'
2  'You've got to clean the car.' 'Who ……………………………………' 'I do.'
3  Sue's getting married. Sarah……………………………………
4  There's going to be a rail strike, or……………………………………
5  'Pete's getting married again.' '…………………………………… from his brother.'
6  'The school's closing.' '……………………………………'
7  She's going to lose the election. Everybody ……………………………………

---

**NOTES**

We often use *so* and *not* after *if*.
    *Granny may come. **If so**, we'll play poker.*     *He may be upstairs. **If not**, try next door.*
We don't use *so* before a *that*-clause or after *know*.
    *I suppose that we'll have to go.* (NOT ~~I suppose so, that we'll have to go.~~)
    *'It's getting late.' 'I know.'* (NOT ~~I know so.~~)

# ellipsis after *and, but* and *or*

**We often leave out** repeated words or phrases after *and, but* and *or*.

*a knife and [a] fork.     She was poor but [she was] honest.*
*You can come with us or [you can] stay at home.*

**leaving out the first of the two**   When two verbs, objects etc are the same, it is not always the second that is left out. We may leave out the first for clarity or simplicity.

*Cats [catch mice] and dogs catch mice.* (NOT ~~Cats catch mice and dogs.~~)
*I can [go] and will go.*

**normal word order**   In informal speech and writing, ellipsis does not usually interrupt the normal word order of a clause. This may happen, however, in a more formal style.

*Peter planned, and Jane paid for, the holiday.* (Less formal: *Peter planned the holiday and Jane paid for it.*)
*Kevin likes dancing and Annie athletics.* (Less formal: *Kevin likes dancing and Annie likes athletics.*)

**1** **Write these sentences with less formal constructions. (Different answers are possible.)**

1   I drove immediately, and Alistair somewhat later, to the Ministry.

.......................................................................................................................................

2   Jane went to Greece and Alice to Rome.

.......................................................................................................................................

3   You seem to be, and she certainly is, ill.

.......................................................................................................................................

4   I have not studied, nor do I intend to study, ancient Greek astronomy.

.......................................................................................................................................

5   The children will carry the small, and the adults the large, boxes.

.......................................................................................................................................

**2** **Put in *and, but* or *or* with one of the verbs from the box.**

| broke   explained   knew   started   stopped   thought   wanted   wanted |

1   At the head of the valley we reached a tiny settlement ............................................. to ask the way.

5   'I know that voice, ........................ ..................... it years ago,' she said.

2   Antonietta sat beside her on the settee .............................................. that a doctor would be along soon.

6   Enid felt she did not have the concentration for advanced driving or painting ............... ................ she could probably try gardening.

3   Then she got really mad ....................................... screaming back at me.

7   They couldn't get in and find the dead woman until they got another key ....................................... the door down.

4   He didn't like her much ................... ................. her to stay.

8   He was very happy with us........................ ......................... to see if the grass was greener elsewhere.

**Note: other conjunctions**   Ellipsis is not normally possible after other conjunctions.
   *She didn't know where she was **when she** woke up.* (NOT ... ~~when woke up.~~)
But subject pronouns and forms of *be* can be left out in certain cases (e.g. *if possible, when arriving, though intelligent*).

# ellipsis at the beginning of spoken sentences

In informal speech (and very informal writing) we often **drop unstressed beginnings** of sentences.

This happens mainly with **articles, possessives, personal pronouns, auxiliary verbs** and *be*, **demonstratives** and introductory *there is*.

*Coffee machine's broken.* (= '**The** coffee machine …')
*Wife's not well.* (= '**My** wife …')     *Need a loan?*     *Can't read this email? Click …*

**1** **Rewrite the sentences with the words that have been left out.**

| are   I   is   it   my   she's ✓   that'll   there's |

▶ Lost her keys again. ..*She's lost her keys again.*.......................
1 You looking for somebody? ...........................................
2 Be £55. ...........................................
3 The boss in? ...........................................
4 Must go. ...........................................
5 No milk left. ...........................................
6 Won't start. ...........................................
7 Sock's got a hole in. ...........................................

**2** **Which words can be left out in informal speech?**

▶ ~~The~~ bus is late again.
1 It won't be ready in time.
2 There's nothing to worry about.
3 You're all well, I hope?
4 Have you seen my coat anywhere?
5 I couldn't understand a word she said.
6 Be careful with that vase.

We only drop pronouns **before stressed words**.

**Need** *some help.*     **Haven't** *heard.*     **Can't** *play.*
BUT NOT  ~~Have heard~~ OR ~~Can play~~. (Affirmative auxiliaries are usually unstressed.)

**3** **Correct (✓) or not (✗)?**

1 I'll see you soon. …
2 Will see you soon. …
3 See you 1. …
4 We're having problems again. …
5 Are having problems again. …
6 Having problems again. …

**4** **Read the conversation and note the examples of ellipsis. Circle some of them.**

FRED:  Morning, Ted. How're you doing?

TED:  Hello, Fred. OK, I suppose. Can't complain. Not raining for once, at least. Damned bus is late again, though.

FRED:  Yeah. See the match?

TED:  Bit of it. Gave up at half-time and went to bed.

FRED:  Don't blame you. Wasn't worth watching. And that ref. Needs a guide dog, if you ask me. What about this strike, then? Think they'll go ahead?

TED:  Won't make any difference to me if they do. Couple of days off work wouldn't hurt. Family OK?

FRED:  Yes. Brother's much better. Be out of hospital at the weekend if all goes well.

TED:  Good news. Give him my best.

FRED:  Will do. Here's my bus, then. See you around.

# the structure of spoken sentences

**simpler structure** Informal spoken sentences are generally simpler than written sentences. They have fewer subordinate clauses, and mostly use a small number of common conjunctions (e.g. *and, but, that, so, because, if, when*).

FORMAL WRITING: *While the region was remarkable for its natural beauty, the family experienced seriously disappointing weather, which continued throughout their stay.*
INFORMAL SPEECH: *The place was lovely, but the weather was terrible the whole time.*

**Passives** are more common in writing than in speech.

FORMAL WRITING: *Customer toilets are situated at the rear of the building.*
INFORMAL SPEECH: *Toilets? Round the back, mate.*

**separating out information** In writing, information is often packed tightly into complex structures (see pages 270–274). This does not necessarily cause problems for readers, who can take their time and read a phrase or sentence several times if necessary. In speech, information is generally separated out and given piece by piece, to make it easier to take in: one can read at one's own speed, but one cannot listen at one's own speed.

FORMAL WRITING: *a carefully constructed progressive three-level course incorporating built-in oral and written revision tests*
INFORMAL SPEECH: *a course with three levels, it's carefully put together, progressive, it's got revision tests, they're oral and written*

**fronting** Spoken sentences may be built up quite differently from written sentences, not necessarily with the order subject-verb-object. Other pieces of information may be moved to the front to give them more importance, or to set the scene for what follows (see page 257).

*Those shirts, you can't get them any more.*
*One of my brothers, his wife's a singer, she says it's really hard to make a living at it.*
*Last Christmas it was, you know Elizabeth, well, she got to us late, …*
*That meeting, I thought I was going to scream.*

**tails** In another spoken structure, the subject comes at the end of the sentence, in a 'tail', with or without an auxiliary. In its place at the beginning there may be a pronoun or nothing at all.

*(He) hasn't a chance, Fred.*     *(She) always gets it wrong, that woman.*
*(They) need a lot of help, some of those children.*     *(I) can't sing a note, myself.*

The subject may be reinforced by an auxiliary,

*Gone mad, you have.*     *Really getting on my nerves, Sylvia was.*
*Like a good thriller, I do.*     *They never keep their promises, the government don't.*

1) **Do you think these sentences were written (W) or spoken (S)?**

1   He took time afterwards to shake hands with staff and customers before emerging to an enthusiastic crowd of hundreds of people who shouted "Congratulations!" and "We love you!". …

2   His last book, OK, the critics liked it, but me, I just couldn't get into it. …

3   A 6ft (1.8m) long pet boa constrictor is on the loose after escaping through a bathroom window in Essex. …

4   The Scottish government says the argument for Scotland gaining more financial powers has to be won in order to grow the economy. …

5   Kids, these days, they just don't know what it's like. …

6   A man I met in a pub, he said, those TV quiz shows, you know, where you can win a million quid, well, it's all fixed, I mean, the contestants, they get to see the questions in advance. …

7   Never smiles at anybody, that woman. …

**2** Change these spoken sentences into a more formal written style. (Different answers may be possible.)

1 People like that I just can't stand.

...................................................................................................................................

2 A lot of good that does me.

...................................................................................................................................

3 What she wanted I never found out.

...................................................................................................................................

4 TV, these days, I never have time to watch anything.

...................................................................................................................................

5 Last for ever, these shoes will.

...................................................................................................................................

6 Crazy, some of these drivers.

...................................................................................................................................

7 Still at school, your kids, are they, then?

...................................................................................................................................

8 That house of theirs, are they ever going to sell it?

...................................................................................................................................

9 1984, I think it was, he started the job.

...................................................................................................................................

10 Sparkling water, listen, can you deliver two dozen bottles, the cheapest you've got?

...................................................................................................................................

11 Friday afternoon, I was watching the match, the doorbell rang, it was this idiot selling insurance.

...................................................................................................................................

12 Harry, his mother, she doesn't approve of his girlfriend, I don't think so, anyway.

...................................................................................................................................

**3** Read the text, and then write a few of the sentences in a more formal style (as if in a written complaint).

> Look, these assistants, I don't know what sort of training they get, but really! Thursday morning, you know that High Street place, Jones, Jenkins, whatever it's called, I don't know, they keep changing, earphones, that was what I wanted, just a pair of ordinary earphones, not much to ask, is it? Well, anyway, I go in, and these two assistants, they're having a good old gossip, hardly like to interrupt them, but I go up to them, and I say, 'Excuse me, but have you got a pair of cheap earphones?' One of them looks at me as if I'm something the cat brought in, the other, he doesn't even bother, and they go straight back to their conversation. Like something in a TV comedy programme. 'You speak English?' I said. Slow and loud. Well, I mean, you wonder sometimes, people like that, don't you? 'Earphones,' I said. 'Where?' 'Oh, you want the earphones department,' the first one said, and off they both went.

...................................................................................................................................

...................................................................................................................................

...................................................................................................................................

...................................................................................................................................

...................................................................................................................................

...................................................................................................................................

...................................................................................................................................

For more about leaving out words at the beginning of sentences, see page 281.

# short answers, reply questions and question tags

*(These structures should be familiar, but it may be worth checking your knowledge.)*

**short answers** We usually avoid unnecessary repetition in answers. A common pattern is *Yes/No* + **pronoun** + **auxiliary**, plus any other words that are really necessary. (*Yes* and *No* alone are often felt to be too short and not polite enough.) We use *do* if there is no other auxiliary.

*'Has Peter arrived?' '**No, he hasn't**.'*
*'Those kids make a lot of noise.' '**They** certainly **do**.'*

**reply questions** (**auxiliary** + **pronoun**) are common in conversation. They are not real questions: just attention signals to show that we are listening and reacting.

*'I've got a headache.' '**Have you?** Let me get you an aspirin.'*

People often answer reply questions, making a three-part exchange.

*'Emma's getting married.' '**Is she?**' '**Yes, she is**. Next month, I think.'*

**question tags** (**auxiliary** + **pronoun**) are added to statements. They can be real questions, used to check one's information; or they can simply be requests for agreement, with no real meaning. The intonation (music of the voice) is different in the two cases. Compare:

*That's Helen, **isn't it?*** (Real question.)

*Lovely day, **isn't it**.* (Request for agreement.)

After negative sentences (including sentences with *never*, *hardly* and similar words), we use non-negative tags.

*It **isn't** right, **is it?***     *He **never** smiles, **does he?***

**1** **Put in suitable short answers, reply questions or question tags.**

▶ 'Can she swim?' 'Yes, ...she can....................'
▶ 'It was a terrible party.' '...Was it?................' 'Yes, it was.
▶ It's hardly rained this summer, ...has it?...................

1 'Are you ready?' 'No,.....................................'
2 'I'm late,....................................' 'Yes,....................................'
3 'We had a lovely holiday.' '....................................' 'Yes, we went to China.'
4 'Have you phoned Julian?' 'Sorry, ....................................'
5 They never try to help,....................................
6 'John likes that girl next door.' '.................................... He's much older than her.'
7 This film isn't much good, ....................................
8 'You haven't paid for the tickets.' '.................................... I sent a cheque.'
9 'I don't understand.' '.................................... I'm sorry. I'll explain it again.'
10 'You don't need a lift, ....................................' '...................................., actually,
....................................'
11 'They got everything wrong. Every single thing.' '....................................' 'Yes, ..............
really............................'
12 'Do we have to pay now?' '...................................., I'm afraid ....................................'

**Question tags** can complete short answers.

*'Lovely day.' 'Yes, it is, **isn't it?**'*

**question tags after imperatives** After imperatives, several question tags are possible: *can you?, could you?, will you?* or *would you?*

*Give me a hand, **can/could you?*** *Wait here for a moment, **will/would you?***

After negative imperatives, the normal tag is *will you?*

*Don't forget, **will you?***

**same-way tags** Non-negative tags are quite common after affirmative sentences. Like reply questions, they express interest, surprise, or some other reaction.

*So you're getting a new job, **are you?** That should be nice.*

Negative tags after negative sentences can sound aggressive.

*So you don't like my soup, **don't you?** Well, you can cook for yourself from now on.*

**negative questions** Note the use of *Yes* and *No* in answers to negative questions (see page 6).

*'Don't you want any more?' '**No**, I don't.'* (NOT ~~*Yes, I don't.*~~)
*'Hasn't the post come?' '**Yes**, it has.'* (NOT ~~*No, it has.*~~)

**Negative short answers** can be used as exclamations to express surprise.

*'I told her exactly what I thought of her.' 'You didn't! Well done.'*

**2** **Choose the best ways of completing the conversation.**

SUE: Peter's done it again!
JILL: He ▶ .hasn't!.............
SUE: Yes, he [1]..........................
JILL: That's the third time, [2]..........................
SUE: At least. Anne's furious. She's gone off to Scotland.
JILL: She [3].........................., [4].......................... she? Well, I'm not surprised, really. I mean, he's a nice guy, but she can't let him get away with that sort of thing, [5]..........................
SUE: No, of course she [6].......................... And that's not all. There's Carl!
JILL: What about Carl?
SUE: Haven't you heard?
JILL: [7].........................., I haven't.
SUE: He told Amanda everything.
JILL: He [8]..........................! He never learns, [9].......................... So what did Amanda say?
SUE: Well, it's funny. She said 'It's OK. I love him, so I don't mind.' I don't believe that for a moment.
JILL: No, nor do I. She'll do what she did last time. Only worse.
SUE: Well, I wouldn't like to be there when she does it, [10]..........................?
JILL: No, I certainly [11]..........................
SUE: Well, nice talking to you. By the way, don't tell Joe I told you about Carl and Amanda, [12]..........................
JILL: No, of course I [13].......................... See you, then.
SUE: See you.

# three kinds of spoken question

**declarative questions** In spoken questions, we do not always use interrogative word order. The rising intonation ('music' of the voice) shows that we are making a question.

*You're working tomorrow?*

These 'declarative questions' are often used to check that we are right about something.

*This is your car?* (= 'I suppose this is your car, isn't it?')
*That's the boss? I thought he was the cleaner.*

This word order is not usually possible after a question word.

*When are you going?* (NOT ~~When you are going?~~)

**1** **Which of these questions are possible (in informal speech)?**

▶ It's lunchtime already? .✓.
▶ Why you are crying? .✗.
1 You're in this evening? …
2 Your wife's Scottish? …
3 You expect me to believe that? …
4 What you are doing at the weekend? …
5 You've got a letter from Ellie? …
6 They won the match? …
7 Where you got that coat? …
8 You saw a ghost? …
9 How you want to pay? …
10 That parcel's for me? …
11 Is Tuesday, the meeting? …
12 When we're seeing Dave? …

**echo questions** To question what has been said, a speaker may simply repeat ('echo') what he/she has heard. A rising intonation is common.

*'I'm getting married.' 'You're getting married?'*

To ask about one part of a sentence, we can repeat the rest of the sentence and put in a stressed question word in place of the part we are asking about.

*'Take a look at that.' 'Take a look at **what?**'*
*'She's invited thirteen people to dinner.' 'She's invited **how many?**'*
*'We're going to Baffinland for our holidays.' 'You're going **where?**'*
*'I've broken the alternator casing.' 'You've broken the **what?**'*

To ask about a verb, or the part of a sentence beginning with the verb, **what** or **do what** is used.

*She set fire to the garage.' 'She **what / did what?**'*

**2** **In these exchanges, which of the replies is/are correct?**

1 'I'm going to New Zealand.'
  'You're going to New Zealand?' …
2 'They've got sixteen children.'
  'They've got how many?' …
3 'I've bought a concrete mixer.'
  'A what have you bought?' …
4 'What are you doing?
  'What I'm doing? Thinking.' …
5 'Are you happy?'
  'Am I happy? I'm over the moon.' …
6 'I've sold your bike.'
  'You've done what?' …
7 'Cassie's going to marry Arthur.'
  'Who she's going to marry?' …
8 'I thought that was really funny.'
  'You thought what was really funny?' …
9 'You can't come in here.'
  'I can't come in here?' …
10 'I gave your phone number to the policemen.'
  'You gave my number to who?' …

**3** Write the father's echo questions.

| SON | FATHER |
|---|---|
| ▶ I'm going to drop out of university. | *You're going to (do) what?* |
| 1 I'm going to Japan. | ................................................ |
| 2 I'm leaving tomorrow. | ................................................ |
| 3 I'll be staying with Maria. | ................................................ |
| 4 I'm going to teach English. | ................................................ |
| 5 I'll make about £5,000 a week. | ................................................ |
| 6 But I'll need £500 for the fare. | ................................................ |
| 7 Can you lend it to me? | ................................................ |

**rhetorical questions** Questions do not always ask for information. A question with an obvious answer, or with no answer, can be an indirect way of pointing something out to somebody. These are called 'rhetorical questions'.

*Do you know what time it is?* (= 'You're late.')
*Who's a lovely baby?* (= 'You're a lovely baby.')
*'I can't find my coat.'* *'What's this, then?'* (= 'Here it is, stupid.')

The expressions *Why should …?* and *How should/would I know?* are quite aggressive.

*'Could your sister help us in the office tomorrow?'* *'Why should she? She doesn't work for you.'*
*'What time does the film start?'* *'How should I know?'*

Negative questions (see pages 6–7) can be rhetorical.

*Haven't I done enough for you?* (= 'I have done enough for you.')
*Didn't I tell you it would rain?* (= 'I told you.')

**4** Write 'translations' of these questions to show what they might really mean. **(Different answers are possible.)**

- ▶ When are you going to grow up? *You're behaving like a child.*
- ▶ What's that thing on your head? *You've got a really funny hat.*
1 Who knows? ................................................
2 What are you doing in my room? ................................................
3 Who's going to clean up all this mess? ................................................
4 Where do you think you're going? ................................................
5 Where's that coffee that I ordered? ................................................
6 What's the use of talking to her? ................................................
7 Why worry? ................................................
8 When is that boy going to get a job? ................................................
9 Haven't you people got a home to go to? ................................................
10 How are you going to pay for all that? ................................................
11 Who cares? ................................................
12 What are you talking about? ................................................
13 What are those things on your feet? ................................................
14 Where's my lunch? ................................................
15 'Give me your phone number.' 'Why should I?' ................................................

→

# three kinds of spoken question (continued)

5 **Complete the conversation with sentences from the boxes. Different answers are possible.**

| Are you crazy?   That's the good news?   You're sure of that?   You've done what?   Would I lie to you? |

**SALLY:** Hi, dear. How was your day?

**BRUCE:** Hi, darling. Well, first the good news. I've resigned.

**SALLY:** ¹...................................................................

**BRUCE:** I've resigned. I'm not going back.

**SALLY:** ²...................................................................

**BRUCE:** Yes it is. I'm going to get a much better job. Twice the salary.

**SALLY:** ³...................................................................

**BRUCE:** Positive. A hundred per cent certain.

**SALLY:** I don't believe you.

**BRUCE:** ⁴...................................................................

**SALLY:** Yes, probably. Well, tell me about it.

**BRUCE:** Well, there's this guy I met in a pub.

**SALLY:** Oh, no! ⁵...................................................................

Anyway, if that's the good news, what's the bad news?

**BRUCE:** Well, you know your new …

6 **If you like, continue the conversation. Put in some declarative questions, echo questions and rhetorical questions.**

..........................................................................................................

..........................................................................................................

..........................................................................................................

..........................................................................................................

..........................................................................................................

..........................................................................................................

'You sold my what to who?'

# politeness: using questions

**requests**  We usually ask people to do things for us by using *yes/no* questions. (This suggests that the hearer can choose whether to agree or not).

*Could you tell me the time, please?*    *Would you mind switching on the lights?*

When we need to be very polite, we often add an apology and/or an explanation. We can also add *possibly*, or use an indirect question.

*I'm sorry to trouble you, but could you **possibly** tell me the way to the station?*
*Excuse me. **I've got to go out for a moment**. **I wonder if** you could watch my bags?*

**imperatives not used**  Adding *please* does not turn an imperative into a polite request.

*'**Please help** me for a few minutes.'  'I'm not your servant.'*

**shops etc**  In shops, restaurants etc we don't always use questions to ask for things (though we quite often do so). Direct orders like *Give me …* can sound quite rude.

*Could I see that dress?*    *I'll have an orange juice, please.*    *I'd like to see the menu.*

**Negative questions** are not used in requests.

*Could you help me for a moment?* (NOT ~~Couldn't you help me for a moment?~~ – this sounds like a complaint: 'Why aren't you helping me?')

But **negative statements** with question tags are common in informal requests.

*You couldn't help me for a moment, could you?*

**Expressions of opinion** can also be made less direct, and so more polite, by turning them into direct or indirect questions. Compare:

*It would be better to fly.* (direct expression of opinion)
*Wouldn't it be better to fly?* (negative question asking for agreement – less direct)
*Would it be better to fly?* (open question – very indirect)
*I wonder if it would be better to fly.* (indirect question)

**1  Imagine you say these sentences to a stranger, or someone you don't know well. Are they probably polite enough (P), or not (NP)?**

▶ Tell me the time, please.  NP
▶ Could you possibly open a window?  P
1  Can't you tell me where the police station is, please?  …
2  Show me some middle-priced watches.  …
3  Excuse me. I wonder if you can help me.  …
4  Please hold this for me for a minute.  …
5  You ought to paint it green.  …
6  Would you mind working late tonight?  …
7  Would it be a good idea to ask your father first?  …
8  Open the door for me, please.  …

**2  One of the authors of this book received this email from a stranger. It's not polite enough for the situation. Can you improve it?**

Dear X, Could you please tell me the difference between *shy* and *timid*? I look forward to hearing from you.    Yours sincerely, Y

# politeness: being indirect

**Questions, suggestions and requests** can be made more polite by using 'indirect' verb forms: for example past instead of present.

*I **wondered** if you **needed** me today.*     *How much **did** you **want** to spend, madam?*

Past modals like *would*, *could* and *might* are often used like this.

*We thought it **would** be useful to ask Joe what he thinks.*
***Could** I ask you to check these figures for me?*
*You **might** see if the people at the town hall have any information.*

**1** **What can you change to make these sentences less direct?**

▶ We wonder if you feel like joining us. ..We wondered ... felt......
1  Can you watch the kids for a moment? ...................................
2  Ann and I wonder if you are here this weekend. ...................................
3  I hope you will find this useful. ...................................
4  It may be a good idea to invite Olivia. ...................................
5  How many rooms do you want to reserve? ...................................
6  Will it be all right if I bring a friend? ...................................
7  You can try the Station Hotel. ...................................
8  Do you want to see the manager now? ...................................
9  Will you tell Harry to come upstairs? ...................................
10  Do you intend to travel tomorrow? ...................................

**Past progressives** give an extra level of politeness.

*I **was wondering** if I could ask your advice.*

**2** **Change the verbs in *italics* to make these sentences less direct.**

▶ We *hope* ..were hoping............................. you *can* ..could............... help us.
1  I *think* ...................................it's ........................... time to get a new dishwasher.
2  I *hope* ...................................you *don't* ........................... mind my asking.
3  We *wonder* ...................................if we *can* ........................... use your phone.
4  *Are* ........................... you looking for somebody?
5  Jan *wonders* ...................................if you *can* ........................... translate this.
6  I *expect* ...................................to get some information from the manager.

**Another way** of making requests less direct is to use a **future** verb form.

*I'm afraid you**'ll need** to fill in this form.*     *I**'ll need** a receipt, please.*
*I**'ll have** to ask you to wait a minute.*     *That **will be** €8.35.*

**3** **Use future forms to make these requests polite. (Different answers are possible.)**

1  Come back on Tuesday.
   ...................................................................................................................
2  Give me two copies.
   ...................................................................................................................
3  Pay in advance.
   ...................................................................................................................
4  £25.60, please.
   ...................................................................................................................

**Structures with *if*** can be used in a similar way.

*It would be nice **if you could phone Anna**.*      ***If you would take a seat** for a moment …*
***If you were to come back this evening** …*

4  **Write a sentence with *if* to ask somebody to do the shopping for you.**
   **(Different answers are possible.)**

.....................................................................................................

**Present progressives** can make statements sound casual and friendly.

*I'm looking forward to hearing from you.* (Less formal than *I look forward …*)
*We're hoping you'll come and stay with us soon.*

5  **Write a sentence that you might put in a letter to a friend, beginning *I'm looking forward to*.**

.....................................................................................................

***quite, maybe** etc*  We can express opinions and intentions less directly, and more politely,
by using softening expressions like *quite, rather, kind of, a bit, maybe* etc.

*He's **quite** rude, isn't he?*      *I find her **rather** bossy, don't you?*

***I think I'll** …*  We can say that we are thinking of doing something, instead of expressing our
intentions directly.

*OK. **I think** I'll go to bed.*      ***I'm thinking** of taking the day off tomorrow.*

***We would like, we are writing to** …etc*  In a formal style, requests, invitations, suggestions etc
are often 'wrapped up' instead of being expressed directly.

***We would like** to invite you to give a talk to our members on 14th June.*
***I'd like** to suggest that we take a vote.*
***I would like** to congratulate you on your examination results.*
***I am writing** to express our appreciation of your generosity.*
***May we** remind you that your subscription is due for renewal on 1st January?*
***This is to** confirm that your payment has been received.*
***Let me assure you** that your request will receive careful attention.*

6  **Use expressions from the box to soften these sentences. (Different answers are possible.)**

| a bit   I think   kind of   maybe   quite   rather   We are writing   We're thinking   would like |

1  It's expensive. ...........................................................................
2  The music's boring. ....................................................................
3  I'll go for a walk. .......................................................................
4  Congratulations on your prize. .................................................
5  I suggest we meet again next week. ............................................
6  We'll sell our house. ..................................................................
7  She's bad-tempered. ...................................................................
8  This meat smells funny. ..............................................................
9  Thank you for your donation. ....................................................
10  Please give a talk to our members. ............................................

# emphasis in speech: stress

**stress** We often want to emphasise one part of a sentence, either to express a strong feeling, or to show a contrast. In speech, this can be done by *stress* – by saying particular words louder and on a higher musical pitch.

*I just LOVE your hair like that!*  *I said TUESDAY, not Wednesday!*
*They really ARE strange people!*  *You HAVE lost weight!*

*Do* is often used with affirmative verbs to show emphasis, if there is no other auxiliary. It can be used with *be* in imperatives (see page 10).

*I DO feel ill!*  *So who DID win in the end?*  *DO sit down.*  *DO be careful.*

**1** Complete the sentences with expressions from the box, and make them more emphatic by using *do/does/did*.

> a lot   for coming late   happy √   interrupting you   it's time to go home
> old cowboy films   on my nerves   Sally for me   to your grandfather

▶ I feel .....*I do feel happy.*.................................................
1 I like ...............................................................
2 Annemarie talked ....................................................................
3 His voice gets ...........................................................................
4 Excuse me for ...........................................................................
5 I think .........................................................................
6 Be polite ...........................................................................
7 I apologise ...........................................................................
8 Say hello to ...........................................................................

**Contrastive emphasis:** stress can show a **contrast** – between false and true, appearance and reality, or a general statement and an exception. The stress is often on an auxiliary verb.

*He said he couldn't swim, but he CAN swim.*
*She thinks I don't love her, but I DO love her.*
*It looks easy, but it DOES need quite a bit of practice.*
*The food wasn't up to much, but the DESSERT was all right.*

We can also use stress to compare what is **expected** with what actually **happens**.

*I said I was going to win, and I DID win.*

**2** Add *do/does/did* if there is no auxiliary, make any other changes that are necessary, and write the words that are stressed.
▶ 'Why haven't you fed the cat?' 'I have fed the cat.' ..*have*.................
▶ I've forgotten his name, but I remember he lives in Bristol. ..*do remember*.......
1 I don't play tennis, but I like watching it. ...........................
2 They're not very interesting people, but they throw great parties. ...........................
3 They gave me an X-ray, and I had a broken rib. ...........................
4 'You weren't listening to me.' 'I was listening to you.' ...........................
5 I told you I could find a room, and I found a room. ...........................
6 Everybody said James would end up in prison, and he ended up in prison. ...........................
7 I don't do much cooking, but I fix breakfast. ...........................
8 I'm not getting much holiday this year, but I will spend a week in Wales. ...........................

**Note:** When we **write down speech**, we usually represent stress by using CAPITALS (as in the above examples, or by *italics*, or by underlining (especially in handwriting).

# repetition

**avoidance of repetition**  In English, we usually avoid repeating words in the same clause or sentence, or otherwise close together, if it can be avoided.

*The ship hit an iceberg. The passengers had to take to the lifeboats.* (better than *The ship hit an iceberg. The passengers had to abandon the ship.*)
*'Lovely day, isn't it?' 'Splendid.'* (better than *'Yes, lovely.'*)

The following paragraph is perfectly grammatical, but feels very clumsy. A careful writer would avoid the repetitions by varying the structure and by using synonyms (e.g. *tried/attempted, summarise/describe briefly, forecast/predict, present/current*.)

*In this report, I have tried to forecast likely developments over the next three years. In the first section, I have tried to summarise the results of the last two years, and I have tried to summarise the present situation. In the second section, I have tried to forecast the likely consequences of the present situation, and the consequences of the present financial policy.*

**ungrammatical repetition**  We normally use pronouns to avoid repeating nouns that have just been mentioned. It is generally ungrammatical or unnatural to use nouns in these cases.

*Dad cut **himself** shaving.* (NOT *Dad cut Dad shaving.*)
*We got that cat because Emma wanted **it**.* (NOT *… because Emma wanted that cat.*)

The same thing happens with other words besides nouns.

*'I'm not hungry.' 'I **am**.'* (more natural than *I'm hungry.*)
*'Do you know if the bank's open?' 'I think **so**.'* (NOT *I think the bank's open.*)
(For more about leaving words out, see pages 276–281.)

**related verbs and nouns**  We usually avoid putting related verbs and nouns together.

*We made wonderful plans.* OR *We planned wonderful things.* BUT NOT *We planned wonderful plans.*
*She wrote an interesting paper.* OR *She did an interesting piece of writing.* BUT NOT *She wrote an interesting piece of writing.*

There are some exceptions in fixed phrases: for example *to sing a song* or *to live a good life*.

**deliberate repetition**  We may of course repeat vocabulary and structures deliberately for emphasis, or for a stylistic effect.

*I'm **very very** sorry.     I want **every room** cleaned – **every** single **room**.*
*First of all, **I want to** welcome you to this meeting. Secondly, **I want to** congratulate you on your success. And thirdly, **I want to** give you details of the day's programme.*

Here are two literary examples. In the first, the writer uses elegant repetition to create a 'grand' effect. In the second, the writer uses deliberately clumsy repetition to reflect the personality of a simple uneducated fisherman.

This is the story of Danny and of Danny's friends and of Danny's house. It is a story of how

(from *Tortilla Flat* by John Steinbeck)

He did not remember when he had first started to talk aloud when he was by himself. He had sung when he was by himself in the old days and he had sung at night sometimes

(from *The Old Man and the Sea* by Ernest Hemingway)

# abbreviated styles

Some styles of writing and speech have their own special grammar rules, often because of the need to save space or time.

**advertisements, notes, instructions**  Small ads and instructions often leave out articles, subject or object pronouns, forms of *be* and prepositions.

*Job needed urgently. Will do anything legal. Call 134522.*
*Single man wants flat Oxford area. Phone 3131312 weekends.*
*Fry onions and celery until soft, add bacon …*

The same kind of thing often happens with informal notes, to-do lists, diary entries, postcards, informal emails etc.

*Gone to hairdresser. Back 12.30.*
*book tickets; call Ann lunchtime; check car service date; fix see Adrian*
*Having a lovely time. Wish you were here.*
*Hi, Phil. Can't make it this evening – problem with Katie. See you tomorrow. Ben.*

**1** **Rewrite these as full sentences with normal grammar.**

1  Open packet other end.

..................................................................................................................

2  See diagram at top of next page.

..................................................................................................................

3  Take car to garage; find baby-sitter for tonight; see Oliver 3.30.

..................................................................................................................

..................................................................................................................

**2** **Can you rewrite this as it might appear in a recipe book?**

Pour the mixture into a large saucepan, heat it until it's boiling, then add three pounds of sugar and leave it on a low heat for 45 minutes.

..................................................................................................................

..................................................................................................................

..................................................................................................................

**txt msgs**  Text messages have their own ways of abbreviating words. Can you rewrite these with ordinary spelling?

▶ c u l8r  *See you later.* .................................................................
1  r u cumin 2day? ...................................................................
2  thx 4 a gr8 party ...................................................................
3  jst 2 let u no ...................................................................
4  wil u b hr Thu eve? ...................................................................
5  RUOK? ...................................................................
6  got ur msg ...................................................................
7  wil b @ bbq @ 9 ...................................................................
8  need mo infmtn ...................................................................

**Note:**  **commentaries** on fast-moving events drop auxiliaries and other less important verbs.
*Goal kick … and the score still Spurs 3, Arsenal 1 … that's Keir … Keir to Parsons, good ball …*
*Parsons running wide … Hargraves takes it, back to Keir, Keir with a cross, and oh, Parsons in beautifully –*
*and it's a goal!*

# news headlines

**News headlines** have their own special grammar. They often consist simply of noun phrases with no verb.

*MORE WAGE CUTS    HOLIDAY HOTEL DEATH*

**Long strings of nouns** are common. Earlier nouns modify those that follow.

*AIRLINE CABIN STAFF STRIKE THREAT*

Strings of nouns like these can be easier to understand if one reads them backwards:

*There is a **threat** of a **strike** by the **staff** who work in the **cabins** of an **airline**.*

**Articles** and the verb *be* are often left out.

*SHAKESPEARE PLAY IMMORAL SAYS HEADMASTER*
*YORKSHIRE SCHOOLBOY WALKS IN SPACE*

**1** **Can you compose a five-word newspaper headline to announce the following piece of news?**

There is a threat of a reduction in wages at a factory that makes furniture.

...........................................................................................................................................................

**verb forms** **Simple tenses** are often used instead of perfect or progressive forms. The simple present can refer to the past. **Infinitives** are used to refer to the future.

*BLIND GIRL CLIMBS EVEREST    STUDENTS FIGHT FOR CHANGES*
*PM TO VISIT AUSTRALIA*

Auxiliary verbs are often dropped from passive structures.

*MURDER HUNT: MAN HELD BY POLICE* ( = '… is being held …')
*SIX KILLED IN EXPLOSION* (= ' … have been killed …')

Note that forms like *HELD, ATTACKED* are usually past participles, not past tenses (which are rare in headlines). Compare:

*AID ROW: PRESIDENT ATTACKED* ( = '… the President has been attacked')
*AID ROW: PRESIDENT ATTACKS CRITICS* ( = '… the President has attacked …')

**2** **Can you translate these headlines into ordinary language?**

1 **HOSPITALS TO TAKE FEWER PATIENTS**

...........................................................................................................................................................

2 **DOG TRAVELS 500 MILES, FINDS OWNERS**

...........................................................................................................................................................

3 **Boy found safe**

...........................................................................................................................................................

4 **BOY FINDS SAFE**

...........................................................................................................................................................

5 MINISTERS WARNED THREE YEARS AGO OVER FLOOD DEFENCES

...........................................................................................................................................................

**Note:** The short words that are common in headlines can often be used as nouns or verbs, so it can be difficult to work out the structure of a sentence. Compare:
- *US CUTS AID TO THIRD WORLD* ( = 'The US is reducing its help…' *CUTS* is a verb, *AID* is a noun)
- *AID CUTS ROW* ( = 'There has been a disagreement about the reduction in aid.' *AID* and *CUTS* are both nouns.)
- *CUTS AID REBELS* ( = 'The reduction is helping the revolutionaries.' *CUTS* is a noun, *AID* is a verb.)

# appendix 1 spelling of grammatical forms

## 3rd person singular present verbs; noun plurals

**Most verbs** add -s:
> *work/works, depend/depends, like/likes.*

**Verbs ending in -s, -x, ch or sh** add -es:
> *hiss/hisses, mix/mixes, catch/catches, push/pushes.*

**Verbs ending in consonant + y** have 3rd person forms in -ies:
> *try/tries, hurry/hurries* BUT *play/plays* (**vowel** + *y*)

**Exceptions**: *goes, does.*

**Noun plurals** are formed in the same way:
> *book/books, bike/bikes, bus/buses, fox/foxes, match/matches, wish/wishes, baby/babies.*

For irregular and special plurals, see page 303.

## -ing forms

**Most verbs** add -ing.
> *start/starting, avoid/avoiding*

**Verbs ending in -e** drop the -e before -ing.
> *hope/hoping, make/making, complete/completing*

**Verbs ending in -ie** have -ying.
> *die/dying, lie/lying*

**Verbs ending in one vowel and one consonant** may double the consonant before -ing: see 'doubling' below.
> *sit/sitting, prefer/preferring*

## regular pasts

**Most verbs** add -ed.
> *start/started, train/trained, develop/developed*

**Verbs ending in -e** add -d.
> *hope/hoped, complete/completed.*

**Verbs ending in consonant + -y** have -ied.
> *try/tried, carry/carried* BUT *play/played* (**vowel** + *y*)

**Verbs ending in one vowel and one consonant** may double the consonant before -ed: see 'doubling' below.
> *stop/stopped, slam/slammed*

## possessives

**Singular possessive nouns** end in 's, plural possessives end in s', irregular plural possessives end in 's.
> *my **brother's** wife    my **grandparents'** house*
> *the **children's** room*

Names ending in -s sometimes have a possessive in s', especially in classical and literary references, but 's is more common.
> ***Socrates'** philosophy    Henry **James'** novels*
> ***James's** aunt*

## comparatives and superlatives (one-syllable adjectives; some two-syllable adjectives)

**Most short adjectives** add -er, -est.
> *old/older/oldest, tall/taller/tallest*

**Adjectives ending in -e** add -r, -st.
> *late/later/latest*

**Adjectives ending in consonant + y** have -ier, -iest.
> *dry/drier/driest, happy/happier/happiest*

**Adjectives ending in one vowel and one consonant** may double the consonant: see 'doubling' below.
> *fat/fatter/fattest, wet/wetter/wettest*

## adverbs of manner

**Most adverbs of manner** add -ly to the corresponding adjective.
> *real/really, complete/completely*

**If the adjective ends in consonant + y**, the adverb has -ily.
> *easy/easily, happy/happily*

**If the adjective ends in -ble**, the adverb has -bly.
> *probable/probably, possible/possibly*

**If the adjective ends in -ic**, the adverb has -ically.
> *chronic/chronically, tragic/tragically*
> Exception: *public/publicly*

## doubling

**Words ending in one vowel and one consonant** double the consonant before -ing, -ed, -er and -est.
> *sit/sitting, run/running, stop/stopped, rob/robbed, fit/fitter/fittest, slim/slimmer/slimmest*
> BUT *read/reading* (two vowels), *start/started* (two consonants), *mean/meaner/meanest* (two vowels), *old/older/oldest* (two consonants).

**In longer words**, *doubling only happens in STRESSED syllables.*
> *forGET/forGETTing, preFER/preFERRed*
> BUT *VIsit/VIsiting, OFfer/OFfered*

*W* and *x* are not doubled.
> *throw/throwing,  fix/fixed*

# appendix 2  active and passive verb forms

| | ACTIVE | | PASSIVE: TENSE OF *BE* + PAST PARTICIPLE | |
|---|---|---|---|---|
| INFINITIVE | *(to) watch* | *(to) write* | *(to) be watched* | *(to) be written* |
| *-ING* FORM | *watching* | *writing* | *being watched* | *being written* |
| SIMPLE PRESENT | *I watch* | *I write* | *I am watched* | *It is written* |
| PRESENT PROGRESSIVE | *I am watching* | *I am writing* | *I am being watched* | *It is being written* |
| SIMPLE PAST | *I watched* | *I wrote* | *I was watched* | *It was written* |
| PAST PROGRESSIVE | *I was watching* | *I was writing* | *I was being watched* | *It was being written* |
| PRESENT PERFECT | *I have watched* | *I have written* | *I have been watched* | *It has been written* |
| PRESENT PERFECT PROGRESSIVE | *I have been watching* | *I have been writing* | ----- | ----- |
| PAST PERFECT | *I had watched* | *I had written* | *I had been watched* | *It had been written* |
| PAST PERFECT PROGRESSIVE | *I had been watching* | *I had been writing* | ----- | ----- |
| *WILL* FUTURE | *I will watch* | *I will write* | *I will be watched* | *It will be written* |
| FUTURE PROGRESSIVE | *I will be watching* | *I will be writing* | ----- | ----- |
| FUTURE PERFECT | *I will have watched* | *I will have written* | *I will have been watched* | *It will have been written* |
| FUTURE PERFECT PROGRESSIVE | *I will have been watching* | *I will have been writing* | ----- | ----- |
| *GOING TO* FUTURE | *I am going to watch* | *I am going to write* | *I am going to be watched* | *It is going to be written* |
| MODAL VERBS | *I can watch* | *I can write* | *I can be watched* | *It can be written* |
| | *I must watch* | *I must write* | *I must be watched* | *It must be written* |
| | *I should watch* | *I should write* | *I should be watched* | *It should be written* |
| | etc | etc | etc | etc |

Passive forms with *be(en) being* are very unusual.

# appendix 3 common irregular verbs

(These are the most common irregular verbs. For a complete list, see a good dictionary.)

| INFINITIVE | PAST | PAST PARTICIPLE | INFINITIVE | PAST | PAST PARTICIPLE |
|---|---|---|---|---|---|
| arise | arose | arisen | go | went | gone/been |
| awake | awoke | awoken | grind | ground | ground |
| be | was/were | been | grow | grew | grown |
| bear | bore | borne/born | hang | hung | hung |
| beat | beat | beaten | have | had | had |
| become | became | become | hear | heard | heard |
| begin | began | begun | hide | hid | hidden |
| bend | bent | bent | hit | hit | hit |
| bet | bet | bet | hold | held | held |
| bind | bound | bound | hurt | hurt | hurt |
| bite | bit | bitten | keep | kept | kept |
| bleed | bled | bled | kneel | knelt | knelt |
| blow | blew | blown | know | knew | known |
| break | broke | broken | lay | laid | laid |
| breed | bred | bred | lead | led | led |
| bring | brought | brought | leap | leapt/leaped | leapt/leaped |
| broadcast | broadcast | broadcast | learn | learnt/learned | learnt/learned |
| build | built | built | leave | left | left |
| burn | burnt | burnt | lend | lent | lent |
| burst | burst | burst | let | let | let |
| buy | bought | bought | lie | lay | lain |
| cast | cast | cast | light | lit/lighted | lit/lighted |
| catch | caught | caught | lose | lost | lost |
| choose | chose | chosen | make | made | made |
| cling | clung | clung | mean | meant | meant |
| come | came | come | meet | met | met |
| cost | cost | cost | mistake | mistook | mistaken |
| creep | crept | crept | pay | paid | paid |
| cut | cut | cut | put | put | put |
| deal | dealt | dealt | quit | quit/quitted | quit/quitted |
| dig | dug | dug | read /ri:d/ | read /red/ | read /red/ |
| do | did | done | ride | rode | ridden |
| draw | drew | drawn | ring | rang | rung |
| dream | dreamt/dreamed | dreamt/dreamed | rise | rose | risen |
| drink | drank | drunk | run | ran | run |
| drive | drove | driven | say | said | said |
| eat | ate | eaten | see | saw | seen |
| fall | fell | fallen | seek | sought | sought |
| feed | fed | fed | sell | sold | sold |
| feel | felt | felt | send | sent | sent |
| fight | fought | fought | set | set | set |
| find | found | found | sew | sewed | sewn |
| fit | fit/fitted | fit/fitted | shake | shook | shaken |
| fly | flew | flown | shine | shone | shone |
| forbid | forbade | forbidden | shoot | shot | shot |
| forecast | forecast | forecast | show | showed | shown |
| forget | forgot | forgotten | shrink | shrank/shrunk | shrunk |
| forgive | forgave | forgiven | shut | shut | shut |
| freeze | froze | frozen | sing | sang | sung |
| get | got | got | sink | sank/sunk | sunk |
| give | gave | given | sit | sat | sat |

| INFINITIVE | PAST | PAST PARTICIPLE |
|---|---|---|
| sleep | slept | slept |
| slide | slid | slid |
| smell | smelt/smelled | smelt/smelled |
| sow | sowed | sown |
| speak | spoke | spoken |
| spell | spelt | spelt |
| spend | spent | spent |
| spill | spilt/spilled | spilt/spilled |
| spoil | spoilt/spoiled | spoilt/spoiled |
| spread | spread | spread |
| spring | sprang | sprung |
| stand | stood | stood |
| steal | stole | stolen |
| stick | stuck | stuck |
| sting | stung | stung |
| stink | stank | stunk |
| strike | struck | struck |
| swear | swore | sworn |
| sweep | swept | swept |
| swell | swelled | swollen |
| swim | swam | swum |
| swing | swung | swung |
| take | took | taken |
| teach | taught | taught |
| tear | tore | torn |
| tell | told | told |
| think | thought | thought |
| throw | threw | thrown |
| tread | trod | trodden |
| understand | understood | understood |
| wake | woke | woken |
| wear | wore | worn |
| win | won | won |
| write | wrote | written |

## American English forms

*Dream, leap, learn, smell, spill* and *spoil* are regular.

*Dive* has an irregular past *dove*. *Get* has a past participle *gotten*, used in the sense of 'obtained' or 'become' (but *got* is used in *I('ve) got*, meaning 'I have').

# appendix 4 punctuation

## the basic sentence
We don't separate the basic parts of a sentence (subject and verb, verb and object, etc).
> *The standard of living of the dock workers was slowly improving.*
> (NOT ~~The standard of living of the dock workers, was slowly improving.~~)
> *Many of them were able to begin buying their own homes.*
> (NOT ~~Many of them were able to begin buying, their own homes.~~)

## before the basic sentence
If we put **long adverbial expressions** (saying *when, where* etc) before the basic sentence, we often use a comma (,). Compare:
> **At that time** *the standard of living of the dock workers was slowly improving.*
> **During the late 1920s and early 1930s,** *the standard of living of the dock workers was slowly improving.*

## after the basic sentence
We don't usually use commas when **adverbial expressions** come **after** the basic sentence.
> *The standard of living of the dock workers was slowly improving* **during the late 1920s and early 1930s.**

## inside the basic sentence
When adverbial expressions come **between** or inside parts of the basic sentence, we usually put commas **before** and **after** them.
> *The standard of living of the dock workers,* **during the late 1920s and early 1930s,** *was steadily improving.*

## noun phrases
We don't usually separate a noun from the adjectives or other expressions that go with it.
> *the mainly foreign labourers* (NOT ~~the mainly foreign, labourers~~)
> *the mainly foreign labourers in the north-eastern docks* (NOT ~~the mainly foreign labourers, in the north-eastern docks~~)
> *the mainly foreign labourers who made up the work force in the north-eastern docks*
> (NOT ~~the mainly foreign labourers, who made up the work force in the north-eastern docks~~)

However, we do use **commas** to separate **non-defining expressions** (see page 210) after nouns.
> *Andreas Bergmeister,* **who established the dock-workers' union,** *…*

## sentences with conjunctions
We often put **commas** in sentences with conjunctions, especially in longer sentences. (See page 254.) Compare:
> *The situation changed* **when** *the export markets began to contract.*
> *The situation changed noticeably for the worse after 1932,* **when** *the export markets began to contract.*

We **usually** use a **comma** if we **start** with the conjunction.
> **When** *the export markets began to contract,* **the situation changed.**

For one-clause sentences with conjunctions (e.g. *Because the world had changed.*), see page 256.

## indirect speech
We **don't put commas** after verbs of saying, thinking etc in **indirect speech**.
> *Many commentators* **declared that** *the economy was in deep trouble.* (NOT ~~Many commentators declared, that~~ …)
> *No one* **knew how** *serious the situation would become.* (NOT ~~No one knew, how~~ …)

We **don't put question marks** (?) in **indirect questions**.
> *Workers asked why they were losing their jobs.* (NOT ~~Workers asked why they were losing their jobs?~~)

## a useful rule: no comma before that
We **don't put commas** before **that** (conjunction or relative pronoun).
> *They did not* **understand that** *the economic* **conditions that** *had existed earlier had disappeared for good.*

## between separate sentences

Between separate sentences (with no conjunction), we use a full stop (.) or a semi-colon (;), but **not a comma** (see page 256). Compare.

*Orders began to dry up,* **and** *most firms started to reduce their work force.* (comma and conjunction)
*Orders began to dry up. Most firms started to reduce their work force.*
OR *Orders began to dry up; most firms started to reduce their work force.*
BUT NOT ~~Orders began to dry up, most firms started to reduce their work force.~~

## conjunctions and adverbs

Note that some linking words (e.g. *consequently, however, therefore*), are **adverbs**, not conjunctions. A sentence beginning with an adverb is **separate** from a sentence before it; a full stop or semi-colon is necessary between the sentences. (For more details, see page 254.)

*Orders began to dry up. Consequently, most firms started to reduce their work force.*
(NOT ~~Orders began to dry up, consequently most firms~~ ...)
*Orders began to dry up; however, some firms tried to carry on as before.*
(NOT ~~Orders began to dry up, however, some firms~~ ...)

## commas between adjectives

Before a noun, we use commas mostly to separate adjectives that say the same kind of thing. Compare:

*a tall, impressive figure     a long, boring speech*
*gloomy economic forecasts     surprising new developments*

After a noun, adjectives are punctuated like a list (see below).

*His speech was long, detailed, boring and irrelevant.*

## lists

We use commas to separate the different things in a list (but not usually before *and* unless the last item is long).

*The developing crisis affected manufacturers, distributors, marketing organisations, banks and credit agencies.*
*... marketing organisations, banks, and some of the major credit agencies.*

## direct speech

Quotation marks ('...' or "...") are used to show direct speech (somebody's actual words). Commas are generally used to introduce direct speech; colons (:) are sometimes used in official reports.

*Mrs Otago said, 'It is essential that we work together.'* (NOT <*It is essential that* ...> OR – *It is essential that* ....)
*The Prime Minister said: 'The Government is doing everything possible ...'*

## figures

We use commas after thousands and millions, and full stops in decimal fractions (see page 311).

*losses of £5,500,000     losses of £5.5m* ( = 'five and a half million pounds')

## colons (:)

Colons are sometimes used to introduce direct speech (see above), and to introduce details and explanations.

*Manufacturing industry was in crisis: in particular, textiles and shipbuilding.*
*British firms were no longer competitive: labour costs had priced them out of the market.*

## dashes (–)

Dashes are common in informal writing. They can be used in the same way as colons, semi-colons or brackets; they can also introduce afterthoughts.

*I really don't know what we're going to do – Joe's out of work, and there's no money coming in.*
*Harry might get a job at the market next month – at least, that's what he says.*

## apostrophes (')

For apostrophes in contractions (e.g. *isn't*), see Appendix 5. For apostrophes in possessives (e.g. *John's*), see page 130. For apostrophes in plurals, see page 303.

## abbreviations (short forms of words)

We use full stops after some abbreviations, like *e.g.* (meaning 'for example'). *Mr* and *Mrs* have full stops in American English, but not usually in British English.

*A high-level meeting between some of those most concerned,* **e.g. Mrs** *Otago, the Industry Secretary,*
**Mr** *Bergmeister, and other union representatives, ...*

# appendix 5 contractions

Contractions like *she's*, *isn't* represent the pronunciation of informal speech.
They are common and correct in **informal writing**, but unusual in formal writing.

| AFFIRMATIVE CONTRACTIONS: PRONOUN + 'M, 'RE, 'VE, 'D, 'LL | NEGATIVE CONTRACTIONS: AUXILIARY VERB/*BE* + N'T | |
|---|---|---|
| I am → I'm | are not → aren't | shall not → shan't |
| we are → we're | is not → isn't | would not → wouldn't |
| she is → she's | have not → haven't | should not → shouldn't |
| he has → he's | has not → hasn't | cannot → can't |
| I have → I've | had not → hadn't | could not → couldn't |
| you had → you'd | do not → don't | might not → mightn't |
| you would → you'd | does not → doesn't | must not → mustn't |
| they will → they'll | did not → didn't | ought not → oughtn't |
| | will not → won't | need not → needn't |

**alternative forms** With *be*, two negative forms are common: *you're not* or *you aren't*, *she's not* or *she isn't* etc. With *have* and *will*, two forms are also possible (*I've not* or *I haven't*, *I'll not* or *I won't*), but the forms with *n't* are more common.

***Am not*** is contracted to ***aren't*** only in questions.
    *I'm late, **aren't I**?* BUT ***I'm not** ready.* (NOT ~~I aren't ready.~~)

*'s* (= *is* or *has*) can be written after pronouns, nouns, question words, *there* and *here*.
    ***It's** dark.*    *Your **brother's** late.*    ***How's** work?*    ***There's** Peter.*    ***Here's** your key.*
*'d* and *'ll* are normally only written after pronouns and *there*; *'re* and *'ve* only after pronouns.

**Don't confuse *it's*** (= *it is/has*) with ***its*** (possessive).
    *Look at that silly puppy. **It's** chasing **its** tail.*

**Don't confuse *who's*** (= *who is/has*) with ***whose*** (possessive).
    ***Who's** the man at the end table?*    ***Whose** coat is this?*

**In very informal speech, *going to*, *want to*, *got to*** and ***have to*** are often pronounced like *gonna*, *wanna*, *gotta* and *hafta*. They are sometimes written like this, especially in American English. *Should have, could have, would have* etc are also often contracted in speech to *shoulda, coulda, woulda* etc, but these are not usually contracted in writing.

**stress** **Affirmative** contractions are **not usually stressed**. When an affirmative auxiliary verb is stressed (for example at the end of a sentence) we don't use a contraction. Compare:
    *'**You're** late.'  'Yes, **we are**.'* (NOT ~~'Yes, we're.'~~)
    *'**He's** forgotten.'  'I think **he has**.'* (NOT ~~'I think he's.'~~)
**Negative** contractions can be stressed, and are possible in any position.
    *'It **isn't** true.'  'No, it **isn't**.'*

# appendix 6 noun plurals: special cases

**common irregular plurals**  Some nouns ending in -f(e) have plurals in -ves.
> calf/calves, elf/elves, half/halves, hoof/hooves, knife/knives, leaf/leaves, life/lives, loaf/loaves, scarf/scarves, self/selves, shelf/shelves, thief/thieves, wife/wives

Other irregular plurals:
> child/children, man/men, woman/women, person/people (less often persons), penny/pence, tooth/teeth, goose/geese, foot/feet, mouse/mice, louse/lice, ox/oxen, quiz/quizzes

**singular and plural the same**  The following nouns do not change in the plural:
> sheep, deer, fish (usually), aircraft, offspring and the names of many animals, birds and fish that are hunted or caught for food or sport (e.g. elk, pheasant, salmon).

Nouns that have both singular and plural in -s:
> barracks, crossroads, headquarters, means, series, species, works (= 'factory')

**nouns ending in -o**  Some nouns ending in -o form their plurals in -s, and some in -es:
> **plural in -s:** commandos, concertos, Eskimos, kilos, logos, photos, pianos, scenarios, solos, sopranos
> **plural in -es:** echoes, heroes, potatoes, tomatoes
> **plural usually in -es:** mosquitoes, tornadoes, volcanoes

**singular uncountable nouns ending in -s**  The following nouns have no plurals:
> news, billiards, draughts, measles

Most singular nouns ending in -ics are also uncountable and have no plurals:
> mathematics, physics, athletics

But politics and statistics can also have plural uses:
> What are your politics?    The economic statistics are terrible.

**after a number**  Hundred, thousand, million etc have plurals without -s after numbers (see page 311).
> two hundred years    five thousand metres    twenty-five billion dollars

**divided objects**  The following plural nouns have no singular:
> glasses, jeans, pants, pyjamas, scissors, shorts, spectacles (= 'glasses'), tights, trousers

To talk about one example we say a pair of (jeans etc).  (NOT ~~a jean~~)

**other plurals with no singular**  Some other plural nouns usually have no singular:
> belongings, cattle, clothes, congratulations, contents, customs (at a frontier), earnings, funds, goods, groceries, manners (= 'social behaviour'), Middle Ages, oats, odds, outskirts, police, premises, regards, remains, riches, savings, scales (for weighing), staff, stairs, surroundings, thanks, troops.

The following expressions are also plural only:
> the British, the English, the Irish, the Welsh, the Dutch, the French, the Spanish

**foreign plurals still used**  The following foreign imports still have their original plurals:
> **-is/-es:** analysis/analyses, axis/axes, basis/bases, crisis/crises, diagnosis/diagnoses, ellipsis/ellipses, emphasis/emphases, hypothesis/hypotheses, neurosis/neuroses, oasis/oases, parenthesis/parentheses, synthesis/syntheses, synopsis/synopses, thesis/theses
> **others:** antenna/antennae, appendix/appendices, bacterium/bacteria, cactus/cacti (or cactuses), corpus/corpora, criterion/criteria, curriculum/curricula, formula/formulae (or formulas), fungus/fungi, nebula/nebulae, nucleus/nuclei, phenomenon/phenomena, schema/schemata, stratum/strata, syllabus/syllabi (more often syllabuses), radius/radii, stimulus/stimuli, vertebra/vertebrae

The plurals data and media are now often used with singular verbs.
> The data **are/is** difficult to interpret.    The media **are/is** too powerful.

**plurals with apostrophes**  Apostrophes are used in the plurals of letters of the alphabet, and sometimes in the plurals of abbreviations and dates.
> She spelt 'necessary' with two **c's**.    **PC's** are getting cheaper. (More usual: PCs)
> Do you remember the **1960's**, Granddad? (More usual: 1960s)

Apostrophes are not correct in other plurals.
> I need some new **jeans**.  (NOT ... ~~jean's~~)

**compound nouns**  Note the following:
> passers-by, mothers-in-law (or mother-in-laws), runners-up

# appendix 7 word order

This section summarises the most important rules of English word order.

## sentences

The basic word order of English sentences is SUBJECT – VERB – OBJECT.

*I play football.* (NOT *I football play.*)

Spoken sentences do not always follow this order (see pages 257, 281–288).

*People like that I can't stand.     Crazy, those kids are.*

## questions

In questions we usually put an auxiliary verb before the subject (see pages 2–3).

***Did you** get my message?* (NOT *Got you my message …?*)     ***Can you** swim?*

'Declarative questions' have a different order (see page 286).

*This is your car?*

Indirect questions usually have the same structure as statements (see page 218).

*I asked him how **he felt**.     They wanted to know if **I was** English.*

However, this is not always true in informal speech (see page 223).

*I asked him how **did he feel**.     They wanted to know **was I** English.* (informal)

Note the word order in formal and informal **negative questions** (see page 6).

***Do you not** feel well?* (formal)     ***Don't you** feel well?* (informal)

## inversion

There are some other cases (besides questions) where the subject-verb order is inverted. For details, see pages 237, 258 and 259.

***Had I** known, I would have changed my plans.     Round the corner **came Mrs Lewis**.*

*Under no circumstances **can we** cash cheques.*

## adjectives

Adjectives and noun modifiers usually go before, not after, nouns.

*an **interesting film**     **chocolate cake**  (NOT cake chocolate)*

Adjectives, and some noun modifiers, can go after *be*, *seem* and similar verbs.

*He seems **happy**.     It's **plastic**.*

Some adjectives only go in one or other place (see page 175).

*a **live** fish.  (NOT an alive fish)     That fish is **alive**.  (NOT That fish is live.)*

For the order of adjectives (e.g. a ***small shiny black leather** bag*), see page 174.

Some participles, and one or two adjectives, follow nouns in reduced relative clauses (see page 211).

*The people **questioned** had seen nothing.* (= 'The people who were questioned …')

*Please ask for full details of the **tickets available**.*

## adverbs

Different adverbs can go in different places in a sentence (see pages 179–180).

***Tomorrow** I'm off to London.     I've **just** had lunch.     She's walking very **slowly**.*

They do **not** usually go **between the verb and the object**.

*I **finished my report yesterday**.  (NOT I finished yesterday my report.)*

*She speaks **Japanese very well**.  (NOT She speaks very well Japanese.)*

Note the position of *always* and *never* with imperatives (see page 10).

***Always** look before you cross the road.  (NOT Look always …)     **Never** give up.*

## prepositions

Prepositions often go **at the ends of questions**, especially in speech (see page 3).

*Who did you go **with**?     What did you buy that **for**?*

Prepositions can also go **at the ends of passive clauses** and (especially in spoken English) **at the ends of relative clauses** (see pages 79 and 212).

*She loves being looked **at**.     There's the woman that I work **for**.*

## exclamations

In exclamations, the adjective, adverb or object comes at the beginning of the sentence, just after *how* or *what* (see page 13).

>*How well she plays!*  (NOT ~~How she plays well!~~)     *What a strange accent he has!*

## phrasal verbs

The objects of **phrasal verbs** (but not prepositional verbs) can often go **between the two parts of the verb** (see page 112).

>*Can you switch the lights off?*  (OR *Can you switch off the lights?*)

**Pronoun objects** always go between the two parts of a phrasal verb.

>*Please switch them off.*  (NOT ~~Please switch off them.~~)

## quite a etc

Note the position of *a/an* after *quite* and *rather* (see page 307), *such*, *so* and *as* (see page 188).

>*It was quite a nice day.*     *We waited rather a long time.*
>*She asked such a strange question.*     *I've never heard so boring a lecture.*
>*It wasn't as bad a journey as I had expected.*

## verbs with two objects

Some verbs that have two objects can be followed by **indirect object + direct object**. Others can't (see page 118).

>*I sent everybody the details.*  (BUT NOT ~~I explained everybody the details.~~)

## so do I etc

Note the word order in structures like *so do I*, *nor do I* (see page 258).

>*My sister works in a bank, and so do I.*  (NOT *... ~~so I do.~~*)
>*I'm not convinced by your arguments, and nor are the others.*

## ago

*Ago* **follows** an expression of **time**.

>*I got here three days ago.*  (NOT *... ~~ago three days~~*)

## enough

*Enough* usually goes **before nouns** but **after adjectives and adverbs**.

>*There isn't enough time.*  (NOT *... ~~time enough~~*)
>*Is the room warm enough?*  (NOT *... ~~enough warm?~~*)     *I didn't shout loud enough.*

# appendix 8  word problems

This section gives brief information about some words that can cause problems even at advanced level, because of the way they are used in sentences or text. For some other words of this kind, see Appendix 9 on pages 308–309, the section on Discourse Markers on pages 262–269, or check in the Index. For fuller information about the grammar of words in general, see *The Oxford Advanced Learner's Dictionary*.

**After all** does not mean 'finally'. It can mean 'contrary to expectations'.
> *I expected to fail, but I passed **after all**.*

It can also be used, especially at the beginning of a clause, to introduce a fact which strengthens an argument.
> *Why take the bus? Let's walk. **After all**, it's only half a mile.*

**Although and though**
These can both be used as conjunctions to introduce afterthoughts or restrictions to what has been said. **Though** can also be used as an adverb at the end of a clause.
> *He's a nice guy – **(al)though** I wouldn't want to work with him.*
> *He's a nice guy – I wouldn't want to work with him, **though**.*

**Anyone and any one**  Note the difference.
> ***Anyone** can sing.* (= 'Anybody …')    *This lift will take four people at **any one** time.* (= 'any single time')

**Anyway and any way**  Note the difference.
> *I don't feel like going out. **Anyway**, it's getting late.* (See also page 266.)
> *'How should I play this?'  '**Any way** you like.'*

**As well as** (meaning 'in addition to') introduces background information that is not the main focus.
> ***As well as** birds, some mammals can fly.* (NOT ~~As well as some mammals, birds can fly.~~)

Note the use of *-ing* forms after *as well as*, and the difference between:
> *She sings **as well as dancing**.* (= 'In addition to dancing, she sings.')
> *She sings **as well as she dances**.* (= 'Her singing is as good as her dancing.')

**Available** can be used not only before a noun, but also after one, like a reduced relative clause (see page 211).
> *Send all the available tickets / **tickets available**.* (= '… tickets that are available.')

**Bet** is often followed by a present tense with a future meaning in an informal style.
> *I **bet** Smith **beats** / **'ll beat** Simmons in the semi-final.*

**Clean** can sometimes mean 'completely' in an informal style.
> *The robbers got **clean** away.*    *Sorry, I **clean** forgot your birthday.*

**Dare** can have modal-verb forms (questions and negatives without *do*, etc, see page 59) or normal verb forms. It is not very common in modern Engish except in the spoken negative *I daren't* and the idiom *I dare say* (meaning 'quite probably').
> *I **daren't** tell him what I think – he'll explode.*    *I **dare say** it'll rain soon.*

**Dead** can sometimes mean 'extremely' or 'completely'.
> *The captain was **dead drunk** at the time of the shipwreck.*    *You're **dead right**.*

**Different** is normally modified by *very*, not by *much*.
> *You're **very different** from your brother.* (NOT ~~You're much different …~~)

**Everyone and every one**  Note the difference.
> ***Everyone** likes her.* (= 'Everybody …')    *He's eaten **every one** of the chocolates.* (= '… every single one… ')

**Fair** can be used as an adverb in some informal expressions: e.g. *play fair* and *fight fair*.

**Fine** can be used as an adverb in informal expressions referring to condition and progress.
> *My mother's **doing fine** after her operation.*    *Pete's **getting on fine** at school.*

**Finished** is often used informally with *be* instead of *have*.
> *Hang on – I'll **be finished** in a couple of minutes.*

**Half**  We often **drop of** after *half*; we usually drop it before *a/an*.
> *He spends **half (of)** the night on his computer.*    *Would you like **half an** orange?*

*Help* is often followed by **object + infinitive without *to*** in active structures. Compare:
> *Can I **help you (to) pack**?*    *The museum **was helped to expand** by a large donation.*

*Home*   We don't use *to* before *home*. In American English, *at* is not common either, and this usage is spreading in informal British English.
> *Are you going **home** now?*    *There's nobody **(at) home**.*

*Hope* is often followed by a present tense with a future meaning in an informal style.
> *I hope you **get** better soon.*

*However and on the other hand*   *However* introduces a modification to what was said before. **On the other hand** is more sharply contrastive: it introduces a new point which is logically opposed to the previous point. *However* signals a change of direction, so to speak, while *on the other hand* signals a U-turn.
> *The climb was tough. **However,** I made it.*   (NOT … *On the other hand, I made it.*)
> *It's a very expensive project. **On the other hand**, it could be very profitable.*

*Indeed*   When indeed modifies adjectives and adverbs, it is normally used with *very*.
> *It was **very** cold **indeed**.*   (NOT USUALLY *It was cold indeed.*)

*It's no use, it's worth*   Note the common use of *-ing* forms with these expressions.
> *It's no use **trying** to explain.*    *It's worth **visiting** the Lake District.*

*Likely* and *unlikely* are very commonly used in a structure with a following infinitive.
> *We're **likely to go** on holiday in March.*    *It's **unlikely to rain** before the weekend.*

*Own*   We don't use *an* before *own*.
> *It's nice to have **a room of your own**.*   (NOT … *an own room.*)

*Possible* can be used not only before a noun, but also after one, like a reduced relative clause (see page 211).
> *It's the only possible solution / **solution possible**.*   (= '… that is possible.')

*Present*   Note the different meanings of *present* before and after a noun.
> *It is difficult to find capital in the **present situation**.*   (= '… the situation now.')
> *Most of **the people present** voted against.*   (= '… the people who were there.')

*Proper*   Note the different meanings of *proper* before and after a noun.
> *She wants a **proper wedding**, in a church.*   (= 'organised as it should be')
> *After trekking through the foothills we finally reached the **mountain proper**.*   (= 'the real mountain itself')

*Quite and rather* usually come **before** *a/an*.
> *I've got **quite an** unusual request.*    *She's had **rather a** shock.*

*Quite* is generally less strong than *rather*. Compare:
> *It's **quite** a good film – you might want to see it.*
> *It's **rather** a good film – well worth seeing, I think.*

For *quite* meaning 'completely', see page 309.
Note the meanings of *rather* in *would rather* and *or rather*.
> *'Coffee?' 'I'd **rather** have tea.'*    *Her name's Anne – **or rather** Anna.*

*Real* is sometimes used instead of *really* in very informal speech, especially in American English.
> *I was **real sorry** to hear about your accident.*    *She's **real nice**.*

*Try and* etc
With *try*, *wait*, *come* and *go*, a structure with *and* can be used instead of an infinitive.
> *I'll **try and get** home early.*    *'Where are we going?' '**Wait and see**.'*
> ***Come and look** at my new painting.*    *Let's **go and have** something to eat.*

The structure is possible in the past with *come* and *go*, but not with *try* and *wait*.
> *I **went and looked** at her painting.*   (BUT NOT *I tried and got home early.*)

*Whom*   In a very formal style, we use *whom* as an **object** in questions and relative clauses.
> ***Whom** did they arrest?*    *For **whom** did she work?*    *The man **whom** they elected did a bad job.*

In an **informal** style, *who* is more normal in questions, and *that* (or nothing) in relatives.
> ***Who** did they arrest?*    ***Who** did she work for?*    *The man they elected did a bad job.*

*Whom* is normal after prepositions.
> *A man **with whom** I once shared a flat told me …*

# appendix 9 prepositions after verbs, adjectives and nouns

These are examples of some common combinations (and some cases where no preposition is used), which may still cause problems at this level. For more detailed information about the grammar of these and other verbs, adjectives and nouns, see the *Oxford Advanced Learner's Dictionary*.

Are you **accusing** me **of** lying?

I'll never get **accustomed to working** at night.

Our dog is terribly **afraid of** thunder.

Nobody **agreed with** me **about** anything.

Lucy was **angry with** her husband **about** the delay.

You have to **apply to** the town hall **for** a permit.

We're **approaching** the frontier.

I **arrived at** the airport just before 8.00.

What time did you **arrive in** Shanghai? (*in* with bigger places)

If I behaved like him I'd be **ashamed of** myself.

The revolutionaries **attacked** the palace.

  BUT There's been **an attack on** the palace.

When did you first become **aware of** the problem?

I'm **bad at** most sports.

**Belief in** supernatural beings is widespread.

Do you **believe in** life after death?

These cups **belong in** the top cupboard.

Who does this coat **belong to**?

Don't **blame** me **for** your problems.

Don't you ever get **bored with** your job?

She's just not **capable of** being unpleasant to people.

The **cause of** the explosion is not yet known.

Are you **certain about/of** the date?

Has there been any **change to/in** the arrangements?

She's always been **clever at** languages.

They **congratulated** her **on** her prize.

**Congratulations on** your success.

The human body **consists** mostly **of** water.

My results **contradict** yours.

My results are **in contradiction with** yours.

The **cost of** a litre of petrol has doubled.

The bus **crashed into** a tree.

He doesn't like people to **criticise** his management.

He doesn't like **criticism of** his management.

The beach is **crowded with** weekend tourists.

There's not much **demand for** pink cars.

Can you give me **details of** the programme?

Our plans **depend on** the weather.

He's still **dependent on** his parents.

  BUT He wants to be **independent of** everybody.

This job's quite **different from** (or **to**) my last one.

I had **difficulty (in)** staying awake.

Have you **discussed** your plans **with** anybody?

Gaul was **divided into** three parts.

Do you often **dream about** work?

When I was young, I **dreamt of being** an explorer.

He was **dressed in** an assortment of old clothes.

They **emphasised** the need for speed.

They put a lot of **emphasis on** the need for speed.

As soon as I **entered** the cave I felt cold.

We've **entered into** an agreement with JJB Ltd.

It was a typical **example of** bad planning.

Let me **explain** my plans **to** you.

The hotel is **famous for** its food and drink.

We're all **fed up with** her bad temper.

Our terrier **fights with** every dog in the street.

I don't feel **fit for** Saturday's match.

Try to **focus on** the most important points.

I'm much too **fond of** chocolate.

**Forgive** me **for** disturbing you.

I'm not **frightened of** hard work.

You should **get off** the bus at the town hall.
  (*get on/off*: public transport)

He said goodbye and **got into** the taxi.
  (*get into/out of*: private and smaller vehicles)

How do I **get to** your house?

I'm not **good at** ball games.

All three men were found **guilty of** armed robbery.

What's **happened to** your hair?

We're all **happy about/with** your decision

Have you **heard about** Jan? She's in hospital again.

Some children have never **heard of** Shakespeare.
  (= They don't even know his name.)

I arrived early in **the hope of** getting a seat.

Who had **the idea of** inviting Annie?
  (NOT … ~~the idea to invite~~ …)

They're planning another **increase in** VAT.

I **insist on** paying.

I don't have much **interest in** politics.

I'm not very **interested in** politics.

John's always been **jealous of** his brother's success.

My girlfriend isn't **keen on** sport.

Have you got the **key to** the cellar?

She's not very **kind to** her children.

He **lacks** concentration.

His work shows **a lack of** concentration.

He **is lacking in** concentration.

Are you **laughing at** my new hairstyle?

It's hard to **live on** my salary.

He **married** a very successful surgeon.

He**'s married to** a very successful surgeon.

What's **the matter with** your sister today?

I try to be **nice to** everybody, but it's hard.

They **operated on** him **for** a heart problem.

Did you **pay** me **for** the train tickets?

Don't forget to **pay** the phone bill.
They **phone** each other every day.
I'm not very **pleased with** my exam results.
Their children are always very **polite to** visitors.
This country is never **prepared for** snow.
The police **prevented** us **from** demonstrating.
I can't believe the **price of** food these days.
You'll need to show me **proof of** your age.
We're really **proud of** our children.
I **ran into** Sue in the supermarket. She sends her love.
What was the **reason for** the delay?
I **reminded** her **about** the meeting.
You **remind** me **of** your father.
We've **replaced** our old car **with** a smaller one.
My children have no **respect for** age.
Who's **responsible for** organising travel?
I'm still not **satisfied with** the way my hair looks.
The customs people **searched** everybody **for** drugs.
I was **shocked at/by** the way he talked.
Stop **shouting at** me. (aggressive shouting)
Can you **shout to** Phil to tell him dinner's ready?
Danish is **similar to** Norwegian.
She **smiled at** me as I walked in.
There's no **solution to** some problems.

I'd like to **speak to/with** the manager.
My sister **specialises in** agricultural economics.
I **spend** too much money and time **on** clothes.
They used plastic as a **substitute for** wood.
I hope you **succeed in** getting your visa.
My teachers had no **success in** teaching me maths.
Older people often **suffer from** arthritis.
I'm not **sure about/of** the exact time of the concert.
I was **surprised at/by** his attitude.
Are you **taking part in** the Christmas concert?
They'll put a **tax on** fresh air next.
I never **think about** the future.
What do you **think of** the new secretary? (opinion)
We're **thinking of** getting a new car. (possible plan)
   (NOT *We're thinking to get* …)
I don't like the **thought of** getting old.
   (NOT … *the thought to get* …)
They **threw** eggs **at** the Minister. (aggressive throwing)
I **threw** the ball **to** Harris.
I never get **tired of** my own company.
She **translates** novels **from** Japanese **into** English.
It's **typical of** him to forget to turn up.
You'll soon get **used to driving** on the left.
Something's **wrong with** the central heating.

# appendix 10  gradable and non-gradable adjectives

## the difference

**Some adjectives are gradable:** you can have **more or less** of the quality. For example, people can be **more or less** *tired* or *interesting*. Some gradable adjectives:

   *tired    interesting    ill    angry    expensive    dangerous    difficult    worried*

**Other adjectives are non-gradable:** they express extreme, **'either-or'** qualities. For example, people are **either** *exhausted* **or not, either** *fascinating* **or not**; we don't usually talk about 'more or less' in these cases (though it is possible). Some non-gradable adjectives:

   *exhausted    fascinating    dead    furious    perfect    starving    ideal    finished*

## adverbs

**Some adverbs** and adverbial expressions usually go only with one or other kind of adjective. **Adverbs of degree**, like *very*, *fairly*, *rather* or *reasonably*, which say 'how much', are used with **gradable** adjectives. **Adverbs which refer to a complete or extreme state**, like *completely*, *absolutely*, *utterly*, *extremely* or *nearly*, are used with **non-gradable** adjectives. Compare:

   *very* tired (NOT ~~completely tired~~)    *completely* exhausted (NOT ~~very exhausted~~)
   *fairly* interesting (NOT ~~absolutely interesting~~)    *absolutely* fascinating (NOT ~~fairly fascinating~~)
   *pretty* ill (NOT ~~completely ill~~)    *completely* dead (NOT ~~pretty dead~~)
   *reasonably* good (NOT ~~totally good~~)    *totally* perfect (NOT ~~reasonably perfect~~)
   *rather* angry (NOT ~~utterly angry~~)    *utterly* furious (NOT ~~rather furious~~)
   *very* hot (NOT ~~nearly hot~~)    *nearly* boiling (NOT ~~very boiling~~)

## quite

In British English, with **gradable** adjectives *quite* usually expresses a moderate degree, like *rather* (see page 307).

   *I'm* **quite tired**. *Maybe I'll go to bed early.*    *She's* **quite ill**. *Should we call the doctor?*

With **non-gradable** adjectives, *quite* means 'completely'.

   *I'm* **quite exhausted**. *I'm going straight to bed.*    *That plant of yours is* **quite dead**.

Note that although *different* is gradable, *quite different* means 'completely different'.

# appendix 11  British and American English

**few differences**  The main differences between British and American varieties of English are in pronunciation and vocabulary; there are very few grammatical differences. The main ones are as follows.

**group nouns**  British English often treats singular group nouns as plural (see page 126). This is uncommon with most group nouns in American English.
> British: *The **team is/are** winning all of **its/their** games.*
> American: *The **team is** winning all of **its** games.*

**adverb position with complex verbs**  In British English, pre-verb adverbs most often go after the first auxiliary, though they may go before an emphasized auxiliary (see page 180). In American English, they more often go before the first auxiliary.
> British: *We have often been asked to help organise conferences.*
> American: *We often have been asked to help organize conferences.*

**present perfect**  The present perfect is mostly used in the same way in the two varieties. However, American English more often uses the simple past with *already* and *yet*, and to announce news (for example with *just*).
> British: *I've already told him.*        American: *I('ve) already told him.*
> British: *Have you eaten yet?*        American: *Did you eat / Have you eaten yet?*
> British: *Ann's just started work.*        American: *Ann('s) just started work.*
> British: *I'm sorry, I've broken a cup.*    American: *I'm sorry, I broke / I've broken a cup.*

Note, however, that British usage in this area is changing under American influence.

**subjunctives**  American English uses subjunctives more often than British English, which often uses ordinary verb forms or *should …* instead (see pages 224–225).
> British: *It's important that she **sees** / **should see** a doctor as soon as possible.*
> American: *It's important that she **see** a doctor as soon as possible.*

**A few irregular verbs** have different forms: see page 299.

**fixed expressions**  On the frontier between grammar and vocabulary, a large number of fixed expressions have differences of preposition or article use in the two varieties. Examples:
> British: *at the weekend    in the team    in hospital    I have toothache*
> American: *on the weekend    on the team    in the hospital    I have a/the toothache*

# appendix 12  numbers

***a/one hundred* etc**  *A* hundred, *a* thousand etc are less formal than ***one*** hundred etc. Compare:
> *I got it for **a thousand** pounds.*
> *The owner originally acquired the painting for **one thousand** pounds.*

We use ***one*** hundred etc when we wish to sound **precise**.
> *It costs exactly **one hundred** dollars.*

We use ***one*** hundred etc, not *a* hundred etc, just before another number or inside a larger number.
> *1,300:* ***one*** *thousand, three hundred*  (NOT ~~a thousand, three hundred~~)
> *$1.75:* ***one*** *dollar seventy-five*
> *four thousand,* ***one*** *hundred and twenty*  (NOT ~~four thousand, a hundred~~ ...)

***three dozen* etc**  *Dozen*, *hundred*, *thousand* etc have **no** *-s* after a number, *few* or *several*.
> *three **dozen** eggs*  (NOT ~~three dozens (of) eggs~~)      *twenty **billion** euros*
> *a few **hundred** times      several **thousand** years*

In other cases we use ***dozens (of)***, ***hundreds (of)*** etc.
> *We've got **dozens of** eggs.      He's done it **hundreds of** times.*
> *They lost **billions** in the financial crash.*

**fractions**  **We write and say common fractions** as follows:
> *⅝: five eighths      ³⁄₁₀ mile: three tenths of a mile*

**Decimal fractions** are written with full stops ('point'), not commas.
> *6.625 (= 6⅝): six point six two five      0.5: nought point five*

Fractions between one and two are treated as plural.
> *Add **1½ pounds** of sugar ...      A mile is about **1.6 kilometres**.*

**quantities**  **Singular verbs** are often used with plural expressions for quantities and amounts (see page 126).
> ***Thirty kilometres is** too far to walk.      **Forty euros seems** expensive for one ticket.*

**kings etc**  **We use Roman numbers** to write the names of **kings**, **queens** and **popes**, and **ordinal numbers** (*first*, *second* etc) to say them.
> *Charles V: Charles the Fifth      Elizabeth II: Elizabeth the **Second**      Pius the **Tenth***

(Roman numbers 1–20: I, II, III, IV, V, VI, VII, VIII, IX, X, XI, XII, XIII, XIV, XV, XVI, XVII, XVIII, XIX, XX)

**dates**  We write and say dates as follows:
> ***writing dates***  *3 June 2010* OR *June 3 2010*  ALSO *3.6.10 or 3/6/10*
> *15 March 1870* OR *March 15 1870*
> ***saying dates*** *the third of June / June the third, two thousand and ten*
> *the fifteenth of March / March the fifteenth, eighteen seventy*

Note: in abbreviated dates American English normally has the month first.

*5.7.09* ='the fifth of July' (British); 'May seven(th)' (American).

**Telephone and credit card** numbers and similar numbers are usually said **one number at a time**.
> *5164933: five one six four nine three three*  (OR ... *double three*)
> *40695: four oh* (OR *zero*) *six nine five*

# answer key

## page 2

**1** 1 ~~the train leaves~~ > does the train leave
2 ~~means 'understudy'~~ > does 'understudy' mean
3 ~~she is~~ > is she
4 Correct.
5 ~~I must to do~~ > must I do
6 Correct.
7 ~~The postman has been?~~ > Has the postman been?
8 ~~Who does live~~ > Who lives
9 Correct.
10 ~~does help you~~ > helps you

## page 3

**2** 1 What did Rob buy?  Who bought a jacket?
2 Who lost his credit card?  What did Oliver lose?
3 What has Kara broken?  Who has broken her leg?
4 What kills flies?  What does this stuff kill?
5 Who caught the first plane?  Which plane did Mike catch?
6 Who collects Chinese paintings?  What kind/sort of paintings does his brother collect?
7 Whose child broke our window?  Whose window did her child break?

**3** 1 What's the article about?
2 Who did she give it to?
3 Who were you talking to?
4 What can I open it with?
5 Who was the letter from?
6 What did she hit you with?
7 Who does your brother work for?
8 What are you thinking about?

**4** 1 Where to?   2 What with?   3 Who for?
4 Who with?   5 What with?   6 Who with?
7 Who to?

## page 4

**1** 1 ~~never is~~ > is never
2 ~~wasn't nothing~~ > wasn't anything
3 ~~not likes~~ > doesn't like
4 Correct.
5 ~~didn't happen~~ > happened
6 ~~do never drive~~ > never drive
7 ~~didn't have~~ > had
8 ~~don't must~~ > mustn't / needn't / don't have to

**2** 1 F   2 E   3 D   4 I   5 J   6 L   7 A   8 B
9 M   10 G   11 C   12 H   13 K

## page 5

**1** 1 ✗   2 ✓   3 ✗   4 ✓   5 ✓   6 ✓   7 ✗   8 ✗

**2** 1 no, entrance   2 not, describe   3 no excuse
4 repaired, not   5 no, revise   6 attend, not
7 not intend   8 worry, Not   9 no, humour
10 cash, no

## page 6

**1** 1 Who didn't they tell?
2 Aren't you well?
3 What didn't we understand?
4 Wasn't the office open?
5 Don't you speak Chinese?
6 Aren't we in the right place?

**2** 1 No   2 Yes   3 Yes   4 Yes   No   6 Yes   7 Yes
8 No

## page 7

**1** 1 Don't you understand?
2 Haven't you read this book?
3 Hasn't Magnus got a work permit?
4 Didn't you get my message?
5 Didn't you turn the lights off?
6 Can't you understand English?
7 Didn't he pass his driving test?
8 Don't you like English food?

**2** 1 Didn't you make a reservation for dinner at 8.00?
2 Didn't Ann pay a 10% deposit with her order?
3 Didn't you say you were going to put a new washer on the tap?
4 Doesn't this account pay 3% interest?
5 Isn't my appointment with Dr Masters at 10.30?
6 Didn't the firm make a profit of half a million euros last year?

## pages 8-9

**1** 1 We don't believe your report of the meeting is quite accurate.
2 I don't suppose you understood the lecture.
3 I don't suppose you know Ruth's whereabouts.
4 I don't imagine John will read the instructions I sent him.
5 I don't think Emma has a driving licence.
6 I don't think I made my intentions clear.
7 I don't suppose you remembered to book our plane tickets.
8 I don't believe the company has got enough funds to continue trading.

**2** 1 She doesn't seem to be ready.
2 I don't expect to be home late.
3 I never want to climb another mountain.
4 It doesn't seem to rain much here.
5 I don't expect to pass the exam.
6 He never wants to get married.
7 The water doesn't seem to be hot.
8 I never want to work with him.
9 I don't expect to be here tomorrow.
10 The heating doesn't seem to be working.

## page 10

**3** 1 Do be careful.   2 Do have some more coffee.
3 Do be back by midnight.   4 Do use my car.
5 Do let me help.   6 Do shut up.   7 Do come again.

## page 11

**4** 1 ✗   2 ✔   3 ✗   4 ✔   5 ✗   6 ✔   7 ✔   8 ✔
9 ✗   10 ✗

**5** 1 press   2 hold down   3 press   4 slide   5 select
6 type   7 receive

## page 12

**1** 1 Let's have   2 Let's tell   3 Let me see / Let's see
4 Let's (not) worry   5 Let's go   6 let's invite
7 Let me think   8 Let's (not) take

**2** 1 ✗   2 ✗   3 ✔   4 ✔   5 ✗   6 ✔

## page 13

**1** 1 What a waste of time it was!
2 How slowly this computer loads!
3 How long the days seemed then!
4 What a big mistake I made!
5 How well we all played on Saturday!
6 How fast the time goes!
7 How boring his poetry is!
8 What a lot of noise those people make!

**2** 1 Wasn't it a waste of time!
2 Doesn't this computer load slowly!
3 Didn't the days seem long then!
4 Didn't I make a big mistake!
5 Didn't we all play well on Saturday!
6 Doesn't the time go fast!
7 Isn't his poetry boring!
8 Don't those people make a lot of noise!

## page 14

**1** 1 F   2 N   3 F   4 F   5 N   6 F   7 N   8 F   9 N
10 N

**2** 1 ~~not hardly~~ > hardly   2 Correct.   3 ~~you are~~ > are
you   4 Correct.   5 ~~you've~~ > have you   6 ~~do not~~
~~these lights work~~ > don't these lights work / do these
lights not work   7 Correct.   8 ~~Answer somebody~~ >
Somebody answer   9 ~~I don't hope it'll rain~~ > I hope it
won't rain.   10 Correct.   11 No > Yes   12 ~~nor~~ > or

**3** Speaker 2.

**4** You have a go …, How romantic …

## page 15

**5** 1 Why is every animal different?
2 Can/Do flying fish really fly?
3 Why is the Earth round?
4 Why is the sky blue?
5 How deep is the Grand Canyon?
6 What is a light year?
7 How do they make bulletproof glass?
8 Why was the Eiffel Tower built?
9 How many stars are there?
10 How do birds fly?
11 Why does cutting onions make you cry?
12 Where do babies come from?
13 Where do you go when you die?
14 Is God real?
15 Who invented football?
16 What makes thunder?
17 What do frogs eat?
18 Why do cats have tails?
19 Why is water wet?
20 What is time?

## page 16

**1** 1 's being   2 'm   3 's being   4 are being   5 'm
6 're being   7 was being   8 's

## page 17

**1** 1 There were
2 Were there
3 There has been
4 Is there
5 there had been
6 there is
7 there isn't
8 there won't be
9 There's (going) to be
10 have there been

**3** 1 There's   2 There's   3 It's   4 There's; It's   5 It's
6 It's   7 There's   8 It's   9 There's   10 There's

## page 18

**1** 1 There must be   2 There seems to be
3 There's nothing   4 There's no point   5 there being
6 there are likely to be   7 There could be
8 There will be; won't there?   9 there to be
10 There were

In these answers, we usually give **either** contracted forms (for example *I'm, don't*)
**or** full forms (for example *I am, do not*). Normally both are correct.

ANSWER KEY **313**

**2** 1 C   2 C   3 B   4 B, F   5 A   6 A   7 D   8 D   9 E
10 C

## page 19

**1** 1 ✔   2 ✘   3 ✔   4 ✘   5 ✘   6 ✘   7 ✔

**2** 1 Yes   2 No   3 No   4 No   5 No   6 Yes   7 No
8 Yes

## page 20

**1** 1 I do think you're mistaken.
2 I do hate the way she looks at you.
3 This room does feel cold.
4 I do like your new shoes.
5 You do work long hours.
6 Mary did need to talk to somebody.
7 We did enjoy the weekend in Scotland.
8 I do apologise for not phoning.
9 She did look depressed.
10 I do wonder if this is the right way.

## page 21

**2** 1 'You don't understand me.' 'I do understand you.'
2 I may not be good at sport, but I do enjoy football.
3 I'll come round this evening, but I do have to get back home early.
4 I'm not sure he speaks English, but he does speak some French.
5 It's a nice car to drive. Mind you, it does use a lot of petrol.
6 I do all the housework, but Peter does help with the cooking.
7 Although he didn't send me a card, he did phone.
8 She doesn't like most music. She does go to jazz concerts sometimes.
9 I told him to see the dentist, and he did have a tooth that needed filling.
10 She's not on this train. She did say 10.15, didn't she?

**3** 1 Italians don't speak Japanese, but they do speak Italian.
2 Banks don't sell beer, but they do lend money.
3 Cats don't eat potatoes, but they do eat mice.
4 It doesn't snow a lot in England, but it does rain a lot.
5 Napoleon didn't fight against China, but he did fight against England.

**4** 1 We do hope   2 We do in fact take good care
3 We do appreciate

## page 23

**1** 1 E   2 D   3 H   4 G   5 L   6 A   7 B   8 I
9 K   10 J

**2** 1 think   2 it's snowing   3 Are you looking
4 don't understand   5 Do you know
6 do you want   7 hate   8 are you driving
9 are you looking   10 don't remember

## page 24

**1** 1 is roasting, peel, put   2 shoots, knocks, is not looking
3 walks, is talking, goes, says

## page 25

**3** 1 interrupt, 'm working   2 get, 'm walking
3 is thinking, makes   4 gets, is blowing

## page 27

**5** 1 is calling   2 are now dying   3 appears
4 are dying   5 finds   6 die   7 take
8 eat   9 also suffer   10 receive
11 is currently investing   12 is having

**6** are looking,  I'm selling

## page 28

**1** 1 depends   2 consists   3 contains
4 don't deserve   5 lacks   6 owns
7 includes   8 imagine   9 recognise
10 means   11 matters   12 owe
13 concern   14 appears   15 deny   16 impress

## page 29

**1** 1 ✘   2 ✘   3 ✔   4 ✘   5 ✘   6 ✔   7 ✔   8 ✔   9 ✘
10 ✘   11 ✘   12 ✔   13 ✘   14 ✘

## page 30

**1** *(possible answers)*
1 We're seeing Sarah this evening.
2 I'm starting fencing lessons next week.
3 We're meeting the accountants on Tuesday.
4 I'm getting the car serviced next month.
5 They're closing the road for repairs tomorrow morning.
6 Everybody's getting a free ticket for tomorrow's concert.
7 The air traffic controllers are going on strike from March 1st.
8 All the train companies are putting their prices up next year.

## page 31

**2** 1 I'll   2 I'll   3 I'm going to   4 I'll   5 I'm going to
6 I'm going to   7 I'm going to   8 I'll

**3** 1 I'll   2 it's going to   3 we're going to
4 he'll probably   5 you'll   6 will
7 there's going to   8 he'll

**4** 1 will start   2 is coming   3 Will you   4 have
5 change   6 is   7 does   8 am playing

**page 32**

**1** 1 I  2 A  3 B  4 G  5 D  6 H  7 E  8 F  9 C

**2** 1 G  2 D  3 E  4 B  5 A  6 C  7 F

**page 33**

**1** 1 shall  2 will  3 will  4 shall  5 Shall  6 will
7 shall  8 will

**page 34**

**1** 1 is to deliver  2 is to inspect  3 are to continue
4 are to get through  5 are to follow  6 are to plan
7 are to bloom  8 are to tidy up  9 are to assemble
10 are to report

**page 35**

**3** 1 When will you be paying the rent?
2 Who will you be inviting?
3 How soon will you be coming back?
4 When will you be going home?
5 Where will you be staying?
6 What time will you be having breakfast?
7 What will you be studying at university?
8 Will you be using the car?

**page 36**

**1** 1 will have hosted  2 will have risen
3 will have driven  4 will have passed
5 will have dropped  6 will have quadrupled
7 will have put on

**page 38**

**1** 1 do you write > are you writing  2 I'm thinking > I
think  3 Correct.  4 is melting > melts
5 How do your tai-chi lessons go? > How are your tai-
chi lessons going?  6 Correct.
7 Correct.  8 It's saying > It says
9 I'm doubting > I doubt  10 Correct.
11 is tasting > tastes  12 Correct.  13 Correct.
14 Correct.  15 I'm lying > I'll be lying  16 Correct.
17 have been > will have been  18 be knowing >
know  19 Correct.  20 would have stayed > would
stay

**2** he's not seeing

**page 39**

**5** Rules 1, 3 and 4 are wrong.

**6** 1 are trying  2 arrives  3 is giving  4 start
5 decide  6 stays  7 is writing  8 is working
9 lives  10 lights  11 loses  12 go out  13 finds
14 hides  15 tell  16 are singing  17 fall

**7** 1 will have been  2 will have tidied  3 read
4 helped  5 taken  6 started  7 will have baked
8 unloaded  9 spent  10 given up  11 cleaned up
12 broken up  13 hidden  14 have spent

**page 41**

**1** 1 met, were working  2 were all playing
3 was going, stopped  4 broke, was skiing
5 was doing, heard  6 were watching, broke, stole
7 sang  8 woke up, were standing  9 made

**2** 1 was running  2 turned out  3 explained  4 ran
5 was feeding  6 was just leaving  7 ran
8 dashed  9 said  10 kept on  11 followed
12 helped  13 caught

**page 42**

**1** 1 A  2 A  3 B  4 A  5 B  6 A  7 B  8 A  9 A

**2** 1 were  2 have disturbed  3 have distributed
4 achieved  5 have seen  6 commented
7 attempted  8 has decided

**page 43**

**3** 1 have clashed, fired  2 has reached, took
3 have identified, had  4 have been, dug

**page 44**

**1** 1 have been talking  2 have been chasing
3 have been farming  4 have been escaping
5 have been behaving  6 have been making
7 have been selling  8 have been crying
9 have been telling

**page 46**

**1** 1 was interpreting  2 was  3 were demonstrating
4 went  5 spoke  6 was drinking  7 gave
8 worked  9 played

**2** had a remarkable amount, were the same age, had the
same birthday, were both very tall, had pretty similar
tastes, liked classical music

**page 47**

**3** 1 was asking  2 was always complaining
3 were wondering  4 was hoping  5 always had
6 was always forgetting  7 was thinking
8 was saying  9 was always bringing
10 was singing

**4** 1 ✔  2 ✔  3 ✗  4 ✔  5 ✔  6 ✔

**page 48**

**1** 1 B  2 C  3 B  4 B  5 B  6 B  7 B  8 B  9 B  10 A

In these answers, we usually give **either** contracted forms (for example *I'm, don't*)
**or** full forms (for example *I am, do not*). Normally both are correct.

## page 49

**3** 1 B  2 A  3 C  4 B  5 B  6 A  7 C  8 B

## page 50

**1** 1 been analysing   2 have been creating
3 have been predicting   4 has (always) assumed
5 have been designing   6 have been substituting
7 has (always) run   8 has been debating
9 has ensured   10 have been wanting

## page 51

**1** 1 applied   2 had published   3 had participated
4 had enclosed   5 had obtained   6 had selected
7 had checked   8 had affected

**3** 1 B  2 D  3 C  4 F  5 A  6 E

## page 52

**1** 1 When I had considered all the alternatives, I decided
to sell my car.
2 When we had looked at eight houses, we were
completely exhausted.
3 When she had explained the problem, there was a
long silence.
4 When I had paid for the meal, I didn't have enough
money for the bus.
5 When everybody had said what they thought, we
voted.

**2** 1 had tried   2 saw   3 had been   4 called
5 had painted   6 had voted   7 came in
8 had sent   9 had telephoned   10 got
11 opened   12 had mapped

## page 53

**1** 1 had been sitting   2 had been holding
3 had been seeing   4 had been expecting
5 had been waiting   6 had been thinking
7 had been crying   8 had been carrying
9 had been playing   10 had been looking
11 had been knitting   12 had been carrying
13 had been going on   14 had been photographing
15 had been watching

**2** 1 G  2 E  3 D  4 C

## page 54

**1** 1 have seen   2 had drunk   3 had been
4 had/have (ever) played   5 had/have had
6 have had   7 had met   8 had/have (ever) seen
9 have asked

**3** 1 A   3 G   3 C

## page 55

**1** 1 A   2 B   3 A, B   4 B, C   5 B   6 A   7 A   8 A, B
9 A   10 B

**2** 1 ✔   2 ✗   3 ✗   4 ✔   5 ✗   6 ✗   7 ✗   8 ✔   9 ✔

**3** A bad   B good   C bad   D bad   E bad   F good

## page 56

**4** 1 arrived   2 was playing   3 were dancing/fighting
4 were playing   5 were fighting/dancing   6 walked
7 tried   8 became   9 were doing   10 picked up
11 smashed   12 were looking   13 reached
14 took out   15 tore   16 said

**5** 1 has been fined, was caught   2 have arrested, found
3 has been, said   4 have discovered, were
5 have shown, were

## page 57

**7** been trying, has gone, did you last feed

## page 59

**1** 1 Correct.   2 ~~to must~~ > to have to   3 Correct.
4 Correct.   5 ~~must~~ > have to   6 ~~mights~~ > might
7 Correct.   8 Correct.   9 ~~stay~~ > to stay
10 ~~to have~~ > have

**2** 1 be understood   2 be tidying up   3 be mugged
4 be planning   5 be opened   6 be getting

## page 60

**1** 1 managed to pass   2 Correct.   3 managed to get
4 Correct.   5 Correct.   6 managed to finish
7 managed to put   8 Correct.   9 managed to get
10 Correct.

**2** 1 can   2 will be able to   3 can   4 will be able to
5 won't be able to   6 can   7 will be able to
8 can't   9 can   10 can

## page 61

**3** 1 can (definitely) smell   2 could see   3 can hear
4 can (distinctly) taste   5 could feel, could not see
6 could smell   7 could hear   8 can (vaguely)
remember   9 can understand

## page 62

**1** 1 too polite   2 not polite enough   3 OK   4 OK
5 not polite enough   6 not polite enough   7 wrong
8 wrong   9 right   10 right

**2** 1 ✗   2 ✔   3 ✗   4 ✔   5 ✔   6 ✗

## page 63

**2** 1 must go to bed.   2 must find out   3 don't have to answer   4 has to vote   5 must throw out   6 must not hit your opponent   7 must come round   8 have to get   9 have to take off   10 must turn down   11 have to pay taxes   12 don't have to go to work

## page 64

**1** 1 should   2 must   3 Should   4 must   5 must   6 should   7 must   8 ought to   9 should   10 should

## page 65

**1** 1 can't   2 should   3 can't   4 must   5 should   6 shouldn't   7 can't   8 should   9 shouldn't   10 can't

**2** 1 will   2 will   3 won't   4 will   5 won't   6 will   7 will   8 won't   9 will   10 won't

## page 66

**2** 1 ✔   2 ✘   3 ✔   4 ✔   5 ✘   6 ✔   7 ✔   8 ✔   9 ✔   10 ✘   11 ✘   12 ✘

**3** 1 can't   2 may not   3 can't   4 may not   5 may not   6 can't   7 can't   8 may not

## page 67

**4** 1 ✔   2 ✘   3 ✘   4 ✔   5 ✔   6 ✘   7 ✔   8 ✔   9 ✔   10 ✘

**5** 1 She may not come to all the meetings, but she knows what's going on.
2 You may have a degree, but that's no substitute for practical experience.
3 I may not know much about art, but I know rubbish when I see it.
4 The government may make impressive promises, but nothing is going to change.

## page 68

**1** 1 could have hit
2 could/might have killed
3 should/would have phoned
4 could/might/would have gone
5 should have been
6 should have put
7 should/could have asked
8 should have taken
9 could/might have died
10 should/could/might have told

## page 69

**2** 1 He may/could/might have forgotten to lock the door.
2 She may/could/might have sent these flowers.
3 The builders may/could/might have finished.
4 I may/could/might have found a new job.
5 Alex may/could/might have changed her mind.
6 Somebody may/could/might have been in my room.
7 We may/could/might have come to the wrong house.

## page 69

**3** 1 Bernie must have had an accident.
2 Luke can't have been shopping.
3 She can't have forgotten.
4 It must have rained in the night.
5 He can't have spent it all.
6 You must have worked all weekend.

**4** 1 can't have gone   2 may not have existed   3 must have been   4 can't have had   5 had to wait   6 can't have understood   7 had to do   8 must have been   9 can't have broken   10 had to get up

## page 70

**5** 1 needn't have hurried   2 didn't need to water   3 needn't have bought   4 didn't need to fill up   5 didn't need to go   6 needn't have studied   7 needn't have bothered   8 didn't need to

**6** must, could

## page 71

**1** (had better)   1 ✔   2 ✔   3 ✔   4 ✔   5 ✔   6 ✔   7 ✘   8 ✔

**1** (be supposed to)
1 Politicians are supposed to serve the people.
2 Teachers are supposed to like children.
3 Business people are supposed to be efficient.
4 Artists are supposed to have a lot of imagination.
5 Mathematicians are supposed to be good with figures.
6 Linguists are supposed to be good communicators.
7 Catholics are supposed to go to mass on Sundays.
8 Old people are supposed to forget things.

## page 72

**1** 1 The car won't start.
2 Would/Will you take a seat?
3 Will you have / Would you like tea or coffee?
4 Would/Will you tell me your name?
5 Nobody will tell us the truth.
6 I will help you.
7 The computer won't recognise my password.
8 The bank won't lend us any more money.
9 Would/Will you sign the form at the bottom?

In these answers, we usually give **either** contracted forms (for example *I'm, don't*) **or** full forms (for example *I am, do not*). Normally both are correct.

ANSWER KEY **317**

**2** 1 will go wrong.  2 won't be enough.
3 will always move faster.  4 will get lost.
5 will misunderstand it.  6 will roll  7 won't go off.
8 will lose.

## page 74

**1** 1 ✔  2 ✔  3 ✘  4 ✘  5 ✔  6 ✘  7 ✘  8 ✘
9 ✔  10 ✘

## page 75

**1** 1 ~~could~~ > managed to  2 ~~could~~ > can  3 Correct.
4 ~~May~~ > Can  5 ~~could~~ > were allowed to
6 ~~mustn't~~ > don't have to / don't need to / needn't
7 Correct.  8 Correct.  9 ~~May you~~ > Might
you / Do you think you may  10 ~~can~~ > may
11 Correct.  12 Correct.

**2** A

**3** B

**4** A

**5** 1 no  2 no  3 no  4 yes  5 yes  6 no  7 no

**6** A

## page 76

**7** 1 No  2 Probably  3 Probably not  4 Yes  5 Maybe
6 Maybe  7 No  8 No  9 Probably  10 Yes

**8** A

**9** A

**10** C

**11** 1 would / used to  2 used to  3 used to

**12** 1 did people use  2 didn't use  3 Did you use
4 didn't use  (used not *is also possible*), did

**13** C

**14** B

## page 77

**15** 1 weigh  2 swim  3 lift  4 jump  5 jump
6 extend  7 live  8 run  9 reach  10 grow
11 dive, stay  12 grow

## page 78

**1** 1 Correct.  2 ~~will told~~ > will be told  3 Correct.
4 Correct.  5 ~~selected~~ > been selected
6 ~~being~~ > been

**2** 1 ~~must to be~~ > must be  2 Correct.  3 ~~been~~ > to be
4 ~~massage~~ > massaged  5 Correct.  6 Correct.

## page 79

**3** 1 Everything will be paid for …
2 by a translator
3 spoken > spoken to
4 Correct.
5 Correct.
6 Who was the new cathedral built by?

**4** 1 ✔  2 ✔  3 ✔  4 ✘  5 ✔  6 ✔

**5** 1 We got burgled  2 Our roof got damaged
3 Not natural with *got*  4 If you get caught
5 I always get bitten  6 Not natural with *got*
7 We all got sent home  8 Not natural with *get*

## page 80

**1** Explanations B and E are right.

**2** 1 B  2 B  3 A  4 A  5 B  6 A

## page 81

**3** 1 I wasn't pleased by George ringing me up at three
o'clock in the morning to tell me he was in love again.
2 I was surprised by Caroline telling me that she had
always wanted to be a singer.
3 We were shocked that nobody was prepared to take
him to hospital.
4 Everybody was irritated that Mary thought she was
better than everybody else.

**4** 1 Applications must be sent to the Central Office before
August 1st. All supporting documentation must be
attached, and a cheque must be enclosed in payment
of the full fee. A stamped addressed envelope must
also be enclosed.
2 Fifty workers were selected at random and given a
thorough physical examination. Blood samples were
taken from all fifty and analysed. No traces of lead
poisoning were found.

## page 82

**1** 1 It was believed that fresh air was bad for sick people.
2 There are claimed to be wolves in the mountains.
3 The man holding the hostages is thought to be heavily
armed.
4 He is said to be in an agitated state.
5 It is suggested that the rate of inflation will rise.
6 She is reported to have died in a plane crash.
7 There are believed to be 6,000 different languages in
the world.
8 It is understood that she left the country on Friday.
9 There is thought to be oil under Windsor Castle.
10 The earth was believed to be the centre of the universe.
11 He is known to have been married four times.
12 It is expected that there will be an announcement on
Friday.

## page 83

**3** 1 Mr Evans was appointed secretary.
2 Louise was considered a sort of clown.
3 Dr Hastings was regarded as an expert on criminal law.
4 The new house has been made much more attractive by the new owners.
5 She was called a witch by the villagers.
6 Professor Martin was elected Vice-President.

## page 84

**1** 1 ✗  2 ✔  3 ✔  4 ✗  5 ✗  6 ✔

**2** 1 frightened  2 surprised  3 stuffed  4 covered
5 surprised  6 known

**3** Number 2 is wrong.

## page 85

**4** A 12, 8   B 1   C 4   D 11, 10   E 9, 3, 7   F 13, 15, 6, 5
G 14, 2

## page 86

**1** 1a 2b 3a 4b 5a 6b 7a 8a 9b

**2** In 1665, an experiment was carried out to investigate the nature of colour. A room was darkened, and a hole was made in the window shutter, so that a narrow ray of sunlight was allowed to enter the room. A glass prism was taken and placed in the ray of light. The result was that the ray was split into a band of colours like a rainbow – a spectrum. When a second prism was placed upside down in front of the first prism, the different colours of the spectrum were recombined into white light. For the first time, the relationship between light and colour had been scientifically demonstrated.

In 1665, Newton carried out an experiment to investigate the nature of colour. He darkened a room and made a hole in the window shutter, so that he allowed a narrow ray of sunlight to enter the room. He took a glass prism and placed it in the ray of light. The result was that the prism split the light into a band of colours like a rainbow – a spectrum. When he placed a second prism upside down in front of the first prism, it recombined the different colours of the spectrum into white light. At last, someone had scientifically demonstrated the relationship between light and colour.

## page 87

**4** (possible answers)
1 He was said to be a friend of the President.
2 He was thought to advise governments.
3 He was believed to have mistresses in three different countries.
4 He was reported to be a mathematical genius.
5 He was understood to speak fourteen languages.

6 He was said to have climbed Everest in winter.
7 He was thought to have a bath with gold taps.
8 He was believed to have lived with wolves.
9 He was reported to run marathons to keep fit.
10 And on top of that, he was understood to be terribly nice.

**5** been

## page 89

**1** 1 to write  2 to have been written
3 to have written  4 to be written
5 not to write  6 to have been writing  7 be writing

**2** 1 writing  2 not writing / not having written
3 being written  4 writing / having written
5 having been written

**3** 1 to live  2 to die  3 to make  4 die  5 die
6 to hear  7 to read

## page 90

**1** 1 you seem to have misunderstood the directions.
2 We were sorry to have upset her.
3 The rain seems to have stopped.
4 I'm glad to have got to know your family.
5 Max was disappointed to have failed his exam.
6 We expect to have moved house before September.
7 Alice was very happy to have left school.
8 I'm fortunate to have grown up bilingual.
9 The terrorists are believed to have left the country.
10 The car appears to have been stolen last night.

## page 91

**1** 1 I would like to have heard what he said when he found the frogs in his bed.
2 He was to have competed in the Olympics.
3 We were to have seen the Grand Canyon.
4 It was to have been a quiet weekend.
5 I meant to have sent her flowers for her birthday.
6 I meant to have tidied the house before the visitors arrived.
7 I would like to have lived in Ancient Rome.

**2** 1 The government was not responsible for giving false information.
2 All three were found guilty of committing armed robbery.
3 I had no memory of having been in his house.
4 Several students were accused of having cheated in their exams.
5 I feel really bad about not sending you a birthday card.

## page 92

**1** 1 look at  2 work  3 explain  4 frown
5 look after  6 clean  7 delay

**2** A wait  B see  C believe  D sit, read  E work
F obstruct  G accept  H steal, beg

In these answers, we usually give **either** contracted forms (for example *I'm, don't*) **or** full forms (for example *I am, do not*). Normally both are correct.

## page 93

**1** 1 to advertise   2 creating   3 to increase
4 to establish   5 reorganising   6 to order
7 to entertain   8 to reverse   9 to convict
10 to extend   11 pretending   12 to compete

**2** 1 afford   2 hesitated   3 intend   4 attempted
5 failed   6 attempts   7 chose   8 tend
9 swear   10 bother

## page 94

**1** 1 to punish   2 accepting   3 polishing   4 to charge
5 smiling   6 drafting   7 worrying   8 climbing
9 to replace   10 juggling   11 to water   12 reducing

**2** 1 appreciate, miss, resent   2 can't face, feel like, mind
3 involve, mention, imagine   4 deny, admit, avoid

## page 95

**1** 1 They need cleaning.   2 It needs mending.   3 It
needs restringing.   4 It needs making.   5 It needs
cooking.   6 It needs servicing.   7 It needs painting.
8 It needs cutting.

**2** 1 appreciate, miss, resent   2 can't face, feel like, mind
3 involve, mention, imagine   4 deny, admit, avoid

## page 96

**1** 1 We didn't expect the visitors to be early.
2 Nobody wanted Alice to resign.
3 I'd like people to listen to me.
4 We need somebody to clean the office.
5 I didn't mean everybody to get upset.
6 I'd prefer your brother to stay with us next week instead.
7 Alex persuaded me to apply for the job.
8 The bad weather caused hundreds of flights to be cancelled.
9 Emma's parents encouraged her to become a doctor.

## page 97

**2** 1 The police believe the jewels to have been stolen.
2 An examination showed the money to be / to have been forged.
3 Copernicus proved Ptolemy to be wrong.
4 My parents considered me (to be) a very strange child.
5 We understand him to be living in France.

**3** 1 people talking, them thinking
2 Mrs Jameson getting
3 customers paying
4 younger people correcting

**4** 1 accused   2 prevented   3 forgave   4 talked
5 congratulated

## page 98

**1** 1 to lock   2 to inform   3 forcing   4 nagging
5 marrying   6 to consider   7 to have, stretch
8 climbing   9 working   10 believing   11 to cancel
12 to collect

## page 99

**3** 1 sending   2 training   3 explode   4 to make
5 to mend   6 to tip   7 visiting   8 to consult
9 blowing   10 looking   11 tuning up
12 changing

## page 100

**5** 1 A   2 A   3 both   4 B   5 both   6 A   7 A

**6** *(possible answers)*
1 to fail   2 in working with children
3 of breaking them   4 to hear Ann's news
5 of getting the job   6 to tell him what I think

## page 101

**7** 1 A   2 A   3 A   4 A   5 A   6 B   7 C   8 A   9 B   10 B
11 B   12 A   13 A   14 A   15 C

**8** 1 tries   2 remember, try   3 afraid   4 regret

## page 102

**1** 1 to invite   2 to take   3 to cross   4 to write
5 to wash   6 to add   7 to post   8 to translate

**2** *(possible answers)*
1 something to sit on
2 something to look at
3 something to eat with
4 something to write with
5 something to cut (things) with
6 something to put things on
7 something to keep money in
8 something to carry water in
9 something to keep clothes in
10 something to write in

**3** 1 for the baby to play with   2 for my father to mend
3 for the whole family to enjoy   4 for the committee
to solve   5 for everybody to walk in

## page 103

**4** 1 The plums are ripe enough to eat.
2 Languages are difficult to learn.
3 Her accent is hard to understand.
4 Andy is difficult to live with.
5 Ice is not easy to drive on.
6 You are impossible to argue with.
7 The river was hard to swim across.
8 Water-colours are hard to paint with.
9 Susie is really boring to listen to.

**5** *(possible answers)*
1 dangerous to sit on
2 hard to eat with
3 uncomfortable to walk in
4 difficult to sleep in
5 impossible to write with
6 uncomfortable to sleep on

**6** 1 ✘  2 ✘  3 ✔  4 ✘  5 ✔  6 ✔

## page 104

**1** 1 It's not a good idea for Emma to study medicine.
2 I'll be happy for you to use my office.
3 I'm anxious for the children to see a good dentist.
4 It's unusual for her to be ill.
5 It's normal for him to play golf at weekends.
6 It would be a mistake for Sue to marry Oliver.
7 Is it possible for your brother to help us?
8 There's no need for the meeting to go on for very long.

**2** 1 It's important for there to be public libraries.
2 It's vital for there to be a good public transport system.
3 It's important for there to be plenty of open spaces.

## page 105

**1** 1 Yes  2 No  3 No  4 Yes  5 Yes  6 No  7 No
8 Yes  9 Yes  10 No

**2** 1 hearing  2 move  3 smoke  4 driving
5 cycling  6 be  7 book  8 playing  9 weeding
10 get

## page 106

**1** 1 I don't understand Maggie wanting to go back home. OR … why Maggie wants …
2 We were surprised at Andy being appointed District Manager. OR … that/when Andy was appointed …
3 I hate him telling everybody what to do.
4 Do you remember me telling you I knew an important secret? OR Do you remember I told you …
5 I'm worried about Alice not wanting to go with us. OR I'm worried that Alice doesn't want …

**2** 1 her arrival  2 their departure  3 our preference
4 your help  5 his refusal  6 everybody's insistence

## page 107

**1** 1 ✔  2 ✔  3 ✘  4 ✔  5 ✘  6 ✔  7 ✔  8 ✔  9 ✔
10 ✘

**2** 1 B  2 A,B  3 A,B  4 A  5 B  6 A,B  7 B  8 A  9 A
10 B  11 A  12 A

## page 108

**4** 1 rejection  2 acceptance  3 agreement
4 complaint  5 request  6 return  7 suggestion
8 criticism  9 advice  10 departure  11 accusation
12 apology

## page 109

**6** to be, to join

## page 111

**1** 1 blue  2 headmaster  3 happy  4 Shorty
5 offensive  6 study  7 regard  8 identified
9 considered  10 sees  11 describe  12 listed

**2** 1 We feel that the price is rather high.
2 I understand that he is interested in cooperating.
3 An examination showed that she was seriously undernourished.
4 Everybody considered that Rogers was the best candidate.

## page 112

**1** 1 Correct.  2 Not.  3 Not  4 Correct.  5 Not.
6 Correct.

**2** 1 PR  2 PR  3 AP  4 PR  5 AP  6 PR  7 AP

**3** into, around, up, out, around, through

## page 113

**4** 1 We talked about it.  2 I put it off.  3 Can you clean it up?  4 She put it on.  5 I'm looking for it.
6 I wrote it down.  7 I sent it back.  8 I stood on it.

## page 114

**1** 1 on  2 into  3 in  4 on  5 on  6 from  7 of
8 on  9 on  10 into  11 into  12 into

**2** 1 about  2 of  3 at  4 to  5 about  6 of
7 about  8 of  9 of  10 about  11 for  12 about

## page 115

**3** 1 –  2 –  3 on  4 to  5 –  6 with  7 on  8 to
9 –  10 –

**4** 1 out of  2 into  3 in  4 with  5 through
6 into  7 for  8 at  9 out of

## page 116

**1** 1 There isn't any more  2 cancelled
3 I can't hear you clearly  4 You're going crazy.
5 rejected  6 see clearly  7 invent
8 criticising their behaviour  9 excites me
10 support me

In these answers, we usually give **either** contracted forms (for example *I'm, don't*) **or** full forms (for example *I am, do not*). Normally both are correct.

**2** 1 a biscuit, a marriage   2 a piece of paper, an onion
   3 a relationship, a branch   4 a bridge, a balloon
   5 a proposal, a suggestion   6 an excuse, a story
   7 a saucepan, a cup   8 a stain, a black mark
   9 an engine, a business

## page 117

**3** 1 further   2 away   3 higher   4 not working
   5 working   6 on paper   7 to various people
   8 into pieces   9 further   10 higher

**4** 1 I'm going to throw this jacket out. I'm going to throw
      it out.
   2 Susie has broken her engagement off. Susie has
      broken it off.
   3 Could you switch the TV on? Could you switch it on?
   4 Please write these figures down. Please write them
      down.
   5 It's time to clear the garage out. It's time to clean it
      out.
   6 I'd like to pay the loan off. I'd like to pay it off.
   7 Do I need to fill this form in? Do I need to fill it in?
   8 You can't turn the clock back. You can't turn it back.
   9 Do you want to play the recording back? Do you
      want to play it back?
   10 I'll think your proposal over. I'll think it over.

## page 118

**1** 2 Throw Sandy the ball.
   3 They offered my brother a promotion.
   4 She reads her children a story every night.
   5 Take the secretary this paper, please.
   7 Shall I make you a sandwich?
   8 I taught Alex's children the guitar.
   9 Pass me the salt, would you?
   11 Sing me a song.

## page 119

**2** 1 Send them to the accountant, please.
   2 I offered it to Helen.
   3 Would you read it to us all?
   4 I've brought these for Tim.
   5 We gave them to the charity shop.
   6 Why don't you send it to a TV company?

**3** 1 Yes   2 No   3 Yes   4 Yes   5 No   6 No
   7 No   8 Yes

## page 120

**1** 1 They get you to go through a metal detector.
   2 They get you to take off your shoes.
   3 They get you to show your passport.
   4 They get you to wait around for ages,
   5 They get you to pay extra for your heavy baggage.
   6 They get you to fasten your seat belt during take-off.
   7 They get you to sit for hours in a small seat.
   8 They don't get you to fly the plane.
   9 They don't get you to sing to the pilot.

## page 121

**3** 1 I didn't have my car stolen, but the wheels were taken
      off.
   2 Have you ever had a letter returned unopened?
   3 Alice (has) had her visa application refused again.
   4 My sister had a short story published earlier this year.
   5 We had our furniture ruined in the flood.

## page 122

**1** 1 head, incompetent   2 impressive, treasurer
   3 as being, average   4 to be, remote
   5 as being, scar

**2** 1 on   2 into   3 in   4 on   5 on   6 from   7 on
   8 –   9 into   10 into   11 into   12 –   13 on
   14 on   15 –

**3** 1 up   2 over   3 off   4 back/away   5 up
   6 up   7 up

**4** *Away* and *back* cannot be prepositions.
   *At* can only be a preposition.

**5** 1 ✗   2 ✔   3 ✗   4 ✗   5 ✔   6 ✗   7 ✔   8 ✔   9 ✗
   10 ✗

**6** 1 C   2 C

## page 123

**7** 1 in   2 up   3 up   4 out   5 up   6 in   7 down
   8 in   9 in   10 out   11 in   12 down   13 round
   14 off   15 up   16 out

## page 125

**1** 1 poetry   2 weather   3 baggage   4 traffic
   5 work   6 money   7 luck   8 progress
   9 furniture   10 evidence   11 research

**2** 1 idea   2 point   3 difficulty   4 change   5 reason
   6 question   7 chance   8 difference

## page 126

**1** 1 have, they say   2 are   3 has   4 are   5 is   6 live
   7 closes   8 are   9 are, they haven't   10 are

**2** 1 ~~has~~ > have   2 ~~are~~ > is   3 ~~other~~ > another
   4 ~~are~~ > is   5 ~~has~~ > have   6 Correct.   7 ~~are~~ > is
   8 Correct.   9 ~~is~~ > are   10 Correct.

## page 127

**3** 1 … is an advantage   2 … that is certain
   3 … leave their coats   4 … has fallen off
   5 … is becoming   6 … on bikes (OR by bike)
   7 … has gone   8 … really small rooms
   9 … their wives   10 … their seats   11 … is often

## page 128

**1** 1 a bicycle thief   2 plant pots   3 pot plants
4 music lessons   5 a hat shop   6 an electricity bill
7 a police car   8 a fish pond   9 a computer
engineer   10 computer engineer training courses

**2** 1 a four-bedroom house   2 a three-hour lecture
3 a 100-euro note   4 two 100-euro notes
5 a ten-mile walk   6 a two-car family

**3** Operate your garage doors, car alarm and home alarm
with one remote control that fits on your key ring.

## page 129

**4** 1 a glass factory   2 a love story   3 the man in the
garden   4 a night club   5 dog food
6 a bird on the roof   7 a folk song
8 a fire at the supermarket   9 music festivals
10 the books on the shelf

## page 130

**1** 1 ✔   2 ✘   3 ✘   4 ✔   5 ✔   6 ✘   7 ✘   8 ✔   9 ✔
10 ✔   11 ✔   12 ✘

**2** 1 Peter's arm   2 the arm of the chair
3 the dog's tail   4 the tail of the hurricane
5 the results of the investigations
6 the students' results   7 the anniversary of the
disaster   8 Harry's birthday   9 the price of the
clothes   10 the students' fees   11 the roof of the
house   12 Eric's family   13 Britain's exports
14 the price of bread

## page 131

**3** 1 Mary's success in her exams boosted her confidence.
2 The economy's growth was slower than expected.
3 Peter's phone call worried us a lot.
4 The treasurer's report on the last six months was
encouraging.
5 The children's punishment was very severe.

**4** 1 a glass factory   2 a toy shop   3 computer discs
4 that cat's tail   5 car papers   6 a telephone
directory   7 a birthday card   8 vegetable
soup   9 Andrew's plan   10 street lamps
11 the firm's problems   12 a bath towel

## page 133

**1** 1 ✔   2 ✘   3 ✘   4 ✔   5 ✘   6 ✘   7 ✔   8 ✔   9 ✘
10 ✘   11 ✘   12 ✔

## page 134

**1** 1 We are too. / So are we.   2 I did.   3 They do.
4 She can.   5 He is

**2** 1 Nobody can sing better than me.
2 It was her that caused the problem.
3 Nobody understood except us.
4 He was the one who/that discovered the solution.
5 We were the ones who/that got left behind.
6 She doesn't panic as easily as I do.

## page 135

**3** 1 I   2 I, LP   3 I   4 W   5 N   6 LP   7 N

**4** 1 W   2 I   3 F   4 N   5 W   6 W   7 N   8 I   9 W   10 N

## page 136

**1** 1 ourselves   2 herself   3 him   4 me   5 each
other   6 herself   7 himself   8 me

**2** 1 –   2 –   3 –   4 herself   5 –   6 –   7 –
8 yourself   9 –, –   10 –

## page 137

**3** 1 me   2 us   3 myself   4 himself   5 her
6 her   7 themselves   8 myself

## page 138

**1** 1 ✘   2 ✘   3 ✔   4 ✘   5 ✔   6 ✔   7 ✘   8 ✘

**2** 1 One has to be fit to do this job.
2 Sometimes you have to keep your opinions to yourself.
3 One needs to leave early if one wants to avoid the
traffic.
4 You can't make an omelette without breaking eggs.
5 You can't teach people anything if you aren't prepared
to learn from them.
6 One can't get an adequate knowledge of a language in
a month.

## page 139

**1 (they)** 1 ✔   2 ✔   3 ✘   4 ✔   5 ✔   6 ✘   7 ✔
8 ✔   9 ✔   10 ✘

**1 (one)** 1 one, sun roof   2 a blue one, buttons
3 throw out, the ones   4 goats', sheep's
5 a big one, transcriptions   6 one, sea level
7 olive, corn   8 a really sharp one

## page 140

**1** 1 ✘   2 ✔   3 ✘   4 ✘   5 ✔   6 ✔   7 ✘   8 ✔
9 ✔   10 ✘

**2** 1 A   2 A   3 A   4 C   5 A   6 B   7 C   8 A   9 A   10 C
11 A   12 B   13 B   14 B   15 C

In these answers, we usually give **either** contracted forms (for example *I'm, don't*)
**or** full forms (for example *I am, do not*). Normally both are correct.

**3** 1 a two-litre bottle   2 a police car
3 a scream of anger   4 a novel about coal miners / a
coal miner   5 a golf club   6 Emma's sister
7 a car factory   8 that dog's tail   9 Correct.
10 Let's have a party.

**4** 1 her   2 Me   3 me   4 us   5 me   6 one   7 shave

## page 141

**5** 1 A   2 C   3 B   4 F   5 A   6 B   7 D   8 E

**6** 1 always, never   2 everything   3 difficult, impossible
4 simply   5 easiest, fool   6 flies   7 diary,
sensational   8 mistakes   9 shoes   10 romance
11 kitchen   12 coffee, thumb

## page 143

**1** a   2 a   3 a   4 a   5 –   6 –   7 –   8 the   9 the
10 –   11 –   12 the   13 a   14 –   15 the   16 –
17 a   18 the   19 the   20 the   21 the   22 –   23 –
24 a   25 –   26 the   27 the   28 the   29 the   30 the
31 a   32 –   33 an   34 the   35 a   36 an   37 the
38 a   39 the

**2** 1 the school > school
2 medical student > a medical student
3 a door > the door
4 The most people > Most people
5 Correct.
6 the North Wales > North Wales
7 the Peter's new job > Peter's new job
8 the very complicated personality > a very
complicated personality
9 Correct.
10 most stupid thing > the most stupid thing

**3** Rules 3 and 6 are the bad ones.

## page 144

**4** 1 gynaecologists   2 estate agents   3 dermatologists
4 horticulturalists   5 surgeons   6 financial advisers
7 paediatricians   8 farmers   9 chefs   10 florists
11 nurses   12 stockbrokers   13 archaeologists
14 zoologists   15 botanists

**5** 1 in garden > in the garden   2 Correct.   3 Correct.
4 Correct.   5 Correct.   6 kitchen > the kitchen
7 gym > the gym   8 Correct.   9 in office > in the office
10 Correct.   11 the work > work   12 the school >
school

## page 145

**6** 1 Wrong; a crazy   2 Wrong; a tourist guide
3 Right; lunch, at breakfast   4 Wrong; a special licence
5 Right; by car, by train

## page 146

**1** 1 ✗   2 ✔   3 ✔   4 ✗   5 ✔   6 ✗   7 ✔   8 ✔

**3** 1 the postage stamp   2 the dishwasher
3 the paper clip   4 the post-it note
5 the bicycle   6 the windscreen wiper

## page 147

**4** 1 ✔   2 ✗   3 ✔   4 ✗   5 ✔   6 ✔   7 ✗   8 ✔
9 ✔   10 ✔

**5** 1 educational philosophy   2 the psychology of
society   3 the painters of France   4 the history of art
5 agricultural development   6 literary study
7 economic theory   8 religious history

## page 148

**1** 1 ✗   2 ✗   3 ✔   4 ✗   5 ✔   6 ✔   7 ✔   8 ✔
9 ✗   10 ✗

## page 149

**2** 1 C   2 A   3 C   4 A   5 B   6 A   7 A   8 C   9 A

## page 150

**1** 1 A   2 A   3 B   4 B   5 A

**2** 1 this   2 this   3 that   4 that   5 that   6 this
7 That   8 This   9 this   10 that

## page 151

**3** 1 Correct.   2 that > that person   3 Correct.
4 Correct.   5 This > This person   6 Correct.

**4** Those who can, do. Those who can't, teach. Those who
can't teach, train teachers.

**5** 1 that, computer   2 these, trip   3 that, bored
4 policies, those   5 Earn, those   6 this, swimming
pool   7 brilliant, that

## page 152

**1** 1 the your > your   2 who's > whose   3 our's > ours
4 their > theirs   5 Correct.   6 it's > its   7 the mine >
mine   8 whose the family > whose family

**2** 1 a cousin of mine   2 this suggestion of yours
3 a colleague of Emma's   4 that translation of Peter's
5 a friend of my mother's   6 these new shoes of yours
7 this latest mistake of the government's   8 a firm
principle of my father's   9 a strange belief of my
sister's   10 some students of mine   11 two recent
films of his   12 this wonderful girlfriend of yours

## page 153

**4** 1 nostrils   2 stomach   3 back   4 eyelash
5 thumb   6 eyebrows   7 trunks   8 tails
9 paws   10 lips

## page 154

**1** 1 –   2 a   3 –   4 a   5 –   6 –   7 the   8 a   9 –
10 –   11 –   12 The   13 –   14 The   15 the   16 –
17 the   18 –, –   19 The   20 –

**2** 1 C   2 C   3 B   4 C   5 B   6 B   7 A   8 B   9 B   10 A

**3** 1 ✗   2 ✔   3 ✔   4 ✗   5 ✔   6 ✔   7 ✔   8 ✗
9 ✗   10 ✔

## page 155

**5** 1 –   2 the   3 a   4 –   5 the   6 –   7 the   8 the
9 a   10 the   11 the   12 the   13 –   14 a   15 a
16 the   17 a   18 the   19 –   20 the   21 the
22 the   23 the   24 the   25 the   26 –   27 the
28 the   29 –   30 The   31 the   32 the / –   33 the
34 the / –   35 –   36 –   37 the

**6** those

## page 157

**1** 1 ✔   2 ✔   3 ✗   4 ✔   5 ✗   6 ✔   7 ✔   8 ✔
9 ✗   10 ✔   11 ✔   12 ✗

**2** 1 Did you understand all of it?
2 Do you want all of us to work late?
3 Kara sends her regards to you all.
4 I'll post them all tomorrow.
5 The dog's eaten all of it.
6 It's the same for us all.

## page 158

**1** all (of) the children   a whole class   a whole coconut
the whole of / all of China   all (of) the islands   all (of)
the luggage   all (of) the meat   all (of) the MPs   the
whole plan   the whole political party   the whole
problem   the whole road system   all (of) the students
all (of) the traffic   all (of) the vegetables

**2** 1 all (of) the country   the whole country
2 all (of) this government   this whole government
3 all (of) that week   that whole week
4 all (of) London   the whole of London
5 all (of) the company   the whole company
6 all (of) our garden   our whole garden
7 all (of) South Africa   the while of South Africa
8 all (of) the cake   the whole cake

## page 159

**1 (both)** 1 ✔   2 ✔   3 ✗   4 ✔   5 ✗   6 ✔

**1 (either... )** 1 either of them   2 either of us
3 Neither child   4 either of these courses
5 Neither of us   6 Neither of the two star players
7 either minister   8 either species

## page 160

**1** 1 every   2 Each   3 player   4 each match
5 each   6 every   7 has   8 says

**2** 1 ✗   2 ✔   3 ✗   4 ✗   5 ✔   6 ✔

## page 161

**1** 1 some   2 some   3 any   4 any   5 any
6 some   7 Some   8 some

**2** 1 ✔   2 ✔   3 ✗   4 ✔   5 ✗   6 ✔   7 ✗   8 ✔   9 ✗

## page 162

**1** 1 some   2 –   3 –   4 some   5 –   6 some   7 –
8 –   9 any   10 –

**2** 1 some water   2 water   3 some water   4 any water
5 water   6 some water   7 any water   8 water

## page 163

**1** 1 /sm/   2 /sʌm/   3 /sm/   4 /sʌm/   5 /sʌm/
6 /sm/   7 /sʌm/   8 /sʌm/

**2** 1 D, C   2 C, D   3 E   4 A   5 F   6 B

## page 164

**1** 1 any help
2 no passport
3 no thief
4 Any complaints
5 any charity
6 not a bird
7 any post office
8 any questions
9 no driver
10 any leftover food

## page 165

**1** 1 Dr Andrews speaks a lot of / lots of languages.
2 There has been a lot of / lots of / plenty of discussion
about the results.
3 The staff have many reasons for striking.
4 The new regulations have caused a lot of / lots of /
plenty of confusion.
5 Many voters stayed at home on election day.
6 A lot of / Lots of / Plenty of English children have
difficulty learning to spell.

In these answers, we usually give **either** contracted forms (for example *I'm, don't*)
**or** full forms (for example *I am, do not*). Normally both are correct.

**1** 1 little  2 a few  3 few
4 little  5 a few  6 a little

**2** 1 only a few / not many friends
2 only a little / not much milk
3 only a little / not much hope
4 only a few / not many answers
5 only a little / not much work
6 only a few / not many cities

**3** 1 the least  2 fewer  3 Fewer  4 less
5 the fewest  6 less  7 the least  8 the fewest
9 the fewest  10 fewer

**1** 1 We haven't got a long enough ladder.
2 We haven't got sharp enough knives.
3 We haven't got a fast enough car.
4 We haven't got enough fresh bread.
5 We haven't got bright enough lights.
6 We haven't got enough hot water.
7 We haven't got enough small screws.
8 You haven't got enough green paint.
9 You haven't got clear enough handwriting.
10 I haven't got enough white T-shirts.

**2** 1 Are there enough eggs for me to make an omelette?
2 Are there enough chairs for us all to sit down?
3 Is there enough coffee for everybody to have some?
4 Is there enough time for me to make a phone call?
5 Is there enough petrol for us to get home?
6 Is there enough money for both of us to get tickets?
7 Are there enough computers for John to use one?
8 Are there enough copies of the book for me to take three?

**1** 1 believe  2 number, were  3 is  4 are
5 amount  6 are  7 large number  8 have

**2** 1 A  2 I  3 D  4 C  5 F  6 G  7 B  8 E  9 H

**1** 1 some of  2 Some  3 any  4 most  5 None of
6 Few of  7 much of  8 Every one of  9 little
10 Most of

**2** 1 ✔  2 ✗  3 ✔  4 ✗  5 ✔  6 ✗  7 ✔  8 ✗  9 ✔
10 ✔  11 ✔  12 ✔

**1** 1 B  2 A  3 C  4 A  5 B  6 A  7 A  8 B  9 C  10 C

**2** 1 Correct.  2 Correct.  3 ~~every~~ > every one
4 Correct.  5 Correct.  6 Correct.  7 Correct.
8 ~~all~~ > both  9 ~~The men both picked~~ > The men
picked  10 ~~some hydrogen and some oxygen~~ >
hydrogen and oxygen

**3** B

**4** B

**5** B

**6** a car

**1** *(possible answers)*
1 deadly  2 cowardly  3 silly  4 ugly  5 unlikely
6 lonely  7 lovely  8 lively  9 friendly
10 monthly

**2** 1 tight  2 clean  3 quiet  4 small  5 carefully
6 short

**1** 1 wide blue eyes
2 black nylon ski pants
3 red woollen cap
4 German climbing boots
5 charming little northern town
6 long cotton jacket
7 heavy dark steel-framed glasses
8 lovely old house
9 strange new American student
10 impressive modern concrete and glass university

**1** 1 little; small  2 live; alive  3 sheer; worrying
4 alone; lonely  5 waking; awake  6 floating; afloat

**2** 1 a different life from this one
2 the first item on the agenda
3 a difficult dialect to understand
4 better singers than you
5 the last delegate to speak

**1** 1 Swedish-speaking Finns
2 fruit-eating bats
3 music-loving people
4 fast-moving traffic
5 hard-working people
6 a never-ending story
7 noise-reducing headphones
8 earth-moving equipment

**2** 1 very  2 very much  3 very  4 very
5 very much  6 very much  7 very
8 very much

## page 177

**1** 1x  2✔  3✔  4x  5x  6x  7x

**2** 1 the Chinese  2 the English
3 the French  4 the Irish
5 the Welsh  6 the Dutch
7 the Japanese  8 the Spanish

## page 178

**1** 1 We were sorry that we missed the concert.
2 I was surprised that you remembered me.
3 We're ready for a holiday.
4 He was aware that he had made a mistake.
5 We're happy to be here.
6 I was furious about the delay to the plane.
7 They were not prepared to wait for a long time.
8 I was anxious to get/find a better job.

**2** 1 to concentrate  2 to sleep  3 to play
4 to accommodate  5 to manage  6 to reach
7 to make/reach

## page 179

**1** 1 He even wears a hat in bed.
2 I only wanted to help you.
3 He even believes in ghosts.
4 My French is even worse than yours.
5 It's only open to members.
6 I even forgot to phone home.
7 I only sing on special occasions.
8 He's only there in office hours.

**2** 1 I think best in the bath.
2 I never worked very hard at university.
3 He wrote his best novels in the 1960s.
4 We're having a meeting here on Tuesday.
5 Please put these carefully on the top shelf.
6 I'm playing golf in Scotland at the weekend.
7 Please take the cat out of here at once.
8 Jenny sang beautifully at Harry's wedding.

## page 180

**1** 1 … always know best …
2 … have never made a mistake …
3 … will never admit …
4 They are usually …
5 They often tell us …
6 Because they invariably know …
7 … they are always right.
8 … they are nearly always wrong.

**2** 1 will probably not
2 is certainly
3 can definitely
4 not always
5 definitely not
6 really doesn't
7 not completely
8 not often

## page 181

**1** A, C, D

**2** *(possible answers)*
1 France is nearly as big as Texas.  2 The United States is not quite as big as Canada.  3 The Eiffel Tower is not nearly as tall as the Petronas Twin Towers.  4 A koala bear is nothing like as dangerous as a grizzly bear.
5 Mars is not nearly as distant as Jupiter.  6 Minus 40° Fahrenheit is exactly as cold as minus 40° Celsius.

**3** pretty as a baby's smile
cold as a banker's heart
deaf as a fence post
fast as small town gossip
slow as grass growin'
useless as ice trays in hell
busy as ants at a picnic
happy as a pig in a peach orchard
big as West Texas

## page 182

**1** 1 most infuriating  2 more efficient
3 more imaginative  4 smoother
5 most peaceful  6 unhappiest
7 dimmer  8 more useful  9 silkiest
10 cleverest  11 most shocking  12 lazier
13 most discouraging  14 denser

## page 183

**1** 1 more and more uncomfortable
2 more and more authoritarian
3 more and more unpredictable
4 smellier and smellier
5 quieter and quieter
6 more and more polluted
7 more and more unpredictable
8 more and more strongly

**2** 1 The more races he wins, the more confidence he gains. The more confidence he gains, the more races he wins.
2 The more he loves her, the more she ignores him. The more she ignores him, the more he loves her.
3 The more she works, the more successful she is. The more successful she is, the more responsibility she gets. The more responsibility she gets, the more she works.
4 The more I cook, the more you eat. The more you eat, the more I cook.
5 The more I go to the gym, the more exercise I take. The more exercise I take, the fitter I get. The fitter I get, the more I go to the gym.

## page 184

**1** 1✔  2x  3✔  4✔  5 ✗  6✔  7✔  8 ✗  9 ✗

**2** 1 taller  2 fuller  3 shorter  4 slower  5 younger
6 older  7 richer  8 smaller

In these answers, we usually give **either** contracted forms (for example *I'm, don't*) **or** full forms (for example *I am, do not*). Normally both are correct.

## page 185

**1** 1 ✗ 2✔ 3✔ 4 ✗ 5✔ 6 ✗ 7✔ 8✔

**3** 1 to eat   2 to graduate   3 to swim, to complete
4 to obtain

## page 186

**1** 1 Correct.
2 ~~very less~~ > much / far / a lot less
3 Correct.
4 ~~far slowly~~ > far more slowly
5 ~~any cleaner~~ > no cleaner
6 ~~even difficult~~ > even more difficult
7 Correct.
8 Correct.
9 Correct.
10 ~~much more~~ > many / far / a lot more

## page 187

**1** 1 He talks a lot
5 I very much like your new flat.
8 There was a lot of rain in the night.

## page 188

**1** 1 … such kind people   2 … such a nice boy
3 Correct.   4 … such a good hotel
5 … so careless   6 Correct.
7 … such nonsense   8 Correct.

**2** 1 too good a story   2 so exciting a year
3 How big a budget   4 so stupid a mistake
5 too polite a person   6 How long a time
7 too small a thing   8 as good a job

## page 189

**1** 1 like
2 both (*as* in formal usage)
3 like
4 both (*as* in formal usage)
5 As
6 like
7 both (*as* in formal usage)
8 both (*as* in formal usage)
9 both (*as* in formal usage)
10 both (as in formal usage)

**2** 1 thoughts   2 looks   3 flutter   4 looks
5 a train   6 car alarms

## page 190

**1** 1 ~~younger~~ > youngest
2 ~~bigger than~~ > as big as
3 ~~such accurate~~ > so accurate
4 ~~more easy~~ > easier
5 ~~as him~~ > than him
6 ~~so long~~ > as long

7 ~~like Chinese~~ > as Chinese
8 ~~slowlier~~ > more slowly
9 ~~so nice~~ > such nice
10 Correct.
11 ~~as me~~ > like me
12 ~~less expensive~~ > least expensive
13 The more cups I break …
14 … more and more interesting

**2** friendly, silly, ugly

**3** 1 B  2 A  3 B  4 B  5 both  6 A  7 B  8 both
9 A  10 both

**4** 1✗ 2✔ 3 ✗ 4✔ 5✔ 6✔ 7✔ 8✔ 9✔ 10 ✗ 11✔ 12 ✗
13 ✗ 14 ✗ 15✔

## page 191

**5** 1 smaller   2 less and less   3 clear   4 larger
5 more recent   6 more probably   7 cold and dry
8 less CO2   9 more favourable   10 few
11 large   12 warmer and wetter
13 more and more   14 greatly   15 not enough
16 mainly   17 unfavourable   18 completely

## page 192

**1** 1 *in* + part of a day, *on* + particular day, *in* + longer
period, *on* + part of a particular day,
*at* + weekend, public holiday, *in* to say how long
something takes

**2** … we usually have/put/use no preposition.

**3** 1 –   2 on   3 in   4 in   5 –   6 –   7 –   8 at
9 –   10 on   11 at   12 in   13 –   14 in   15 in
16 on

## page 193

**1 (in and on)** 1 on   2 in

**2** 1 on   2 on   3 in, on   4 on   5 on/in   6 in
7 on   8 on

**1 (at)** 1 at   2 at   3 in   4 at   5 at   6 in   7 at
8 in   9 at   10 at

## page 194

**2** (*possible answers*)
1 for boiling water
2 for cutting wood or metal
3 for lifting things
4 for putting out fires
5 for keeping valuable things safe
6 for holding papers together
7 for making holes
8 for cooking
9 for taking corks out of bottles
10 for holding things tight

## page 195

**1** 1 I 2 F 3 W 4 I 5 I 6 I
7 F 8 I 9 W 10 F

## page 196

**1** 1 that 2 for the fact that 3 that
4 of the fact that 5 to the fact that
6 for the fact that 7 that

**2** 1 ~~about~~ 2 ~~of~~ 3 can't drop 4 can't drop
5 ~~on~~ 6 can't drop 7 ~~at~~ 8 can't drop

## page 197

**1** 1 between 2 between 3 among

**2** 1 until 2 by 3 by the time 4 till, until

**3** 1 during 2 for

**4** 1 attractive, for 2 by, realises 3 habits, during
4 till/until, tomorrow 5 Between, evils 6 war, by
7 surprised, for 8 strange, during 9 Love, between
10 among, advice 11 until, interval

## page 198

**1** 1 by 2 with

**2** 1 by 2 with

**3** 1 besides 2 except

**4** 1 opposite 2 in front of

**5** 1 with, gun, with 2 except, taxes 3 Besides, not
4 with, help 5 By, boss 6 government, except
7 rain, by 8 besides, criminals

## page 199

**1** A 1 in 2 of 3 on 4 – 5 on 6 out of / through
7 at 8 at
B 1 at 2 in 3 for 4 at 5 at
C 1 on 2 on 3 in 4 from 5 to 6 from 7 –
8 in 9 with
D 1 through 2 – 3 at 4 after 5 on 6 at
7 off 8 – 9 at 10 at/in 11 in 12 to 13 for
14 on

## page 201

**1** 1 ✗ 2 ✔ 3 ✔ 4 ✗ 5 ✔ 6 ✗ 7 ✔ 8 ✔

**2** 1 after/when 2 when 3 when/after 4 where
5 when 6 although 7 Although 8 where
9 when/after 10 because 11 and because 12 so

## page 202

**1** 1 Should I wash or dry-clean this jacket?
2 You can come with me or wait here.
3 Do you speak English, German or Chinese?
4 I've written and posted six letters this morning.
5 I'm depressed because I've worked all day and
achieved nothing.
6 These people will service, clean and polish your car.

## page 203

**1** 1 This drug can reduce both inflammation and pain.
2 Either you'll leave this house or I'll call the police.
3 Either he didn't hear me or he deliberately ignored
me.
4 He writes both teaching materials and computer
manuals.
5 Either they have gone to bed or there's nobody at
home.
6 Conrad either commutes to London or lives there; I
forget which.
7 Your car needs both a service and some urgent
repairs.
8 He either lied to me or he lied to Jenny. / He lied to
either me or Jenny.

## page 204

**1** 1 will find, go 2 have, will write 3 Will you stay,
takes 4 will be, recognises 5 will go, go
6 will give, finds 7 will ask, want 8 will find,
are 9 win, will have 10 arrive, will phone

**3** 1 would be able, thought 2 would, was, knew
3 would never do, went 4 would be, had, wanted
5 would hit, talked 6 would tell, thought
7 would be, could, liked 8 would not give, asked
9 would mean, spent

## page 205

**4** 1 was, had not helped, needed 2 has been, lasted
3 have usually liked, worked 4 has done, needed
5 talks, is thinking

**6** 1 ~~it is~~ 2 ~~I was~~ 3 ~~you are~~ 4 ~~he or she is~~ 5 ~~it is~~

## page 206

**1** 1 It's time we took a break.
2 It's time you watered the garden.
3 It's time you washed the car.
4 It's time Jenny got up.
5 It's time we went to the theatre.
6 It's time we cleaned the windows.

**2** 1 'I'd rather we talked tomorrow.'
2 'I'd rather you came at ten.'
3 'I'd rather you didn't.'
4 I'd rather you phoned her tonight.'
5 'I'd rather we played poker.'
6 'I'd rather we spoke Spanish.'

In these answers, we usually give **either** contracted forms (for example *I'm, don't*)
**or** full forms (for example *I am, do not*). Normally both are correct.

## page 207

**2** until, come up      when, fills up

## page 208

**1** 1 ~~which~~ > who
2 ~~will interest~~ > which will interest
3 Correct.
4 ~~who~~ > which/that
5 ~~that it opens~~ > that opens
6 ~~everything what I read~~ > everything (that) I read
7 Correct.
8 Correct.
9 Correct.
10 ~~refuse it~~ > refuse.

**2** 4 is the bad rule.

## page 209

**3** 1 cannot be dropped   2 ~~that~~   3 ~~that~~
4 cannot be dropped   5 cannot be dropped
6 ~~that~~

**4** 1 can't read   2 one you can't understand
3 one you can't solve   4 one you can't satisfy
5 one you can't forgive   6 can't avoid
7 you can't see coming   8 something you can't do without

**5** 1 What   2 that   3 what   4 what   5 that   6 that

## page 210

**1** 1 the others   2 identifying   3 identifying
4 non-identifying

**2** 1 no commas
2 no commas
3 … Warwick, which is a long way from the sea.
4 My cousin Julie, who is a fashion designer, has gone …
5 no commas
6 … 'Black Island', which was really good.

**3** 1 no change   2 no change   3 ~~that happened~~
4 ~~which~~   5 no change   6 no change   7 no change
8 ~~The man that looks~~   9 no change   10 ~~which~~

## page 211

**1** 1 The students taught by Oliver
2 Cars parked in the street
3 the girl talking to Patrick
4 those books piled up
5 the birds singing
6 plastic used for packaging
7 people studying full-time
8 posted in 1986
9 the books requested, those in stock
10 the tickets available

**2** 1 F   2 J   3 N   4 H   5 L   6 P   7 A/F   8 C

## page 212

**1** 1 No. An extinguisher is something you put out a fire with.
2 No. An umbrella is something you keep yourself dry with.
3 No. A bucket is something you carry water in.
4 No. An axe is something you cut wood with.
5 No. A saucepan is something you cook soup with.
6 No. A piano is something you play music on.
7 No. A freezer is something you keep things cold in.
8 No. Glue is something you stick things together with.

**2** *(possible answers)*
1 An extinguisher is something with which you put out a fire.
2 An umbrella is something with which you keep yourself dry.
3 A bucket is something in which you carry water.
4 An axe is something with which you cut wood.
5 A saucepan is something with which you cook soup.
6 A piano is something on which you play music.
7 A freezer is something in which you keep things cold.
8 Glue is something with which you stick things together.

**3** *(possible answers)*
1 the place you were born in   2 the place you live in
3 a place you find books in   4 a person you work with
5 a person you work for   6 a person you are married to

## page 213

**4** 1 Joe Peters, with whom my father plays golf, has just opened a restaurant.
2 This bracelet, for which I paid £5, is apparently very valuable.
3 Martin Oliver, for whom I am working at the moment, is a very successful farmer.
4 Our little village school, in which I learnt to read and write, has been turned into a museum.
5 The committee have appointed a new treasurer, Peter Barnes, in whom I have no confidence.
6 Hutchins had an operation on his knee, after which he was unable to play for three months.

**5** 1 at which time   2 in which case
3 after which disturbing experience
4 at which point   5 in which pleasant post

## page 214

**1** 1 A   2 B   3 C

**2** *(possible answers)*
1 whose plants don't grow.   2 whose children are unhappy.   3 whose patients die.   4 whose books don't sell.   5 whose students learn nothing.
6 whose tourists get lost.   7 whose food is uneatable.
8 whose lion eats him.

## page 215

**3** 1 which  2 what  3 which  4 what  5 which
6 what  7 which  8 which

## page 216

**1** 1 A, C  2 A, B  3 A, B, C  4 A, C  5 A  6 B, C  7 A

**2** 1 No  2 No  3 Yes

**3** 1 They showed me some shoes whose price tag made me go pale.
2 I once had a friend from Norway whose grandfather had been a famous explorer.
3 We had a dog whose main interests were sleeping and eating.
4 We stayed in a lovely hotel whose dining room had a view of the Grand Canyon.
5 I once lived next door to a woman whose son is now a famous rock star.
*(Commas are also possible in these sentences – see page 210.)*

**4** 1 A tool with which you make holes is called a drill.
2 A tool with which you make metal smooth is called a file.
3 A tool with which you take the tops off bottles is called a bottle-opener.
4 A tool with which you grip things is called a pair of pliers.

## page 217

**5** The Emperor Julius Caesar, who was on his way to the Senate for an important meeting, was assassinated earlier today by a group of conspirators led by Marcus Junius Brutus, who, like many of the Roman population, had become dissatisfied with Caesar's assumption of absolute power.

Marco Polo, who left Venice in 1269, has returned together with his father Niccolò and his Uncle Maffeo Polo, who accompanied him on his travels. The Polos claim to have spent over 20 years in China, where Marco served as adviser to Kublai Khan, travelling extensively through his empire as an ambassador.

William of Normandy, whose army defeated the English forces at the Battle of Hastings on October 14th, was crowned king of England today in Westminster Abbey, in succession to King Harold, who was killed in the battle.

News has just reached us that General George Armstrong Custer, who was attempting to put down a revolt by a coalition of Indian tribes, has been killed in a battle on the Little Bighorn River, where his troops were outnumbered and wiped out.

## page 219

**1** 1 needed  2 have  3 was  4 that  5 she
6 would  7 where the police station is?
8 if she's awake  9 said

**2** 1 ✘  2 ✘  3 ✘  4 ✔  5 ✔  6 ✘  7 ✘
8 ✔ (or needed)

**3** but he **didn't** want to tell me very much
fed up with living **there**
perhaps he **would** start looking for a job
with **his** girlfriend
**girlfriend** (no question mark)
He **said** everything was fine
I asked what **he thought**
too busy **that** week
there wasn't much I **could** do for him
I don't think I **will** see him

## page 220

**1** 1 sacrifice, was
2 is/was, contemporaries, was
3 contained, soul, continued, could, preserve
4 was, possessions, afterlife
5 reincarnation, are
6 planet, has/had
7 continent, was
8 are/were, microscopic
9 are/were, independent

## page 221

**2** *(possible answers)*
1 had better  2 needn't  3 should  4 should
5 would have  6 would have  7 must
8 had better

**4** 1 D  2 E  3 C  4 G  5 H/E  6 I  7 A

## page 222

**1** 1 … that they accepted my claim
2 ~~about if~~ > about whether
3 ~~suggested to have~~ > suggested having
4 Correct.
5 … objected that I wasn't ready.
6 Correct.
7 ~~if~~ > whether
8 Correct.
9 Correct.

## page 223

**2** 1 evidence  2 proof  3 agreement  4 lie
5 exaggeration  6 refusal  7 confusion  8 claim

## page 224

**1** 1 clarify  2 direct  3 provide  4 realise, put
5 not be  6 take on  7 be  8 consider

In these answers, we usually give **either** contracted forms (for example *I'm, don't*) **or** full forms (for example *I am, do not*). Normally both are correct.

## page 225

**3** 1 should think   2 should be   3 should want
4 should forget   5 should not care   6 should lose

## page 226

**1** 1 ~~that~~   2 ~~that~~   3 Can't drop 'that'   4 ~~that~~   5 ~~that~~
6 Can't drop 'that'   7 ~~that~~   8 Can't drop 'that'
9 ~~that~~   10 Can't drop 'that'

**2** 1 The fact that nobody would tell me anything added
to my difficulties.
2 The fact that we had comprehensive insurance made
things much easier.
3 The fact that his father knew the President helped to
keep him out of jail.
4 The fact that I spoke three languages helped me to
work abroad.
5 The fact that she had a small child was taken into
account at her interview.

## page 227

**1** 1 Where she lives is not important. / It is not important
where she lives.
2 You can do the job how you like.
3 Our arrangements will depend on what time she
arrives.
4 I don't know when he was born.
5 Can you ask what they want?
6 Why they are here is not at all clear. / It is not at all
clear why they are here.
7 I'll spend my money how I choose.
8 Whether he knows/speaks French doesn't matter. /
It doesn't matter whether he knows/speaks French.

**2** 1 whoever pays the bills   2 whoever wants it
3 whatever you want   4 whatever you say
5 Whoever gets this job   6 Whoever wins /
Whichever team wins

## page 228

**1** *(possible answers)*
1 It's your task to steal the secret formula.
2 It's amazing what she can do with a few leftovers out
of the fridge.
3 It's strange how they all disappear when it's time to
do some work.
4 It upset everybody that he kept swearing at the referee.
5 It doesn't interest me what you think.
6 It's a pity that so few people came.
7 It's typical of him to forget to buy the tickets.
8 It's exciting when a baby starts talking.
9 It's probable that we'll be a little late.
10 It's nice being back home.

## page 229

**3** 1 it   2 it   3 –   4 it   5 it   6 –   7 –   8 it
9 it   10 it

**4** 1 hate it   2 owe it   3 appreciate it   4 leave it
5 take it

## page 230

**1** 1 A, B   2 A   3 B   4 A, B   5 A, B   6 B   7 A, B   8 A, B
9 A, B   10 A   11 B   12 B   13 A   14 B   15 A, B

**2** *(possible answer)*
I told Carl that we needed to talk, but he said he couldn't
talk just then. So I said we'd better talk soon, and asked
him if that afternoon would be OK, but he said it wouldn't.
I asked him what he was so busy with, and he said he had
a lot of urgent work. I told him he couldn't keep avoiding
things, and he said I was in a bad temper. I asked him if
he wanted to know why, and he said he didn't think so.
So I told him he could either listen to me or find another
girlfriend, and he said that was a really difficult choice. So
I said I wasn't taking any more of that nonsense, and he
asked me to close the door on my way out.

## page 231

**3** 1 the Zulus   2 the Sumerians   3 the Navajo
4 The Norse people

## page 233

**1** 1 stops, pass   2 filled, form, don't   3 wins, election
4 factory, closes down   5 sell, will reduce,
expenditure   6 buy, shares   7 will decide, get,
estimate   8 has forgotten, reservation, won't

**2** 1 would tidy up   2 would bake   3 was/were not
4 would redecorate   5 cared about   6 would go
sailing   7 converted   8 joined

## page 234

**3** 1 could/might play   2 might feel   3 might go
4 could/might get   5 could understand   6 might
taste

**4** 1 'd realised, 'd have sent   2 would have been, 'd
asked   3 wouldn't have happened, 'd thought
4 'd gone, would have waited   5 would have cost, 'd
carried on   6 hadn't gone away, 'd have gone
7 hadn't done, would have done   8 'd fallen in, 'd
have been   9 'd married, would have got
10 'd known, 'd have done

## page 235

**1 (unless)** 1 You can have the car tonight unless Harry
needs it.   2 I'll do some gardening unless it rains.
3 He'll pass the exam if they don't ask him about
Shakespeare.   4 He's usually pretty good-tempered, if
people don't ask him for money.   5 I can't understand
Spanish unless you speak very slowly.   6 Unless they
mend the road soon, there's going to be an accident.

**2** (if and in case) 1 brand-new, in case   2 If, rusty
3 sprinklers, in case   4 automatically, if
5 mobile, in case   6 If, message

## page 236

**1** 1 will sign   2 will solve   3 will agree   4 will cure
5 will check   6 will improve   7 will accept
8 will write down

**2** 1 If it wasn't for the/my cat, I wouldn't have anybody /
would have nobody to talk to.
2 If it hadn't been for my mobile phone, I would have
been unable / wouldn't have been able to get help.
3 If it hadn't been for your mother, things would have
been OK.
4 If it wasn't for chocolate, I wouldn't eat too much.
5 If it hadn't been for old Mrs Perkins, the bank robbers
would have got away.

## page 237

**3** 1 if necessary   2 If in doubt   3 if ever   4 if any
5 If anything

**4** 1 should / happen to run into
2 should / happens to turn up
3 should / happen to have
4 should / happen to run out of
5 should / happen to feel like

**6** 1 Had she asked
2 Were we to close the department
3 Had the soldiers invaded
4 Had you waited another week
5 Were our finances in better order
6 Should the tax inspector enquire

## page 238

**7** 1 if stylish   2 If that's your idea   3 If Jones has
dropped out   4 if tedious   5 if I have to knit it

## page 239

**1** 1 I wonder if it would be better to wait until tomorrow.
2 If she had asked me, I would have told her to go
home.
3 What would you have said if one of your children
had done that?
4 If you need a drink, there's some beer in the fridge.
5 You should not park there. *(various other answers
possible)*
6 I would not be surprised if she just went back home
one of these days.

## page 240

**1** 1 B   2 A, B   3 A, B   4 A   5 A, B   6 B

**2** 1 am trying   2 was watching   3 As   4 packed
5 was getting

## page 241

**5** 1 A   2 B   3 A   4 B   5 B

**7** 1 A, B   2 A   3 A   4 B   5 A

## page 242

**8** 1 A   2 A, B   3 B   4 A, B   5 A

**10** 1 A, B   2 B   3 A, B   4 A, B   5 B

## page 243

**1** 1 Whoever   2 whatever   3 whatever/whichever
4 wherever   5 whenever   6 However
7 However/Whenever   8 whoever   9 Whenever

**2** 1 however rich they are   2 However you travel
3 Whatever you say   4 Whatever problems you have
5 Whenever I see you   6 Whatever time you turn up

**3** 1 No matter what   2 No matter what/which
3 No matter how   4 No matter what
5 No matter when   6 No matter how

## page 244

**1** 1 No wanting to upset everybody, I said nothing.
2 On Friday George arrived, bringing news from the
Irish cousins.
3 The dog rushed round the room, breaking one
priceless ornament after another.
4 Knowing what he liked, I sent him a large bouquet of
orchids.
5 Fried in butter, it should taste delicious.
6 A train caught fire near Oxford, causing long delays.
7 Not being in a hurry, I stopped for a coffee and a
sandwich.
8 Having lost all his money, he had no way of getting
home.

**2** 1 sipping   2 watching   3 stolen   4 provided
5 protected   6 belonging   7 checking   8 satisfied
9 stopping   10 getting   11 shooting   12 walking

## page 245

**3** 1 Mrs Perkins   2 Josie   3 I   4 Sandra   5 the
children   6 I

**4** 1 ✔   2 ✘   3 ✘   4 ✔   5 ✔   6 ✘

**5** 1 The fire   2 her doll   3 smoke   4 The school hall
5 Her smile   6 the treasurer

In these answers, we usually give **either** contracted forms (for example *I'm, don't*)
**or** full forms (for example *I am, do not*). Normally both are correct.

## page 246

**1** 1 After analysing   2 After ... rearranging
3 Before applying   4 Since qualifying
5 Before signing   6 After abandoning

**2** 1 since   2 On/After   3 while/when   4 Besides
5 before/when   6 when/while   7 On/When
8 before   9 after   10 In

## page 247

**1** (possible answers)
1 in order to keep dry   2 so as to keep warm
3 so as to have some company   4 in order not to get
lost   5 so as not to forget it   6 in order to wake up
early   7 so as to meet people   8 in order to get fit
9 in order to lose weight   10 so as to get more exercise

## page 248

**1** 1 Correct.   2 ~~unless he has an accident~~ > if he doesn't
have an accident   3 ~~In case~~ > If   4 Correct.
5 Correct.   6 Correct.   7 ~~If you in doubt~~ > If in
doubt   8 Correct.   9 Correct.   10 ~~even~~ > even if

**2** 1 B   2 A, B   3 A   4 A, B   5 A   6 A   7 B   8 A   9 A
10 A, B

**3** 1 F   2 I   3 N   4 I   5 N   6 F   7 N   8 I

## page 251

**1** 1 A   2 B   3 A   4 A

**2** 1 D   2 C   3 B   4 A   5 F   6 E

## page 252

**1** 1 All Sandra's jewellery was stolen (by burglars).
Sandra had all her jewellery stolen (by burglars).
2 I had my palm read by a fortune-teller.  A fortune-
teller read my palm.
3 The central heating was put in by Jenkins and Fowler.
Jenkins and Fowler put in the central heating.
4 My blood pressure was checked by the doctor. I had
my blood pressure checked by the doctor.
5 My neighbour, who's a mechanic, serviced the car.
I had the car serviced by my neighbour, who's a
mechanic.
6 The house was looked at by a qualified surveyor. A
qualified surveyor looked at the house.

**2** 1 Everybody admires Oliver.
2 A man in the market sold me a faulty hair-dryer.
3 Mrs Lopez taught me Spanish.
4 My sister lent me the money I needed.
5 Everybody laughs at Joe's stories.
6 Over 20 million people died in/ because of the flu
epidemic in 1918–19.

## page 253

**1** 1 It   2 This   3 This   4 it   5 This   6 This   7 it, It

**2** 1 this   2 it   3 That   4 That   5 this   6 it

## page 254

**1** 1 ...a question; then
2 ... your order as soon as ... / ... your order, as soon
as ...
3 ... attention; also ...
4 ... cold and ... / ... cold, and ...
5 ... decision, because ...
6 ... than C; therefore ...
7 ... tickets, so ...

**2** 1 She has considerable musical ability, but her
technique is poor.
2 Nobody liked him; however, everybody agreed that
he was a good manager.
3 It is a reliable and economical car; however, its
performance is disappointing.
4 Simpson was not playing at his best, but he
managed to win the match.
5 The house is in reasonable condition; however, the
roof will need some repairs.

## page 255

**3** 1 The bank is very inefficient; also, the staff are
remarkably rude. / ... very inefficient. Also ...
2 We bought a map; then we set off to explore the town.
/ ... a map. Then ...
3 There had been no investment for years; consequently,
the railways were in a terrible state. / ... for years.
Consequently ...
4 The people are friendly; on the other hand, it is difficult
to get to know them really well. / ... friendly. On the
other hand ...
5 We walked down to the beach area; there we found the
men we were looking for. / ... beach area. There ...

**5** 1 He had little talent; his sister, on the other hand, was
a brilliant musician. / ... was a brilliant musician, on
the other hand.
2 The hospital was understaffed; the standard of care,
in spite of that, was excellent. / ... was excellent in
spite of that.
3 Andrew overslept; the whole family, as a result,
missed the plane. / ... missed the plane as a result.

## page 256

**6** 1, 2; 3; 4; 5; 6, 7, 8; 9, 10, 11;

## page 257

**1** 1 All the information you need I am putting in the post today.
2 Any item in our catalogue we can supply and deliver.
3 How she got the gun through customs they never found out.
4 The kitchen we are planning to redecorate in the autumn.
5 Last for ever, these shoes will.
6 (A) very good lesson we had this morning.
7 (A) fat lot of good that does me!

## page 258

**1** 1 F 2 N 3 W 4 F 5 F 6 N 7 W 8 F 9 W

**2** 1 He was not able to start walking again until July.
2 I had hardly got into the house when he started shouting at me.
3 The world has never faced a crisis of this order.
4 I only found out later where they had gone.
5 We not only lost our money; we also wasted out time.

## page 259

**3** 1 The people in the village were so friendly that we soon felt completely at home.
2 Harold went into the civil service, as most of the students in his year did.
3 Emma learnt much more quickly than the other children (did).

## page 260

**1** 1 It was Mary who/that was supposed to interview the new students today.
It was the new students that Mary was supposed to interview today.
It was today that Mary was supposed to interview the new students.
2 It was Paul who/that met his bank manager in prison.
It was his bank manager that Paul met in prison.
It was in prison that Paul met his bank manager.
3 It was Henry's dog that dug up Philip's roses yesterday evening.
It was Philip's roses that Henry's dog dug up yesterday evening.
It was yesterday evening that Henry's dog dug up Philip's roses.
4 It was Mrs Hawkins who/that lost an earring in the supermarket.
It was an earring that Mrs Hawkins lost in the supermarket.
It was in the supermarket that Mrs Hawkins lost an earring.

**2** 1 It's not butter we need, it's sugar.
2 It was a van I bought, not a car.
3 It's not Joseph who's/that's the Director, it's Maggie.
4 It was her address I forgot, not her name.
5 It's not stamps he collects, it's coins.
6 It's Sam I love, not you.

## page 261

**1** 1 What I want is more time to think.
2 What I need is something to eat.
3 What she hated was his possessiveness.
4 What I have never understood is how aeroplanes stay up.
5 What I did was (to) call the police at once.
6 What she does is (to) teach English in prisons.

## page 263

**1** 1 First of all 2 Regarding 3 Now 4 Right
5 In conclusion 6 By the way 7 For one thing
8 As far as the repairs are concerned
9 As for, finally, in short

**2** 1 For one thing 2 First of all / For one thing
3 as for 4 as far as 5 Speaking of

## page 264

**1** 1 On the whole 2 apart from Hungarian
3 Consequently 4 Similarly 5 In some cases
6 Broadly speaking 7 As a result

**2** 1 On the other hand 2 Despite that 3 Mind you
4 Look 5 On the contrary 6 After all 7 Still
8 Look here

## page 265

**3** 1 It is true / Certainly / Of course, Nonetheless / Still / Even so / But
2 certainly, Nonetheless / Still / Even so
3 Of course / Certainly / It is true, Still / Even so
4 Of course / Certainly / It is true, Still / Even so
5 Granted / Of course / Certainly / It is true, Nonetheless / Even so

**4** 1 ~~Also~~ 2 ~~For example~~ 3 ~~in other words~~
4 ~~For instance~~ 5 ~~In particular~~

## page 266

**1** 1 honestly 2 No doubt 3 At least 4 I'm afraid
5 or rather 6 Let me see. 7 Apparently 8 Frankly
9 so to speak 10 I suppose

**2** 1 it was one of them. 2 I'm really not hungry.
3 it's better than sleeping in the car.

## page 267

**3** *(possible answers)*
1 Actually 2 in fact 3 To tell the truth 4 actually
5 In fact 6 Well

**4** 1 You see 2 you know 3 you know 4 You see
5 You know

In these answers, we usually give **either** contracted forms (for example *I'm, don't*) **or** full forms (for example *I am, do not*). Normally both are correct.

## page 268

**1** 1 in conclusion   2 As far as   3 to a great extent
   4 Turning now   5 As regards   6 In general
   7 on the contrary   8 Briefly / Broadly speaking
   9 or rather   10 Broadly speaking / Briefly
   11 It is true that   12 what is more

## page 269

**3** 1 Incidentally   2 To tell the truth   3 You know
   4 sort of   5 Frankly   6 all the same   7 you see
   8 mind you   9 As I was saying   10 By the way
   11 As for   12 anyway

## page 270

**1** B

**2** 1 that was parked outside the front gate
   2 after he had completed his discussions with the
   bank manager
   3 if you have difficulty in deciding your next course of
   action
   4 (in the enquiry office) on the second floor of Robinson's

## page 271

**3** 1 Some papers that a dustman found …
   2 A picture that a schoolboy bought …
   3 She insisted that she thought that he knew that she
   was on the train.
   4 If the details that you provided …
   5 The man that the terrorists bought the guns from …
   6 … claims that reporters hacked into their phones.
   7 A girl that Helen was at school with …
   8 The ladies that men admire …
   9 … and the money that money makes …

**4** 1 B   2 A   3 E   4 F   5 D

## page 272

**7** Many of the gold and silver objects which were
   excavated from the 3000-year-old royal tombs
   resemble items of jewellery which are still made today
   by craftsmen who are trained in the traditional skills.

**8** 1 a separatist who was accused   2 Police who were
   called   3 Three immigrants who were returned

## page 273

**10** 1 Yes   2 Yes   3 No

## page 274

**1** *(possible answers)*
   1 a long, awfully boring, badly delivered lecture that
   sent me to sleep
   2 the really tall, slightly balding, highly skilled motor
   mechanic who worked on my car
   3 the terribly noisy, extremely irritating, badly brought
   up children who live next door
   4 a hastily planned, incompetently commanded,
   unnecessary invasion that caused massive loss of life
   5 a pleasantly furnished, light and airy apartment with
   a splendid view of the sea and within easy reach of
   the town centre

## page 275

**1** 1 Yes   2 Yes   3 No   4 No   5 No   6 Yes

## page 276

**1** 1 …'I am.'   2 … I did today.   3 '… I would have
   been.'   4 … but I do.   5 …'It certainly does.'
   6 … please do.   7 …'Yes, it is.'   8 … and Sue
   doesn't either.

**2** 1 thought the whole thing was too absurd
   2 think the whole thing was too absurd
   3 come round
   4 come round
   5 ready to take offence
   6 ready to take offence
   7 want to quarrel
   8 want to say another thing about it

## page 277

**3** 1 E   2 C   3 A   4 D   5 B

## page 278

**1** 1 afford to   2 used to   3 mean to / intend to
   4 was going to / meant to / intended to
   5 need to   6 seems to   7 intend to   8 hope to

**2** 1 to   2 to   3 to   4 (to)   5 –   6 (to)   7 (to)
   8 to

## page 279

**1** 1 I'm afraid so.   2 I don't think so.
   3 I don't suppose so. / I suppose not.
   4 I hope so.   5 I believe so.   6 I hope not.
   7 I'm afraid not.

**2** 1 So I see.   2 says so   3 told me so.
   4 so it said on the news   5 So I understand
   6 So I hear – that's terrible. / So I understand.
   7 says so.

## page 280

**1** 1 I drove to the Ministry immediately, and Alistair (drove there) somewhat later.
2 Jane went to Greece and Alice went to Rome.
3 You seem to be ill, and she certainly is.
4 I have not studied ancient Greek astronomy, nor do I intend to.
5 The children will carry the small boxes, and the adults (will carry) the large ones.

**2** 1 and stopped   2 and explained
3 and started   4 but wanted   5 and knew
6 but thought   7 and broke   8 but wanted

## page 281

**1** 1 Are you looking for somebody?   2 That'll be £55.
3 Is the boss in?   4 I must go.   5 There's no milk left.
6 It won't start.   7 My sock's got a hole in.

**2** 1 It   2 There's   3 You're   4 Have you   5 I   6 Be

**3** 1 ✔   2 ✗   3 ✔   4 ✔   5 ✗   6 ✔

**4** Not raining, Damned bus, See the match?, Bit of it, gave up, went to bed, Don't blame you, Wasn't worth watching, Needs a guide dog, Think they'll go ahead?, Won't make any difference, Couple of days, Family OK?, Brother's much better, Be out of hospital, Good news, Will do, See you around.

## page 282

**1** 1 W   2 S   3 W   4 W   5 S   6 S   7 S

## page 283

**2** (possible answers)
1 I just cannot stand people like that.
2 That does me a lot of good.
3 I never found out what she wanted.
4 I never have time to watch anything on TV these days.
5 These shoes will last for ever.
6 Some of these drivers are crazy.
7 Are your children still at school?
8 Are they ever going to sell their house?
9 I think it was in 1984 that he started the job.
10 Can you deliver two dozen bottles of the cheapest sparkling water that you have?
11 On Friday afternoon when I was watching the match the doorbell rang. It was someone selling insurance.
12 I do not think that Harry's mother approves of his girlfriend.

**3** (some sentences: possible answers)
I do not know what sort of training your assistants get.
On Thursday morning I visited your store to buy a pair of earphones.
Two assistants were talking.
I asked if they had a pair of cheap earphones.
One of them looked at me unpleasantly, the other did not even bother.
They went straight back to their conversation.
It was like something in a TV comedy programme.

## page 284

**1** 1 I'm not.   2 aren't I? you are   3 Did you?
4 I haven't.   5 do they?   6 Does he?   7 is it?
8 Yes, I have.   9 Don't you?   10 do you? Yes … I do
11 Did they? they … did   12 Yes … you do.

## page 285

**2** 1 has   2 isn't it?   3 has   4 has   5 can she?
6 can't   7 No   8 didn't   9 does he   10 would you?
11 wouldn't   12 will you   13 won't

## page 286

**1** 1 ✔   2 ✔   3 ✔   4 ✗   5 ✔   6 ✔   7 ✗   8 ✔
9 ✗   10 ✔   11 ✗   12 ✗

**2** 1 ✔   2 ✔   3 ✗   4 ✗   5 ✔   6 ✔   7 ✗   8 ✔
9 ✔   10 ✔

## page 287

**3** 1 You're going where?   2 You're leaving when?
3 You'll be staying with who?   4 You're going to what? / You're going to teach what?   5 You'll make how much?   6 You'll need how much?
7 Can I (do) what?

**4** (possible answers)
1 Nobody knows.   2 You shouldn't be in my room.
3 You should clean up all this mess.   4 Come back.
5 You haven't brought my coffee.   6 It's no use talking to her.   7 There's nothing to worry about.
8 That boy should get a job.   9 It's time for you to go.
10 You can't afford all that.   11 I don't care.
12 I can't understand you.   13 Those are very funny shoes.   14 You haven't made my lunch.
15 I don't want to.

## page 288

**5** (possible answers)
1 You've done what?   2 That's the good news?
3 You're sure of that?   4 Would I lie to you?
5 Are you crazy?

In these answers, we usually give **either** contracted forms (for example *I'm, don't*) **or** full forms (for example *I am, do not*). Normally both are correct.

## page 289

**1** 1 NP  2 NP  3 P  4 NP  5 NP  6 P  7 P  8 NP

**2** *(possible answer)*
Dear X
I'm sorry to trouble you, but I have a question that I can't find the answer to, and I wonder if you can help me. Could you possibly tell me the difference between *shy* and *timid*?
I look forward to hearing from you.
Yours sincerely, Y

## page 290

**1** 1 Could  2 wondered, were  3 hoped, would
4 might  5 did you want  6 Would, brought
7 could  8 Did  9 Would  10 Did

**2** 1 was thinking / thought, was  2 was hoping /
hoped, didn't  3 were wondering / wondered, could
4 Were  5 was wondering / wondered, could
6 I was expecting

**3** *(possible answers)*
1 I'll have to ask you to come back on Tuesday.
2 I'll need two copies.
3 I'm afraid you'll need to pay in advance.
4 That will be £25.60, please.

## page 291

**6** *(possible answers)*
1 It's kind of expensive.
2 The music's quite boring.
3 I think I'll go for a walk.
4 We are writing to congratulate you on your prize.
5 We're thinking of meeting again next week.
6 Maybe we'll sell our house.
7 She's rather bad-tempered.
8 This meat smells a bit funny.
9 I would like to thank you for your donation.
10 We are writing to ask if you would give a talk to our members.

## page 292

**1** 1 I do like old cowboy films.
2 Annemarie did talk a lot.
3 His voice does get on my nerves.
4 Do excuse me for interrupting you.
5 I do think it's time to go home.
6 Do be polite to your grandfather.
7 I do apologise for coming late.
8 Do say hello to Sally for me.

**2** 1 do like  2 do throw  3 did have  4 was
5 did find  6 did end up  7 do fix  8 will

## page 294

**1** 1 Open the packet at the other end.
2 See the diagram at the top of the next page.
3 Take the car to the garage; find a baby-sitter for tonight; see Oliver at 3.30.

**2** Pour mixture into large saucepan, heat until boiling, then add three pounds sugar and leave on low heat for 45 minutes.

**3** 1 Are you coming today?
2 Thanks for a great party.
3 Just to let you know.
4 Will you be here (on) Thursday evening?
5 Are you OK?
6 (I) got your message.
7 (I) will be at (the) barbecue at nine.
8 (I) need more information.

## page 295

**1** 1 FURNITURE FACTORY WAGE(S) CUT THREAT

**2** 1 Hospitals are to take / will take fewer patients.
2 A dog travelled 500 miles and found its owners.
3 A/The boy has been found safe.
4 A boy has found a safe.
5 Ministers were warned three years ago about flood defences.

# index